MISSION COLLEGE
LEARNING RESOURCE SERVICE

DATE DUE

MAY 2 1 1987			
DEC 1 4 1993			

DEMCO 38-297

COMPUTER MANAGED INSTRUCTION
Theory and Practice

COMPUTER MANAGED INSTRUCTION

THEORY AND PRACTICE

FRANK B. BAKER

UNIVERSITY OF WISCONSIN

EDUCATIONAL TECHNOLOGY PUBLICATIONS
ENGLEWOOD CLIFFS, NEW JERSEY 07632

Library of Congress Cataloging in Publication Data

Baker, Frank B
   Computer managed instruction.

   Bibliography: p.
   Includes index.
   1. Computer managed instruction. I. Title.
LB1028.46.B23   371.3'9445   77-24006
ISBN 0-87778-099-4

Printed in the United States of America.

Library of Congress Catalog Card Number:
77-24006.

International Standard Book Number:
0-87778-099-4.

First Printing: February, 1978.
Second Printing: June, 1983.

Preface

The early years of an emerging field, such as computer managed instruction (CMI), are often the most interesting. During this period, the basic logic is established and the framework of the field defined. Typically it is also a time when the literature is meager, the level of technical documentation inadequate, and the questioning of underlying rationale rare. During my early involvement in CMI, circa 1966, these deficits did not pose a problem, as CMI systems were being developed primarily to show the feasibility of the use of the computer to support the management of individualized instruction. By the mid 1970's, it was clear that CMI was viable and had the potential for making an impact upon all levels of education. However, this potential was being reduced by the limited and scattered literature available to those persons interested in CMI. In the summer of 1974, I decided to write a book pulling together the available literature and describing the existing CMI systems. Shortly thereafter, I attended the NIE-IBM conference on the Short-Term Potential of CMI; the proceedings of this conference form the keystone of the literature on CMI cited in this book. Attending this conference also drastically changed the emphasis I had planned for the book. The various formal and informal sessions made me realize that CMI was being viewed in terms of the procedures performed by the computer rather than in terms of the management functions performed by the teachers. While understandable, the former emphasis struck me as odd for a field labeled Computer Managed Instruction. It was quite clear that an underlying conceptualization of instructional management was missing. As a result, the emphasis of the present book was shifted towards the educational aspects of CMI rather than the computer-based procedures. In doing so, it quickly became apparent that CMI encompasses a broad range of educational issues, each of which is worthy of several books. In order to keep the magnitude of the book reasonable with respect to these issues, a six-part model for CMI was employed throughout the book. This model was used to keep the reader aware of the scope of CMI while not overextending the discussion of each part. The model also serves to put the computer-related aspects of CMI in their proper context.

Because of the nature of CMI systems, persons ranging from classroom teachers to computer programmers tend to get involved in their creation and use. Such a range poses a problem in terms of the intended audience of the book. One would write quite different books on CMI for computer specialists, classroom teachers, or school administrators. The approach taken was to attempt to appeal to the widest possible audience. Thus, with the exception of Chapter Five, and possibly Chapter Seven, the book was intended for a rather general audience of persons in the field of education. Chapter Five describes a specific CMI computer program in considerable detail and was intended for the computer specialist. It was included to provide such persons with an insight into the nature of CMI computer programs, their logic, and their magnitude. Such documentation is very rare; however, I felt it was necessary in this instance to fully portray CMI. Chapter Seven also deals with computer-related issues but at essentially a nontechnical level.

While the literature contains descriptions of specific CMI systems, it does not contain a description of the process through which such systems were developed. Because CMI systems are often developed by local school districts, and individual instructors, it was felt the complete history of specific CMI system would provide valuable guidance. Thus, Chapter Four presents a case study of the Sherman School Project, complete with its problems and successes. Since such case studies are rare, it is hoped it will give the reader a unique insight into the developmental processes involved in creating a sophisticated CMI system.

Despite the author's long involvement in the Sherman School Project, this book is not about the project. However, the influence of the project is seen in the book's orientation towards elementary school CMI systems. Although CMI systems are used at all academic levels, they share approaches, techniques, and underlying issues with the elementary school systems. In addition, the CMI literature dealing with other than the elementary school setting is extremely sketchy and provides a meager basis for an extended discussion. Hopefully, the present emphasis will elicit a clear enough recognition of the major factors that the reader will be able to generalize the discussion to other academic settings.

The present book has two goals: First, to provide the reader with the conceptual framework for CMI as an educational system. The intent was to provide the reader with a "Gestalt" for CMI broader than the computer-related procedures currently emphasized. Second, to initiate a dialogue leading to a definition of instructional management. Such a definition will need to encompass a conceptualization of the teacher as a manager as well as identify an underlying management philosophy.

While the author is solely responsible for the contents of this book, his view of CMI has been shaped by a number of persons. As a consultant to the Southwest Regional Educational Laboratory (SWRL) during the mid 1960's, I was introduced to CMI by Drs. Harry Silberman and Jack Bratten of System Development Corporation. At the same time, two colleagues of mine at the University of Wisconsin, Professors Vere DeVault and Allan Kelley, each developed CMI systems. In 1971 an unusual set of circumstances occurred which led to the Sherman School Project described in Chapters Four and Five. The staff of Sherman School, Dr.

Anthony Farina, Principal, were instrumental in converting a student project into an operational CMI system. Mrs. Berdella Grass was the driving force behind the project and contributed in many ways, not the least of which was providing the determination that the project would succeed. During the Title III phase of the project, Mr. John Chapin was literally everywhere at once keeping the project functioning. Most of Chapter Four and parts of other chapters are based upon the steady flow of working papers, proposals, and status reports generated by him. Although the MICA computer program was the result of a class project, its subsequent refinement, enhancement, and extension has been the work of Mr. Thomas Lorenz and his small but dedicated group of programmers. Chapter Five rests upon the software documentation generated by these programmers over a multiple-year period. The author has benefited from extended discussions about the logic of CMI with Dr. Richard E. Schutz, Director SWRL, and Drs. Sidney Belt and Dennis Spuck of the Wisconsin R & D Center for Cognitive Learning. Dr. Leo Anglin, Kent State University, gave an early version of the book a much appreciated critical review that contributed much to its final form. The author is indebted to Dr. George DeHart of Westinghouse Learning Corporation for providing the materials on PLAN* and to his staff for a review of the sections of Chapter Three dealing with PLAN*. Their timely and responsive assistance is greatly appreciated. Mrs. Connie Shelhamer flawlessly typed the many drafts of the book despite the author's illegible handwriting. The contributions of all these persons were instrumental in providing the author with the experience, motivation, and support needed to write the book.

Frank B. Baker

April, 1977

Table of Contents

List of Figures

Chapter V
Figure

Chapter VII
Figure

List of Tables

COMPUTER MANAGED INSTRUCTION
Theory and Practice

Chapter One

Introduction to CMI

Since the turn of the century, the individualization of instruction has been an elusive goal for educators. The interest in this topic has arisen, peaked, and subsided a number of times in this period. Although the forces determining this cycle are complex, underlying interest in individualization never completely disappears. Consequently, when favorable conditions exist, the cycle begins anew. Such was the case in the early 1960's when new curricula, instructional models, and approaches to individualization were beginning to be developed. It quickly became clear that one of the most troublesome facets of these instructional schemes was their management. Within the classroom a dynamic situation exists in which each pupil is employing a different set of instructional materials, proceeding at his own rate, and with a unique pattern of achievement. As a result, information as to the instructional status of each pupil is needed by the teacher to keep abreast of events in the classroom. Manual processing of the instructionally related data by teacher aides and students proved unsatisfactory in keeping up with the flow of information emanating from the classroom. In addition, the aggregation and summarization of the data needed by the teacher for management purposes was not readily accomplished by manual means. Thus, by the mid 1960's, it was clear that efficient, effective, and timely processing of instructionally related data was fundamental to the management of individualized instruction. The failure of many past attempts at individualization could also be ascribed to the lack of such processing. At roughly this same point in time, the commercial and industrial sectors had successfully made the transition to computer-based data processing in support of a variety of management functions. This use of computers was perceived by a number of educators as a reasonable model for the support of the management functions associated with the individualization of instruction. Consequently, the developers of schemes for individualized instruction began to use the modern digital computer to perform the necessary data processing. The resulting combination has become known as computer managed instruction (CMI). The origins of this terminology are obscure, but as early as 1965 most persons working in the area were using the mnemonic CMI, and it appeared in the literature a few years later (Brudner, 1968). It appears the terminology arose naturally among these workers to differentiate the new approach from the existing computer aided instruction (CAI) systems. Whatever the origin, the computer managed instruction label is firmly entrenched in the literature, despite Cooley and Glaser's (1968) and Baker's (1971a) admonitions about the undesirable connotations of the terminology. The latter author suggested computer based instructional management systems (CBIMS), which is more descriptive, but CMI appears to be in the lexicon.

The year 1967 marked the beginning of literature dealing with computer managed instruction. In that year, two papers by Flanagan (1967a,b) described the basis of his Program for Learning in Accordance with Needs (PLAN), and a paper by Coulson (1967) described the design of System Development Corporation's Instructional Management System. By 1968, a number of papers describing operational CMI systems had appeared. Four of these systems: Individually Prescribed Instruction/Management Information System (Cooley and Glaser, 1968); Computer Managed Systems of Mathematics Instruction (DeVault, 1968); PLAN (Flanagan, 1968); and Instructional Management System (Bratten, 1968; Silberman, 1968) were designed for use in the elementary schools. One system, Teacher Information Processing System (Kelley, 1968) was intended for use at the college level. These five systems were developed completely independently of one another in widely separated geographical locations. Yet, as Baker (1971a) has shown, these pioneering CMI systems shared a common conceptual basis, suggesting that forces were at work within the educational community that led rather naturally to the concept of computer managed instruction.

The five pioneering CMI systems generated considerable interest among educators and the field began to grow at a modest pace. Because CMI systems tend to be developed to meet the needs of a given teacher or group of teachers in a local school district, college, or university, information on existing CMI systems has been difficult to acquire. One of the goals of the conference on the "Short-Term Potential of Computer Managed Instruction" was to provide a vehicle for better exchange of information on CMI systems. This conference, held Nov. 6-8, 1974, and jointly sponsored by the National Institute of Education and IBM Corporation, brought together nearly forty persons actively involved in CMI and related systems. The conference revealed widespread interest in CMI and highlighted the diversity of existing CMI systems. From the proceedings of this conference (Mitzel, 1974b) and a number of other sources, the author has compiled the list of CMI systems appearing in Appendix A. Perusal of this list reveals that one can document somewhat under 30 systems—and no claim is made for the completeness of the list. The author suspects there are at least as many operational CMI systems whose existence has not been noted in the literature. The documented CMI systems span a number of different dimensions. Some are designed to meet the needs of a single instructor (see Allen, Meleca, and Meyers, 1972; Countermine and Singh, 1974; Kelly, 1968) in a single course. Others support several different courses, many instructors, and large numbers of students (see Flanagan, Shanner, Brudner, and Marker, 1975; Johnson and Mayo, 1974). The academic level of the instruction managed via CMI spans the complete range. There are CMI systems for the elementary school (Belt and Spuck, 1974; Chapin, Lorenz, Anglin, and Grass, 1975; Connally, 1970; and Wiel, 1973), for high school (Knipe, 1973; Morgan and Richardson, 1972), for Vocational schools (Danforth, 1974), for colleges and universities (Allen, Meleca, and Meyers, 1972; Dick and Gallager, 1972; Judd and O'Neil, 1974; Kelley, 1968; Merrill, 1974), and for military technical training schools (Howard, 1974; Johnson and Mayo, 1974; Mayo, 1974; Rockway and Yasutake, 1974). It should be noted that the U.S. Air Force Advanced Instructional System (Rockway and Yasutake, 1974) has been funded at the ten million dollar level, although the majority of the funds were for the development of course materials. In addition to CMI systems, recent years have seen the development of computer-based systems employing certain aspects of CMI but having different goals in mind. The most interesting of these are the "course management" or "study management" systems. These systems (see Anderson, Anderson, Dalgaard, Weitecha, Biddle, Paden, Smock, Allessi, Surber, and Klemt, 1974; DeNio, 1974) are essentially computer-administered testing systems that report test results to the students and teachers.

Although the growth of CMI has been rather modest since 1967, it has a number of characteristics indicating that its long-term growth potential is excellent. Lippey (1974a) has suggested three tests to be met if a computer-based innovation is to become part of the educational scene. Test 1: Was the application independently developed in several locations to meet local needs? CMI passes this test easily, as the majority of systems listed in Appendix A were developed to meet local needs. Test 2: Were most implementations initiated by classroom instructors? Again CMI passes, as most of the college level and some of the elementary school systems were initiated by individual instructors. Test 3: Are the operating expenses in most cases met by local funding practices? Other than an occasional funding under Title III, the majority of CMI systems use local funds to support their operations. Insofar as Lippey's tests are concerned, CMI as a field appears to be robust.

CMI also possesses some other characteristics contributing to what seems to be a slow but well-grounded growth rate. First, CMI is characterized by a large number of small systems, suggesting it is not a difficult area to which to gain entry. The resources in terms of time, computer support, and funds appear to be within the grasp of many individuals in a variety of situations. Second, CMI systems tend to be developed by classroom teachers and college instructors rather than by professional educational innovators or computer manufacturers. This is especially important, since teachers are extremely wary of those who sell instructional elixirs. They have much more confidence in educational schemes arising out of the classroom.

Overall, CMI appears to have a firm rooting within the educational scene. Some systems have been in use for many years, others have been phased out, and new systems have been created. A significant feature of the CMI movement (if one can call it that) is that it has been a rather low-keyed effort attracting very little of the publicity of the kind associated with CAI (Scanlon, 1974). Consequently, it has not attempted to live up to unrealistic promises. Unfortunately, it has also not attracted any significant funding from agencies such as NSF, USOE, NIE, or the military— who provided the massive, but futile, funding of CAI. Perhaps, following Lippey's (1974a) third test, this has been beneficial, since CMI has been forced to develop within a self-supporting frame of reference. The characteristics of CMI systems suggest that CMI probably will not peak quickly and fade quickly, as have many other educational innovations.

Underlying Themes

Although CMI systems appeared in the educational community rather suddenly in the late 1960's, such systems have their roots in some long-term themes embedded in the fabric of American education. These themes are discussed briefly below to provide a context for CMI. Certain of these themes will be explored in somewhat greater detail in later chapters. The first of these themes is that of individualization. It would appear that educators have a deeply ingrained intuitive feeling there is some means by which education can be optimized for individual students. In modern terminology, this constitutes a belief in aptitude-treatment interaction. This belief is held despite some evidence (see Cronbach and Snow, 1969) disputing its benefits. Over the years, many different approaches to individualization have been tried. The 24th Yearbook of the NSSE (Wipple, 1925) describes schemes, such as the Winnetka Plan and the Dalton Plan, developed during the early 1900's. A generation later, another NSSE Yearbook (Henry, 1962) was again devoted to individualization. This latter yearbook appeared just before computer-aided instruction became widely known, hence does not reflect the impact of computer technology. Recently, the same organization sponsored a book on systems of individualized education (Talmadge, 1975) describing three of the most widely used elementary school systems. Interestingly, all three involved CMI. Many different dimensions of individualization, such as student interests, learning styles, learning modality, ability, rate of progress, etc., have been employed in the individualization of instruction. Of these, only individualization with respect to rate of progress appears to have been implemented consistently. In fact, rate of progress is the only dimension of individualization implemented in the majority of CMI systems listed in Appendix A. Since 1970, a very high level of interest in the individualization of instruction (see Weisgerber, 1971a,b) has been reached. Local school districts are heavily committed to individualization, individualized curricula have been developed for many subject matter areas, and individualization has been the focus of considerable research and federal funding.

The second theme underlying CMI is behavioral objectives. Due to the work of Gagné (1965), Glaser (1967), Mager (1962), Popham (1969), and others, considerable emphasis has been placed upon performing a "Task Analysis" of a curriculum or subject matter area and breaking it down into a set of specific "behavioral objectives." These objectives then are the basis for instructional segments designed to enable the student to attain the objective, where attainment is usually defined as a test score exceeding some arbitrary value. The small book by Mager (1962) was instrumental in popularizing behavioral objectives with classroom teachers. Ralph Tyler (1950, 1964) has also been a leader in the behavioral objectives movement. Although using much of the same vocabulary and basic paradigms, his approach has emphasized objectives at a higher level of abstraction than those derived from Mager (1962) and others.

The impact of the behavioral objectives movement can be seen at all educational levels. College courses are fractionated into units that are further subdivided into objectives. Large lists of objectives are created for elementary school subjects (see Glaser, 1967; Popham, 1969; Westinghouse Learning Corporation, 1973a). Technical training is based upon lists of job-related objectives to be mastered (see Danforth, 1974; Mayo, 1974; Rockway and Yasutake, 1974). Within the present educational milieu, the role of behavioral objectives can best be described as ubiquitous. Despite its modern appearances, the roots of the behavioral objectives movement can be traced to Bobbitt (1913). His adaptation of Taylor's (1911) "Scientific Management" to education is the philosophical basis underlying most present-day discussions of behavioral objectives.

The third theme underlying CMI is educational technology. The impact of technology upon the daily lives of ordinary citizens during the past seventy-five years has been dramatic. To a large extent, many of the primary achievements of the 20th century have been technological in nature. Much of this technology has been scrutinized by educators for its potential in instruction. With each new level of technology has come a corresponding group of enthusiastic educators expounding its promise of dramatic change in education. In the past, we have seen waves of enthusiasm associated with educational movies, radio, and television crest and subside (Scrivin, 1975). Twenty years ago the wave was teaching machines and programmed instruction; ten years ago it was CAI. The technology theme in education has been well documented up to 1967 by Saettler (1968). In the recent past, the digital computer has been the focus of technology and its use in education. The ability of the computer to be programmed and to control peripheral devices has given educators an extremely powerful technology to exploit. Computers were still in their early stages of development when the first educational application, Computer Aided Instruction, was put into operation (see Coulson, 1961). In a very real sense, the digital computer and its associated technology represents an increase in educational potential of many orders of magnitude over previous technologies. Considerable funding has been expended by both private industry and governmental agencies to achieve this potential. Projects such as the Stanford CAI project (Suppes and Morningstar, 1972), the University of Illinois PLATO project (Bitzer, Hicks, Johnson *et al.*, 1967), and the MITRE/Brigham Young University TICCIT project (MITRE, 1974) have been the recipients of many millions of dollars. The latter two received five million dollars each from NSF in recent years. Despite this rather handsome level of funding, the impact of CAI upon the educational community has been minimal. A large number of CAI projects have been initiated with much fanfare, only to fade away quietly. The underlying causes for the limited impact are complex; but, as early as 1963, Baker pointed out that in order to achieve any educational leverage via computers, their unique capabilities would need to be exploited (also see Kopstein, 1970, for a discussion of the underlying causes for the limited success of CAI). One of the unfortunate features of classical CAI has been its proclivity to be the electronic equivalent of programmed instruction. Baker (1971a) also points out that the development of CMI systems was to some degree a result of the recognition by educators that the educational potential of CAI was not going to be realized in the foreseeable future. Consequently, they turned to other models of computer usage within education.

These three basic themes have converged, and the result is CMI. The behavioral objectives movement has yielded a particular style of curricular plan. Individualization has provided new instructional paradigms matched to the characteristics of the curricular plans. The combination has produced a unique educational environment and exposed a set of problems related to the management of instruction in this environment. However, CMI holds considerable promise for solving these problems. This promise is based upon a technology that can provide a data processing capability sufficient to meet the needs of teachers conducting programs of individualized instruction.

Towards a Definition of CMI

In the paragraphs above, CMI has been treated as if it were a coherent concept with a precisely stated definition. Unfortunately, this is not the case. The definitions of CMI are as diverse as the number of existing systems since CMI is somewhat like Topsy in that it "just grew." Baker (1971a) observed common capabilities for testing, diagnosing, prescribing, and reporting in the early systems. Scanlon (1974) indicated educational programs employing CMI would: call data at periodic intervals; use the computer to track pupil progress; schedule student learning activities; supply clerical assistance and management data to teachers; and provide administrators with evaluation information. Mitzel (1974b) attempted to define levels of CMI as a function of whether the computer was used in batch or interactive mode. Finch (1972) approached defining CMI by contrasting what was done under CMI with what was done under CAI with regard to student/computer interaction, decision-making requirements, lesson material storage, and other factors. These approaches to defining CMI have quite different perspectives; and the definition problem can be compounded further by inspection of Appendix A, which reveals there is little in common among some CMI systems other than the use of the computer.

Because of the existing diversity in what constitutes CMI, it is probably futile to attempt a precise definition. Rather, what is needed is a CMI concept to provide a framework to encompass a variety of computer-based instructional management systems. The underlying purpose of this book as a whole is to develop such a conceptual framework for CMI. To initiate this process, the paragraphs below restrict the domain by indicating what is not CMI and what is CMI at a rather global level.

First, what CMI is not can be shown easily. CMI is not Computer-Assisted Test Construction. CATC systems focus upon the creation of tests upon request from computer-based item pools. For example, the system developed by Kotin, Lin, and Jameson and reported by Lipson (1974) is a CATC system, not a CMI system. CATC has been the subject of a book edited by Lippey (1974b), and the distinction therein between CATC and CMI is quite clear. However, both Lippey (1974b) and Baker (1974b) indicated in separate chapters that CATC can be a component of a CMI system providing teachers with a test generation capability. CMI systems due to Merrill (1974), Griesen (1973), and Egan (1973) have integral CATC components. One can argue successfully that tests and test scores are fundamental to a CMI system; however, CATC systems provide the teacher with too limited a level of managerial support to qualify as CMI.

A number of supplemental systems described in Appendix A are actually Computer Administered Testing (CAT) systems and as such do not qualify as CMI systems. Systems such as those due to Anderson *et al.* (1974a) use the computer to administer end-of-unit tests to the student via an interactive terminal and inform him of his test results. The title applied to these CAT systems by Anderson *et al.* (1974a) is Study Management Systems (SMS). It is quite likely there will be a growing number of study management systems appearing in the near future, as they represent a mid-way position between CATC and CMI. The grounds on which the author rules CAT systems out of the CMI context is one of managerial support, since they provide the teacher with little more than test results.

Another related type of system is the achievement monitoring system, such as Comprehensive Achievement Monitoring (Gorth, O'Reilly, and Pinsky, 1974) and Student Achievement Monitoring (Oakland Schools, 1972). These systems are primarily concerned with test scoring and reporting procedures. Although much of the data provided by these systems is similar to that under CMI, the use of the data is different. The achievement monitoring systems focus upon curriculum evaluation, while CMI concerns itself with instructional management. O'Reilly and Hambleton (1971) attempted to use CAM as a CMI system but with limited success. Consequently, achievement monitoring systems are not CMI, even though the latter can perform most of the functions of the former.

The final non-CMI approach is CAI. There has been considerable dialogue among those interested in educational uses of computers as to whether CAI or CMI is the superordinate level of computer usage in education. Some persons argue that CMI is simply a degraded version of CAI in which the instruction takes place away from the computer. Such could be the case if CAI systems clearly had a well-developed managerial component. Examination of most CAI systems shows that, if any managerial component is present, it is considered a minor facet of the system. For example, the managerial aspects of the Stanford CAI project were added only when the shift was made from CAI to drill-and-practice. Other than Baker's (1971a) comments, discussion of the management aspects of the drill and practice system is confined to the teacher's manuals (Jerman, 1969). CAI systems also are disqualified as superordinate to CMI systems on the grounds of their view of the teacher's role. Under the classical CAI model, the teacher is allowed to be either an interested bystander or a resource person to call upon when the CAI system can't get a student to learn. Admittedly, in recent years CAI has moved away from the electronic implementation of programmed instruction inherent in classical CAI. The modern view of CAI is that it can be an effective instructional medium for specialized segments of a curriculum. Thus, the trend is to use the computer for segments of instruction involving modeling, simulation, and complex calculations rather than presenting a whole semester's work (McLean, 1973). Consequently, the author's strongly held view is that CAI is simply one of the educational resources managed by the teacher via CMI. This view also is counter to that of Cooley and Glaser (1968) and Silberman (1968), who viewed CMI as a stepping stone to viable CAI. However, CAI developers have begun to take notice of CMI and are considering the managerial aspects of instruction, but no CAI system known to the author approaches the managerial support provided the teacher by the most rudimentary CMI system. Thus, as currently implemented by most developers, CAI is not CMI.

Now that what CMI is not has been described, it remains to be seen what CMI *is*. From the author's point of view, CMI is a total educational approach in which a computer-based management information system is used to support the management functions performed by the teacher. This totality encompasses the educational goals, the curriculum, the instructional model, the teacher, and a management information system. Most of the discussions of CMI have tended to focus upon the computer-related aspects of CMI and have not looked at the total context. There is also some confusion in the literature as to who is the beneficiary of the inclusion of a management information system under CMI. It is the author's view that the computer component within CMI exists for the benefit of the teacher, not the student. The computer-based aspects of CMI are for the benefit of the student only insofar as they enable the teacher to improve the quality of education the student receives. This view is quite divergent from that of many CMI implementers. A number of CMI systems described by Mitzel (1974b) are based upon a learner-oriented conceptualization, but such an orientation is a carry-over from programmed instruction and CAI. The concept of CMI as learner-oriented is a weak one with limited growth potential. The real power of CMI lies in its ability to provide the teacher with a management information system capability to be used within the context of a total educational program. To conceptualize CMI as learner-oriented is to seriously divert the primary thrust of CMI.

The difficulties in defining CMI also stem from the implementation orientation of existing systems. The early CMI systems (Baker, 1971a) were developed primarily to help classroom teachers cope with the mass of detailed information generated by programs of individualized instruction. As a consequence, the design of CMI has focused on providing a clerical level of support concerned with test scoring, recording the number of objectives achieved, and the time it takes to complete instructional units. Clerical help at this level is highly situation-specific, and the detailed support needed can vary widely from curricula to curricula. Because of this, what appears to one system implementer to be a viable approach is of little value in another context. The real danger of this focus is that the CMI concept becomes too firmly identified with this detailed level of clerical support for the classroom teacher. One can very quickly run out of instructionally related clerical tasks to be allocated to the computer. When this point is reached, the clerical support version of CMI has reached the upper bound of its growth potential and will quickly stagnate at that level of conceptualization.

Another aspect of the difficulty in defining CMI results from the meeting of the three themes of individualization, behavioral objectives, and technology in CMI. This juncture has forced the recognition of the teacher as a manager. Teachers obviously have been managing their classrooms for many generations; however, the computer component of CMI forces the managerial component of a teacher's job to the foreground. Teachers and CMI designers alike are faced with deciding the issue of what the teacher manages: an instructional process akin to a production line, a curriculum, or an educational program. A number of different points of view can easily be adopted, each of which leads to quite different conceptualizations of what is being managed and what kind of a CMI system is needed. Assuming the teacher is a manager raises a second major issue, namely, the determination of the management goals of a teacher. Should they manage the classroom so as to maximize some output variable, such as units completed or scores on a standardized achievement test, or to manage so as to achieve the underlying goals of education or to optimize the self-realization of each pupil? Again, different managerial goals lead to different views of CMI. At the present time, it is not at all clear what management functions or goals are inherent in a teacher's job. Under classical management theory, as used in industry (Massie, 1965), a number of managerial functions are defined and the manner and degree to which they are performed can be a function both of the size of the organization and the level of the manager within a management hierarchy. Whether there are analogies to the managerial functions of the commercial world within the teacher's managerial role needs to be determined. Finally, the search for a definition of CMI involves ascertaining the "Management Philosophy" upon which one wishes to base the teacher's managerial role. One needs to look seriously at whether or not the roots of CMI should be in the "Scientific Management" theories of Taylor (1911) as applied to education by Bobbitt (1913). Many teachers would be affronted by the concept of the school as a factory, yet most CMI systems have their instructional management component based upon this management philosophy.

The role of the teacher as a manager is also highly dependent upon the level of the educational institution. At the elementary school level, the teacher deals directly with students and works cooperatively to some degree with other teachers. Thus, the teacher primarily manages an instructional process in which the teacher is directly responsible for the lowest level of detail in that process. At the college level, the professor may lecture to large classes, and the direct student contact is the teaching assistants. In this case, the professor has managerial responsibility over those who conduct much of the actual instruction. The managerial roles of the college professor and the elementary school teacher have certain commonalities, yet there are significant differences that could lead to quite different approaches to CMI for them.

Summary

The development of the field of CMI since its inception in the mid-1960's has proceeded at a modest pace. A basic question is whether this pace will continue or whether CMI will follow the boom-and-bust pattern of so many technology-oriented educational innovations. A basic premise of this book is that a firm conceptual framework must be developed for the field of CMI. Such a framework would provide a context for the design of curricula and the development of instructional models, and for the management information systems needed by teachers in their rediscovered managerial role. Due to many factors, such a conceptual framework does not exist; thus, it is the author's strategy to use the chapters of this book to further its development. In Chapter Two, the components of CMI, both educational and technological are examined as they occur in existing systems. Then, two CMI systems are analyzed relative to the components defined in Chapter Two. The Sherman School project is used as a case study, in Chapter Four, to illustrate the iterative process by which a rather sophisticated CMI system was developed. To provide both educators and computer specialists with an insight into the technical characteristics of CMI computer programming, the MICA computer program used in the Sherman School Project is described in detail in Chapter Five. These first five chapters essentially describe CMI as it exists (circa, 1977). The next two chapters examine some of the major issues that need to be faced in order for CMI to become an integral part of the educational scene. Chapter Six examines the educational side of CMI, with emphasis upon the teacher as a manager. Chapter Seven discusses some of the technological aspects of CMI related to creating and maintaining viable computer support for instructional management. The final chapter is the author's overall view of the status of CMI and the lines along which it is likely to develop in the future. Hopefully, the end result for readers will be a conceptual framework for CMI that will serve them well in their own educational environment.

Chapter Two

The CMI Concept

The relatively few attempts to model CMI have been either procedurally oriented (Spuck and Owen, 1974) or structurally oriented (Hsu, 1974). In the former case, the sequence of events such as test scoring, achievement profiling, diagnosing, and prescribing are specified and a functional flow diagram used to show the interrelationships among the various procedures. Under the latter approach, the structure of the computer programs and computer hardware components are described. The computer programs receive the data and store it in computer memory; the number and nature of the files in the data base and the sequence of computer processing are shown. In both the procedural and structural approaches, the resulting models are highly specific to the particular CMI system. Consequently, a large number of such models would need to be examined to elicit some general idea of CMI. However, such an approach would not result in a total system view of CMI, as these procedural and structural models, when they exist, are rather limited in scope. Consequently, the goal of the present chapter is to develop a conceptualization of CMI as a total educational system. Such a conceptualization is needed, since most developers of CMI systems have focused their attention upon the mechanics rather than the concepts. Without a conceptual framework, it is difficult to compare CMI systems and define lines of past and future development. The conceptualization of CMI developed below has been based primarily upon existing practice, and with a few exceptions does not attempt to indicate what CMI *should be.*

The basic building block of any educational program is some form of a curriculum plan in one or more subject matter areas. Such plans define the subject matter in a course and delimit the scope of the course. The degree of formalization of a curricular plan varies from simply selecting a textbook to highly detailed plans where the smallest curricular detail is specified. From an operational point of view, the curriculum plan exists in the form of a set of chapters, modules, units, or behavioral objectives that encapsulate the subject matter content. Thus, over the time frame of the course, these segments of course content are studied by the students. Given a curricular plan, an instructional model is employed to specify how the curriculum is to be implemented in the classroom or other instructional setting. The instructional model essentially defines the strategy by which the curriculum is to be delivered to the student. The instructional model could be the traditional lecture approach, or student centered, or one of any of a number of models. To a large degree, the instructional model determines the roles played by both the teacher and the students within the educational setting. Students achieve objectives, attain concepts, and complete units of instruction as a function of the curricular plan. They read textbooks, listen to lectures, confer with the teacher, sequence their activities, and are assessed according to the dictates of the instructional model. The teacher's role can be both instructional and managerial. In the former role there is a responsibility for "teaching," whether it be for classroom groups or individual students. In the latter role, there is a responsibility for insuring the smooth and effective functioning of the educational program, while assuring that acceptable levels of quality and quantity of education are obtained. The introduction of individualization into an educational program brings with it a host of problems for the teacher, in both the instructional and managerial roles. To cope with these problems, the digital computer was introduced to provide the teacher with a management information system. The computer provides a powerful vehicle for data processing, data storage, and report generation to be employed by the teacher in both the instructional and managerial roles. When a computer component has been added to the educational milieu, the result is typically referred to as Computer Managed Instruction. Because computer support has been added to an existing educational situation, many persons view CMI as being synonymous with the computer-based procedures. It is the author's view that CMI is an educational system composed of the following six components: curricular plan, instructional model, diagnosis and prescription, management, reporting, and computer. Each of these components plays an important role within the CMI concept, and there are interdependencies among them unique to CMI. For discussion purposes, the first four have been labeled the educational components; and the last two, reporting and computer, as the computer components. Since the six components will be used as the basis for describing and comparing the various approaches to CMI throughout the book, each is discussed in greater detail below.

Curricular Plan

Curricular plans are the end product of a deliberate design process performed by textbook writers, educational research and development centers, school districts, and individual teachers. Such plans specify the subject matter, content, academic level, fractionalization of content, and structure and interdependencies of the elements of the plan. One consequence of the behavioral objectives theme underlying CMI is that curricular plans are often the result of a "task analysis" of a given subject matter area. A subject, such as elementary school mathematics, is broken down logically into successively smaller conceptual units until some minimal element is reached. Depending upon one's point of view, these minimal elements are called behavioral objectives, concepts, teaching-learning units, or frames. The analogy of curricular fractionalization to a piece-parts breakdown of a television set or a work breakdown of a production line worker's job is direct. In the present book, the minimal curricular elements shall be called "units." Such unitization breaks down the curriculum into usable segments and also provides a convenient vehicle for communication related to the curriculum. When the teacher refers to Unit 6, the unit label conveys considerable information from the teacher to the pupil. Data such as its content, relative position in the curriculum, etc., are understood by the teacher and the pupil. To the pupil it may mean the physical instructional materials, another educational hurdle to jump, or another accomplishment. The reduction in communication load for both the student and the teacher provided by the unitization of the curriculum is considerable.

Once a task analysis has broken down the curriculum into "units," the curriculum designer is free to restructure these units in a way which he feels is most advantageous. The units can be arranged in logical sequences, such as chronological in social studies; by major topics in a science course; or in the building block fashion typically found in mathematics courses. At least five different curricular structures are employed in the curricular plans associated with CMI systems; these are shown in Figure 2.1. The linear structure is one in which the total curriculum is arranged in a unit to unit sequence. Within a linear curriculum there are no optional sequences for a student to follow. All students start at unit 1 and proceed sequentially to the last unit. The curricular plan used in the Sherman School Project, described in Chapter Four, has a linear structure. The strand structure is a variation of the linear arrangement in which the curriculum is divided into major areas. Within each of these areas, i.e., strands, several units are arranged in a linear order and a student may work on a unit within one or more strands concurrently. Eventually, the student should complete the last unit in each strand. The elementary school mathematics curriculum employed by DeVault *et al.* (1969) employed the strand structure. The block structure is one in which the curriculum is broken down into major topics, or blocks, and a

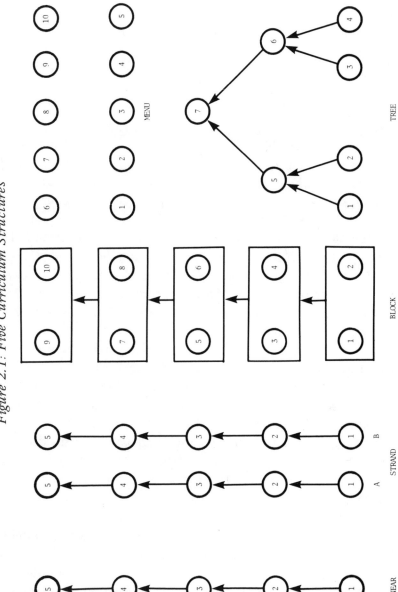

Figure 2.1: Five Curriculum Structures

number of units exist within each block. However, within a block there is no structure to the unit. A student is free to take the within-block units in any order until the block is completed. The elementary school science curriculum employed by PLAN* (WLC, 1973a) essentially has a block curricular plan. The most sophisticated curricular plan is one employing a tree structure. Under this plan, each unit is considered a node or a vertex in a graph and the lines connecting the nodes are edges. Diagramatically, the curricular plan appears like the root system of a tree with the trunk at the top and the root endings at the bottom. Typically, the units appearing at the bottom of the tree are considered to be prerequisites to those above them. Figure 2.1 shows a simple tree structured curricular plan where Units 1 and 2 and 3 and 4 are prerequisites to Units 5 and 6, which are prerequisites to Unit 7. The Developmental Mathematics Program (Romberg and Harvey, 1969) supported by the WIS/SIM system (Belt and Skubal, 1974) employs a rather elaborate tree structured curricular plan. Tree structured curricula can be quite complex, and the student can be working simultaneously on units on several different branches. When tree structured curricular plans are employed, they generate a considerable bookkeeping task for the teacher in terms of where each student is within the curriculum plan and in terms of whether all the prerequisites have been met for a given unit. The final curricular plan employed by CMI systems is what might be called a "menu" plan. Under this plan the total course is divided into modules or units that are unstructured. The student is free to select any module to study. When it is completed, he is free to select from the "menu" of remaining modules. The menu plan is quite common at the college level and has been employed by Allen, Meleca, and Meyers (1972); Countermine and Singh (1974); Judd and O'Neil (1974); and Merrill (1974).

  A direct link exists between the curricular plan and the form of individualization of instruction employed. Some CMI systems are based upon curricular plans that provide a degree of flexibility in the order in which a student may take the units, the exception being a linear curriculum. Thus, in addition to rate of progress, a degree of individualization can be provided in the sequence in which a student undertakes the units. In the strand structure, he can be at different places in each strand. Within blocks, no required order is imposed. Under a tree structure, a student may skip around with regard to units but must complete prerequisites before proceeding to a higher level in the tree. A given student may be at a very high level in one part of the tree and a low level in another. Few CMI systems have reported using different curricular plans for each student. Under such differentiated plans, each student studies only those units from the curriculum plan meeting his particular educational goals. Glaser (1967) indicated he felt curricular plan differentiation was not a viable concept in basic skills courses such as those taught in the elementary school. Thus, IPI and many other CMI systems for the elementary school level make no provision for student specific curricular plans. One CMI system supporting differentiated curricular plans is the Computer Managed Individualized Instruction System (Danforth, 1974) used in a vocational school. Its curricular plans were based upon task analyses of the occupations the students intend to enter. Thus, for each occupation there was a specific set of units to be accomplished. Presumably, individual curriculum units could appear in the curricular plans for more than one occupation. The degree of differentiation afforded an individual student within the curricular plans associated with most CMI systems is quite low. Most of the linear, strand, block, and tree structured curricular plans require each student eventually to complete the total curricular plan. The exception is those plans (Morgan and Richardson, 1972) where a student's course grade depends upon the number of curricular units completed, or those where there are core units and optional units (Allen, Meleca, and Meyers, 1972).

Although the mechanics of differentiated curricular plans to meet each student's educational goals can easily be handled by many CMI systems (see PLAN*, for example), the educational philosophy attendant to curricular plan differentiation typically is not employed.

The structure of the curricular plan has implications for the designer of CMI computer programs. The greater the number of units in the curriculum, the greater the amount of instructionally related data generated in the classroom. The more complex the structure, the greater the amount of record-keeping necessary to track the student through the curricular plan. For example, under a tree structured plan, a student may concurrently be working on several units, and he may not proceed to a higher level unit until all of its prerequisites are completed. Thus, the task of monitoring the student's progress becomes involved. Highly fractionalized curricular plans result in larger files in the computer's memory as well as in additional computer programming to handle the files and monitor students.

Instructional Model

The instructional model is the design for the scheme used to implement a curricular plan in the classroom or other instructional setting. As such, it specifies the functional flow of the educational program, the roles of teachers, assistants, and students, and the educational philosophy being implemented. The instructional model implicitly underlying most of the elementary school level CMI systems is one formulated by Glaser (1969). CMI systems at academic levels other than elementary school often employ the model without referencing it. An earlier version of this instructional model was a 14-point instructional model (Glaser and Reynolds, 1964) based upon a behavioral objectives approach to programmed instruction.

The instructional model was reported in abbreviated form by Cooley and Glaser (1968); the six parts are as follows:

"1. The goals of learning are specified in terms of observable student behavior and the conditions under which this behavior is to be exercised.

2. Diagnosis is made of the initial capabilities with which the learner begins a particular course of instruction. The capabilities that are assessed are those relevant to the forthcoming instruction.

3. Educational alternatives adaptive to the initial profile of the student are presented to him. The student selects or is assigned one of these alternatives.
4. Student performance is monitored and continually assessed as the student proceeds to learn.
5. Instruction proceeds as a function of the relationship between measures of student performance, available instructional alternatives, and criteria of competence.
6. As instruction proceeds, data are generated for monitoring and improving the instructional system."

As a verbal model, it a very good conceptualization of the basic instructional cycle of programmed instruction and its counterpart—classical Computer Aided Instruction (CAI). It specifies quite clearly what is to be done relative to the instructional cycle for a given curricular unit. In addition, Glaser's sixth point, specifying that the instructional system shall collect data to facilitate its own improvement, is an important concept. The basic deficiency of the Glaser instructional model is its lack of attention to instructional goals above the behavioral objective level. Krathwohl and Payne (1971) have indicated this is a general failing of the behavioral objectives approach. Glaser's own implementation of his six-point model in IPI (Cooley and Glaser, 1968; Glaser, 1967) is very heavy on the mechanics of the unit-of-instruction cycle, with mastery of behavioral objectives being the primary educational goal. The IPI implementation is dominated by unit pretests, unit posttests, and curriculum embedded tests (Hambleton 1974). Closer examination of the model shows that such a heavy emphasis upon assessment is probably inevitable, as three of the six points are assessment dependent.

One outcome of employing the Glaser instructional model, whether used explicitly or implicitly, is a CMI system built around the unit-of-instruction cycle. This cycle appears in a number of different forms, each of which reflects the particular educational context of the CMI system. The basic unit-of-instruction cycle due to Glaser (1967) employed a pretest to determine which objectives in the unit the student had already mastered. Then, instructional procedures for the remaining objectives within the unit are implemented. During the course of study, the student must pass a test (curriculum embedded test) for each of the remaining objectives. When all such tests are passed, the student takes a post-unit test covering all objectives in the unit. When a test score above the defined mastery level (85 percent) is achieved, the student is given credit for the instructional unit. CMI systems due to Connally (1970), Cooley and Glaser (1968), and Morgan and Richardson (1972), have used this unit-of-instruction cycle. Essentially, the same unit-of-instruction cycle, without the curriculum embedded tests, has been employed by Allen, Meleca, and Meyers (1972), Dick and Gallager (1972), and Judd, O'Neil, Rodgers, and Richardson (1973). The most simplified version of the unit-of-instruction cycle consists of the instructional procedures for the unit followed by a posttest. CMI systems such as PLAN* (Flanagan *et al.*, 1975; Westinghouse Learning Corporation, 1973a) and those due to Belt and Spuck (1974), Countermine and Singh (1974), Danforth (1974), and Kelley (1968) employ this version. In all versions of the unit-of-instruction cycle, test results are used diagnostically; the student receives a remedial prescription or a new unit.

At the college and university level, CMI implementers use the Keller Plan rather than Glaser's model as the basis for their instructional models. The Keller Plan has its origins in reinforcement psychology. It is a scheme for self-paced, self-directed study at the college level, often called "personalized instruction" (Sherman, 1974). The basic tenets of the Keller Plan were presented in a paper with the unique title "Goodbye Teacher" (Keller, 1968). The paper outlined an instructional model developed by two Brazilian and two North American psychologists as part of the attempt to establish a psychology department at the University of Brasilia. Keller (1968) reported that this model was first implemented at Columbia University in the Winter of 1963. The Keller Plan is designed to implement a college course individualized with respect to rate of progress where the students engage primarily in self-directed study. The contents of the plan are as follows:

1. The subject is divided into units of instruction that have a defined sequence. The students study these units on their own.
2. Students are required to achieve mastery on the posttest for each unit.
3. Lectures and laboratory demonstrations are available only to those students who have demonstrated mastery on the prerequisite units.
4. A hierachy of an instructor, a graduate student classroom assistant, laboratory assistants, and undergraduate proctors are used to provide the students with study materials, to administer and score tests, and to provide assistance to individual students upon request.
5. There is a final examination covering the whole course that constitutes 25 percent of the student grade. The remaining 75 percent is based upon the number of units and laboratory exercises completed. Each student must complete a minimum number of units to receive a grade.

A Keller Plan fits very nicely into the framework of most large classes, where typically a professor lectures, and teaching assistants conduct quiz or laboratory sessions. What the Keller Plan essentially does is redistribute these human resources so as to achieve a greater level of student contact. At the same time, it shifts a greater burden upon the student to be responsible for his own study of the course content and for maintaining progress through the sequence of units. The instructional units under the Keller Plan appear to be larger than the behavioral objectives used at the elementary school level. However, some college level CMI systems (Allen, Meleca, and Meyers, 1972; Griesen, 1973) employ behavioral objectives within the larger instructional units. Although the Keller Plan individualizes upon the rate of progress dimension, it establishes a minimum number of units to obtain a grade and bases better grades on completion of more instructional units.

The CMI systems due to Allen, Meleca, and Meyers (1972) and Griesen (1973) are modeled quite closely to the Keller Plan although neither references Keller. The Teacher Information Processing System due to Kelley, described in Chapter Three, approximates the Keller Plan, even though its independent design was completed prior to Keller's article. The recent study management systems (Anderson *et al.*, 1974a) also borrow heavily from the Keller Plan. The author has had many discussions with persons developing college level CMI systems, and generally they indicate the Keller Plan is their instructional model.

The relationship of the instructional model to individualization is an important one for CMI. Inspection of Appendix A reveals that the majority of existing CMI systems were designed to individualize only with respect to rate of progress, since all students pass through the same curricular plan. This holds across academic levels, as examples of rate of progress schemes can be found at the elementary school level (Chapin, Lorenz, Anglin, and Grass 1975; Cooley and Glaser 1968); at high school level (Morgan and Richardson, 1972); and at the college level (Dick and Gallager, 1972). The CMI systems supporting military training programs (Mayo, 1974; Rockway and Yasutake, 1974) were explicitly designed to individualize on rate of progress, as in this training context, time is literally money. Despite an occasional attempt at developing instructional models facilitating other forms of individualization, the preponderance of CMI systems individualize solely on the rate of progress dimension. This attests to the enormous difficulties, both theoretical and practical, of individualizing on additional dimensions.

Diagnosis and Prescription

The twin procedures of diagnosis and prescription are the keystone of most instruction. The teacher must diagnose the present status of the student and prescribe some educational activity that hopefully will alter the student's status in a desired way. These functions are performed by every classroom teacher many hundreds of times each day as the teacher interacts with students. In the typical classroom situation, the teacher relies upon knowledge of: the curriculum, the particular pupil, the range of student achievement in the particular subject, and the available resources in order to judgmentally perform diagnosis and prescription. Under these conditions, the accuracy of the diagnosis and the appropriateness of the prescription are a function of the teacher's experience and sensitivity to the information derived from the classroom situation. The consistency of performance over time of even highly perceptive and skilled teachers can be variable for a given pupil as well as across pupils. It is at this level where Glaser's instructional model makes a significant contribution. Diagnosis and prescription are explicitly called for in points two through five of his model. Diagnostic and prescriptive procedures were an integral part of the early CMI systems (Baker, 1971a), yet many of the systems listed in Appendix A do not include both procedures. The diagnostic procedures of most CMI systems are based primarily upon the results of criterion-referenced tests administered as part of the unit-of-instruction cycle. The pre- and posttests are used to determine whether or not objectives have been mastered. Hambleton (1974) has investigated the diagnostic procedures of a number of CMI systems and found that instructional diagnoses consisted simply of a list of objectives mastered or nonmastered. The level of diagnostic information provided by such a list is at a rather crude level of detail. Such diagnoses do not in any sense diagnose why the student has not mastered the given objective; they merely indicate the status of the student relative to the curricular structure. No CMI system makes diagnostic use of the pattern of achievement data, such as topics appearing in more than one unit that a student consistently has difficulty mastering. Again, this seems to be due to the behavioral objectives approach with its emphasis upon mastery of individual objectives. Under PLAN* (WLC, 1973a) and IPI

(Cooley and Glaser, 1968) a broad form of diagnosis is provided by placement tests. PLAN* employs placement/achievement tests for modules at each grade level in each of four subject matter areas. These tests enable a student to bypass teaching-learning units that have been mastered previously. IPI employs a placement test to place students at an appropriate unit within the set of units. Two CMI systems, PLAN* and WIS/SIM, can employ assessment procedures not based upon test scores. Under both, teachers can certify that a pupil has achieved a particular objective or demonstrated a particular skill. These teacher certifications are treated as equivalent to mastery of a unit posttest.

Two classes of prescriptions can be made on the basis of a diagnosis, forward and remedial. If a student has completed some segment of the curricular plan successfully, he will receive a forward prescription assigning the next unit, module, etc. If the assessment procedures reveal that a student has not mastered certain objectives, or has not understood a unit or module, he receives a remedial prescription. A remedial prescription can be simply to restudy the material, but more commonly it is the assignment of some educational activity or resource to aid the student in achieving a satisfactory level of performance. When referring to prescriptions, most CMI implementations tend to consider them to be remedial in nature. Thus, a diagnosis is a list of objects or units not mastered, and a prescription becomes a corresponding list of educational activities or resources. Ideally, these resources should be linked very closely to the particular diagnosis. For example, if a student did not master the objective of two-digit addition, there should be a prescription that would be optimal for enabling the student to master the objective. However, one of the commonalities of present CMI systems is that the basis upon which prescriptions and diagnoses are connected is entirely judgmental. Teachers or curriculum developers are responsible for the matching of educational activities or resources with a given diagnosis. In addition, the realities of the classroom and of economics usually reduce the range of prescriptions to educational vehicles such as textbooks, work books, and various pencil and paper activities. A number of CMI systems (see Allen, Meleca, and Meyers, 1972; Flanagan, 1969; Mayo, 1974) provide a range of prescriptions via the media of presentation. In these cases, the instructional material can be presented via audiotapes, filmstrips, movies, or television. In most cases, the differentiation of the prescriptions is simply in the media used, as the content or instructional approach is the same. The concept of highly individualized prescriptions is severely constrained by one's ability to conceptualize such prescriptions and to create the appropriate educational resources. In addition, there are financial constraints, further restricting the level of resources available for developing prescriptive materials on a large scale.

Some CMI systems employ prescriptions differing somewhat from those described above. Kelley (1968) prescribes attendance at other professors' lectures, conferences with teaching assistants, and release from certain course requirements. Under WIS/SIM (Belt and Spuck, 1974) prescriptions consist of assignment to instructional groups, and the teacher chooses how to handle remediation for the group of students. Hsu (1974) displays a list of available instructional options based on the diagnoses, and suggests a sequence of objectives to be learned. Only one CMI system (Connelly, 1970) has reported an attempt to take aptitude-treatment interaction into account when prescribing. In the Conwell School CMI project, the instructional materials for each curricular unit were categorized by reading level, aptitude level, learning style—consisting of three distinct sensory pathways, visual, auditory, and kinesthetic—and cognitive style—abstract or concrete. A battery of tests was administered to provide a profile of each student on these dimensions. Instructional packets were developed for each instructional unit and were characterized by various combinations of these attribute values. Teachers were responsible for coding the available packets using these attributes. Hypothetically, there could have been 72 different packets for each segment of an instructional unit. However, in actual practice a much smaller number was available. When prescribing, a matching algorithm was employed which attempted to obtain the best fit between the pupil's profile and the attribute values of the instructional packets. This algorithm first tried to obtain a perfect match and iteratively removed attributes from the matching process until a match was obtained.

Given the importance of diagnosis and prescription at the unit-of-instruction level, it is surprising that CMI systems such as PLAN*, WIS/SIM, ILS/*CMI (Egan, 1973), and that due to Judd *et al.* (1973) do not involve the computer in the prescriptive process. In these CMI systems, the teacher judgmentally makes prescriptions based on diagnostic reports. The diagnosis and prescription process is automated in CMI systems due to Allen, Meleca, and Meyers, (1972); Bratten (1968); Chapin *et al.* (1975); Cooley and Glaser (1968); and Countermine and Singh (1974). In these systems the teacher's judgments have been stored in the computer's data base; and, when an objective is failed, the previously determined prescription is obtained and printed by the computer for the teacher to use. The Sherman School Project (Baker 1974a; Chapin *et al.*, 1975) employs a "menu selection" approach where the computer displays a list of seven possible prescriptions for each objective and the teacher selects the one he or she feels is best for the particular student. Hsu (1974) uses a similar approach.

Diagnosis and prescription as it exists in present CMI systems is not very sophisticated. None of the CMI systems employs patterns of student performance or instructional history over time to develop diagnoses, although Kelley (1968) provides the capability. Similarly, the prescriptions generally are judgments as to what the student should do for remediation of a deficiency. Although implementation of these judgments is automated in some systems, they are still one-to-one relations between an objective missed and an educational activity or resource. The underlying problem here is one of a lack of a real theoretical basis for both diagnosis and prescription. Both procedures are highly specific to given curriculum plans and instructional models. Even those CMI systems emanating from well funded research and development centers do little better than CMI systems developed by local school districts in regard to diagnosis and prescription. It appears to be a "state of the art" problem. However, CMI does offer a straightforward means of collecting data on diagnosis and prescription, hopefully to provide some data upon which to base better procedures.

Management

One of the primary causes of the emergence of CMI systems was a recognition of the unmanageability of highly unitized, rate of progress, individualized instructional schemes. Once such a scheme was initiated, the pupils quickly spread themselves over the curricular plan; the instructionally relevant data for each pupil was different; and each pupil needed a considerable amount of managerial attention. The mass of instructional data, the lack of uniformity in pupil activities, and the individual differences among students severely taxed the teacher's managerial skills. More than any other factor, the asynchronous movement of students though the curricular plan at their own rate created a changed managerial role for the teacher. Despite this basis, the CMI literature pays scant attention to the teacher as a manager. Baker (1971a) observed the lack of emphasis upon managerial aspects in the pioneering CMI systems. In 1974, Mitzel indicated this was still the case, even though many more CMI systems had been developed. Such a state of affairs seems to be rather peculiar in light of the label "Computer Managed Instruction." The author was unable to find a single paper due to persons associated with the development of a CMI system dealing explicitly with the management component. Only the paper due to Kooi and Geddes (1970) looked at CMI from the teacher's point of view, and devoted a few paragraphs to the teacher and management. The majority of articles on CMI written by systems implementers focus upon the mechanics of supporting the teacher as a manager, but neglect to define the specific managerial functions fulfilled by the teacher.

An additional peculiarity of the CMI literature is the rarity with which the managerial goals of a given CMI system are explicitly stated. An examination of the literature for implicit rather than explicit managerial goals reveals two managerial goals implicit in the design of most CMI systems. First is the maximization of student achievement at the minimum level of the curricular plan, i.e., mastery of behavioral objectives, attainment of concepts, etc. The second implicit managerial goal is that of maximizing pupil flow through the curricular plan. This goal underlies the numerous CMI systems individualizing on the rate of progress and is the *raison d'etre* of military training CMI systems. Because of these anomalies in the CMI literature, the paragraphs below attempt to define the levels of management that appear to be implicit in CMI.

Within the educational setting, the teacher performs management functions at three levels: instructional, course, and program. The choice of labels for these three levels was somewhat arbitrary, but they do have some correspondence to the curriculum literature. Figure 2.2 diagramatically depicts the relationships among the three levels.

At the instructional level the teacher performs managerial functions associated with the unit-of-instruction cycle. When a unit is assigned to a student, the teacher must determine if the prerequisites for the unit have been met. The pretest must be administered and scored, and a mastery or non-mastery decision made on each objective within the test. For those objectives failed, the teachers must decide what prescription to employ for each. The necessary resources, whether books, films, etc., must be located and made available to the student. While the student is engaged in the prescription, the teacher monitors his progress to keep the student on task and to clarify any ambiguities in the tasks. Once the student completes the assigned task, the posttest is

Figure 2.2: Three Levels of Management

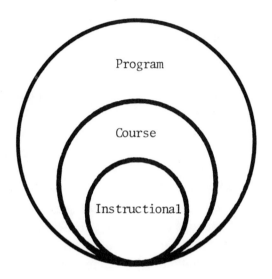

administered and the process repeats, either for a set of remedial prescriptions or for the next unit in the sequence. From a managerial point of view, the teacher is responsible for this cycle being conducted properly. Although the basic cycle is simple, it occurs asynchronously for each of the pupils in the class; the starting times are different, as are the contents of the units. When multiplied by the number of pupils in a class, the lack of synchronization leads to a considerable management load at the instructional level. However, a high proportion of the managerial load is more procedural than instructional in nature.

The course level of management is concerned primarily with the productivity of the CMI system in a specific course or subject matter area. The teacher is responsible for the students completing units and proceeding through the curriculum plan at a reasonable rate under the instructional model employed. Thus, the course level of management is concerned with student scheduling, pacing, and expectations. For example, PLAN* uses a Program of Studies

(POS) to assign a series of instructional units to a student. The POS enables the teacher to assign a set of units to a student, and the computer-generated reports keep the teacher informed of the student's progress relative to the POS. Danforth (1974) also uses a program of studies approach in a vocational school setting. WIS/SIM (Belt and Spuck, 1974) establishes performance expectations in terms of the number of units a given student is expected to complete during the semester. Thus, the teacher can relate student progress to the expectation. IMS-3 (McManus, 1971) provides teachers pacing information relative to the curricular plan to assist teachers in completing the plan by the end of the school year. Egan (1973) keeps track of students relative to an instructional flow chart associated with each subject matter. Schedules such as the above become part of the information base a teacher uses to formulate managerial decisions at the course level. If a student does not complete a sufficient number of units within a given period of time, the teacher is aware of the discrepancy. The teacher can then amend the plan, assign the student other remedial activities, or take other appropriate actions to remedy the situation. Silberman (1968) has commented upon the conflict between a teacher's desire for students to master the educational content and externally imposed pressures to complete curricular plans by the end of the school year. This is the case even in individualized rate of progress schemes, as it is implied that progress will be made. The course level management functions performed by teachers are often aimed at attempting to achieve a reasonable balance between mastery and progress. In some CMI systems it is explicit that progress will be made. The Keller Plan and CMI systems due to Allen, Meleca, and Meyers (1972) and Morgan and Richardson (1972) assign grades on the basis of units completed. The pacing function of course level management employs data such as the number of units completed, the date the unit was assigned, and the program of studies. Through such data, it is possible to identify dawdling students, and students who can not achieve a given objective. The teacher must then make course level decisions as to how to manage the students in the best manner to achieve progress. The final facet of course level management within the classroom is that of resource allocation. Because students are distributed throughout the curricular plan and within the instructional model, some balance is needed in the way instructional resources are used. In most situations, only a finite amount of resources, such as texts, filmstrips, specialized equipment, and human resources are available. Thus, if students' needs for these resources are not managed, the whole instructional process can degrade due to queues and conflicting demands for the same resources. The teacher needs to manage both the allocation of resources and the distribution of students needing these resources in order to have an effective instructional program. In vocational schools and military training programs, where specialized and often expensive equipment is used, resource allocation at the course level is an especially important function. The AIS system (Rockway and Yasutake, 1974) makes explicit provision for such resource allocation as a management function. Chapin (1975) has also discussed the resource problem within the context of an elementary school CMI system.

From the literature, it would appear that the management in CMI is primarily course level management. The instructionally related data collected and the reports generated by a wide range of CMI systems are designed to support the course level of management.

The third level of management is the program level, where the teacher is concerned with the educational program of a student or group of students. Management responsibilities at this level encompass all of the courses constituting the educational program under a teacher's jurisdiction. Issues such as the attainment of higher level educational goals, the balance of time and other resources across the several courses, curricular improvement, interaction of the courses, and the quality of the educational program underlie program level management functions. Since the majority of CMI systems involve a single course under a single instructor, the program level of management is essentially non-existant. However, Bolvin (1974) indicated that CMI systems must move in the direction of the program level of management in order for the teacher to truly manage. Although certain CMI approaches (see Chapin *et al.*, 1975; Countermine and Singh, 1974; Kelley, 1968; and Merrill, 1974) can support several different courses, they do so on an independent basis rather than on an across-course basis. Only PLAN* encompasses multiple courses under a single teacher; but despite the generation of reports for multiple subject areas, PLAN* does not provide direct support for the teacher at the program level of management. During the 1975/1976 school year, WIS/SIM employed a curricular plan where the science units had prerequisites in the mathematics curriculum. Unless a student had completed the appropriate units in mathematics, he was not able to initiate a given science unit. One aspect of program level management, curricular improvement, is provided for in a number of CMI systems, although on a single course basis. CMI systems such as those reported by Belt and Spuck (1974), Chapin *et al.* (1975), Cooley and Glaser (1968), Flanagan *et al.* (1975), and Judd *et al.* (1973), have incorporated the sixth point of Glaser's model into their designs. These systems use test results, item analysis, and end-of-year student history data to evaluate the curricular plan and the instuctional model. Typically, such evaluations are made during the summer with changes incorporated for the next school year. These annual reviews also encompass the computer component. Changes in data collection, reports, and procedures are implemented to improve the total CMI system. Chapter Four provides an account of this process as it was performed in the Sherman School project.

Because the management component of CMI has essentially been ignored in the literature, a major portion of Chapter Six has been devoted to the historical and conceptual roots of this component. This was done in the belief that the ultimate level of sophistication of CMI is going to depend upon the conceptualization of the management component. The area is too important to be implicitly defined via use.

Computers

Within the CMI concept, the educational components have the dominant role, while the computer component plays a supportive role. In most situations, the curricular plan and the instructional model for an individualized course existed and the computer component was "added on." The computer was viewed as a vehicle for performing a number of clerical and data processing tasks that were the keys to successful implementation of an individualized course. Although the computer component plays a key role in CMI, there is considerable variation in the way in which this role is fulfilled. In a given situation, the actual functions performed by the computer component are dependent upon the computer capability available to the implementer as well as the design of the CMI system. In the paragraphs below, the primary functions performed by the computer are discussed and the major approaches to using the computers for CMI are described. Again, the plan has been to look across rather than within individual CMI systems and to develop a composite picture of the computer component.

The primary role of the computer component in the majority of CMI systems is to collect, store, and report instructionally related data. In order to do this, the following five functions are performed: (1) *Data collection.* Instructionally related data, such as test scores, objectives mastered, units completed, resources employed, etc., are recorded on or transcribed to a computer-compatible medium. The most widely used input medium consists of test answer sheets or cards that can be scanned by an optical mark reader. The item responses are detected by the scanner and transmitted (input) to the computer (see Baker, 1971b, for a discussion of this technology.) Data other than assessment results are entered into the computer via optically scannable sheets or cards, keyboard terminals, or in the form of punched cards.

(2) *Data storage.* The dynamic data collected from the instructional setting is stored in the computer along with static data such as the curricular plan, lists of student names, assessment instruments, and student groupings. The totality of this data forms what computer specialists call a data base. The data base is the core element of the computer component of all CMI systems, and a major portion of the computer programs in the computer component are associated with the creation, maintenance, and use of the data base. The data base consists of a number of different files each storing a class of information used by the CMI system. Files commonly employed are a student history file, a curriculum file, a test file, and a class roster file. In Chapter Five, detailed specifications of the set of files employed by the MICA CMI computer program (Behr *et al.*, 1972) are presented. The data base can be stored in one of a number of different computer storage devices. The particular device depends upon the specific computer, but the most popular device is disk memory, with a few systems using magnetic tape storage. The design of data bases for management information systems is a sophisticated endeavor and is the key to the efficiency, cost, and flexibility of a CMI system. (3) *Automated diagnosis and prescription.* A relatively few CMI systems include functions to perform diagnosis and prescription automatically when assessment results are received. For each diagnostic outcome, a prescription exists in the data base that can be extracted on a simple table look-up basis and reported, thus relieving the teacher of a routine repetitive instructional level task. (4) *Data processing.* The primary advantage of computer supported data processing over manual procedures is the facility of the computer to organize, aggregate, and summarize data. Computer programs can be written to organize the data in various ways to make certain functions more efficient. The summarization of data extracted from a variety of sources within the data base is a simple task for the computer but a nearly impossible task for manual procedures. In addition, it is a straightforward task to develop computer programs to perform particular data analyses, such as

correlating variables, matching patterns, and grouping students. (5) *Reporting.* All of the data collection, storage, and processing capabilities are focused upon the generation of reports for use in instructional management. The computer component includes computer programs to generate the various reports employed. The computer can easily report data in one format, restructure the data, and report it again. Much of the power of CMI systems stems from their ability to exploit the data base and generate the reports needed for management purposes. Because of this, reporting has been identified as a separate component of the total CMI system and is discussed in greater detail in a separate section.

An interesting phenomenon observed in classrooms operated under CMI is that these five computer related procedures become a focal point for both students and teachers. Students are responsible for preparing a variety of computer compatible media, such as optically scanned answer sheets or cards. Both students and teachers use the computer generated reports. They also become dependent upon the computer for the daily conduct of the classroom and are sensitive to the reliability of the computer component.

The operational procedures related to the use of the computer component depend upon the type of computer system available and mode of operation employed by the CMI system. The two basic modes of computer utilization are "batch" and "time-sharing." Under the "batch" approach, the instructionally related data is collected in the classroom in either raw form or on a computer compatible medium. The data is then physically transported to the computer facility where it is entered into the sequence of "jobs" to be processed by the computer. The CMI data processing is simply one of many hundreds or thousands of jobs performed by the computer during the course of the day. The CMI reports are produced on the high-speed printers of the computer facility and upon completion must be physically transported back to the classroom. CMI systems such as those due to Danforth (1974), Kelley (1968), and Steffenson and Read

(1970), employ the batch approach. The major disadvantage of the batch approach is the slow "turn around" time, i.e., the time between creation of the data in the classroom and the receipt of the reports by the teacher. This can vary from as little as three hours (Kelley, 1968) to ten days (O'Reilly and Hambleton, 1971). The advantage of the batch approach is that it is the lowest cost mode of computer utilization. A variation of the batch approach, Remote Job Entry (RJE), is used by nine of the CMI systems listed in Appendix A. Under the RJE approach, a computer input device and a computer output device are located in the school building and are connected to a physically distant computer via telephone lines. The input device is commonly an optical mark reader that processes the test answer sheets. The output device can be any one of a number of printing mechanisms, such as a keyboard terminal or low speed line printer (for examples see Belt and Spuck, 1974; Rockway and Yasutake, 1974; and WLC, 1973b). Procedurally, the use of the RJE is identical to the batch approach. The difference is that the data is no longer physically transported to the computer facility. It is submitted to the computer directly from the school. Similarly, under RJE, the reports are printed at the RJE terminal in the school and are available immediately upon completion. The data and request for data processing submitted via the RJE approach are entered into the queue of jobs to be performed by the computer facility just as if it were submitted at the computer facility. Thus, the actual processing is simply another batch job as far as the computer facility is concerned. The advantage of the RJE approach is the elimination of the delays associated with physically transmitting materials to and from the computer facility. This convenience is achieved via computer peripherial equipment costing roughly $6,000 to $10,000 and a telephone connection to a computer capable of supporting RJE terminals. Southwest Regional Laboratory (McManus, 1971) has performed an interesting study comparing the various manual and automated schemes for getting data from the classroom to the computer and returning the reports.

The "time-shared" approach to computer usage involves what is commonly called "interactive" computing. Typically, a device such as a keyboard terminal or a cathode ray tube display is connected via telephone lines to a computer. When a person using the terminal types in data, requests a report, or performs other actions, the computer recognizes the action as a demand for service and performs the required data processing within a few seconds. Thus, under the "time-sharing" approach the terminal operator conducts a dialogue with the computer. The nature of the dialogue depends on the design of the particular CMI system. The MICA system (Behr *et al.*, 1972), described in Chapter Four, requires a teacher to enter all test results and requests for reports via a cathode ray tube display. The reports are printed by a small printer attached directly to the display terminal. A number of CMI systems use optical mark readers (see Countermine and Singh, 1974) as the input device in conjunction with a keyboard printer or CRT display. This approach simplifies the entry of student responses to assessment instruments. Under a fully interactive CMI system, the terminal is connected to the computer during the entire class period and the resources of the computer are available whenever the teacher or a student needs them. Hsu (1974) employed a scheme where interactive terminals were used at the end of the school day to enter the day's data.

The advantage of the "time-shared" approach is that it places the full capability of the computer component at the disposal of the teacher or terminal operator. Data can be entered as it is created in the classroom. A teacher can examine a student's history file before making an instructional decision in the classroom. Reports can be printed upon demand when the teacher feels a report is needed rather than on a schedule or waiting over-night for it to be delivered. In addition, the interactive mode is generally much simpler for a teacher to use, there are no forms to fill out, no delays between request and result, and the computer is obviously under the teacher's control. All of these advantages are obtained at some economic cost, and the capability for supporting a "time-sharing" mode of operation has become available widely only recently. "Time-sharing" requires specialized computer hardware and very sophisticated computer operating systems to perform the computer scheduling and resource allocation needed to conduct "time-sharing" operations.

For the most part, CMI systems employ a computer facility that is not dedicated to CMI, and a high proportion of all CMI systems use the computer facilities of a college or university. These computer facilities normally support a wide variety of users: students learning to use computers, faculty research, and administrative data processing as well as CMI. Such a situation has the advantage of providing a sophisticated level of computer capabilities, while having the disadvantage of considering CMI as only one of many uses of the computer. Only the military (Howard, 1974; Rockway and Yasutake, 1974) appear to have the financial resources necessary to dedicate computer facilities to strictly instructional purposes. At least one CMI system (Morgan, 1974) shares a large-scale computer, an IBM 370/168, with the administrative data processing group of a local school district. Two commercial CMI systems are available (PLAN* and TRACER, Capson, 1974) but there is no data available on the degree to which the computer facilities involved are dedicated to the CMI operations. CMI implementers have been quite adept at employing the most sophisticated computer hardware available. Within the existing systems one can find use of desk-top optical scanners, cassette recorders, and a variety of CRT displays and hard copy printers. This array of peripheral devices is inter-connected to computers ranging from mini-computers to the largest computers available. Thus, there is no lack of sophistication among CMI implementers as regards computer technology.

The final aspect of the computer component within CMI is its cost-effectiveness. One of the salient features of CMI is the good fit between what the computer is called upon to do and its capabilities. Under CMI the computer is doing what it does best, namely, data collection, data processing, and data storage. These procedures are well understood and can be performed efficiently by a wide variety of computers. This is in sharp contrast to CAI, where the computer is used to present instruction and is doing what it does least well: communicate with many different people on an individual basis. In the case of CMI, one computer terminal in a classroom can be used by a teacher to manage dozens of students, and one remote job entry terminal in a school can be used to process hundreds of students each day. The net result is that CMI is a cost-effective use of computers in education. Operational costs can be tenths of a cent per pupil per day under batch access and about seven cents per day where interactive access is employed.

Reporting

The reporting function is a key part of a management information system, whether it is employed in industry, government, or the schools. Any functioning organization generates a considerable mass of raw data from its daily operations. Some of this data has been organized. In the school setting, raw test scores can be arranged in rank order to impart knowledge of a student's relative standing in a group. The unit engaged in by a given student can be juxtaposed against his program of studies to show his relative progress. Beyond simply organizing data, the reporting component also summarizes data in order to depict the situation from a broader perspective. The raw data can be aggregated from a number of points of view, and summary statistics calculated and reported. Summary information, such as number of units completed per week by each pupil, mean and variance of test scores, and number of posttests administered per unit, can be reported and used by the teacher to make decisions. When data has been organized, summarized, and reported, the manager can use the reports to elicit patterns of performance and underlying trends. A good example is the standardized grade placement of the Stanford Drill and Practice system (Jerman, 1969) that enables a teacher to observe if a student is working above or below his average grade placement. Attempting to elicit such trends or patterns on a judgmental basis in the classroom is very difficult if not impossible in most situations. For managerial purposes, the usefulness of the data is greatly enhanced by the manner in which it is summarized, organized, and reported. Also, summary reports have the potential for revealing the nonobvious characteristics of the classroom situation.

Examination of the reports generated by the various CMI systems shows that their number and composition depend upon the subject matter, the curricular plan, the instructional model, and the level at which the teacher manages. To obtain a coherent picture of the reporting component, one needs to look at the complete set of reports for each CMI system in some detail. However, such an examination will be delayed until the next chapter, where two different CMI systems will be presented. In the present case, a cross-section of reports will be examined in relation to their use at each of the three levels of management. To do so is a bit awkward, as it takes the report out of context; and the CMI system designer typically did not have the three levels of management as a design guide.

At the instructional level of management, the primary reports employed are those dealing with data collected during the unit-of-instruction cycle. The data is usually the result of the various assessment instruments. Test results are commonly reported in their raw form (see Anderson *et al.*, 1974a; Griesen, 1973; Judd *et al.*, 1973) along with an indication of whether or not the unit or objectives were mastered. Students as well as teachers typically receive these test result reports. A number of systems report the test results and also provide a prescription for each non-mastered objective. CMI systems due to Chapin *et al.*, (1975), Countermine and Singh (1974), Kelley (1968), and Mayo (1974), provide such prescription reports directly to the student in the form of "tear off" sheets retained by the student. These prescription reports inform the pupil as to the outcomes of the assessment and what he is to do next. Often the report is used as the basis for a dialogue between the student and the teacher to determine the best course of action. The teacher can also examine an aggregate prescription report (see Kelley, 1968) to evaluate how a group of pupils perform on the test. When certain concepts or objectives are not achieved, instruction can be modified to attempt to rectify the problem before the deficits accumulate in the educational program. For example, if in a chemistry course, the aggregate prescription report shows that few students mastered the concept of valences, the professor may wish to devote extra lectures or laboratory sessions to the concept before proceeding. Rather than generating prescription reports, WIS/SIM (Belt and Skubal, 1974) produces instructional grouping reports. These suggest how the teacher should group students for instructional purposes. A student history report appears in many variations within CMI systems and can be used at all three levels of management. Depending upon the CMI system, the student history report may simply list the units completed up to the date of the report. Additionally, it may show test results, diagnoses, prescriptions, tests taken, dates of instructional decisions, and similar detailed data. At the instructional level of management, the student history report and assessment results can be the basis for the making of daily instructional decisions. For example, a student history report may indicate a student has taken three posttests on a given unit and not achieved mastery. Consequently, the teacher may decide to chat with the student to determine the basis for the pattern of failures. Because the student history report covers a reasonably long time interval, often the school year to date, it allows the teacher to make daily instructional decisions within the total context of the pupil's efforts. Thus, the reports used at the instructional level of management enable the classroom teacher to see the present educational context for a pupil or group of pupils and to make detailed-level decisions appropriate to that context.

Course-level management reports are an integral part of existing CMI systems. The two nearly universal reports are the group report and the unit report. These reports provide the teacher with an overview of what each pupil is doing at a given point in time. They are employed primarily for determining a student's status relative to the curricular plan. The group report lists pupils' names in alphabetical order within some administrative group such as classroom, homeroom, or within an instructional group. The name of the unit and the date it was assigned to the student follows each student's name. Often, additional information such as the assessment procedure to be used at the end of the unit is included. The group report enables the teacher to evaluate the educational status of individual students or groups of students from a single report rather than attempting to extract such information from a set of student history reports for the individual students. The unit report essentially inverts the information of the group report. The major heading is the unit and under it are listed all students assigned the unit and the date the unit was assigned. In some cases (Behr et al., 1972), units are ordered by the number of students engaged in the unit, in order to draw the teacher's attention to the most popular unit.

In addition to status reports, such as the group and unit reports, progress reports are also used. Periodic reports generated on a weekly or other basis are used by PLAN* (WLC, 1973b), Danforth (1974), and Griesen (1973) to list the objectives or units completed by the student during the time interval or up to the date of the report. Two systems, IMS-3 (McManus, 1971) and WIS/SIM (Belt and Spuck, 1974), keep track of pupil progress relative to an expected number of units to be completed. Several systems (see Belt and Spuck, 1974; Chapin et al., 1975) use a report listing those students who have not had any interaction with the computer based aspects of the system since a given point in time. Teachers use this report to identify students who have been absent or are not making progress for some reason. Only IMS-3 aggregates student data over group, class, school, and school district to provide overall course evaluation data in much the same manner as CAM (Gorth et al ., 1974) and SAM (Oakland Schools, 1972).

From the characteristics of the reports used at the course level of management, primarily the group and unit reports, it is clear that they are used to manage throughput. The majority of the reports either give a student's status at a certain point in time or locate him relative to the curricular plan or unit-of-instruction cycle. These reports are used by the teacher to perform the scheduling and pacing functions associated with a management goal of maximizing throughput. Since the program level of management has received little attention in present CMI systems, it is not surprising that no reports were designed for use at this level. The pattern has been to use instructional and course level reports to manage individual courses rather than educational programs.

The six components of a CMI system described above do not exist as independent entities. The nature of each component is determined to a large part by its interaction with the other components. The curricular plan has an impact upon the design of the data base of the computer component. The mode of computer usage can depend upon the instructional model. Diagnosis and prescription is a function of the curricular plan as well as of the instructional model and has a considerable interdependency with the computer component. The management component is a function of all of the remaining components, since it depends upon reports which in turn depend upon the data generated in the classroom. While these are but a few of the immense set of interactions, they clearly illustrate that CMI is an educational system rather than simply the computer support added onto an existing instructional scheme. Because CMI is a system, these six components and their interactions provide a frame of reference for examining existing CMI approaches as well as for the design of future CMI systems.

The Scale of CMI Systems

The scale of a CMI system is important from both an educational and a technological point of view. The majority of

CMI systems were created as small-scale systems designed to meet the needs of a single instructor and a small number of students. However, if CMI is to become an integral part of the educational scene, large-scale systems capable of handling many different courses, thousands of pupils, and hundreds of instructors must come into general use. From a technological point of view, small-scale systems are reasonably straightforward to conceptualize and implement. As the scale increases, so do the demands upon computer storage, processing, and communication capabilities. Accompanying these increased demands are technological problems in data base design, file maintenance, and computer hardware that must be solved to achieve large-scale CMI. In the paragraphs below an attempt is made to define three levels of scale of CMI so that the related educational and technological issues can be attended to in later chapters.

Small-Scale CMI

A small-scale CMI system is one in which a single course is managed by a teacher or group of teachers. The popularity of this scale system is attested to by noting that 23 of the 28 CMI systems listed in Appendix A were classified as small-scale. CMI systems due to Allen, Meleca, and Myers (1972), Dick and Gallager (1972), Judd and O'Neil (1974), and Kelley (1968) are representative. Because small-scale CMI systems deal with one course at a time, they also tend to involve relatively few students. Although some college level course enrollments can approach a thousand, enrollments are typically a few hundred or less. The development of the computer programs needed to support a small-scale system are easily within the means of a single instructor. The necessary software often can be developed and maintained by an instructor with student help. In addition, the magnitude of the data base can be kept within reasonable bounds by balancing the amount of data stored per pupil against the total number of pupils. Since many small-scale CMI systems have been developed within a college or university context, access to medium- to large-scale computers is common. Thus, the developer has a choice as to the mode of computer usage to employ. An additional characteristic of small-scale CMI systems is that the operational costs are small in absolute terms. Because of this, they often can be supported directly by departmental or local school funds. Small-scale CMI systems represent an important facet of CMI, as they are the entry point for most schools, teachers, or instructors into CMI. As such, they constitute the base level of support and interest in the field.

Medium-Scale CMI

Medium-scale CMI systems are those in which one or more courses are independently managed by a number of different instructors employing a common set of computer software within a single school or institution. Such systems require multiple computer access, either RJE or interactive, to a single computer. Finding clear-cut examples of medium-scale CMI is a bit difficult. Systems such as that due to Merrill (1974) support many courses, but do it via customized computer programs for each course. Although TIPS (Kelley, 1968) could support multiple courses, it appears to have been used only to support single courses and instructors. The best examples of medium-scale CMI systems are those due to Danforth (1974) and Rockway and Yasutake (1974). The former encompasses a range of different job preparation courses, and uses eight interactive terminals for student inter-actions, all under a common computer. The latter encompasses three courses, many instructors, employs a large number of interactive and RJE terminals, and involves many thousands of students at any point in time. The immediate consequence of having a medium-scale CMI system is the increase in the size of the data base. It is magnified both by the number of courses and by the number of students. The complexity of the computer programs also increases due to the use of a common program. In addition to the complexity arising from multiple sets of students, technical issues such as software re-entrance become important. When a CMI system is both of medium-scale and moderately sophisticated, it will require considerable resources, especially when the time-sharing mode is used. In Chapter Seven, it will be seen that the computer component of a medium-scale CMI system is not a simple extension of a small-scale system. Rather, it involves a completely different set of design criteria and approaches.

The lack of many examples of medium-scale CMI systems appears to be a function of the state of the development of the field. However, as the small-scale systems demonstrate their utility, more medium-scale systems will be needed to handle the load.

Large-Scale CMI

In order to qualify as a large-scale CMI system, there must be multiple courses, multiple instructors, and multiple institutions involved, all operating on a single computer under a shared set of CMI software. The primary characteristic is the total size of the system. Large-scale CMI systems can be school district-wide, college-wide, or serve multiple institutions that are geographically distant. The two examples of large-scale CMI systems are PLAN* (Flanagan, 1969; Flanagan et al., 1975) and the NAVY CMI systems (Johnson and Mayo, 1974; Mayo, 1974). While there may be no difference between the educational components of a medium- and large-scale CMI system, the computer component of a large-scale system must cope with a much greater mass of data. This mass results from multiple curricula and from the large number of students involved. PLAN*, for example, supported four subject matter areas and involved 40,000 elementary school pupils during the 1973-74 school year (Flanagan et al., 1975). At this scale, only a very large computer dedicated to CMI could support a sophisticated, interactive approach to CMI, and such resources are beyond the economic capabilities of most CMI implementers. Consequently, the large-scale CMI systems must be brought within the realm of economic feasibility. This has been accomplished by two techniques. First, the remote job entry mode of computer utilization is employed. This approach allows the data from many classrooms to be entered via a single station, and the data from many such stations are consolidated into the job queue of the central computer. This provides a considerable reduction in the scale of the time-sharing capability needed to support large numbers of teachers. The price paid, however, is to divorce the classroom teacher from interactive access to the computer as a management tool. Consequently, the interval between the collection of instructional data and the availability of reports based upon the data is similar to that achievable under RJE procedures. The second vehicle for reducing the scope of the computer component of large-scale CMI systems is limiting the amount of data collected and stored per pupil. The smaller the amount of data, the smaller the data base, and thus the faster the data processing and the lower the overall cost. The mass of data and the associated computer usage can also be reduced by not automating certain functions in the instructional model. For example, PLAN* does not involve the computer component in the prescriptive process. Given the multiple curricula, the wide variety of instructional materials employed, and the total number of instructional units involved, the creation, storage, and maintenance of prescriptions would be prohibitively expensive. Thus, in addition to other features, large-scale CMI systems are characterized by the need to keep operational costs within reasonable bounds.

The distinctions among small-, medium-, and large-scale CMI systems are rather arbitrary. Also, the distinction between a medium-scale and a large-scale system is not very sharp. Despite these issues, the classification scheme provides a convenient framework for describing and comparing CMI systems. Consequently, it will be used in conjunction with the above-noted six CMI components to describe CMI systems in the rest of the book.

Summary
Due to the lack of an existing conceptual framework for

CMI, the present chapter has identified six components of a CMI system. These components have encompassed both the educational and computer aspects of CMI, since it is the author's view that CMI is a total educational system rather than simply the computer-related features. Although a variety of curricular plans are possible, the most common are linear sequences involving instructional units and behavioral objectives. The two most popular instructional models are those due to Glaser (1967) and Keller (1968), both of which are built around rate of progress through the curricular plan as the dimension of individualization. While diagnosis and prescription are important functions, they tend to be based upon judgmental connections between objectives failed and conventional remedial activities. Only in a few cases were these two procedures automated by a CMI system. The computer component in existing CMI systems has been conceptualized as the vehicle for relieving the classroom teacher of the clerical tasks associated with individualized instruction. Because of the ability of the computer to process data, the reporting component is the key to providing the teacher with management information. A variety of computer-generated reports is used at the instructional and course levels of management. However, a program level management is rarely encountered in present CMI systems; hence, few reports for this level are generated.

The base level of support and interest in CMI is founded upon the small-scale CMI system. A reasonable number of small-scale systems have been documented, and they provide a school's entry point into CMI. Because the interest in CMI is still at a relatively low level, there are not many medium- and large-scale CMI systems. In addition, the rather large developmental costs have limited the number of these systems.

While the present chapter has not defined CMI, it has attempted to provide a conceptual framework. The remainder of the book will employ this framework extensively to bring some order into how one views CMI.

Chapter Three

Some Representative CMI Systems

In the previous chapter the commonalities as well as the diversity of the various CMI systems were used to establish a six-component description of CMI. However, such an approach does not take into account the total context of a given CMI system and the interaction among the components. Consequently, one loses the flavor or philosophy of an individual system. In order to capture this, two CMI systems will be described in the present chapter, and a case study of an additional system will be presented in Chapter Four. The selection of the three systems was based on a number of considerations. First, the systems selected represent different points on the dimension of academic level. Second, representatives of small-, medium-, and large-scale CMI systems were chosen. Third, the systems chosen were documented at a level sufficient to form a basis for the description. The last point was especially troublesome as, beyond a rudimentary user's manual, most of the CMI systems are very poorly documented.

The example systems fulfilling the above requirements were: the Teaching Information Processing System (TIPS), (Kelley, 1968, 1973), the Sherman School System (Chapin *et al.*, 1975), and Program for Learning in Accordance with Needs (PLAN*) (Flanagan, 1969; Flanagan *et al.*, 1975; Westinghouse Learning Corporation, 1973b). TIPS is a good small-scale CMI system for college level courses. It is both one of the systems that pioneered the CMI concept and a widely used system. PLAN* is an excellent large-scale CMI system for use in the public schools. Although PLAN* can be used at the elementary, junior high school, and high school level, only the elementary school level will be described below. PLAN* also is one of the pioneering CMI systems and is unique in being offered as a commercial product by a major corporation, Westinghouse Learning. Of the five early CMI systems described by Baker (1971a), only TIPS and PLAN* have been in continuous use since 1967. The discussion of a medium-scale CMI system will be deferred to Chapter Four, where a case study of the Sherman School system is presented to illustrate the process through which CMI systems are developed. The design philosophies underlying these three systems are distinct; hence, they represent quite different approaches to CMI. The descriptions of all three systems will be based upon the six components defined in Chapter Two.

Teaching Information Processing System (TIPS)

TIPS was developed by Professor Allen C. Kelley of the economics department of the University of Wisconsin and was first used in the fall of 1966. TIPS was developed independently of the other early CMI systems. It originated in Kelley's desire to improve the conduct of his own introductory economics courses. The early development of TIPS was supported primarily by local funds. Subsequent funding has been received from several foundation sources. Since Kelley's original work, a number of other college level CMI systems (seven systems in Appendix A) have been developed. Each of these and the recent course study management systems have their roots in TIPS.

Kelley (1968) reported four design goals for TIPS. These were: (1) Provide a more formalized system for feedback of performance information from staff to students. In the typical large college class the quantity and frequency of performance information received by the student is not sufficient for most students to know where they stand in the course. Often the delay between assessment and student receipt of the results is such that it does not affect the students' study habits or level of effort. (2) Provide student performance information to the staff in a timely fashion. The teaching staff also needs information on student performance so that discussion or quiz sessions can be planned, lectures can be adjusted to meet needs of the students, and available resources can be allocated appropriately. (3) Provide a degree of personalization in the absence of a capability to provide a highly individualized instructional program. A common complaint of students in large lecture classes is the lack of personal attention they receive. At best a few students ask questions of the professor during and after class. The small-group sessions run by teaching assistants provide some personal contact, but their quality and usefulness is highly variable. In addition, the resources to develop and implement highly individualized courses at the college level are extremely difficult to acquire. Thus, TIPS was designed to provide an attainable level of personalization within the context of a large college class. (4) Develop a vehicle that would provide data for research on methods of undergraduate instruction. The TIPS effort has been characterized by a continuing research effort (see Kelley, 1968, 1973) where the research draws heavily upon the student performance and student description data maintained by TIPS.

Curricular Plan

The data base employed by the TIPS system does not contain a description of the curricular plan in use. As a result, the relationships among the curricular units must be maintained by the instructor external to TIPS. It appears as though it was assumed that a linear curricular plan was to be employed. The course would be divided into time periods, units, or modules that follow one another in a defined sequence. Within each curricular segment there can be a number of concepts, principles, or objectives the students must attain. Although not explicitly stated, Kelley (1968) appears to have divided his economics courses into time periods. Shakhashiri (1975) employed TIPS in a freshman chemistry course divided into eight major topic areas. In both cases, the curricular segments had a linear structure.

Instructional Model

The instructional model embedded in TIPS is the traditional college paradigm, a professor lecturing to large classes several times per week with graduate teaching assistants conducting discussion or laboratory sections one or more times per week. Superimposed upon this is a unit-of-instruction cycle employing a survey quiz. At the end of each curricular segment, all students take a 10-12 item survey quiz requiring about five minutes of time. The quizzes are ungraded and do not count towards the student's grade. The test results are used diagnostically, and prescriptions are generated informing the student of his strengths and weaknesses. The basic unit-of-instruction cycle with its survey quiz posttest is repeated roughly 10 to 12 times per semester. The actual number is determined by the professor; TIPS places no requirements in this regard. In addition to the survey quizzes, there are the regular graded midterm and final examinations. There is a high degree of similarity of the instructional model employed by TIPS and the Keller Plan. The two were actually developed in the same period of time, both were described in articles appearing in 1968, yet it is clear that the two authors were unaware of each other's efforts. Kelley (1968) was interested in showing in an empirical way that TIPS was beneficial to students and staff. His articles did not emphasize the instructional model aspect of TIPS other than to explain what TIPS was. Keller (1968) expressed a much greater interest in the procedural aspects of his instructional approach and its intuitive advantages as a model for conducting college classes. The two salient differences between the models is that Kelley (1968) did not envision TIPS as a vehicle for self-paced independent study by the students, and Keller did not employ a computer to support his approach. There are, however, basic similarities in the two approaches.

Diagnosis and Prescription

The diagnostic procedures under TIPS are based upon decision rules involving both student performance data and classificatory data. The performance data consists primarily of the results yielded by the ungraded survey quizzes. Within a survey quiz, one can allocate one or more items to a concept, objective, etc., within the curricular segment. Thus, the student can receive a total test score and a number of subscale scores for each survey quiz. The data base design enables one to assign these scores to specific data record locations by variable name. In addition, classificatory data, such as the student's age, major, quiz section, etc., can be stored in a similar fashion. TIPS provides a clever mechanism for defining decision rules whose outcomes are linked to messages printed for the student, teaching assistant (TA), and professor. These messages can be prescriptions or messages of an informational nature. The decision rules employ a scheme allowing one to define limits on the values of variables and to connect these limits via the logical operators AND and OR. The actual decision rule procedures implemented in TIPS use a card image oriented scheme that is not well suited to illustrative purposes. Hence, in the examples given below, a more programming-like approach has been taken to explain how the decision rules work. The simplest form of a decision rule compares the numerical value of a variable with a given value; if the comparison is met, a message is printed. For example, IF (Test Score < 3), then message (2). The decision rule can be made more complex by checking for a value lying within a range and through the use of logical operators in the following way: IF ($2 <$ Subscale score (2) < 3 OR Total Score > 6), then message (9). The decision rules can involve both student performance variables and student classificatory variables such as in the following example: IF (Econ Major AND Test Score < 9), then message (6). It is also possible to use performance data from more than one survey quiz as well as data from the graded midterm exams in a decision rule.

Using the TIPS diagnostic procedure, a professor can implement diagnostic logic to fit a given situation with ease. Because the generality of the data base scheme, the decision rules can employ essentially any data to which the professor has access and which is stored in a student's data record. The decision rule mechanics are simple and flexible, and provide a very powerful diagnostic procedure. It would appear that TIPS contains the most sophisticated diagnostic procedures of any of the CMI systems listed in Appendix A.

As used by Kelley, prescriptions are in the form of messages that are printed in the reports when the logic of a decision rule has been met. The messages are composed by the professor; they can be whatever he feels is appropriate to the related decision rule. When used prescriptively, the messages can specify a variety of educational activities. Kelley has used prescriptions such as: conference with the students' quiz section leader, attendance at lectures by visiting professors, participation in seminars, writing short papers, and release from certain course requirements. This approach requires the professor to have a good knowledge of campus activities in order to draw upon them for prescriptive purposes. It also means such prescriptive messages must be entered into the data base shortly before the survey quiz is to be administered. Under CHEM TIPS (Shakhashiri, 1975), the prescriptive messages related the survey quiz items to specified pages in the textbook to restudy, and assigned a variety of audio-visual materials available in a freshman chemistry resource room. In addition to prescriptive messages, informational messages can be printed via TIPS for all students or selectively for a subset of students in accordance with a decision rule. These messages can inform the students of a social event, draw their attention to the fact that the midterm examination is next week, or tell them to read a specific chapter in the text before the next lecture.

Procedurally the decision rules and corresponding messages as well as the survey quiz answer key are entered into the data base as a data set associated with a specific survey quiz. The TIPS system allows one to enter the set of information for each quiz at any time. It can be done dynamically just before each quiz, or all such sets can be entered at once in the beginning of the course. The latter procedure can reduce the timeliness and uniqueness of the prescriptions but also reduces the pressure to meet a deadline in the midst of other activities.

Reports

The TIPS approach employs three basic reports; a student report, a teaching assistant report, and a professor report. In addition, the latter report can contain a number of special tabulations of certain data. The student report is in the form of a computer printout given to each student as soon as the computer completes processing of the results of a survey quiz. The purpose of the report is to inform the student of his performance on the survey quiz and to provide the prescriptive messages. The heading of the report contains the usual identification information, student name, professor name, quiz section number, and the section leader's name. The body of the report presents the total test score, a table showing the correct response plus the student's response to each question in the survey quiz, and the messages resulting from processing the student's data via the decision rules. The reports are returned to the students via a "pigeon hole" system enabling each student to pick up his own report. Figure 3.1 shows a typical student report produced by TIPS.

The teaching assistant report is designed to provide the section leader with summary data from the survey quiz for the students in a section. The report heading identifies the course, the professor, the section, and the section leader. The number of students in the section and the class are reported along with the numbers in each that took the specific survey quiz. Average scores for each subscale within the quiz are reported by section and total class. An item analysis table reports the correct answer, the percent correct response in the section and class, the percent in the section choosing each alternative item responses, and the number not responding. A list of names of students in the section

Figure 3.1: TIPS Student Report

```
TIPS - SURVEY  6,12/2/76              ADAMS,HARRY
DESCRIPTIVE STATISITCS               ID  1234567890
EDPSY 561,PROF JONES                 SECTION  2,MR BETZ


YOU ANSWERED 6 OUT OF 10 QUESTIONS ON THIS SURVEY.
THE FOLLOWING TABLE SUMMARIZES YOU ANSWERS AS WELL AS THE CORRECT
ANSWERS FOR THIS SURVEY. YOU ARE URGED TO MAKE SURE THAT YOU UNDER-
STAND THE NATURE OF ANY INCORRECT RESPONSES WHICH YOU MADE.

      TABLE OF RESPONSES

QUES.  YOUR   CORR.     QUES,  YOUR  CORR.      QUES  YOUR  CORR.
NUMB.  ANSW.  NUMB.     NUMB.  ANSW. ANSW.      NUMB. ANSW. ANSW

  1,    2      2        5.     1     4            9,    2     2
  2,    3      3        6,     3     3           10,    4     6
  3,    2      4        7,     3     3
  4,    2      2        8,     2     4

FORMULA CALCULATIONS (QUESTIONS 3,5)
   YOU NEED TO BECOME BETTER ACQUAINTED WITH THE CALCULATION
   OF VARIANCES AND STANDARD DEVIATIONS. DO PROBLEMS 9-20 OF THE
   SUPPLEMENTAL HAND OUT SHEET. ALSO REREAD CHAPTER 6 IN HAYS.

SUMMATION ARITHMETIC (QUESTION 8)
   YOU ARE HAVING DIFFICULTY APPLYING THE RULES OF SUMMATION
   ARITHMETIC. DO DRILL AND PRACTICE EXERCISES ON SHEET 6 AND
   REREAD APPENDIX A OF HAYS.

INTERPRETATION OF NUMERICAL VALUES (QUESTION 10)
   YOU DO NOT HAVE A GOOD CONNECTION BETWEEN THE NUMERICAL
   VALUES OF DESCRIPTIVE STATISTICS AND THE DISTRIBUTIONAL
   CHARACTERISTICS THEY REPRESENT.  USE STAT*CONCEPT EXERCISE 3
ON THE COMPUTER TERMINAL UNTILL YOU DEVELOP A BETTER FEEL.

SPECIAL MESSAGE
   YOU SCORED BELOW THE MEAN ON THE MID-TERM EXAMINATION. YOU
   MAY BENEFIT BY ATTENDING THE STATISTICS LABORATORY SESSIONS
   HELD M-W-F AT 2,30-4,30.
```

is provided; for each student the messages contained in that person's student report are identified. This table is followed by a listing of the decision rule and the corresponding message. It also specifies how many students received the given message. Figure 3.2 depicts a TA report as generated by TIPS.

The professor report is identical in form to the TA report, the major differences being that the tables of average scores and the item analysis data are based on the total class. The professor report omits the history of student names and messages received. It does contain the list of messages and the number of students receiving each message. An abbreviated verson of the professor

Figure 3.2: TIPS TA Report

```
        TEACHING ASSISTANT SUMMARY OF STUDENT PERFORMANCE    PAGE 1
12/2/76     EDPSY 561 - PROFESSOR HENRY JONES
                SURVEY  6 - DECEMBER 2,1976
TA   MR BETZ
SECTION AND TIME  2, 1.20 F

NUMBER OF STUDENTS                                      24    50
NUMBER TAKING SURVEY  6,DESCRIPTIVE STATISTICS          24    50

                    TABLE OF AVERAGE SCORES
                                        AVERAGE PCT. CORRECT
                                          SAMPLE       CLASS
                                          (N=24)      (N=50)
G155 -- SURVEY 6,ALL 10 QUESTIONS          58.2        57.8
G175 -- QUESTIONS 1,2(CONCEPTS)            70.7        74.0
G176 -- QUESTIONS 3,4,5(CALCULATIONS)      79.0        80.0
G177 -- QUESTIONS 6,7,8(FORMULAS)          33.3        36.7
G178 -- QUESTIONS 9,10(INTERPRETATION)     41.6        40.0
```

```
                        ITEM ANALYSIS TABLE
                PERCENT        PERCENT IN SAMPLE SELECTING
NO.   ANS.      CORRECT         ALTERNATIVE RESPONSES
              SAMPLE  CLASS                                   NO
              (N=24)  (N=50)     1    2    3    4    5      RESP.
 1     3        83      80       4   83   13    0    0        0
 2     3        63      68       8    0   63   25    0        4
 3     4        75      78       4    4    8   75    0        8
 4     2        83      82       4   83    4    4    0        4
 5     4        67      80       8    8   13   67    0        4
 6     3        33      44      13   21   33   33    0        0
 7     3        25      32      13   21   25   37    0        4
 8     4        33      34      29   29    0   33    0        8
 9     2        54      46      13   54   17   13    0        4
10     1        50      34      50   25   21    4    0        0
```

```
                CONFIGURATION OF MESSAGES RECEIVED
                BY EACH STUDENT IN THE SAMPLE
        STUDENT NAME                      MESSAGES
                                 A    B    C    D    E
 1   ADAMS,HARRY                 NO  YES  YES  YES  YES
 2   BOLTZ,GEORGE               YES   NO   NO   NO   NO
 3   CRAMER,ANN                 YES  YES   NO  YES  YES
 4   DAVIS,MAX                   NO   NO  YES  YES  YES
 5   EPSTEIN,MAURICE            YES  YES  YES   NO   NO
 6   FISCHER,RON                YES  YES   NO  YES   NO
 7   GALLAND,ALBERT             YES  YES  YES  YES  YES
 8   HERTZ,BARBARA              YES   NO  YES  YES   NO
 9   INBERG,SYLIVA              YES  YES   NO  YES   NO
10   JOHNSON,BETTY               NO  YES  YES  YES   NO
11   KELLY,PAT                  YES  YES  YES   NO  YES
12   LEWIS,JACK                 YES   NO  YES  YES   NO
13   MORGENSTERN,JASON          YES  YES   NO  YES  YES
14   NEWELL,DENISE              YES  YES  YES   NO  YES
15   ORGANICK,ROBERT            YES  YES   NO  YES   NO
16   PEPPER,JAMES                NO   NO  YES  YES  YES
17   QUILLING,MIKE              YES  YES  YES  YES   NO
18   ROBERTS,SALLY               NO  YES   NO  YES  YES
19   ROPIER,DAN                 YES  YES  YES  YES   NO
20   SUNDQUIST,ALVIN            YES   NO  YES  YES  YES
21   STERNBERG,PAUL             YES  YES  YES  YES   NO
22   TIMMINS,VICTORIA           YES  YES  YES   NO  YES
23   THOMAS,JOANNE              YES  YES   NO  YES  YES
24   ZINK,WILLIAM               YES   NO  YES  YES   NO
```

Figure 3.2
(continued)

20 STUDENTS MET THE FOLLOWING CRITERIA

         G175 FROM 0 THROUGH 1
AND THEREFORE RECEIVED MESSAGE A

    CONCEPTS
         YOU HAVE NOT LEARNED THE BASIC CONCEPTS UNDERLYING DESCRIPT-
         IVE STATISTICS. ATTEND ALL STATISTICS LABORATORIES THIS WEEK.
         ALSO USE STAT*CONCEPT EXERCISE 3 ALONG WITH HAYS CHAPTER 6.

17 STUDENTS MET THE FOLLOWING CRITERIA

         G176 FROM 0 THROUGH 2

AND THEREFORE RECEIVED MESSAGE B

    FORMULA CALCULATIONS
         YOU NEED TO BECOME BETTER ACQUAINTED WITH THE CALCULATION
         OF VARIANCES AND STANDARD DEVIATIONS. DO PROBLEMS 9-20 OF THE
         SUPPLEMENTAL HAND OUT SHEET. ALSO REREAD CHAPTER 6 IN HAYS.

16 STUDENTS MET THE FOLLOWING CRITERIA

         G177 FROM 0 THROUGH 2

AND THEREFORE RECEIVED MESSAGE C

    SUMMATION ARITHMETIC
         YOU ARE HAVING DIFFICULTY APPLYING THE RULES OF SUMMATION
         ARITHMETIC. DO DRILL AND PRACTICE EXERCISES ON SHEET 6 AND
         REREAD APPENDIX A OF HAYS.

19 STUDENT MET THE FOLLOWING CRITERIA

         G178 FROM 0 THROUGH 1

AND THEREFORE RECEIVED MESSAGE D
    INTERPRETATION OF NUMERICAL VALUES
         YOU DO NOT HAVE A GOOD CONNECTION BETWEEN THE NUMERICAL
         VALUES OF DESCRIPTIVE STATISTICS AND THE DISTRIBUTIONAL
         CHARACTERISTICS THEY REPRESENT. USE STAT*CONCEPT EXERCISE 3
         ON THE   COMPUTER TERMINAL UNTILL YOU DEVELOP A BETTER FEEL.

12 STUDENTS MET THE FOLLOWING CRITERIA

         G164 EXAM 2 SCORE LESS THAN 30

AND THEREFORE RECEIVED MESSAGE E

    SPECIAL MESSAGE
         YOU SCORED BELOW THE MEAN ON THE MID-TERM EXAMINATION. YOU
         MAY BENIFIT BY ATTENDING THE STATISTICS LABORATORY SESSIONS
         HELD M-W-F AT 2.30-4.30.

report containing the information through the item analysis table is called the course summary report. Figure 3.3 shows a course summary report as generated by TIPS.

The reporting system of TIPS is based upon a table scheme. The student report contains an individual performance table showing how the student responded to the quiz. The TA and professor reports are based upon a table of average scores, an item analysis table, and a listing of decision rule based messages. In the TA report, the data for the section is reported and in the professor report, the data for the complete class is given. Such a table driven approach greatly simplifies report generation, as the format of the report is consistent; only the numerical values and headings need to be changed.

Figure 3.3: TIPS Course Summary Report

```
12/2/76

               PROFESSOR SUMMARY OF CLASS PERFORMANCE
          EDPSY 561 - PROFESSOR HENRY JONES

                 SURVEY 6 - GIVEN 12/2/76
                                                CLASS
     NUMBER OF STUDENTS                           50
     NUMBER TAKING SURVEY 6,DESCRIPTIVE STATISTICS  50


                 TABLE OF AVERAGE SCORES

                                         AVERAGE PCT. CORRECT

                                            CLASS
                                            (N= 50)
     0155 -- SURVEY 6 ALL 10 QUESTIONS        57.8
     0175 --QUESTIONS 1,2(CONCEPTS)           74.0
     0176 -- QUESTIONS 3,4,5(CALCULATIONS)    80.0
     0177 -- QUESTIONS 6,7,8(FORMULAS)        36.7
     0178 -- QUESTIONS 9,10(INTERPRETATION)   40.0
```

			ITEM ANALYSIS TABLE					
		PERCENT	PERCENT IN CLASS SELECTING					
NO.	ANS.	CORRECT	ALTERNATIVE RESPONSES					
								NO
		CLASS	1	2	3	4	5	RESP.
		(N= 50)						
1	2	80	2	80	8	8	0	2
2	3	68	12	8	68	8	0	4
3	4	78	0	6	12	78	0	4
4	2	82	6	82	2	8	3	2
5	4	80	4	0	10	80	0	6
6	3	44	26	16	44	10	0	4
7	3	32	12	28	32	24	0	4
8	4	34	18	12	38	34	0	2
9	2	46	22	46	22	8	0	2
10	1	34	34	14	20	30	0	2

Management

The management of instruction under TIPS is primarily at the instructional level with a small amount of course and program level management. Due to the structure of college level courses, the student is responsible for a considerable portion of the instructional level management. The student report lets the student know how well he is learning the course content. The prescriptions and other messages inform the student as to what he can do to remediate difficulties, or what he can do to extend his knowledge of the content. The student is responsible for actually implementing most of the prescriptions, allocating study time, and making use of the available resources. The teaching assistants serving as section leaders also are involved at the instructional level of management. The TA report shows the section leader the level of performance of his section and the messages employed in the student reports. The section leader can use the report to plan the next quiz section, review the recent survey quiz, and assist students with common difficulties. When messages requiring individual conferences with students have been used, the section leader knows how many students to expect. The TA report also shows which students have not taken a survey quiz. The section leader can use this information to follow up on students and determine why they missed taking the quiz. Examination of reports over several survey quizzes and establishment of specific decision rules can be used to identify students who are not performing at reasonable levels for a period of time. Such students can be given additional help within the section or through special help sessions. Techniques such as these also provide a degree of course level management.

The managerial role of the professor in a large college-level class is quite different from that of an elementary or high school teacher. The primary difference is that the professor has limited direct contact with the students; this role is delegated to the section leaders who meet with small groups of students. The professor is responsible for lecturing, designing the curriculum, implementing the instructional model, and supervising the teaching assistants. He can use the TA reports as the basis for discussions with TAs relating to the conduct of individual sections. The reports can also be used to compare sections and identify groups needing additional attention, or perhaps a section leader that is not doing an adequate job. The supervision of subordinates is an important aspect of CMI at the college level. Such management cuts across both the instructional and course levels, as the teaching assistants are directly involved in instruction as well as course level management. The professor must insure at the course level that a reasonably uniform curriculum is offered to all students enrolled, regardless of which sections the student attends. To do so, he must supervise the section leaders and monitor their performance on the job. Through the class summary report, the professor can determine the achievement level of the class as a whole. If survey quizzes reveal common misunderstandings, the lectures can be modified to approach the subject from another point of view, new resources can be made available, and section leaders can be instructed to emphasize the topic in the next sessions. The item analysis tables from the several quizzes can be used to improve the survey quizzes themselves before they are used again.

There is little emphasis in TIPS upon a throughput model; for example, TIPS does not have a direct capability to track a given student through the curricular plan. The emphasis is upon student achievement and on providing a means for both students and staff to keep informed as to this variable. The management procedures are aimed at maintaining an acceptable lower bound on student achievement.

Computer

The computer component of TIPS consists of batch mode programs written in FORTRAN and executed at a university's computer center. All input to the computer facility is via punched cards; output is via the line printer. Depending upon the local computer facility, TIPS can be run via conventional batch mode or Remote Job Entry; in either case the procedures are the same. The data collection procedures used originally by Kelley employed optically scanned answer sheets, and the scanner produced punched cards that were then transported to the computer facility for use. Due to a change in equipment, Shakhashiri (1975) was unable to use the optical scanner, and manual key punch procedures were used to transform the item responses to punched card format. Such a procedure is slow and expensive; therefore, a much better procedure would be to employ a desk top optical scanner (DATUM 1973) connected to the computer via telephone lines to scan the answer sheets and store the item responses directly in computer memory. The use of the scanner in time-sharing mode eliminates a major bottleneck in the TIPS procedures and greatly reduces the overall "turn around" time. The optical scanner can only input the test item responses; thus, all other input, such as decision rules, messages, and student descriptive data, must be entered via punched cards or a keyboard terminal.

The data base capability employed by TIPS is one of the most sophisticated reported for CMI systems. The data base record for each student can contain up to roughly 2,000 data elements. These data elements can be of two classes: (1) performance data, such as total and subscale scores on survey quizzes, or scores on midterm and final examinations, and (2) attribute data, such as student age, sex, major, laboratory session, etc. TIPS allows the user of the system to define each data element and assign it a label. For example, G160, may be the total test score on survey quiz six. Once defined, that data element is the same in all student records. One may define a new data element at any time, as long as there is available space in the student record. The two major data classifications are further subdivided into sets of data elements having specific characteristics. The attribute file assigns a certain range of data element labels to the following classes of data: primary student identification attributes, alphanumeric attributes, coded attributes, integer attributes, and decimal attributes. Thus, if one employed grade point average as an attribute, it must be assigned a data element label from those allocated to decimal attributes. The performance data is subdivided into integer and decimal subsets. Although these subdivisions limit the number of data elements of a given type that can be employed, the total number of labels available under each classification is more than enough for most purposes. The data element definition and labeling scheme is very flexible and allows the user to define the data rather than having it predefined such as in the case of most CMI systems. The labels assigned to each data element also are used in the decision rules. Taking our earlier example, IF (Test Score < 3), Message (2), would become IF (G160 < 3), Message (2). This enables the user to put any defined data element into the decision rule mechanism.

The data of TIPS also stores the answer key for each quiz, the decision rules, and messages for each quiz. These three types of information are stored by quiz, and there does not appear to be any capability to use the information across quizzes other than through replication. Depending upon the particular computer facility, the data base can be stored on magnetic tape or disk. Because TIPS is a low activity level system, once a week, the normal practice would be to store the whole TIPS software package on tape and load it to disk on the day it was to be used. When all the processing is completed, the whole system can be copied from disk to tape again and saved as a new master file. TIPS also implements a rudimentary data analysis capability that is user-directed. The user can define a data element in terms of an arithmetic operation upon previously defined data elements. For example, capabilities are provided for summing variables and calculating a percentile rank. The derived variable can then be used in the same manner as any other variable.

The table based approach to report generation simplifies the computer programming, yet provides a good degree of flexibility in report generation. Because of the need to give each student an individual student report and the somewhat lengthy messages employed, TIPS tends to produce a moderate volume of printed output. Due to speed of printing and cost considerations, this printing is done on the computer facility's high-speed line printers. At the present time, it does not seem feasible to produce TIPS reports via low-speed printers employed in a time-sharing mode. If TIPS were used for a small class, say 50 students or fewer, then interactive report generation might be feasible. The net effect of report printing at the central computer facility along with the use of punched card input is that the turn-around time for TIPS is what can be achieved under batch mode procedures. By using student couriers to send answer sheets to the optical scanner, carry the punched cards to the computing center, and returning the printed reports, Kelley achieved a three hour turn-around time. Using the on-line optical scanner for data input instead of the courier, one should be able to reduce turn-around to less than an hour.

The reported operational costs for TIPS have varied quite widely. Kelley (1968) reported data processing costs of roughly $1.00 per student per semester. At that time there was no charge for optical scanning and producing the punched cards from the answer sheets. CHEM TIPS (Anonymous, 1974) reported a cost of 50 cents per student per quiz, which is quite high. However, the students' item responses were manually key punched. Shakhashiri (1975) reported that CHEM TIPS was costing roughly 12 cents per student per survey quiz. He was using a UNIVAC 1110 computer, but still key punching the item responses. When one adds the cost of student help to insure that the mechanics of the TIPS approach are supervised, reports distributed, etc., he reported a cost of less then $2.00 per student per semester.

The published articles dealing with TIPS (Kelley, 1968, 1973; Freyman, 1973; Shakhashiri, 1975) have emphasized the impact of TIPS upon students and have reported the results of research studies. Unfortunately, a technical description of the computer programs supporting TIPS has not been published. Consequently, it is difficult to document the capabilities of TIPS and their evolutionary development. The description of the computer component presented above was developed through discussions with persons who actually use TIPS. Thus, the description is incomplete, but not inaccurate. Hopefully, Kelley will publish a complete technical description of the TIPS computer software, as it is both innovative and sophisticated as far as CMI systems are concerned.

Summary of TIPS

The TIPS system adds two dimensions of feedback into the high-enrollment college lecture class. It provides students with a continuing set of information they can use to decide whether their efforts are appropriate to the course. The ungraded survey quizzes and the corresponding student reports provide this feedback. In addition, the prescriptions and other messages provide some direction to the student as to how to remediate deficiencies exposed by the survey quizzes. The student reports coupled with the quiz sections and their graduate student leaders provide an improved degree of personalization as opposed to individualization in a large college class. The teaching assistant reports and the professor report provide feedback to the staff as to student performance. This information can be used managerially in a number of ways to make both lectures and quiz sections more adaptive to student performance. As a CMI system, TIPS focuses primarily upon the instructional level of management with little emphasis upon course or program level management. The lack of the latter is strictly a function of TIPS being a college level system where individual professors are not involved in across subject matter area management in the manner of elementary school teachers.

Due to the conceptual simplicity of TIPS, the ability to define data elements, the decision rule approach to diagnosis, and the prescriptive messages, TIPS is in reality a general-purpose CMI system for the college level. It is not tied to any particular subject matter. It can be employed with a number of different instructional models other than the lecture-quiz section approach from which it derived. Although TIPS has been in continuous use since 1966, it could be updated technologically quite easily. For example, the use of desk top scanners to feed survey quiz results directly to computer storage could significantly improve TIPS turn-around time. In addition, the use of interactive terminals to enter the decision rules, messages, etc., associated with each survey quiz would simplify the survey quiz preparation procedures.

The rather wide range of operational costs suggests that these costs are more a function of computer center billing rates and cost of data preparation than of the execution of the TIPS computer programs. However, the high degree of generality in the TIPS data base procedures coupled with a tape oriented computer facility would contribute to some of the operational costs.

TIPS is an excellent small-scale CMI system with considerable inherent adaptability to college level courses. The operational procedures are sufficiently simple that college instructors should be able to master them easily. TIPS is a good example of how a well conceptualized data base makes the remainder of a CMI system straightforward to implement. Most present-day college level CMI systems owe a great deal to TIPS.

Program for Learning in Accordance
with Needs (PLAN*)

Project PLAN was conceptualized by John C. Flanagan, of the American Institutes of Research, as an educational system to rectify the deficiencies revealed by his project TALENT. In an article titled "Functional Education for the Seventies" (Flanagan, 1967a), he presented the global design and the goals of his educational system. Similar but less comprehensive descriptions are also presented in Flanagan, 1967b; Flanagan, 1968; Flanagan, 1969; Flanagan, 1970; and Flanagan, 1971. The approach taken by Flanagan was essentially a "systems approach" in which he took into account educational goals, student needs, subject matter content, and the teacher.

Flanagan described his functional model as follows: "The functional model being developed begins with the tentative plans for educational objectives to be attained by each individual, assists him in attaining those objectives through the use of specially designed modular segments of learning activities, and continuously monitors his progress with respect to the attainment of these objectives. In the process the student and teacher are provided with the services of a computer as an information processing, storage, and retrieval tool" (Flanagan, 1967a). This functional model was one of those that helped shape the basic CMI concept as described in Chapter Two. Flanagan (1967a) elaborated upon this model by describing five components that needed to be developed to put his educational system into operation. The first component was the formulation of detailed educational objectives. He felt there should be a wide variety of objectives defined so they could be used to meet the educational goals for each student. Flanagan (1968) takes issue with those who define educational objectives at a trivially detailed level. He views educational objectives as existing at a level above those usually emanating from the behavioral objectives movement. He also emphasized goal differentiation. The total set of educational objectives comprises a pool from which objectives are selected to meet individual student needs. The second component was the development of a set of procedures for assessing the performance of students in a number of areas. Under PLAN, he employed placement instruments, end-of-unit posttests, achievement tests in subject matter areas, and Developed Ability Performance Tests (DAPT) (Flanagan, 1971). The PLAN achievement tests were given after completion of a group of modules to test achievement and retention beyond the unit posttests. The Developed Ability Performance Tests were used to measure long-range goals, such as reading comprehension, arithmetic reasoning, etc., and were administered in the spring of the year. The third component was the allocation of instructional methods and materials to segments called "Teaching-Learning Units" (TLU's). These units were to consist of a set of objectives requiring two to three hours' work each and the whole unit would require roughly two weeks of study by the typical student. The idea was to have sufficient different teaching-learning units for each segment to accommodate individual differences among students. The number of alternative TLU's available for a given curricular segment originally was six to eight (Flanagan, 1967a) and became two or more (Flanagan, 1971) later. Each teaching-learning unit made use of existing curricular materials, alternative media, etc. Flanagan (1967a) explicitly excluded the development of new curricula materials from his scheme, feeling the evolution of existing materials via PLAN was preferable to creation of new materials. Although the definition of a TLU included the related resources and activities, it was up to the teacher to decide how to employ them with regard to an individual student, following the guidelines given. The fourth component involved a set of methods and materials for guidance and individual planning. The TALENT data had shown that the schools do very little to help the student take responsibility for his own educational development. There are many facets to this issue. At the lowest level, it involves the choice of teaching-learning units to study, at higher levels it involves course planning and real-life decision-making. Flanagan's writings placed great emphasis upon this aspect of PLAN; but other than the mechanics of generating a Program of Studies, it appears not to have become an operational aspect of PLAN. The final component needed was the data processing support provided by the computer. Flanagan (1970) has described the computer component in some detail. He used a medium-scale computer, IBM 360/50, in a remote job entry mode with an optical mark card scanner (IBM 2956) to collete data from the classroom, and an automatic typewriter (IBM 2740) to print reports and other information. He used one such RJE station per school building, but envisioned having one in each classroom. The use of an on-line typewriter as a report printing mechanism severely limits the volume of reports that could be printed. The computer was viewed primarily as providing clerical level support to the teacher in terms of data collection, storage, and report generation. One of the most interesting aspects of PLAN, as developed by Flanagan, was the generation of a program of studies (POS) for each student by means of the computer. Originally the POS consisted of all the modules a student was to study for the complete year. The development of a POS involved a three-step procedure. The first step was placement of the student within the curricular plan in a given subject matter area. This was based on modules completed the past year and the results of PLAN achievement tests. The next step was the establishment of a quota of modules to be completed by the student that year. The quota was based upon the number of modules completed the past year and the results of the Developed Ability Performance Tests. Third, the selection of specific modules and teaching-learning units within the module was made appropriate to the student. Appropriateness was based upon data collected from the student, his parents, and his teacher. Dunn (1970) reported the 1970 specification for creating a POS consisted of over 200 pages of instructions plus 400 pages of tables and coded module descriptions for 1,200 modules. A simplified version of POS generation was coded for the IBM 360/50; it required roughly ten seconds of CPU time to produce a POS.

One of the difficulties with the literature on PLAN up to 1971, when new articles on PLAN ceased to be forthcoming, is that it is difficult to separate Flanagan's global design from what was actually implemented. Dunn (1970), for example, describes the development of the POS over the first four years. In the first year, once a student was placed in a course by level, all students took the same course in the same order. In the second year, the student and the teacher jointly planned what TLU's a student would use and what order they were to be taken. Such planning was repeated quarterly throughout the school year. In the third year, the computer was used to generate tentative POS's for each student based on prior data collection via PLAN. The fourth year, the module posttests were available, as were PLAN achievement tests and the DAPT for use in creating the POS. Such a developmental pattern is inherent in the creation of any large educational system, but Flanagan's (1971) description of the POS was not achieved until the fourth year.

Although the basic functional model developed by Flanagan for PLAN does not differ greatly from other contemporary CMI systems, his was a much more comprehensive conceptualization. His emphasis was upon the educational aspects and what could be done for the individual student (see Wright, 1970, for a comprehensive listing of the educational goals of PLAN). What Flanagan proposed was educationally sound and reflects a careful analysis of what he felt was needed as far as an educational system was concerned. To implement such a scheme on a large-scale basis places one in direct contact with both the realities of the classroom and of economics. Due to these factors, the implementation of PLAN as conceived by Flanagan was an educational development effort of considerable magnitude.

The original development of PLAN (Flanagan, 1967a; Flanagan *et al.*, 1975) was a troika arrangement with American Institutes for Research (AIR) doing the system planning, management, and providing the behavioral scientists to design, develop, and evaluate PLAN. Teachers from the 14 school districts involved were to formulate the educational objectives and prepare the teaching-learning units under AIR direction. Westinghouse Learning Corporation was to contribute the technologists and media specialists to make use of modern technology. The literature of PLAN for the period 1967-1971 is based upon the educational system resulting from the combined efforts of these three groups. Beginning in 1970 PLAN was marketed by Westinghouse Learning Corporation as a service to the schools on a commercial basis. In July, 1970, total responsibility for PLAN, now called PLAN*, was assumed by Westinghouse Learning Corporation (WLC) (Flanagan *et al.*, 1975). By 1974, some 60,000 students in 64 school districts and one foreign country were using PLAN* (DeHart, 1974). Since 1970, PLAN* has undergone a major redesign to improve its feasibility and marketability. The basic functional model has been retained, as has the terminology, although some of the terminology does not have the same implementation as it had in the past. For example, the complex POS generation procedures have been abandoned; at present a POS is simply a short list of objectives in a subject matter area the student is to master. The version of PLAN* described below is that for the elementary school and is based upon the following documents: The 1973 and 1975 editions of "PLAN* Curriculum Overview," the 1973-74 edition of the "PLAN* Computer Manual," and the sales brochure called "PLAN* An Individualized Learning System." The discussion also draws heavily upon the definitive description of PLAN*, as an individualized system of education, due to Flanagan, Shanner, Brudner, and Marker (1975). In addition, a visit was made to an elementary school employing PLAN* in grades one through six. As was the case with the previous CMI system, PLAN* will be described relative to the six CMI components of Chapter Two. Because PLAN* encompasses a wide variety of activities, and due to space limitations, the description given below will endeavor to convey the essence of PLAN* rather than present a definitive description of all aspects of PLAN*.

Curricular Plan

The "PLAN* Curriculum Overview" manuals provide curricular plans for the four subject matter areas: Language arts, mathematics, science and social studies. Each subject matter area is divided into eight achievement levels, corresponding roughly to the usual grade level. Within each achievement level there are approximately 40 to 45 educational objectives. Associated with each objective is one or more Teaching-Learning Units (TLUs). There can be up to five different documents associated with each TLU, depending upon the objective. There is always an Objective Sheet, shown in Figure 3.4, that specifies the educational objective and contains a sequence of instructions the students follow when studying the objective. The Instructional Guide supplements the

Figure 3.4: PLAN* Objective Sheet

Different Names for a Number   2229-1

TEACHER DIRECTIONS

OBJECTIVE

Find different combinations for a given number.

MATERIALS

Elementary School Mathematics Book 2, Addison-Wesley, 1971
Elementary School Mathematics Book 2, Teachers' Edition
Sets and Numbers 2, L. W. Singer Co., 1969
Sets and Numbers 2, Teacher's Edition
Flash Cards, Addition, Subtraction and Multiplication, Ideal
Math Balance, Selective Educational Equipment
magic slate—this is a general purchase
small thin box
beans
transparent kitchen wrap
felt pen
masking tape
Activity Sheets 1 and 2

PREPARE

3T   Collect several small boxes or ask the children as they start work on this TLU to bring one from home. Hosiery boxes are ideal, but a shoe box will work as well. Activity Sheet 1 gives directions for making a Sum Box.

6   Select from the three boxes of flash cards all combinations of your choice that equal 5 numbers.

DIRECTIONS

1   Students are challenged to find as many equations as possible that equal 10. These equations should be addition and multiplication equations (excluding subtraction because of the nature of the math balance). The children should be encouraged to add two or more addends.

3   Each Sum Box will represent a number of the child's choosing, depending on how many beans are placed in it. As the box is shaken back and forth, the beans distribute themselves on either side of the center line, representing two addends of the total number represented. The child shakes the box and writes an equation for the addends he sees. He repeats this process six times. He should be cautioned that no beans may rest on the line. Check the accuracy of his equations. Since students make Sum Boxes with different sums, you may want to set up a display area so that they may work with other sums.

(Courtesy Westinghouse Learning Corporation.)

Objective Sheet by providing the student with reading material related to the objective. A TLU can have one or two Activity Sheets, each of which specifies a particular task the student is to perform. The Activity Sheets are designed to assist students in applying what they are learning. The Teacher Direction sheet contains the objective and a list of educational materials used in the TLU. These materials can be pages in one or more textbooks, filmstrips, audio recordings, and various other audio-visual media. The sheet also contains brief instructions to the teacher regarding the unit as well as directions for administering the assessment procedure. The final component of the TLU is an assessment procedure which can be either a computer-scored multiple choice test or a teacher-scored test. The composition of the TLU in terms of these five basic documents is not consistent. At each level of each of the four subject areas, a matrix is presented specifying which sheets and assessment instruments are available for each TLU.

The curricular plans, or curricular strategies in PLAN* terminology, all use the objective as the basic curricular entity. The actual curricular plan varies as a function of subject matter and level, and often two plans are defined at a given point. The only constant feature across all curricular plans is the use of orientation and placement TLU's at the beginning of each level. Because of the wide variety of curricular strategies employed by PLAN*, it is not possible to define a single underlying curricular plan. Instead, representative, but not necessarily inclusive, curricular plans from each of the subject matter areas are described below. In language arts, different curricular plans are employed in the primary levels (levels 1-3) and in the remaining levels (levels 4-8). At the primary level, the nearly 200 reading objectives have been arranged into sequences corresponding to each of five commonly used reading programs. The language skills objectives are integrated into the various reading program sequences at the appropriate points. At levels 4-8 of language arts, a strand structured curricular plan is employed to introduce grammar, and the reading program includes both reading skills and literature. Two different curricular strategies are provided at each level. Strategy 1 splits the objectives into groups of seven to ten associated with a Placement/Achievement test. The groups of objectives must be studied in the same order as the tests are numbered. However, within a group, the objectives may be attacked in any order. On occasion, some objectives may have prerequisites but the situation is identified. Strategy 2 classifies the same objectives by language skill and reading categories. At all eight levels there is a TLU document inventory specifying what documents are used by the TLU corresponding to each objective.

The 1973 mathematics program employed a strand structure up to level seven and a block structure at level eight. Within levels one to four the mathematics program employs two different strands. One is based upon the *Elementary School Mathematics* text; its approach was deductive, concrete, and number oriented. The second used the *Math Workshop* text; its approach was inductive, abstract, and pattern oriented. The objectives in each sequence are the same but the TLU's differ depending upon the strand, although some TLU's are common to both. At levels five, six, and seven there is a single sequence within each level, and the objectives are divided into groups of five to ten under a Placement/Achievement test. Both the objectives under a test and the tests must be taken in sequence to preserve the structure. At level eight the same scheme is employed except that the tasks need not be taken in a given order. At all levels of the mathematics program, the objectives are also listed by content categories with prerequisite order shown where appropriate. The 1975 mathematics program has a strand structure for levels 1-8. The objectives within the strands were based upon the *Holt School Mathematics, School Mathematics Concepts and Skills*, and *Mathematics Around Us* textbook series for grades 1-8. As was the case in language arts, two curricular plans were presented, one a strand structure keyed to Placement/Achievement tests, the other a block plan keyed to content areas.

The curricular plan for levels 1-8 of science has a block structure within each level. A block corresponds to a science topic such as magnetism or weather. Within each block are a number of objectives that generally may be studied by the student in any order. A Placement/Achievement test is associated with each topic. In some cases an objective within a block may have prerequisites, which are indicated in the block definition.

The social studies curricular plan provides for two curricular strategies within each of the eight levels. Strategy 1 associates a group of objectives with a Placement/Achievement test; there are three to six such groups at each level. The objectives under a P/A test are in rough order chronologically where appropriate. Strategy 2 organizes the same objectives under topics cutting across the groupings established for strategy 1. In both cases the curricular plan employed is a block structure within achievement levels.

From the above it can be seen that PLAN* employs two basic curricular plans—the strand and the block—with variations on each. Strands go across achievement levels, while the block structure always employs blocks at a single achievement level. Within a block, the objectives often are treated as a short strand or can be arbitrarily ordered. In the latter case, occasional prerequisites to given objectives are designated.

One of the features of the curriculum plans supported by PLAN* is that teachers may add their own local objectives and associated TLU's to the existing structure. Thus, objectives can be added to increase the emphasis in a given area, topics of local interest can be included, and a teacher can adjust the curricular structure to a personal approach to a topic. The ability to add local objectives to the provided curricular plans is very important in terms of teacher acceptance of an externally imposed curriculum. It provides the teacher with a mechanism to reduce the restraints perceived to be imposed by someone else's curricular plan. It is probably more a psychological issue than an educational one, as the curriculum plans provided are well conceived. PLAN* also allows the teacher to define a complete course in a subject matter area. A special form is used by the teacher to list the TLU's constituting the course. This mechanism provides the teacher with the ability to custom design a course that is independent of any of the curricular strategies provided by PLAN*.

Instructional Model

The instructional model employed by PLAN* is a unit-of-instruction cycle based on groups of objectives. The instructional model is applied independently to each group within each achievement level of the four subject matter areas. The basic unit-of-instruction cycle consists of a pretest used to place the student within the group of objectives, a teaching-learning unit for each objective with a mastery test for the objective, and a posttest used to determine if the student has performed well enough to terminate the group of objectives. It should be noted that this unit-of-instruction cycle is the same as that specified by Glaser's model, discussed earlier.

Each achievement level within a subject matter area is initiated via an orientation and placement TLU. This TLU provides the student with some preliminary exposure to the subject matter and the procedures used at that achievement level. Once this TLU is completed, the unit-of-instruction cycle for a group of objectives is initiated by generating a Program of Studies (POS) for each student. There are two options for POS generation that are linked to the two curricular strategies usually available at an achievement level. The first, used at the intermediate level, is tied to the group of objectives defined by the Placement/Achievement tests, and a POS is automatically generated and stored by the computer. The second allows the teacher to specify a POS for each student via a card input scheme, and is not dependent upon the Placement/Achievement test. The unit-of-instruction cycle employing the first POS option is described below.

The unit-of-instruction cycle begins with a student being administered a Placement/Achievement test as a placement test. When the student responses are processed by the computer, a POS is generated automatically for those objectives within the group for which the student does not have prior mastery. The POS is printed as part of the daily report received by the teacher and is stored in the student's data record in the computer. The POS is simply a list of the TLU identification numbers. Once the student has the POS, he obtains the TLU associated with the first objective he is to study. The student follows the sequence specified by the TLU. He studies independently, works with other students, employs audio-visual media, and gets help from the teacher or teacher's aide. Upon completion of the sequence, the posttest for the TLU, called an objective test, is taken. Depending upon the subject matter area and achievement level, this posttest can be either computer scored or teacher scored. If the results meet the criterion for mastery, the objective is marked completed and the student moves on to the next objective in his POS. If the test was not mastered, the teacher assigns the student remedial activities. Alternatively, the teacher can certify the objective mastered and the student proceeds to the next objective on his POS. When a student completes the last TLU on his POS, the teacher assigns the Placement /Achievement test as an achievement test in the form of a posttest. The same test is used for placement and achievement purposes. When used as an achievement test, the results are reported on the teacher's daily report. The achievement results are not stored in the student's data record by the computer. If the teacher is satisfied with a student's performance on the posttest, the Placement/Achievement test for the next group of objectives at the achievement level is administered for placement purposes and the unit-of-instruction cycle begins anew.

An interesting feature of the PLAN* assessment procedure is the use of either computer-scored or teacher-scored objective tests with a TLU. The former are used in all areas where multiple choice items can be employed. The latter are used when the objective can be achieved via a written product or project requiring a teacher's evaluation. The two approaches enable PLAN* to adapt to a wide range of assessment needs.

Diagnosis and Prescription

Under the PLAN* instructional model, diagnosis and prescription occurs at the group of objectives level in conjunction with the Placement/Achievement tests, and at the TLU level in conjunction with the objective tests. When used as a pretest, the scoring of the Placement/Achievement test results in a student's POS for that group of objectives. The actual student responses to the items in the Placement/Achievement test and their correctness are not reported to either the student or the teacher. The rationale is that the test performs a placement function relative to the objectives encompassed by the grouping, and the POS constitutes both a diagnosis and a prescription. When used as a posttest, the Placement/Achievement test is considered an achievement test, and thus the number of items answered correctly for each objective is reported. The teacher uses this information diagnostically. He or she must decide whether the level of achievement is adequate for the given pupil and if the group of objectives is to be considered completed.

Within a TLU, PLAN* uses diagnosis and prescription procedures based upon the objective test. The only diagnostic information yielded by the computer-scored test is whether or not the objective was mastered. The computer component does not print remedial prescriptions for the items answered incorrectly on the objective test. It is the teacher's responsibility to create a remedial prescription for the student. As was the case with the Placement/Achievement test, the actual student item responses are not reported for diagnostic purposes. For the case of teacher-scored objective tests, the teacher has the student responses and can use them diagnostically. In both cases, prescription is done judgmentally by the teachers.

Not having detailed diagnosis and prescription procedures at either the TLU objective test level or at the achievement test level greatly simplifies the PLAN* computer procedures, as a significant data storage and processing task would be associated with automating diagnosis and prescription. The PLAN* approach also eliminates the enormous effort needed to create and maintain prescriptions for each pattern of test results and pupil characteristics. Given the scope of subject matter, the number of curricular strategies, and the large number of students involved, the diagnosis and prescription scheme employed by PLAN* seems to be an economic necessity. In addition, it also reduces the impact of PLAN* upon normal classroom practices, by having teachers continue the use of their own clinical prescriptive procedures supplemented by the Teacher Direction Sheets.

Reporting

The system of reports employed by PLAN* uses the objective as the basic data element. Three primary reports (the Daily Report, the Weekly Report, and the Periodic Progress Report) keep the teacher informed as to the status of each student in each of the four subject matter areas. These reports are supplemented by other computer printouts useful from a management point of view. The Daily Report is a working document generated every day to keep both students and teacher informed as to each student's status. The Daily Report comes in three different versions, called options by PLAN*, and a teacher can specify which of these three options is to be received on a given day of the week. The several Daily Report options reflect in various ways the type of actions that have taken place. Some of these are the result of students having taken tests, while others are the result of teacher actions related to the student's POS. The Teacher Card enables a teacher to define a POS, certify objectives, and request a report of student progress. These are implemented via a set of six commands on the Teacher Card that can be selected. ENTRY allows the teacher to assign up to five objectives to a student by recording the identification number of the objectives on the card. REPLACE permits the teacher to replace an existing list of objectives by those specified on the Teacher Card. ADD is used to place additional objectives on a student's current POS. The DELETE command enables the teacher to delete up to five objectives from the student's current cumulative record regardless of their status. The TEACHER CERTIFY command enables the teacher to designate an objective as completed, or a Placement/Achievement test as mastered. The PROGRESS command has four choices, one for each subject matter area. When selected, it results in a listing of all objectives completed, tested, and started since the last Periodic Progress Report. With these commands in mind, the Daily Report options are described below.

Option 1 shows only the information resulting from processing.the computer cards (test results and Teacher Cards) submitted the previous day. The report is divided into three sections. The first lists students in alphabetical order and reports any transactions relating to the POS resulting from the teacher's use of the Teacher Card commands. It also lists objectives assigned by the computer as a result of a student having taken a Placement or Achievement test. The use of the PROGRESS command results in a listing of the objectives a student has started, completed, or been tested on during the current progress period (six periods per year). The second section lists the students who have completed an objective on the previous day. The third section lists students for whom the teacher has used the certify option or who did not pass an objective test taken on that day and will need to be certified or retested. The salient feature of this option is that it deals, except for the progress data, with the previous day's results.

Option 2 is used to obtain a picture of a student's current status. It contains all of the information of the previous option, but it also contains a listing for each student of the most recent objectives completed, started, tested, scheduled, and deleted. In contrast to Option 1, the data base is searched back in time until the most recent objective in each status category is found. However, the data is not time tagged and the teacher has no direct way of knowing the recency of a given data element. The next three objectives in a student's POS are also reported. If a completed objective is the last one in a POS, a warning message is printed. The second and third section of the Daily Report are the same under options 1 and 2 and are based on the previous day's results.

Option 3 is a combination of Option 1 and what has been called the Unit Report in previous chapters. It is basically an Option 1 report with an additional list inserted in the first section. This listing contains for each objective the names and status—completed, tested, started, and scheduled—of each student assigned that objective. See Figure 3.5.

The Weekly Report shows for each student in the class what objectives were completed during the previous week. It also shows how many objectives the student has completed thus far in the school year in the particular subject matter area. If a student has not completed an objective during the week or longer, a message is printed after the student's name to alert the teacher. The Weekly Report is generated automatically each Friday and is printed as an extra section on the Daily Report received by each teacher on Monday.

The Periodic Progress Report is sent to a PLAN* school six times a year and is a cumulative record of each student's progress. A separate Periodic Progress Report is generated for each student in each of the four subject matter areas. The report lists identification numbers of objectives completed prior to the reporting period. It then reports the identification number and wording of objectives completed, started, and scheduled during the period. The date an objective was started or completed is also reported. At the bottom of the report, the next three objectives on the student's POS are shown. Several alternatives are available for the Periodic Progress Report. Instead of using objective wording, the titles of the TLU's can be reported. Upon request, the Periodic Progress report for all four subject matter areas can be consolidated into a single report. A special version of the Periodic Progress Report is generated at the end of the year. This Final Progress Report lists only the identification number and objective wording for those objectives a student has completed during the school year.

Figure 3.5: PLAN* Daily Report

```
D A I L Y   R E P O R T          MATHEMATICS      02 MR. APILLINARO                OCTOBER 12,1974
ADAMO MARY BETH   (1213)   STARTED 2429-1*  ADDED 2442-1, 2448-1, 2425-1
BYNOE DEBBIE      (1612)   ADDED 2443-1, 2444-1, 2448-1  DELETED 2401 1, 2402, 2406-1
NOBILE DONNA      (1418)   ENTRY 2242-2, 2240-2, 2215-2
ORTIZ ELIZABETH   (0084)   REPLACE 2338, 2342-1, 2337-1, 2334-1
PAENOZZI ANTHONY  (6529)   REGISTRATION CANCELLED, ALL OTHER ACTIONS IGNORED
SERIPERRI VITO    (6588)   2943 PLACEMENT TEST RESULTS SUGGEST THE FOLLOWING OBJECTIVES FOR STUDY
                           2430 TIME                           2444 DISSECTING THE CIRCLE
                           2441 SUGAR CUBES AND VOLUME         2450 TAKING A PLANE INTO SPACE
                           2408 ABC -- POINT, LINE, PLANE
TAYLOR HELEN      (7121)   STARTED 2448-1*
                           2941  ACHIEVEMENT TEST RESULTS 2426 2/3  2425 2/2  2434 0/2  2405 1/2
                           2417 3/3  2416 3/4 2401 3/3
WALKER NED        (1410)   PROGRESS - COMP (16) 2429-1, 2434-1, 2442-1  TESTED 2448-1
                           STARTED 2425-1  SCH 2431, 2407, 2411-1, 2419-1, 2417-1,2416-1,2449-1,
                           2446

        THESE OBJECTIVES WERE COMPLETED
ADAMO MARY BETH  50004*   CHITES CHARLES   2323-1*   GENSINGER JOHN  2438-1T
POWERS JANE      2440-1   SERIPERRI VITO   2438-1    WALKER NED      2442-1

        TEACHER CERTIFY OR HAVE STUDENTS RETEST THESE OBJECTIVES
ORTIZ ELIZABETH  2429-1*  SERIPERRI VITO   2440-1    WALKER NED      2448-1*
```

(Courtesy Westinghouse Learning Corporation.)

Two types of special notices are printed by the PLAN* computer component. The first type, for the building administrator, contains five sections. The first section acknowledges the entry of new students into the system; it assigns each a student number. The second section confirms that locally developed objectives are now included in the computer's data base. Section three lists the independent activities ready for use. Section four lists the objectives, supplies, and the packets of sheets used by students as part of the TLU that have been ordered and the purchase order number. The final section lists the computer-related supplies, cards, and input forms on order. The second type of special notice is appended to a teacher's daily report. It acknowledges any changes a teacher has made in the specification of which option of the Daily Report is to be received on a given day, simply listing the new configuration of options by day of the week.

Management

Under PLAN*, the instructional level management procedures focus upon that part of the unit-of-instruction cycle dealing with objectives. The student is scheduled for an objective; it is started; when ready, the student takes an objective test; and, finally, the objective is completed. The TLU associated with each objective defines the instructional sequence followed by the student when pursuing the objective. There is a considerable dependence upon self-management by students at the instructional level. Once assigned an objective, the student assumes responsibility for following the specified instructional sequence, using the various resources required, and working with other students when called for by the TLU. In addition, the students use mark sense computer cards as answer sheets for the computer-scored objective test. The teacher plays a supervisory role in addition to an instructional role in relation to the students working on the various TLU's. In this supervisory role, the teacher assists students in following the instructional sequence; allocates the resources;

and provides whatever other support the students may require. The Teacher Direction sheet assists the teacher in performing this supervisory role. Both students and teachers use the Daily Reports to perform instructional level management. The student can: determine what he or she is to be working on in each of the four subject matter areas: decide when he or she should have a conference with a teacher; and see when to check his or her results on tests. The teacher can use the Daily Reports to keep track of where each student stands relative to an objective. The teacher will have to determine whether to retest each student, prescribe different resources for restudy, or certify the objectives as completed. The Daily Report can also be used to plan a day's activities. If a number of students are starting the same TLU, they may be called together for a period of group instruction or cooperative effort. It also lists students needing conferences; thus, a schedule of conferences can be established for the day. The Weekly Report can be used to identify students who have not completed any objectives. The teacher can meet with each student to find the source of difficulty.

Course level management under PLAN* is aimed at individualization with respect to rate of progress. The management procedures used to implement a throughput model are based upon curricular strategies, Placement/Achievement tests, and Programs of Study. The unit-of-instruction cycle employed at the course level of management is based loosely upon a group of objectives. The grouping is defined by the two curricular strategies usually available at an achievement level within each subject matter area. Which strategy is used depends upon the teacher's approach; both may be used by different students within the class. The basic vehicle for course level management is the Program of Studies generated from the results of a placement test or manually by the teacher. Any POS can be modified by the teacher by adding, deleting, or replacing objectives to create a POS that is a closer fit to a given student's needs. A common POS can be assigned to several students to create classroom groups. Regardless of how the

POS was created, it defines a sequence of objectives in a subject matter area the student is to master. The Daily Reports, Weekly Reports, and the Periodic Progress Reports all provide the teacher with information on the student's progress. The primary information is a listing of objectives completed. Only the Daily Report shows when a POS in a given subject matter has been completed. The Periodic Progress Report also shows the next three objectives on a student's POS in a given subject matter area. The teacher can use the status information in these three reports to monitor the rate of progress of each student.

Despite the curricular segment orientation of the curricular strategies, the course level management procedures tend to ignore the segments. Although the Daily Report shows when a POS is completed, neither it nor the Weekly or Periodic Progress Reports provide a listing of groups of objectives completed. Both of these latter reports show only individual objectives completed. The net effect, from a course level management point of view, is that the POS provides only a short-term management vehicle, with no means for managing the total course in a subject matter area other than via individual objectives. The identification numbering schemes for the objectives do specify the subject matter and the achievement level of the objective. However, other than the student roster produced at the beginning of the school year, none of the PLAN* reports presents a course level summary of the sequence of groups of objectives for a student or the sequence of POS's that were used. Much of this information must be gleaned from the several Periodic Progress Reports. The author suspects that the lack of emphasis upon managing a student's progress through a course in a subject matter area stems from the curricular flexibility built into PLAN*. The several curricular strategies in the curriculum overview document are high level guides for the teacher, who is free to use or modify them at will. The result is that the course defined for any two students does not need to be the same; thus making reporting of progress relative to a predetermined course a difficult matter. The associated problems were eliminated by PLAN* by keeping the reporting based upon individual objectives. The teacher must then assume the course level management burden for keeping track of a student with respect to curricular segments completed and progression from one achievement level to another through the given subject matter. The underlying course level management philosophy seems to be that if one manages the small curricular segments defined by the POS's on a continuous basis, the overall course management takes care of itself.

One of the strong features of PLAN* is that it encompasses four subject matter areas within a single CMI system. As such it is one of the few elementary school systems that have the potential for program level management as defined in Chapter Two. At the present time (1977), PLAN* treats the four subject matter areas as independent entities. The Daily Reports and Weekly Reports are generated separately for each subject matter area. Only the Periodic Progress Report has an option that places data for all four subject matter areas on a single report so that the pattern of achievement of a given student across areas can be seen. There does not appear to be any across-data interdependencies, such as a social studies objective having a language arts prerequisite. If such were the case, the teacher would need to manage across subject matter areas at a program level. Although PLAN* does treat the four subject matter areas independently, the fact that they are under a common CMI system allows some program level management. The foremost of these is a balancing effect across the areas. When a student working in science finds that the materials needed are all in use, he can simply set his science TLU aside and work on a TLU in another subject. The ability to switch smoothly from one TLU to another greatly diminishes queues related to resources and minimizes a student's idle time. An incidental benefit is that the student learns how to adapt to changing conditions and to use time wisely (Wood and Lewis, 1974). Since PLAN* is used nationwide in a highly heterogeneous set of classrooms, curriculum improvement is a delicate operation. PLAN* achieves its universality by being somewhat "loose" at the curricular level and depending upon widely adopted textbook series. Consequently, curriculum improvement must retain this looseness, yet correct deficiencies that have some commonality across the user community.

Computer

The PLAN* computer component is based upon the batch mode of operation using the remote job entry approach. A central computer, an IBM 370/155, is located in Iowa City, Iowa, and two different RJE schemes are used. Under the first and most common approach, an IBM 3735 terminal is used with an IBM 2956 optical mark card reader and an IBM 3286 printer. The RJE terminal is connected directly via telephone lines to the central computer. The second approach uses a mini-computer connected via telephone lines to the central computer. The mini-computer, usually a Hewlett Packard 2100, has a number of RJE terminals connected to it. The RJE terminal configuration is a W-400 optical mark card reader, a programmable storage control unit, a modem, and a small printer. The advantage of the mini-computer approach is that the mini-computer can perform a number of data editing and preprocessing tasks at the local level, thereby relieving the central computer of a considerable work load. The mini-computer also acts as a data concentrator by collecting the data from many RJE terminals, reformatting it, and sending it to the central computer. In Chapter Seven, a more detailed discussion of the use of networks of computers for CMI is presented. The computer programs underlying PLAN* are written in ANS COBOL, Version Four, and require at least 110K bytes of memory and two tape units, 20 million characters of disk storage, and a line printer (DeHart, 1974). Since the programs are written in a standard programming language, they can be run on a number of different computers. Consequently, the PLAN* computer programs can be leased or purchased from Westinghouse Learning Corporation for use on a school district's own computer.

Figure 3.6: PLAN* Student Card

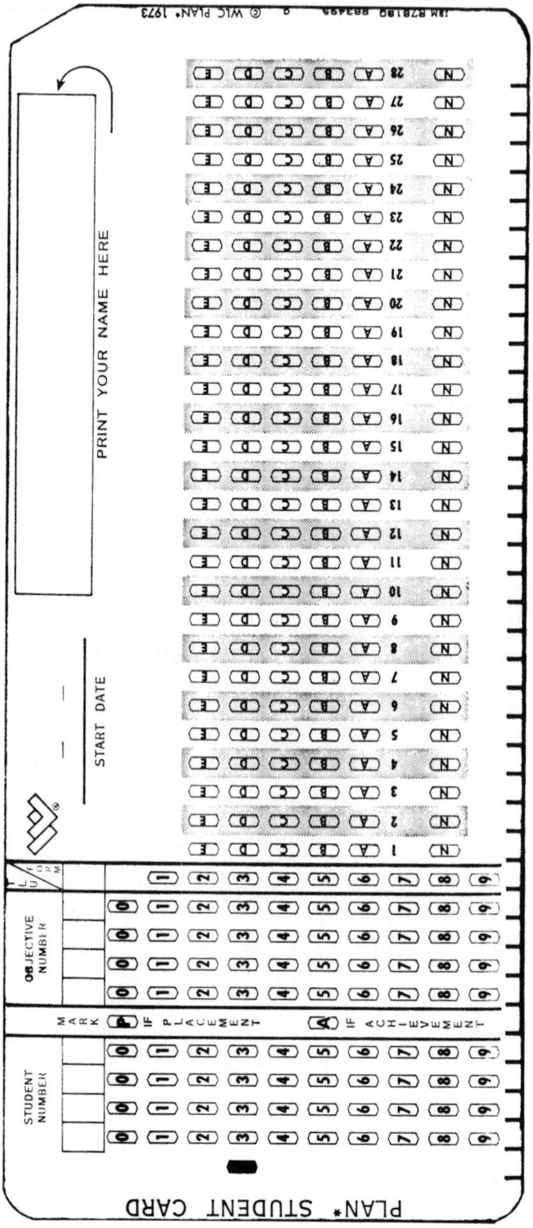

(Courtesy Westinghouse Learning Corporation.)

The data collection procedures of the computer component employ forms at the beginning of a school year to collect information such as student names, teacher daily report options, titles of independent activities, and definition of local objectives. These forms are sent to the central computer facility where they are key punched and the data entered into the data base. The daily transactions between the classroom and the computer component are conducted via Hollerith sized cards that can be read by the optical mark readers in the RJE terminals. There are seven different cards, each with a preprinted form on it. The information is entered on the card by filling in the appropriate marking position with a lead pencil. The seven different cards serve three different purposes. Three cards, the achievement analysis card, the registration card, and the teacher card, are concerned with the mechanics of entering students into the system and controlling the Program of Studies. Two cards, the primary card and the student card, are used to enter students' item responses to objective and Placement/Achievement tests into the computer; these cards are marked by the students. Figure 3.6 depicts a student card. The last two cards, batch start card and batch end card, are used to identify batches of cards submitted via the RJE terminal.

The card-based data collection system is well designed, is easy to use, and provides considerable capability in a compact form. During the course of a school day, the teacher fills in cards to record various transactions. Students fill in cards for tests taken. At the end of the day the cards from a classroom are collected and delimited by batch start and end cards. The total set from all classrooms are pooled and taken to the RJE terminal where an operator runs the cards through the card reader. Two quality control procedures are performed. As each batch of cards is read, mechanical errors in reading are detected and an immediate editing summary is printed describing the problems. The operator can correct certain of the problems and resubmit the cards. Cards with unresolved errors are returned to the teacher. Cards successfully read are subjected to internal consistency checks by comparing the data, such as objective number, etc., with the data base. Any errors found in this process are printed as an error report appearing at the top of a teacher's daily report. These two editing procedures insure that only valid information is entered into the computer files.

The available documentation of the PLAN* computer software does not describe the data base design. The following description has been provided by the staff of Westinghouse Learning Corporation. Three major files are maintained: a student history file, a curricular file, and a school file. A record in the student history file is maintained for each student registered. This record contains data such as student name, student identification number, school identification number, and all units of work (objectives) assigned—whether completed, scheduled, or in progress. The curriculum file contains information related to the four subject matter areas and the corresponding assessment procedures. For each objective the name, subject area, answer key for the objective test, and the minimum passing score are stored. Answer keys and minimum passing scores are also stored for the Achievement/Placement tests used with groups of objectives in the four subject matter areas. Additional information is retained to identify local school objectives and independent activities. The school file contains both descriptive and administrative data relating to the school. For example, the vector of teacher report options by day and the data, such as supplies ordered, appearing in the special activities report are stored. At the high school level, the school file also contains descriptive information for courses beyond the four PLAN* areas.

The reports generated by the PLAN* computer component are created at the computer facility and transmitted to the RJE terminals. In the case of the IBM 3735 terminal, the reports are captured on an internal link and then printed. When a mini-computer is connected, it receives all the reports for the RJE terminals connected to it. If the mini-computer has disk storage, the reports are stored and printed when requested by the RJE operator. Without auxiliary storage, the mini-computer would simply act as a distributor and cause the reports to be printed as they are received. The PLAN* procedures are such that the data processing cycle is performed overnight, with the reports delivered to the teachers in the morning before classes begin. The overall print load per classroom under PLAN* is modest. Each Daily Report is only one to three pages, depending upon the option, and there is one such report for each subject matter area per teacher. A print load of 12 pages per teacher per day is very reasonable. Other reports, such as the Periodic Progress Report, are produced on a low frequency basis and involve only 30-40 students a time. Only the Periodic Progress Report, covering all four subjects, would be of moderate size, especially near the end of the school year.

Summary of PLAN*

The version of PLAN* described above is the result of an iterative development process spanning many years. The original rather visionary conceptualization due to Flanagan (1967a) has been tempered by the realities of the classroom and the economics of public education. The result is a CMI system retaining much of the original educational system philosophy yet having a decidedly practical implementation. The need for PLAN* to be acceptable to teachers in a wide variety of school settings imposes design constraints not imposed on other CMI systems. Small-scale CMI systems, for example, can be tailored to a given teacher and even to a specific course. A large-scale CMI system such as PLAN* must provide considerable generality, yet do so in a manner acceptable to the schools both educationally and economically. The educational acceptability is achieved by PLAN* through the flexibility provided in the various curricular plans. The curricular strategies provided are those commonly used in the schools and do not constitute a radical departure. In addition, the TLU's allow the teacher much leeway at the instructional level. Hence, the curricular plans have considerable face validity. The ability of the teacher to restructure the curricular strategy as seen fit also reduces the feeling that an external curriculum has been imposed. The implementers of PLAN* have also astutely minimized the external imposition factor as well as the data base problem by retaining teacher judgment as the basis for prescriptive procedures.

To be successful, the management procedures associated with CMI must provide the teacher with sufficient gain to make the additional work load worthwhile. PLAN* achieves this balance by managing rather closely at the objective level and rather loosely at the course level. Emphasis upon the objective level is a good fit with most teachers' interest in daily classroom concerns. The POS provides a good short-term management vehicle for both teachers and students. The POS gives sufficient curricular segmentation to provide some student motivation, while giving teachers a curricular frame of reference. Anecdotal reports from visitation to schools employing PLAN* indicate two effects. First, PLAN* impacts upon teachers by having them assume a much more managerial role than in conventional classrooms. Second, PLAN* enables good teachers to achieve the level of individualization they desire but could not achieve without a CMI system. At the same time, PLAN* tends to upgrade weaker teachers by providing a well-designed supportive educational system. A small research study by Wood and Lewis (1974) shows that students under PLAN* have more personal contact with teachers, spend more time working alone, and less time in instructional groups than under IGE (Klausmeier, 1975) or traditional instruction, suggesting that PLAN* does change classroom practice. The economic acceptability of PLAN* is due to both the use of existing instructional materials, with a minimum of expendables, and the design of the computer component. Flanagan's (1967a) concept of not creating new materials and relying on existing educational resources has been a key element in the design of PLAN*. For example, in both reading and mathematics, the curricular plans are based upon widely used textbook series. The major curricular materials added by PLAN* are the documents associated with the TLU's. These documents come in the form of pads which are reasonably priced. PLAN* makes contractual provisions for school districts themselves to print these expendable materials if desired. The computer component has also been designed to minimize costs. The use of batch mode, card based data collection, low volume of reports, and overnight processing all contribute to economic feasibility. Over the years there has been a dramatic drop in the per pupil per year cost of using PLAN* in a school district. In 1971, when the complex computer based POS for a school year was employed, the cost was $180 per pupil per year. In the fall of 1973, the cost was $42 per pupil if the full complement of PLAN* services was employed (PLAN* Newsletter No. 7, April, 1973). Thus, the iterative development procedures have been very effective in reducing costs.

It is the author's judgment that other persons developing large-scale CMI systems would do well to study PLAN* very closely. The designers and implementers of PLAN* have faced and met most of the educational, computer, and economic issues involved in large-scale CMI.

Chapter Four

A CMI Case Study:
The Sherman School Project

Although many CMI systems exist, the developmental process by which they come into existence and the procedures used to bring them to their present state are rarely documented. The published descriptions of CMI systems tend to describe the system at one point in time. If a later description of the system appears, it usually does not give the rationale for the changes made. Consequently, in addition to describing the Sherman School CMI System, a major purpose of the present chapter is to document the origins, operational history, and developmental pattern of the system. In order to do so, it is necessary to present a baseline description of the system as it existed at the beginning of the first year of operation via the six CMI components used in Chapters Two and Three. This description is followed by a discussion of the pattern of growth and change over the next three years. To put the total project in perspective, the descriptions are preceded by the brief project history. The history identifies the participants and establishes the project chronology.

Project History

The Sherman School CMI project had its inception in 1969 when the fourth and fifth grade teachers at Sherman School decided to individualize their mathematics courses. The teachers developed a curricular plan, an instructional model, instructional materials, and assessment instruments. The associated data collection and processing procedures were performed by manual means. Records were kept on 3 x 5 cards, retained by the students, and in teachers' grade books. The initial results of the individualized mathematics program were excellent; student attitudes improved dramatically, achievement rose, and teachers were pleased with their system. Each year, the total program was examined and improvements made on the basis of experience. By the 1971/72 school year, it had become evident to the staff that the work load associated with the diagnosis of test results and the prescription of remedial work was becoming a limiting factor on the effectiveness of the instructional system. At this point, the staff recognized the need for some form of computer support to relieve them of manual record-keeping procedures and to increase the efficiency of the prescription process. These needs were made known to the administrative data processing section of the school system; however, their computer was not capable of providing the level of support needed. Hence, the need was recognized, but not met.

In the Fall of 1971 one of the members of the staff of the administrative data processing section enrolled in the University of Wisconsin course titled "Hardware/Software Systems for Instructional Use" (Baker, 1973). The purpose of this course was to teach the design and implementation of computer-based instructional systems. The particular goal was to construct a computer-based instructional management system. Early in the course, the staff member mentioned that the Sherman School mathematics program needed computer support and might be the basis of a class project. The class visited Sherman School for a day, observed the mathematics program in operation, talked to the staff, and collected information. On the basis of this visit, the students decided to develop the computer programs necessary to provide Sherman School with a CMI capability. The result of this two-semester effort by a team of six graduate students (three from computer science, three from education) was a computer program called MICA (Managed Instruction with Computer Assistance) described in detail in Chapter Five. The final examination in the course was to demonstrate the system and make a presentation to the Sherman School staff. It should be noted that the MICA program contained nearly 4,000 lines of FORTRAN code and represented a significant programming effort. The students conceptualized the total program, developed a complete data base management capability, and created the interactive procedures enabling the teacher to use a computer terminal for the prescription process, as well as doing the actual computer programming. Thus, by the Spring of 1972, the computer-based aspects of a CMI system existed.

During the Fall of 1972, one of the students who was on the development team worked with the Sherman School staff to implement a small data base from actual pupil data. Early in the Spring of 1973 a computer terminal was made available to the Sherman School staff for exploratory and demonstration purposes. The MICA system and the data base were put "on line" to the University of Wisconsin UNIVAC 1108 computer and the staff could use the system as they desired. The computer terminal was in Sherman School for six weeks and was used approximately 20 times during this period. Staff response was uneven, but generally enthusiastic about proceeding. Late in the Spring of 1973 a meeting was held involving the Sherman School staff, Madison Public Schools central office staff, and the author. At this meeting it was decided to put the CMI system into operation for the 1973/74 school year. Through the efforts of a number of persons, funds were obtained to support the project. Although these funds were modest, $4,000 from the Madison Public Schools and $7,500 from the Teacher Corps, they were sufficient to carry the project through its first year of operation. These funds were used for three purposes: data base creation, computer programming support, and purchasing of computer time for operational use of the system. Data base creation was a major effort, since none of the curricular information was in a computer compatible format. During the Summer of 1973, a team of teachers extended the current pool of prescriptions until seven prescriptions existed for each objective in the curricular plan. By late August, 1973, the complete data base had been constructed and stored in the computer and the computer programs were in working order. The first year of operation was devoted to "shaking-down" all six components of the CMI system.

Near the end of the first year, the Department of Public Instruction, State of Wisconsin, announced it was allocating a segment of Title III funds to Computer Managed Instruction. As the result of the evaluation of a number of competitive proposals, roughly $250,000 was awarded to the Madison Public Schools to support the Sherman School Project over a three-year period, 1974-1976. The three goals of the Title III effort were (1) to expand the use of the CMI system to additional subject matter areas; essentially, this meant using the MICA software to support courses other than fourth and fifth grade mathematics; (2) extend the capabilities of the MICA computer programs from a small-scale to a medium-scale CMI system; and (3) accomplish the transition of operational use of the CMI computer component from the University of Wisconsin UNIVAC 1108 computer to a medium-scale computer to be selected by the Madison Public Schools. Due to the increased level of funding, the informal working group that was the project through its first year was replaced by a project director, Mr. John Chapin, and a staff of programmers led by Mr. Thomas Lorenz, and secretaries and educational specialists.

The major tasks of the second year of operation, the first under Title III funding, were to compare the operation of the Sherman School Mathematics Program with and without a computer component and to further refine all six components of the CMI system. The outcomes in these two areas are described in a later section of this chapter. During the third year, the use of the CMI system was extended to six schools geographically distributed over the city. Some of these schools had used the Sherman School Mathematics Program in past years, while others had not. The schools were selected on the basis of the willingness of the staff to participate, student body characteristics, and a commitment of some local school funds to the project. During this year, the transition from a small-scale to medium-scale CMI system was to be accomplished. Again, a subsequent section in the present chapter describes these efforts. The final year of Title III funding was devoted to inclusion of other subject matter areas under the CMI system in a few of the six schools and making the transition to a new medium-scale computer to be selected by the school district. Due to the recency of these events, they are not discussed in detail in this chapter.

The Baseline CMI System

As initially implemented, the Sherman School CMI system consisted of the fourth and fifth grade mathematics program used in previous years, supplemented by a computer component. During the time period devoted to the mathematics program, the students from six classrooms were treated as a single group of 165 pupils. A unique instructional paradigm similar to that of a medical clinic was employed, where each of the six teachers performed a specific function. The most troublesome aspect of this paradigm had been the prescription function, where a teacher assigned students remedial work. Thus, the major role of the computer was to support the teacher in performing this function. However, the computer also provided a series of reports to aid the team. A computer terminal was placed in the school and used interactively by a teacher in the time-sharing mode. Of the several elementary school CMI systems described in Appendix A, only the Sherman system uses the computer this way. Under the classification scheme presented earlier, the baseline system is a small-scale CMI system, since it supports a single course in a single school.

Curricular Plan

The subject matter encompassed by the curricular plan is fourth and fifth grade mathematics. The teachers had studied these two courses as presented in five different textbook series and restructured them into 30 instructional units. Each instructional unit covered a particular segment of the mathematics courses and included a number of objectives within the segment. The number of objectives included in a given unit was quite variable, ranging from 3 to 70, but typically from 9 to 12. A study guide, consisting of a package of instructional materials prepared by the Sherman School staff, was associated with each unit and used to introduce the student to content of the unit. In most cases, the study guide existed in the form of printed materials and as an audio-tape. In the computer programs, these two study guide forms are referred to as the instructional methods. In addition to the curricular segments accompanied by the study guides, there were six review units, each covering the objectives in the previous five study guides. The curriculum plan had a linear structure with all students proceeding from study guide 1 to study guide 30, with the six review units interspersed every five study guides. Within the curricular plan, a "spiral staircase" approach was used, so that many mathematical concepts, skills, etc., appeared at multiple points in the curriculum to consolidate skills, add sophistication to the concept, and provide review. Associated with each curricular unit, a study guide in Sherman School terminology, were one pretest and three posttests to be used to determine whether the objectives within the unit had been mastered.

Instructional Model

The instructional model employed at Sherman School employs the common pretest, instruction, posttest unit-of-instruction cycle. For each curricular unit, the following cycle occurs. The student is assigned a study guide to read or to hear. He then is administered a unit pretest covering the objectives included in the unit, where each objective is represented by three or more test items. The test is scored by a teacher's aide in the following fashion: items within an objective are scored using an answer guide and can result in no, partial, or full credit for an item. On the basis of the results for the set of test items, the objective is then scored as pass or fail. The test items vary widely in type and involve computation, diagrams, reading passages, etc., and are not amenable to machine scoring. For each objective failed, the student receives a prescription in the form of an assignment. Upon completion of the tasks specified by the prescription, the student takes the unit posttest. The posttest is structurally similar to the pretest and is scored in the same manner. Again, failed objectives result in a prescription, and an alternative form of the posttest is used for the next testing. This basic cycle is repeated for all 30 units and the six review units.

The instructional model for the unit-of-instruction cycle is implemented via a unique instructional paradigm. The basis of this paradigm is the abandonment of self-contained classrooms in favor of specialized uses of the physical space and reallocation of the roles of the teaching staff. The 165 pupils normally assigned to the six classrooms constituting the fourth and fifth grades are treated as a single group for the mathematics period. Individual pupils proceed from room to room as required by their activities. Teachers perform the function associated with a particular room. It should be apparent that the model is akin to that underlying a medical clinic where physical spaces serve specialized functions and patients move from place to place as they need the services of those spaces; each space is staffed by a specialist.

The second floor of Sherman Elementary School contains six classrooms, which are all used during the period of time assigned to mathematics. Figure 4.1 depicts the uses to which each room was put and the personnel assigned to the room. Three of the rooms are designated study rooms and have a teacher in them. These rooms are used by the students to read study guides and to work on remedial assignments. One room is a testing room where pupils take pretests and posttests. A teacher's aide scores the tests. A teacher is in the testing room to assist pupils having questions regarding the tests. The testing room also contains the audio-tape equipment used by the students to listen to the study guides rather than read them in a study room. The seminar room

Figure 4.1: Sherman School Space and Personal Allocation, Fall, 1973

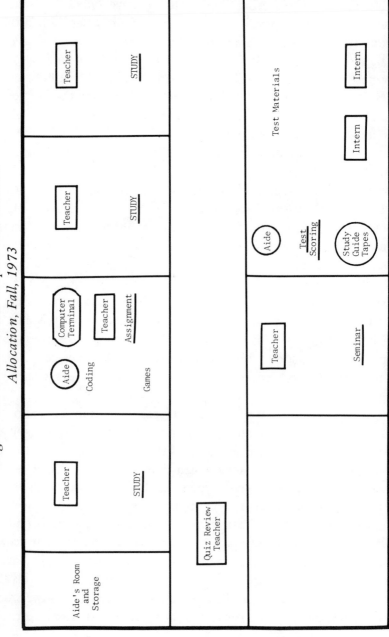

is used to enable a teacher to present topics of interest to a group of students. The remaining classroom is devoted to a number of activities. In this room, the assignment teacher diagnoses test results and uses the computer terminal to assist in the prescription of remedial activities. A teacher aide codes test results for computer input. The room is also used by students engaged in mathematical games. Due to physical space limitations, one teacher used the hall as a place to review students' work and to determine if they are ready to take unit tests. The aide's room contains various instructional materials, and the teacher aide assists students in obtaining those called for in their prescriptions. To clarify the operation of the instructional paradigm, the path of a typical student is described below.

The sequence begins with a pupil being assigned a unit by the assignment teacher using the computer terminal. The number of the unit assigned is stored in the student's record in the computer's data base. The pupil obtains the study guide material from the aide's room and proceeds to one of the study rooms and reads the material. Alternatively, he can listen to it via an audio-tape machine in the testing room. In both cases, a teacher is present to assist the student by answering questions and providing explanations. Upon completion of the study guide, he goes to the testing room, where he locates the appropriate pretest and takes the test. The teacher aide scores the test and marks objectives as passed or failed. The pupil takes his test paper to the assignment room, where the assignment teacher examines the results and uses the computer terminal to enter the identification number of the objectives failed. The computer terminal displays the lists of prescriptions corresponding to the objectives failed, and the teacher selects prescriptions he or she feels are appropriate to the student. The selected prescriptions are also written on the student's 3 x 5 card. The teacher gives the student the appropriate book or books. Often the assignment teacher also provides the student with a brief explanation of what is to be done. The pupil proceeds to the study room to perform the tasks specified by the prescription. Upon completing the prescribed assignment, he leaves the study room and shows the quiz teacher in the hall what has been done. The teacher examines the assignment and judgmentally determines if the pupil is actually prepared to take a posttest. If not, the pupil returns to the study room for additional study. If his subject matter topic is the one currently being presented in the seminar room, he may join the seminar group rather than use the study room. For those who proceed to the testing room, the procedure is the same as for the pretest. When a pupil obtains an adequate score on the posttest, the next study guide in the sequence is assigned by the assignment teacher at the computer terminal. Each of the 165 pupils proceeds through both the unit-of-instruction cycle and the curricular sequence at his own pace. Although the whole process appears rather mechanical, there is considerable student-teacher interaction at every stage of the instructional sequence. A teacher is always available for assistance and a high level of rapport is maintained.

Diagnosis and Prescription

The Sherman School CMI system places a heavy emphasis upon diagnosis and prescription. Since the instructional units are quite large, only 30 units covering two school years, a student is not likely to pretest out of a unit nor master all objectives in a unit on the first posttest. Consequently, the major portion of the unit-of-instruction cycle focuses upon diagnosis and prescription. During the years prior to adding the computer component, prescriptions were created judgmentally by the teachers for each student on each test. However, an effort was made to record these prescriptions with a view towards creating a prescription book at some point in time. These prescriptions and those created during the Summer of 1973 were stored subsequently in the prescription file of the computer's data base. The prescriptions consisted primarily of pages in one of the five different mathematics texts available in the school. The section of the textbook assigned included both instructional material and problems or exercises related to the objective. The textbooks embodied several different approaches to mathematics as well as different levels of difficulty.

One of the constraints imposed by the Sherman School staff upon the design of the CMI system was that the computer makes no educationally related decisions. In particular, the diagnosis and prescription procedures would not be automated. In order to meet this constraint, yet use the computer to eliminate the bottleneck existing in the diagnosis and prescription procedures, it was decided to use a "menu" selection approach. The computer would merely present the assignment teacher with a list of prescriptions for each objective failed. The assignment teacher then would select one or more prescriptions from the list and inform the student and the computer of the selection. The menu approach enabled the assignment teacher to make the educationally related decision and use the computer as an information retrieval and storage device. Under these procedures, diagnosis consisted simply of a listing of objectives failed on the test. In some cases, a prescription was not selected for an objective even though it was failed. Often, the teacher's inspection of the test paper could lead her to believe that the student had an adequate understanding, hence, no prescription was needed. Figure 4.2 shows a typical prescription sequence as performed by the assignment teacher at the computer terminal. The teacher activates the prescription computer program via the /P command. Then the student identification number is entered via the keyboard, and the computer responds with the student's name. The computer asks for the name of the test for which results are to be entered; pretest for study guide #9 in the example. The teacher then enters the identification numbers of the objectives marked as failed on the student's answer sheet. The computer replies by listing the eight prescriptions associated with each failed objective. Prescriptions one through eight belong to objective two, pairing members of sets; and prescriptions #9 through #16 to objective #9, associative properties multiples of 10 to 100. The numbering scheme simplifies the teacher's selection of the prescriptions from the list. Due to an oversight in

Figure 4.2: Typical Assignment Sequence at Console

```
MICA READY
/P
~
?STUDENT #
83
?ROBERT JONES

?TEST NAME
PRE9
?RESULTS
2,9.

~
?REMEDIAL PRESCRIPTIONS:
? 1. PAIRING MEMBERS OF SETS
? 2. MSM4P100-103
? 3. EM4P61
? 4. NDM4P16-17
? 5. *ESM4P104-106
? 6. MSM3P205-207
? 7. MSM5P100-101
? 8. MSMWB4P34-35
? 9. ASSOC PR MULT OF 10-100
?10. MSM4P116
?11. EM4P63,162
?12. M4P80-81
?13. NDM4P104,110[5]
?14. *EEM4P176-178
?15. ESM4P136-137
?16. ESM5P50-51

?ACTIVITY #
1,2,9,10.
~
?AVAILABLE POST-TESTS:
? 1. PT9A
? 2. PT9B
? 3. PT9B

?TEST #
1
PRESCRIPTION SELECTION COMPLETED.
```

the computer program design, the first prescription in the set of eight is the name of the objective. Thus, the teacher must always select the first prescription in the set, so that the name of the objective failed is stored in the student's data base record. In the example, the teacher selected only one prescription for each objective in response to the computer's ?ACTIVITY query. When the student completes the assigned activities, he will be in a position to take the unit posttest. Therefore, at the present time, the teacher also assigns him one of the three available posttests; posttest 9A in the example. Within the teacher-computer dialogue, all teacher entries made via the keyboard are entered into the student's data base record and stored. The actual entries are simply one or two digit numbers so the dialogue proceeds quite quickly. Although the prescriptions are rather cryptically encoded, the abbreviations used, such as MSM for the *Modern School Mathematics* textbook, are readily understood by both teachers and students. Once the process is completed, the teacher writes the prescriptions and the posttest assigned on the student's 3 x 5 card and the student retains this card as his record of what he is to do. If necessary, the assignment teacher also modifies the prescription to fit the student. Typical modifications are assigning fewer problems than are contained on the specified pages or assigning fewer pages. These prescriptive procedures achieve a reasonable degree of individualization, since the assignment teacher knows the instructional approach and difficulty level of each textbook as well as the characteristics of each student. Thus, by selecting an appropriate prescription and adjusting it to each student, individualized assignments result.

The computer supported diagnosis and prescription procedures described above were identical to those in use in prior years. Employing the computer in the process had three effects. First, it insured that seven prescriptions were available for each objective, and that all prescribing was done via these prescriptions. Second, the prescription received by each student was recorded in the data base and thus could be used for reporting purposes.

Third, it systematized the prescriptive process through the use of a well-defined teacher-computer dialogue.

Reporting

The reporting component of the Sherman School CMI system was originally designed to be used only in the "Batch" mode. However, during the early demonstrations, it was found that the major reports were more useful when obtained via the computer terminal in the classroom. The computer programs were changed so that the routine reports could be generated interactively. The three primary reports included in the baseline system were: the Student History, the Unit Report, and the Group Report. These three reports were designed to assist the teachers in performing instructional and course level management functions. Each of the reports is described in some detail below.

The Student History Report contains all the instructionally related information generated by the assignment teacher-computer dialogue as the student proceeds through the instructional paradigm. The intent of the report was to provide a teacher with a detailed instructional history of each student. The mechanism for requesting the report allows the teacher to specify the starting date for the data to be included in the report. If the teacher were interested only in the last month's history, the appropriate date could be entered to exclude all prior data. The Student History Report can be requested for a single student or for all students in an administrative group such as a homeroom. The Student History Report is simply a print-out of the student's record in the student history file formatted to make it easy to read. Figure 4.3 shows a typical Student History Report. The report header contains the name of the teacher requesting the report, the date the report was generated, and the cut-off for the data reported. The body of the report consists of organized blocks of data for each curricular unit assigned to the student. The data reported for each curricular unit are: the name of the unit, the date it was assigned, and the study guide method—printed or audio-tape. For each test assigned

Figure 4.3: Student History Report

```
REPORT REQUEST?
S,MR JONES,05/25/76,805,S


STUDENT HISTORY REPORT
**********************

    DATE: 09/08/76    REQUESTED BY: MR JONES
    ACTIVITIES SINCE:   5/25/76

RICHARD RICH          ID:       805    HR : HR 2    SHERMAN MATH

UNIT 3-2      STUDY GUIDE   1    4/11/76 TO  9/ 8/76    47 DAYS
   PR 3-2        5/ 7/76 (DATE RECORDED)
   MULT-EVEN 10'S/100'S BY 1 PL  1
    1 SBM(4)     P. 140 (1-12)
    3 EA(4)      P. 248 (1-4 TOP)
   MULT-2 PL BY 1-NO CARRYING     2
    2 EMW(4)     P. 31 PROB (1,3)
   MULT-2 PLACE BY 1-CARRYING     3
    5 NDM(4)     P111(4-6)1ST 3 INROW
   TA 3-2

UNIT 6-1      STUDY TAPE    3    1/ 1/76 TO  9/ 8/76   107 DAYS
   PR 6-1        5/ 7/76 (DATE RECORDED)
   SET LISTING/SET DESCRIBING    1
    1 MSM(4)     P.1,2
   TA 6-1
```

within the curricular unit, the date assigned and the identification number of the objectives failed are reported—along with the prescriptions and posttest assigned. This block of data is repeated for each unit. The whole data set can be repeated for each student in an instructional group, if that option were selected. In the latter case, the students' data sets would appear in student number order. A special version of the Student History Report, called a Participant Report, shows all transactions occurring on a single day.

The Unit Report is a listing of the students currently assigned to each curricular unit. An option is provided to report all units that are active at the time of the request, or to report only a specified unit. The report was designed to assist the teachers in deciding what topics were to be presented in the seminar room. Figure 4.4 shows a typical Unit Report. The report header contains the name of the teacher requesting the report and the

Figure 4.4: Unit Report

```
U,MR JONES,UNIT 13

UNIT REPORT
***********


     DATE: 09/08/76          UNIT 13        REQUESTED BY: MR JONES
                           # OF      # ASSIGNMENTS BY OBJ
                           DAYS-TESTS  1 2 3 4 5 6

     HOMEROOM 23                                   MRS WALLEN
     BILL BROWN            42    3      2 2 2 2 3 0
     HARRY HECK            37    1      1 1 1 1 1 1
     ROBERT ROBERTS        17           0 0 0 0 0 0
     SALLY SMALL           26    2      0 2 1 0 0 1
     SIBEL SMITH           20    1      0 1 1 1 0 0
     SUZANNE SMEDT         42    3      1 0 0 2 3 3

     HOMEROOM 24                                   MISS SCHNEIDER
     ALBERT ALMET          21           0 0 0 0 0 0
     CHARLES CHURCH        37    3      0 0 0 0 0 3
     PETE PETERSON         25    2      0 0 0 0 1 2
     WILLY WILLIAMS        21    2      0 2 2 0 0 0

     HOMEROOM 26                                   MRS GRASS
     BOB BAKER             57    4      1 2 3 1 3 2
   · MILLY MILES           34    3      1 1 3 1 0 3
     OLE OLSEN             18    1      0 0 0 0 1 0


     COLUMN    SHORT    FULL                       RELATIVE
     NUMBER    NAME     TITLE                      DIFFICULTY

       1        1       1 PL MULT THROUGH 10,000'S      9%
       2        2       MULT-2 PLACE TIMES 2/3 PLACE   16%
       3        3       MULT-2 PL TIMES 3 PL WITH 0    20%
       4        4       DIV OF 100'S-0 IN 2/3 PL QUO   12%
       5        5       DIVISION BY EVEN 10'S          18%
       6        6       100'S DIVIDED BY 10'S          23%
```

date the report was requested. The body of the report consists of the name of the curricular unit, the number of students assigned to the unit, followed by a list of student identification numbers and student names in ID number order. If the "all units option" is selected, the block of data for each active unit is reported in number of students assigned order. Thus, the unit with the most students enrolled is first, and that with the least is last. The teachers specified this order should be used to simplify their use of the report.

The Group Report lists pupils by homerooms or other instructional groups and shows what curricular unit is assigned to each student. The report was intended to be used by homeroom teachers to monitor the status of their own pupils. Figure 4.5 contains a representative Group Report.

The report header shows the name of the teacher requesting the report, the current date, and the identification number of the group. The body of the report is a listing of student names, identification numbers, name of the curricular unit, instructional method, the name of the test currently assigned, and the date the unit was assigned to the student. The students are listed in student identification number order.

The three primary reports used by the Sherman School CMI system are those common to many other CMI systems and were decided upon after a study of reporting practices of a number of CMI systems. During the course of the first semester's operation, the teachers requested that two additional reports be added to the set of reports. These were a Contact Report and a Test Report. The Contact Report was designed to identify students who had not had any contact with the assignment teacher since a given date. Figure 4.6 contains a copy of a Contact Report.

The report header shows the name of the teacher requesting the report and the date defining the beginning of the report period. Through use of the date, the report can extend back in time as far as the teacher desires. For example, the report could cover the past week or the past 42 days. The body of the Contact Report is organized by students within the instructional group. The identification number of each group is followed by a list of names and identification numbers of students who have had no entries in their student history record since the date specified. The current unit, instructional method, test, and date they were assigned are reported for each student. The date of assignment can precede the cut-off date, as the student may have begun a unit before the cut-off date and had no subsequent contact with the assignment teacher.

The Test Report was intended to facilitate the curriculum improvement cycle by providing item analysis data on the unit

Figure 4.5: Group Report

```
MICA READY
G,MR WEBER,,G
INVALID INPUT: G,MR WEBER,,G

MICA READY
/R


REPORT REQUEST?
G,MR WEBER,,G

GROUP REPORT
************
```

```
DATE: 09/08/76   TEST                    SHERMAN MATH
MR. WEBER                TEST GROUP 1
```

	GRADE	ID#	ACTIVITY	DAYS SINCE	METHOD	NEXT TEST	DAYS SINCE
JOHN LITTLE	4	792	REVIEW 1-2	33	TEST	PR R1-2	33
JOHN BIG	4	793	UNIT 15-2	48	STUDY GUIDE	TA 15-2	1
	4	793	UNIT 8	48	STUDY GUIDE	TB 8	3
JOHN MEDIUM	4	794	REVIEW 6-1	48	TEST	PT R6-1	48
JOHN SMALL	4	795	UNIT 3-2	69	STUDY GUIDE	PASS	69
JOHN LARGE	4	796	UNIT 23-1	16	STUDY GUIDE	PR 23-1	16
	4	796	UNIT 12-2	16	SEMINAR	PR 12-2	16
	4	796	UNIT 11-2	47	STUDY GUIDE	TB 11-2	34
MARY PETITE	4	797	UNIT 4-1	65	STUDY GUIDE	TC 4-1	65
MARY HUGE	4	798	UNIT 6-1	107	STUDY GUIDE	PR 6-1	107
	4	798	UNIT 4-1	107	STUDY GUIDE	PR 4-1	107
JANE PLAIN	4	799	UNIT 6-1	12	STUDY TAPE	TC 6-1	12

```
GROUP REPORT
************
```

```
DATE: 09/08/76   TEST                    SHERMAN MATH
MR. LORENZ               TEST GROUP 2
```

	GRADE	ID#	ACTIVITY	DAYS SINCE	METHOD	NEXT TEST	DAYS SINCE
JANE PRETTY	4	800	UNIT 10-2	39	STUDY GUIDE	PR 10-2	39
	4	800	UNIT 1-1	31	STUDY GUIDE	PR 1-1	31
	4	800	UNIT 2-2	38	STUDY GUIDE	PR 2-2	38
SADIE SMALL	4	801	REVIEW 2-1	41	TEST	PT R2-1	41
	4	801	UNIT 4-1	17	SEMINAR	PR 4-1	17
	4	801	UNIT 2-2	41	STUDY GUIDE	PR 2-2	41
TOM THUMB	4	802	UNIT 2-1	21	STUDY GUIDE	PR 2-1	21
	4	802	UNIT 4-1	21	STUDY GUIDE	TA 4-1	21
	4	802	UNIT 19	47	STUDY GUIDE	TB 19	47
TOM SHORT	4	803	NOTHING				
RICHARD POOR	4	804	UNIT 10-2	107	STUDY GUIDE	TA 10-2	107
	4	804	UNIT 8	107	STUDY TAPE	PR 8	107
	4	804	UNIT 7	106	SEMINAR	PR 7	106
RICHARD RICH	4	805	UNIT 3-2	47	STUDY GUIDE	TA 3-2	29
	4	805	UNIT 6-1	107	STUDY TAPE	TA 6-1	29
SAM CLEMENCY	4	806	UNIT 8	65	STUDY GUIDE	TB 8	65
SALLY SEASHELL	4	807	NOTHING				
PETER PUMPKINEATER	4	808	NOTHING				
MARY CONTRARY	4	809	UNIT 21-1	49	SEMINAR	TB 21-1	49
	4	809	REVIEW 5	49	TEST	PT R5	49
	4	809	UNIT 16-1	49	SEMINAR	PASS	48

Figure 4.6: Contact Report

```
REPORT REQUEST
C,MR JONES,06/01/76

CONTACT REPORT
**************
```

MR JONES			DATE 06/01/76		
	ID	ACTIVITY	METHOD	TEST	DAYS
HOMEROOM 63					SINCE
BILL BROWN	42	UNIT 10-2	STUDY GUIDE	PR 10-2	7
HARRY HECK	37	UNIT 19	STUDY GUIDE	PR 19	1
ROBERT ROBERTS	17	UNIT 10-3	STUDY GUIDE	TC 10-3	1
SALLY SMALL	26	UNIT 16-1	STUDY GUIDE	PR 16-1	4
HOMEROOM 64					
ALBERT ALMET	21	UNIT 10-1	SEMINAR	PR 10-1	11
CHARLES CHURCH	37	UNIT 10-3	STUDY GUIDE	PR 10-3	5
HOMEROOM 65					
BOB BAKER	57	UNIT 4-2	FILM STRIP	PR 4-2	1
OLE OLSEN	18	UNIT 18-2	STUDY GUIDE	TA 18-2	4

Figure 4.7: Test Report

```
REPORT REQUEST
T,MR JONES,UNIT 1-1,ALL,,

MR JONES                                    DATE 06/1/76

UNIT  1-1     STUDY GUIDE  1      PR  1-1  TOTAL NUMBER TAKEN  144

ITEM NUMBER              1     2     3     4     5
CORRECT RESPONSES       68    78    50    46    47

UNIT  1-1     STUDY GUIDE  1      TA  1-1  TOTAL NUMBER TAKEN  126

ITEM NUMBER              1     2     3     4     5
CORRECT RESPONSES      106   108    77    68    77

UNIT  1-1     STUDY GUIDE  1      TB  1-1  TOTAL NUMBER TAKEN   78

ITEM NUMBER              1     2     3     4     5
CORRECT RESPONSES       73    72    58    60    58
UNIT  1-1     STUDY GUIDE  1      TC  1-1  TOTAL NUMBER TAKEN   30

ITEM NUMBER              1     2     3     4     5
CORRECT RESPONSES       26    20    18    30    24
```

pre- and posttests. In contrast to the preceding reports, the Test Report can only be generated under the "Batch" mode. Figure 4.7 shows a Test Report for one unit.

Test Report options allow the requester to specify the set of test data to be printed. One can request the data for a specific test, for a given study guide, or for all tests associated with a given study guide. The maximum number of objectives in the tests involved must also be specified. The report header contains the name of the requester, the name of the curricular unit, the study guide method, the name of the test, and the total number of times the test was administered. For each test reported, a table is presented containing the number of times each objective in the test was passed. Although the data reported is at a crude level, it has proven useful to the teachers in evaluating the unit tests.

The scheme for requesting reports via the interactive terminal is very simple and is consistent across all reports. To request a report, a letter identifying the report, the requester's name, and the date are all that is required. Some reports have options, selected by number or name. Most reports can be limited in their scope to a student, a group of students, or by the period of time covered. Consequently, the size of the reports is reasonably small and can be printed via the print unit attached to the display terminal. If necessary, all reports can be produced via the batch mode at the central computer facility. Large reports, such as end-of-semester or end-of-year Student History Reports for all students and test report for all units, are produced under the batch mode. One of the excellent features of the EXEC-8 operating system for the UNIVAC 1108 is that a computer program can be run under either batch or time-sharing mode with no changes in the program.

Management

The management component of the Sherman School CMI system is quite different from that of other CMI systems. Because of the instructional paradigm employed, the instructional and course level management functions performed by a single teacher in the usual elementary school classroom are shared among six teachers. Each is responsible for performing a particular instructional function and the management procedures associated with it. At the instructional level of management, such fractionalization is convenient. However, at the course level it is not, as no single teacher would be responsible for monitoring student progress. At this level of management, the six teachers form a management group with the lead teacher as the group leader.

The instructional level of management focuses upon the diagnosis and prescription procedures of the unit-of-instruction cycle. The assignment teacher performs the major role in the process, assigning curricular units and tests, and selecting prescriptions. The assignment teacher essentially manages the overall unit-of-instruction cycle for all 165 students in the two grades. Due to the distribution of students over the curricular units and within a unit, not all 165 students are contacted in a single day. The assignment teacher can generate a Student History Report for a given student to assist in making decisions in the prescription process. However, this is done rarely due to the relatively slow speed of the interactive printer. The remaining five teachers perform primarily instructional roles, but each contributes to the unit-of-instruction cycle. The teacher in the testing room assists the students in locating tests, answer sheets, and audio-tapes for the study guide. The three teachers in the study rooms assist the student more closely than was done by the assignment teacher. Thus, each teacher while performing a specific function contributes to the instructional level of management.

The goal of course level management is to individualize with respect to rate of progress through a common curricular plan. Under the Sherman School system, the course level management is performed both by individual teachers and jointly by them as a management group. Since only mathematics instruction is conducted via the CMI system, students return to their regular homeroom classes for other subjects. Thus, each teacher is responsible for approximately 30 students. The group report is used by each homeroom teacher to determine the status of his or her own pupils in the mathematics program. As the full group of students flows through the instructional paradigm, each teacher comes into repeated contact with students from his or her own homeroom. During these contacts, the teacher performs course level management functions for his or her own students in addition to instructional level functions associated with the teacher's specific role in the mathematics program. The teacher also monitors his or her own homeroom students' progress in the mathematics program for grading and other purposes. The homeroom teachers have used Student History Reports in each semester's parent-teacher conferences and as the basis for filling out report cards which are primarily progress reports. The Contact Report is used by homeroom teachers to locate students who get "lost" in the system, usually spending excessive time in the study rooms. It is also used to identify students who have been absent from school.

When operating as a management group, the teachers use the Unit Report to decide what topics should be presented in the seminar room during the next week. They identify troublesome curricular units and plan how to assist students through these units. The group discusses the operation of the total system and makes adjustments in the functions performed in the various rooms to improve operations. In addition, individual students who are having difficulty are identified, and each teacher is alerted to the nature of the problem. Thus, as the student comes into contact with a teacher, specific assistance can be provided.

Because the Sherman School CMI system encompasses only mathematics, there is no program level of management as defined in Chapter Two. The one facet of program management that is performed is curriculum improvement. Each summer, a group of teachers works to improve the curriculum. The reports used in this process are the Unit Report and the Test Report. The unit report for the last day of class shows the distribution of students over the curricular plan and is a measure of the throughput for the year. The test report shows the frequency with which each objective was mastered. Due to a number of factors, the curriculum improvement cycle is an important aspect of the Sherman School Project; it is discussed in greater detail later in this chapter.

In contrast to most CMI systems, where each teacher acts as a separate manager, the management responsibilities in the Sherman School CMI system are shared by the six teachers. Instructional level and some course level management functions are performed by each teacher; and as a group they perform the majority of the course level and limited program level management functions. The overall results of this unusual management arrangement have been good.

Computer

The Sherman School CMI system was designed from its inception to employ the time-sharing mode of computer operation. The computer component was structured to provide the classroom teacher an easy-to-use, flexible, yet powerful interaction with the computer via a terminal in the classroom. Only the creation of the data base at the beginning of each school year and a few of the more lengthy reports employ the batch mode. All daily transactions between the school and the computer are conducted via an interactive terminal. Figure 4.8 presents the hardware configuration used by the teacher in the classroom. The primary unit is a Hazeltine 2000 alphanumeric display consisting of a cathode ray tube and a keyboard. The computer displays information on the tube screen, and keyboard entries made by the teacher also appear on the screen. A Hazeltine printer is connected to the display unit, and all data displayed on the screen are also printed. The printer is used primarily to diagnose operational difficulties and generate reports. The display unit is connected to the UNIVAC 1108 computer via an acoustic coupler and telephone lines.

Once the data base has been constructed, all data is collected

Figure 4.8: Computer Terminal Configuration

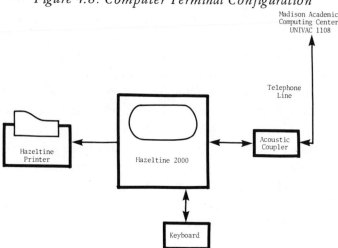

via the use of the interactive terminal. Under operational conditions, the assignment teacher is the only person who enters data, but any teacher can use the terminal for report generation. As was mentioned above, the computer-teacher dialogue, except requesting of reports, is via menu selection procedures. Lists of possible actions are presented, and the teacher simply enters the sequence number of the selection desired. The computer programs employed by the system are written in FORTRAN IV, with some use of FORTRAN V for execution on the University of Wisconsin's UNIVAC 1108. Because these programs and the data base are the subject of Chapter Five, they will not be described in detail here.

The data base design employs six files divided into student-related and curriculum-related files. The first group consists of the Student History File, the Student Data File, and the Group File. The Student History File has a record for each student in the mathematics program. The record contains the dynamic, instructionally related data entered by the assignment teacher. The Student Data File has a record for each student containing the static data such as name, birthdate, sex, grade, instructional group, and attendance zone. The Group File contains a record for each homeroom group, listing the students in the homeroom. The Group File is created from data in the Student Data File. The second collection of files consists of the Unit File, the Prescription File, and the Dictionary File. The Unit File contains the curricular plan, and defines each unit in terms of its prerequisites, pretests, posttests, and study guide methods. The Prescription File stores the criteria by which a given prescription is selected and links them to the prescriptions stored in the Dictionary File. The MICA software actually implements a more general diagnosis and prescription capability than is used by Sherman School, and the design of the Prescription File reflects this more general capability. The Dictionary File consists of lists of names of entities used by the other files. An indexed sequential file scheme was used and the data elements in the other files are index numbers into the entities in the dictionaries. Only the Dictionary File contains the actual prescriptions, unit names, test names, etc., as they appear in reports and at the interactive terminal. The dictionary scheme solved the vexing problem of cross-file linkages in the data base. The design of the data base also facilitates adding new elements to the files when needed.

The conceptualization, implementation, and documentation of the original MICA computer program required roughly 36 man-months of effort, and approximately $3,000 of computer time was used. The cost of transforming the original MICA program into a production program was $6,000 for programming effort and $2,000 for computer time, including creation of the initial data base.

Operational Experience with
the Baseline System

The decision to put the CMI system into operation was made late in the Spring of 1973, and a number of activities were initiated to meet the target date of August 27, 1973. The foremost of these was to build a prescription file. The Sherman School staff had kept an informal record of prescriptions for a number of years; however, it was incomplete and not in a form usable for computer input. Three teachers were employed during the Summer to perform the significant task of creating up to seven prescriptions for each objective of each test for the 30 study guides and six review sessions. These prescriptions were then recorded on MICA input forms and subsequently keypunched by a service bureau. The result of the efffort was a set of over 11,000 prescriptions, of which somewhat over 2,000 were unique.

The MICA computer programs were only partially checked out during the Spring demonstration, and a number of hidden faults in the programs had been uncovered. To compound the problems, the last student familiar with the MICA program was leaving school. Fortunately, the Teacher Corps funding provided a computer programmer who was able to work with that student for a two-month period. During this period, known software deficiencies were corrected and the basis for eventual "clean up" of all the software was established. At this point in time, there was considerable concern over the possibilities of computer failures and subsequent loss of data entered by the teacher at the terminal. To mollify these concerns, a magnetic tape backup scheme was designed and implemented. Every transaction altering the contents of the data base was recorded on magnetic tape. In addition, manual data collection forms were designed and printed so that in case of system failure, the equivalent of teacher terminal actions could be recorded and transferred to punched cards. Through the combination of the magnetic tapes and the punched cards, it was possible to recover from nearly all forms of computer system failure.

Once the prescriptions were created and keypunched, a roster of next year's students was obtained and a list of study guides prepared. Then it was possible to build the data base. With the exception of some keypunch problems due to poor communications among those involved, the data base building went very smoothly. By mid-August, all files were created and stored in the computer's mass memory. A special printout was produced in which the prescriptions were listed by study guide, by test, and by objective, enabling teachers to do assignments manually when the computer was down for repairs.

The final step, in setting up, was inservice training for the teachers who were to use the system. A manual of operating procedures was prepared and printed. A few days prior to opening of school, an afternoon was devoted to showing the teachers how to turn on the system, log in with the computer, and put MICA into operation.

The target date of August 27, 1973 had been met, and both Sherman School and the computer component were ready to go into operation. The lead teacher was to be the assignment teacher during the initial phases of operational use and would be the person employing the computer terminal. After the first few days, devoted to getting school organized, the teachers simply turned on the terminal and began to use the computer to manage the mathematics program.

First Semester, 1973/74. The first two weeks of operation were very nearly the last! The UNIVAC 1108 computer went into a period of erratic operation and failed with great regularity during the mathematics class period. The computing center staff had decided to install a new version of the operating system containing numerous errors, most of which caused the system to fail. The telephone company installed a telephone line of dubious quality that would hang up the computer line at inopportune moments due to spurious noise signals. Finally, the university anti-bomb threat scheme precluded getting the phone connection back once the line noise had hung up the line from the terminal end. As is obvious, the number of days the computer-based components functioned was less than one-half. The teachers dutifully filled out manual data collection forms, and each night the computer programmer worked through the night to bring the data base up to date via batch runs. Another major problem anticipated by the

Sherman School staff, but not by the computer staff, was that all 165 pupils were started at Instructional Unit 1. Due to these problems, the lead teacher was the only teacher to use the computer terminal during the first several months of operation. With the passage of time, the technical difficulties subsided and by mid-November the system failure rate was very low and an acceptable level of service was achieved. Unfortunately, the computer is used by the total University and the usual heavy end of the semester work load reduced the reaction speed of the machine during December.

Data related to the first semester's operations had been collected via a number of techniques. The system analyst spent many hours in Sherman School observing the mathematics program in operation and recording relevant data. He also met many times with the Sherman School staff to collect teacher comments related to system operation and system improvements that were needed. The University of Wisconsin Computing Center has a rather detailed cost accounting procedure, and accurate records were maintained by the computer programmer related to operational computer costs and the sources of the costs. In addition, everyone involved viewed the project from their own professional vantage point and provided a wealth of informal observations, estimates, and intuitions as to the state of affairs.

During the first months of operation, the systems analyst collected data pertaining to the utilization of the computer terminal and the rate of pupil flow through the instructional sequence. The data presented in Figures 4.9 and 4.10 clearly document the technical difficulties encountered and their impact. Figure 4.9 depicts the pattern of computer terminal operation. The dashed line below the 50-minute limit indicates the number of minutes the computer terminal operated during the mathematics class period. The solid line shows the total amount of time the terminal was used on a given day, including the time during the class period. Any portion of the dashed line below the 50-minute line implies that a computer system failure occurred and the

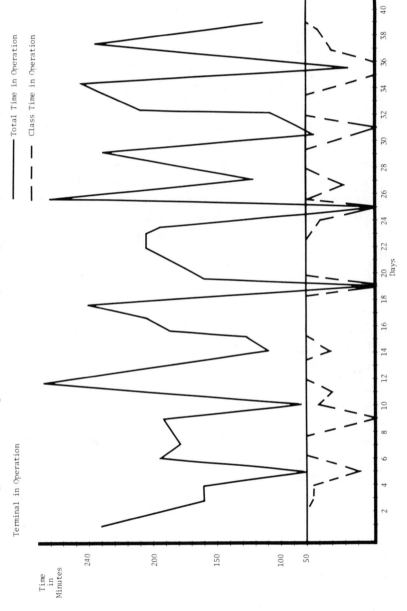

Figure 4.9: Computer Terminal Operating History, First 40 Days

terminal was not available for some portion of the class period. The solid line touching the base indicates the computer system never became operational on that day. During these first 40 days, the terminal was being used exclusively for the assignment process; hence, if operating perfectly, the dashed line, the solid line, and the 50-minute line should have coincided. Clearly a great deal was amiss. Twenty of the 40 days the terminal was operated for the full class period. On the remaining 20 days, some form of computer failure was encountered, and complete failure to achieve terminal operation occurred on six of these 20 days. The interactive computer terminal never failed; all failures were due to the computer system or telephone line problems.* Thus, the probability of some form of technical difficulty occurring during the class period was 50 percent, hardly a reliable system. Subtracting the value of the in-class use of the terminal from the total use value for a given day is the amount of time the terminal was used for assignment purposes after class. The after-class use exceeds the in-class use nearly every day and on some days this use exceeded three hours. The after-class use reflects two problems. First the pupil flow was greater than the teacher at the console could process. Second, when a computer failure occurred one day, the backlog was processed the next day. The latter backlog was due in part to the assignment teacher's deciding that the filling out of manual forms for a batch run during the night involved too much teacher time. Consequently, after the first few days, the manual forms were not used and the teacher used the terminal to complete the assignment process after class. One might add, at the cost of many missed meals.

The data in Figure 4.10 is based upon the number of pupils given assignments during the class period and the number waiting

---

*The actual computer may have been operating, but either a telephone connection could not be maintained, or the length of time of proper computer operation was too short to accomplish useful work due to operating system software failures.

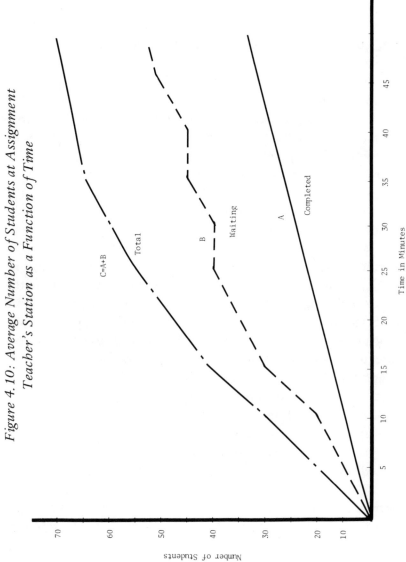

Figure 4.10: Average Number of Students at Assignment Teacher's Station as a Function of Time

for assignments. The data was collected at five-minute intervals and then averaged over a number of days. The line labeled A is the average number of pupils receiving assignments and is linear. At the end of a class period, roughly 24 pupils had on the average received assignments. The line labeled B is the average number of pupils waiting for assignments as a function of time and is reasonably linear. At the end of the class period, approximately 40 pupils were waiting for assignments. The line labeled C is the sum of the values of A and B at each time interval and represents the total pupil flow.

The data shows students completing tests roughly once a minute, while the assignment teacher at the computer terminal was completing a pupil once every two minutes. The pupil flow was roughly twice that expected by the MICA designers, who envisioned a flow of only 30 pupils per class period rather than the 60 that occurred. One consequence of the ratio of waiting pupils to processed pupils was that those pupils entering the assignment room after the first 20 minutes had no chance of receiving an assignment. Their test papers were collected and the assignments made after class by the teacher using the terminal, recorded on the 3 x 5 card, and given to the pupil the next day—a procedure similar to that used under the previous manual system when overload occurred. The rather high pupil flow was a direct consequence of both fourth and fifth graders starting at Unit 1. An additional factor was that many students worked on mathematics assignments at home and were using the class period only to take tests on material done at home, reflecting the pupils' enthusiasm for mathematics.

The high frequency of computer-related failures seriously reduced the available computer processing and the number of pupils processed. However, even with full computer availability, as was the case for most of the month of November, 1973, the assignment teacher was not able to process 60 pupils. Rates of 34-45 pupils per period were achieved in mid-semester, when the computer was lightly loaded and the telephone lines behaved.

Although some improvements were made during the course of the first semester, the data collected during the first weeks of the project exposed two primary areas of concern. First, the total amount of computer terminal time used each day for assignment purposes had to be reduced until it matched the class period. The existence of a persistent overload was not acceptable. Second, the pupil flow through the instructional sequence was too high. Achieving a better match between the implementation of the mathematics program and the processing capacity of the computer component would require both curricular and technical changes.

In summary, the first semester operations were a qualified success. The total CMI system, including its educational and computer components, was made operational on time; the computer performed the functions it was designed to do; and a significant portion of the instructional management process was implemented. The reaction of the pupils to the terminal was good, and they delighted in seeing their names appear on the display unit screen. No hostile reactions were reported, and little fear of the computer was observed. Teacher reactions were also favorable to the use of the computer. A number of teachers commented that the overall operation of the mathematics program was the best ever, and they would like the system expanded to include other subject matter areas. A facet of this reaction was due to the fact that only the terminal operator can update student records, thus freeing other teachers from what was previously a joint effort to keep assignments up to date. Because the assignment teacher now had a list of alternative prescriptions for each objective in a test, it was possible to make assignments from any of five textbooks. Teacher comments indicated that for the first time, extensive use was being made of multiple texts by the pupils. Technical difficulties plagued the effort, and the survival of the project was the result of the complete dedication of the Sherman School staff to the goal of a viable CMI system. Without this staff dedication, the very real technical problems could have terminated the project.

Second Semester, 1973/74. As was the case with the first semester, the first few weeks were a technical disaster. The University Computing Center replaced the UNIVAC 1108 with a UNIVAC 1110. These two computers had identical software characteristics so there was no software conversion involved. The MICA programs ran on the 1108 one day and the 1110 the next. The underlying problems were threefold: First, the computer had been ordered with only 32K of high-speed memory, and this proved insufficient. Second, the machine had a dual Central Processing Unit (CPU) configuration, and one CPU would not function. Third, the operating system was defective and prone to collapse. Despite a three-month overlap in 1108, 1110 operations, these problems did not surface until the full University computing load was placed on the 1110. The end result was a pattern of computer utilization similar to the first 40 days. In contrast to the first semester, a prolonged period of high utilization was never achieved. At one point, a complete week of operation was lost due to a combination of technical and administrative problems. The primary benefit of the switch to the UNIVAC 1110 computer was a major realignment of computer usage rates that were highly favorable to the time-sharing mode of operation. For example, the cost of connect time was reduced from $4 to $1 per hour. The new rates cut the cost of using the system roughly in half. By early in the second semester, most of the deficiencies of the curricular plan, instructional paradigm, and computer component were painfully apparent. As a result, it was decided to finish the school year with the system as it existed. Only the minor improvements would be implemented when it appeared feasible. Major attention would be devoted to modifying the total system to improve the match between the educational and the computer components.

At the end of the first year of operation, the average number of curricular units completed per student was 12. Four students were on unit 2, and nine students had finished all 36 units. The frequency distribution peaked at unit 12 and tailed off rather rapidly towards the higher numbered units. The majority of pupils were working on units in the range from number 8 to number 17 at the end of the school year.

During the first year of operation, the teachers made less use of the reports than had been intended. The most popular report was the Contact Report, generated at the end of each week. Group and Unit Reports were generated only occasionally. Student History Reports were used for parent-teacher conferences but were difficult for parents to understand. By the end of the school year, the assignment teacher was a skilled computer terminal operator, but felt the role was more clerical than instructional. Due to the limited use of reports, most of the instructionally related data so carefully entered by the assignment teacher was archival in nature. It was clear that better use of the reports was needed and that the computer terminal operator's role needed changing.

Improving the System, 1973/74

There were a number of interests focused upon first year's operations of the CMI system at Sherman School. The school staff was interested in obtaining a level of computer support that would enable them to effectively manage the mathematics program. The Madison Public School's central office was interested in determining how well the CMI approach worked with the mathematics program and in ascertaining its potential for other educational programs within the school district. The Laboratory of Experimental Design (University of Wisconsin) was concerned with the continued development of the MICA software package on the basis of its actual use in the classroom. The Teacher Corps project was interested in the application of MICA to teacher training. These interests resulted in the formation of a very loosely organized working group monitoring the Sherman School Project during the first year of operation. The working group consisted of the following staff: the principal and lead teacher from Sherman School; the East area coordinator, a systems analyst, a curriculum coordinator, the director of research and development, the director of the administrative data processing group, and his assistant from the Madison Public Schools; and a computer programmer and the director of the Laboratory of Experimental Design. In addition, one staff member from the University's Teacher Corps project was in the group. The working group met roughly every two months to discuss current efforts and plan future activities. The working relationships among the various group members was very informal and the lines of communication were informal almost to the point of being tenuous at times. During the first year, there was no project management per se. As the basic trend of work to be done evolved from day-to-day operations and from the infrequent group meetings, each subgroup went about what it felt needed to be done. There were three major areas of work: system analysis, curricular improvement, and technology. The efforts in these areas of necessity overlapped and complemented each other; consequently, no subgroup worked exclusively in one area, yet particular subgroups worked primarily in areas of their own expertise. When major decisions concerning the fate of the project were to be made, the group had a meeting, and the area coordinator kept the group on task until the decision was reached.

The overall goal established by the working group was to evaluate the Sherman School Project as a system and make recommendations that would improve the system.

System Analysis. Three primary problem areas were exposed by the first year's operations: an overloading of the assignment teacher, a mismatch between curricular details and the computer processing, and the need to reduce operating costs. The problem of assignment teacher overload focused attention on the sources of the overload. The initial area receiving attention was that of the functions being performed at the console by the assignment teacher. Some of these functions were instructional in nature, while others were clerical, involving the use of the computer terminal. When a pupil appeared at the console, he brought with him a scored test. Unfortunately, the identification number of a given objective was not the same on all tests for a given instructional unit and did not correspond with the number used by MICA to locate the prescriptions for the objective. The teacher used a book to obtain the number correspondence so that the objective could be identified to the computer. Early in the year, a procedure was initiated whereby a student intern or other person manually converted these numbers on the answer sheet before the student appeared at the terminal. However, this was only a palliative measure and did not solve the basic problem which was inherent in the inconsistent ordering of objectives on the printed tests associated with each unit.

When remedial prescriptions were selected, the teacher inspected the textbook and "filtered" the prescription to make the work assigned an appropriately sized task for the individual pupil. The teacher then gave the pupil the textbook. The teacher also recorded the prescription on the pupil's 3 x 5 card, and the pupil departed. In the meantime, the assignment room contained 10-30 pupils waiting for assignments, as well as pupils using the room to play mathematical games under the assignment teacher's supervision.

It was abundantly clear that the assignment teacher performed far too many functions, and the whole process needed to be re-examined. Ideally, the pupil should bring to the console a workload the assignment teacher can dispatch quickly. The pupil should leave the console with an individualized assignment. All the pupils needing such service should be accommodated during the class period. There was some tendency to use technological enhancements of the computer terminal to achieve greater productivity by the assignment teacher. Some gains can be made by this means, such as shifting from a 110 baud telephone line to a 300 baud line, but the gains are marginal relative to the total problem. The major improvements must be achieved via the curricular and procedural areas.

In the curricular area, the primary concern was the lack of precision in the prescriptions stored in the prescription file and used by the assignment teacher. The prescriptions tended to specify rather large sections of a text, and often the assignment teacher needed to make a more specific assignment for each pupil. The number of objectives covered by each unit, hence, included in the pre- and posttests, was too large, ranging from a minimum of 3 to a maximum of 70 with an average 8.8 and standard deviation of 8.8. It is here that a significant mismatch with the MICA computer program occurred. The computer terminal can display at most six sets of prescriptions per screen; however, the screen can be refilled any number of times. Teachers did not like multiple screen displays due to the time it takes to fill the screen and the necessity of manually recording the identification numbers of prescriptions selected from previous screen displays before the whole set of selections are entered via the keyboard. Thus, to be most effective, each test should cover no more objectives than can be displayed simultaneously at the terminal. An additional facet of the prescription problem was that each objective was allowed only eight prescriptions. Due to an oversight in the MICA design, as noted earlier, the first prescription was used to store the name of the objective and must always be assigned as a prescription. The teacher is then free to choose one or more of the remaining seven. The Student History File record was designed to hold up to 14 prescriptions per test, but up to seven of these may be just the objective names. The end result was that the assignment teacher had a relatively restricted field within which to prescribe. At a maximum, one prescription could be made for each of seven objectives or six prescriptions for each of two objectives. The high pupil flow also was due partially to a pupil's not being given assignments for all objectives missed. Each time he appeared at the console, prescriptions were made for only those objectives the assignment teacher chose. The original concept was that all objectives missed would be prescribed at one time and a pupil would take a posttest only when he felt he had mastered the whole unit. Inspection of the test results showed about two-thirds of the missed objectives were bypassed when making assignments during the first semester, and this ratio was reduced somewhat later in the year. Thus, the pupil might take two or three posttests before all objectives of a unit were covered. As a result of this practice, the Student History File contained only a subset of the objectives actually missed by a pupil on a given test.

From a procedural point of view, the most obvious queue occurred at the assignment teacher's station, but observational data collected by the systems analyst revealed the quiz teacher was also the head of another queue. The purpose of the quiz teacher was to insure each pupil was actually prepared to take the assigned test before entering the testing room. Queues of students formed at this station, and it was not uncommon for 10-20 pupils to be waiting for the quiz teacher to assist them. The same data also showed too many activities were being conducted in the testing room, and the use of the audio-tape version of the study guide was inconsistent with the testing occurring in the room. The teacher in the testing room was performing a dual role supervising testing and assisting with study guides.

The operation of the computer terminal during the first year revealed a number of areas requiring technical modifications to both the MICA program and to computer-related procedures. Early in the first semester, changes were made to increase the speed of the system and to reduce operational costs. Later in the semester, additional reports requested by the teachers were implemented. Throughout the whole year, the MICA software underwent a continuous "clean up" to improve the quality of the programming, which was basically very good. Cost data were collected for each computer run during the first semester, and some aggregate data is reported in Table 4.1.

There were three main sources of operational computer costs: file storage charges, interactive use of the computer (Demand) by the assignment teacher, and batch runs for file maintenance and report generation. The major portion of the file charges were due to the Student History File, 165 tracks at a cost of 2.5 cents per track per day plus a 10 cents per file per day

Table 4.1

1973 First Semester Computer Costs

	Cost Per Day	Total
File Storage	$6.16	$ 505.17
Terminal Usage	9.29	761.43
Batch Runs	1.50	122.94
	Semester Total	$1,389.54

	Days	**Files**	**Demand**	**Batch**	**Totals**
Aug.	5	24.00	64.31	1.13	89.44
Sept.	20	180.35	213.30	21.73	415.38
Oct.	23	125.66	189.28	36.56	351.50
Nov.	19	96.86	202.39	28.00	327.25
Dec.	15	28.30	92.15	35.52	205.97
Totals	82	505.17	761.43	122.94	$1,389.54

charge. A number of other files were maintained at these rates, resulting in a total storage of $6.16 per day and a total cost for storage of $505.17 for the first semester. Early in the semester a procedure was initiated whereby each Friday the files and programs were copied onto magnetic tape, the mass storage released, and the files reloaded on Monday. The procedure saved about $10 per weekend in file charges. One of the design deficiencies of the MICA computer programs contributing to file costs was the data base design. No provision had been made for dynamic growth of the Student History File. The file had been designed with a fixed record format that could hold a year's data for a student. At the beginning of the year, each record was nearly empty; yet, file storage charges were paid for the full record.

During the first semester, a significant proportion of the operational costs was associated with activating the MICA program and files for the day's use. When the assignment teacher signed onto the computer, the computer programs and a number of files were transferred from disk to core memory. The back-up tape from the previous day was mounted; and, if necessary, the files were updated via the information on the magnetic tape. These initialization procedures cost nearly $5 each time they were performed. To reduce these costs, the recording of each transaction on the back-up magnetic tape was abandoned in favor of copying the Student History File from disk to tape at the conclusion of each day's use of the computer terminal. This magnetic tape would be used only if a system failure occurred between two days' use of the computer. The new approach to protecting the system against a computer failure reduced the cost of initializing the MICA programs and files from $5.00 to $1.50 while providing ample file protection against a computer failure. The batch run costs were relatively small and included the cost of a daily run to produce the back-up tape, the "Friday-Monday" procedures, generation of large reports, and some file maintenance. The total first semester batch costs were $122.94. The cost of using the computer terminal interactively (Demand) was a function of the initialization costs, how long the computer was used (connect time at $4/hr.), and the actual computing performed. After the magnetic tape back-up procedures were changed, these costs varied from $4 to $24.85 per day, with an average cost of $9.20 per day. The aggregate of all computer operational costs during the first semester, 1973/74, was $1,389.54, for an average per day cost of $16.95 and an average per pupil per day cost of slightly over 10 cents.

Other than the noise-induced disconnecting of the telephone line, which was solved by installing a conditioned line, the most troublesome technical problem was recovery from computer system failures. The MICA software was designed around the menu selection procedures, and the assignment teacher could recover easily from self-induced problems. When the computer system failed, a vast array of possible messages appeared at the console, most of which were meaningless. Even experienced computer users have difficulty responding to the conditions described by these messages and recovering in a reasonable fashion. Since the teachers had no experience in this regard, system failures were catastrophic events. At first, the assignment teacher simply hung up the phone, waited, and reinitialized the MICA system at a considerable cost. After a few months, the assignment teacher, with some assistance from the programmer, learned to differentiate absolute failures from recoverable failures and was able to cope with the common failures of both types. Protecting the "naive" user from system-induced failures is a problem plaguing all interactive use of the computer, and in the first year was never solved completely.

The improvement of the basic MICA computer program was a continuous effort. The original MICA program was written by six students whose programming expertise varied from only one prior course to professional experience. Consequently, the quality of the implementation was highly variable. In addition, one programmer did not follow the ground rules used by the others and produced highly idiosyncratic programs. As a result, the report module was completely restructured during 1973/74 to facilitate the efficient creation of new reports as the need occurred. A large number of subroutines throughout MICA were either rewritten or cleaned up to yield better code. During the second semester, the idiosyncratic modules were replaced with all new programs following the ground rules. Internal changes were made to take into account whether the Hazeltine 2000 terminal or a keyboard-style terminal was in use, thus preventing difficulties with Hazeltine commands giving the keyboard terminals illegal directions.

Another software effort of the second semester of 1973/74 was to provide a dictionary file maintenance capability. The original MICA program neglected to do so, and often it was necessary to be able to correct spellings of prescriptions, pupil names, add pupils, etc., in an efficient manner. Such a capability increased the flexibility of the system considerably.

It is clear from the nature of the technical changes that the MICA computer programs were developed in an evolutionary manner from a homework project into a production program. To make such a transition without the program degenerating into a complex of overlaid changes tailored to specific situations was very difficult. Each change was evaluated on the basis of its present value, future utility, and impact upon the total software package.

Summary of First Year of Operation. The first year of operation was one of learning what was involved in using a CMI system in an ongoing instructional program. Many insights were gained into how the computer support could best be employed within the mathematics program. The teaching staff had developed confidence in their ability to collect instructional data, and to store and retrieve it via the computer terminal. They learned that the contents of the reports were accurate. It was also quite clear that many features of the curricular plan and instructional model that carried over from the manual system were not compatible with the use of computers. However, there was no evidence of the mathematics program and its instructional paradigm being basically incompatible with the computer component. On the contrary, the overall fit was excellent, and the basic framework of the educational and computer components were to be retained. During the second semester of 1973/74, most of the planned modifications to be made to the Sherman School CMI system were documented by the working group. The system analyst and the Sherman School staff worked on the educational component. The computer programmer and the systems analyst laid out the modifications to the MICA program necessitated by the changes in the educational component.

Prior to implementation of the changes arising from the first year's experience, the Title III funding was received, thus insuring adequate staff and funds. Since the Sherman School Mathematics Program was used in six other schools in the East attendance area, a working team of one teacher from each school was assembled for the Summer of 1974 to implement the changes to the educational components. Due to the relatively minor nature of the changes to the computer software, these were implemented early in the Summer on the basis of agreed upon documentation defining the changes in the educational component.

The Second Year

The second year of operation, 1974/75, was the first under the Title III funds and was to mark the transition of the project from an informal effort to a formal project. While the Sherman School work was to continue to be at the leading edge of the developments, major administrative and technical efforts were to be initiated to meet the goals of the Title III proposal. During the second year, three primary tasks were accomplished. First, the baseline CMI system was modified on the basis of the first year's experience, and this modified system was used operationally in Sherman School. Second, the Sherman School Mathematics Program would be used in another elementary school, but with improved manual procedures. The intent was to determine the contribution of the computer to an individualized instructional program. Third, the initial planning was performed underlying expanding the use of the CMI system in multiple schools. These efforts and their outcomes are described in the sections below.

CMI System Design Changes

The analysis of the first year's operation resulted in changes in three areas, the structure of the curriculum, the role of the assignment teacher, and diagnosis and prescription. The mathematics curriculum was restructured into 63 units by subdividing existing units and creating new ones where required. A major consideration in the restructuring was to achieve greater compatibility with the computer component. To this end, the new curricular units had a minimum of four objectives, and a maximum of nine; most had six, with the new study guides written to match the new units. Unit pre- and posttests were rewritten so that the same objectives were tested in the same order in all four tests associated with a given unit. The magnitude of the test construction effort can be seen in the total number of items needed. There are 32 test items for each objective and 300 objectives for a total of 9,600 items. Redesigning the tests corrected the problem of recoding the objective numbers, as was done during the first year. The first three units in the new curricular plan each were composed of six survey tests. These tests were to function as a pretest and as a placement vehicle to spread students over the first few units. The intent was eliminate the problems encountered when all students started at Unit 1. Each of the survey tests covered up to 18 objectives, the number in roughly three instructional units. The set of 18 tests spanned all 300 objectives in the total curricular plan.

The new curricular plan covered the same material and objectives as in the past. The changes were primarily structural to achieve greater uniformity in number of objectives per unit and to impose a greater degree of systematization upon the pre- and posttests. Reducing the span and number of objectives within a unit was also aimed at allowing a student to complete a unit via a single posttest, rather than successive testing of subsets of objectives; thus, reducing the pupil flow encountered during the first year.

The unacceptable overloading of the assignment teacher was attacked by completely redesigning the role. The instructional functions of the assignment teacher were transferred to the quiz teacher. The computer terminal operator functions were assigned to a teacher aide. To achieve the split, it was necessary to automate the diagnosis and prescription process so that the teacher aide could perform these procedures. It was also necessary to expand the role of the quiz teacher, now called the review/quiz teacher. Under the new scheme, there were three review/quiz teachers who, with the student, reviewed each test taken while the teacher aide generated the prescriptions via the computer terminal. As was the case in the past, these teachers retained their function of determining whether a student was ready to take a test. This function was enhanced by providing a capability for review/quiz teachers to add prescriptions to those assigned by the computer. Other changes in the roles of teachers resulted from moving the study guide audio-tapes from the testing room to the seminar room, eliminating the need for a teacher in testing rooms. The allocation of the Sherman School staff for the second year was three teachers as review/quiz teachers, two teachers in study rooms, and one teacher in the seminar room. One teacher aide served as the computer terminal operator, and the aide in the testing room was retained. Figure 4.11 shows the space and personnel allocation for the second year of operation.

Diagnosis and Prescription. Significant changes were made in the diagnosis and prescription component for the 1974/75 school year. Experience had shown the existing prescriptions needed considerable tailoring for them to be useful for a given student. The assignment teacher had also noted most prescribing was a rather routine procedure. Coupled with the known overload upon the assignment teacher, it was concluded that the diagnosis and prescription process could be automated. In order to automate these procedures and have a teacher aide perform them, a system was devised for rank ordering the prescriptions for a given objective. The first prescription in a set was always the name of the objective. The second prescription was different for the pretest and each of the three posttests. This prescription was established as the "best" one for this objective and the particular test. The third prescription was for process and practice, exploring concepts and providing practice. The fourth provided drill exercises. The fifth was a remedial process and practice prescription. It provided a presentation of the concepts in simpler terms than in the third prescription. The sixth was remedial practice having simple drill and practice exercises. The seventh level prescription was a

Figure 4.11: Space and Personnel Allocation, Second Year

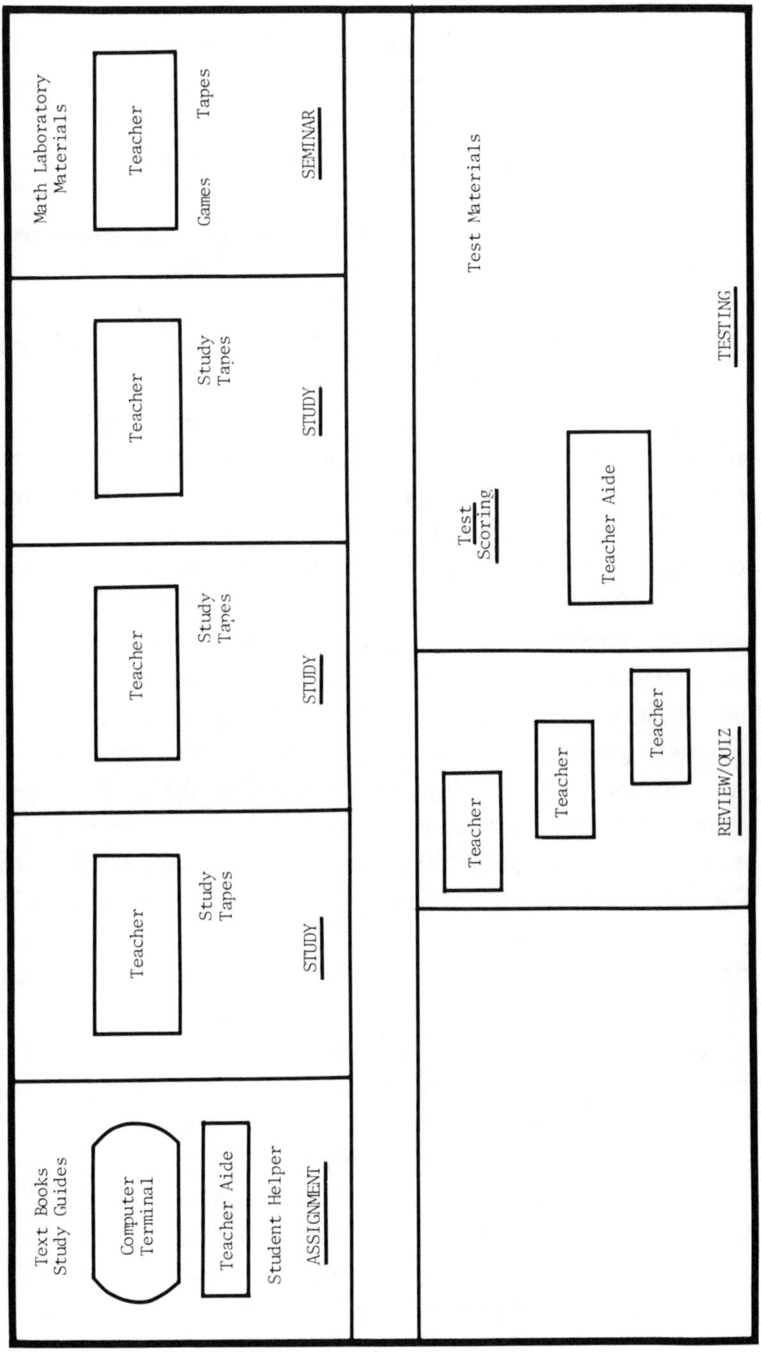

Math Laboratory Materials

Teacher

Games   Tapes

SEMINAR

Teacher

Study Tapes

STUDY

Teacher

Study Tapes

STUDY

Teacher

Study Tapes

STUDY

Text Books
Study Guides

Computer Terminal

Teacher Aide

Student Helper

ASSIGNMENT

Test Materials

TESTING

Test Scoring

Teacher Aide

Teacher

Teacher

Teacher

REVIEW/QUIZ

laboratory experience involving a variety of materials. The lowest rank-ordered prescription, the eighth, was the seminar where the student could receive help on a one-to-one basis. The prescriptions for any objective would be displayed at the computer terminal in this rank order. The rank ordering also simplified the interpretation of prescriptions by the teachers, since they simply needed to know the seven categories rather than several thousand individual prescriptions. Other than the "best" prescription, all prescriptions for an objective were the same for the pretest and three equivalent forms of the posttest. Automation of the prescription process was as follows: In response to the computer's request (see Figure 4.12), the teacher aide enters the identification number(s) of the failed objective(s), the computer selects the name of the objective and the "best" prescription and stores them in the student's record in the Student History File. At the same time, the computer prints the full list of prescriptions and the identification numbers of those assigned via the hardcopy device attached to the computer terminal. This "tear-off" sheet is given to the student, and it replaced the 3 x 5 cards employed in the past. The use of the "tear-off" sheet also enabled the quiz teacher to make additional prescriptions for the student at a later time by circling identification numbers on the "tear-off" sheet. Prescriptions, made by the computer or by another quiz teacher, were preceded by an asterisk on the printout so they were not assigned twice. When all assigned prescriptions were completed, the student leaves the tear-off sheet with the computer terminal operator, who uses it to up date the Student History File. This approach enabled the quiz teacher to prescribe, yet keep the student's record in the data base accurate. It was also instrumental in splitting the assignment teacher's role between the teacher aide and the quiz teacher. Figure 4.12 contains an example "tear-off" sheet.

Because computer system failures resulted in the creation of a considerable backlog of work relating to diagnosis and prescription, a fast prescribing mode was implemented. Using this mode, the terminal operator can prescribe for a student in roughly 20 seconds and a backlog can be disposed of quickly.

Figure 4.12: Student "Tear-Off Sheet"

```
MICA READY
/PR
STUDENT NUMBER ?
793
WHICH IS BEING ENTERED ?
    1.   UNIT 15-2
    2.   UNIT 8          ?
1.
ENTER DATA OF TA 15-2  FOR JOHN BIG                    HR: HR 1
1,5

INSTRUCTIONAL ASSIGNMENTS:

A      1        FRACTIONS TO MIXED NUMERALS
    1   MSM(6)    P.213 (15-28)
    2   M(4)      P.194-195
    3   MSMW(4)   P94(11-22)95(23-34
    4   EEM(4)    P.332-333
    5   EA(5)     P.204
    6   SBM(5)    P.202
    7   SEMINAR   15-2 (1)

B      5        ADD MIXED-DIF DEN-FRAC LESS1
    1   EM(5)      P.252(ADD ONLY)
    2   EA(5)      P.220-221
    3   MSM(6)     P.218 (ADD ONLY)
    4   EM(5)      P.249,326 SET 9
    5   MSMD(4)    P.74 PROB.(15-30)
    6   MSMR(6)    P.31 (ADD ONLY)
    7   SEMINAR    15-2(5)

SELECTIONS ?
A1,B4


* * * * * * * * * * * * * * * * * * * *
*
*     STUDY LIST   09/08/76
*
* JOHN BIG                 SHERMAN MATH   HR 1
*
*    CURRENT UNIT    NEXT TEST
*    UNIT 15-2       TB 15-2
*
*   ASSIGNMENTS TO DO
*
* 1    FRACTIONS TO MIXED NUMERALS
*      MODERN SCHOOL MATHEMATICS(6)
*         P.213 (15-28)
*
* 5    ADD MIXED-DIF DEN-FRAC LESS1
*      ELEMENTARY MATHEMATICS(5)
*         P.249,326 SET 9
*
* IF YOU PASS THE NEXT TEST, GO ON TO UNIT 15-3    STUDY GUIDE
*
* * * * * * * * * * * * * * * * * * * *
```

Instructional Sequence. The composite effect of the changes appeared in both the unit-of-instruction cycle and the instructional paradigm. Figure 4.13 shows the functional flow diagram for the resulting unit-of-instruction cycle.

After the first series of survey tests are administered in the homerooms, the typical sequence of steps in the instructional process will be as follows:

Step 1. A student enters the test room, where he takes the appropriate test from the cabinet. The student also picks up the Unit Objective Missed List (UOML). The student will have his "tear-off" sheet from the computer terminal (the bottom half of which contains the assigned prescription and his student number). The student fills in the information at the top of the Unit Objective Missed List before handing in his test to the aide to be corrected. After correcting the test, the teacher aide indicates on the UOML the objectives not mastered by the student. More than one mistake out of five items will be considered nonmastery on an objective. At the bottom of the UOML, the aide stamps the date the test was taken. The aide staples the UOML to the student's portion of the "tear-off" sheet.

Step 2. Both of these sheets are taken to the terminal room where they are placed in a basket for the terminal aide to process. After the student has dropped off the UOML, he takes the corrected test to a teacher in the review/quiz room. There the student and the teacher discuss the test in a one-to-one situation.

Step 3. The student leaves the review room (leaving the test there) and goes to the terminal room, where the aide will have previously entered the test result data and generated a new "tear-off" sheet for the student. Normally, the computer will select the best prescription for the student automatically. If the required books are not present, alternative prescriptions could be selected on the basis of what texts are available. In the terminal room there also is a student helper who takes the printout from the terminal and finds the book corresponding to the prescription for the *first* objective missed by the student. The student helper

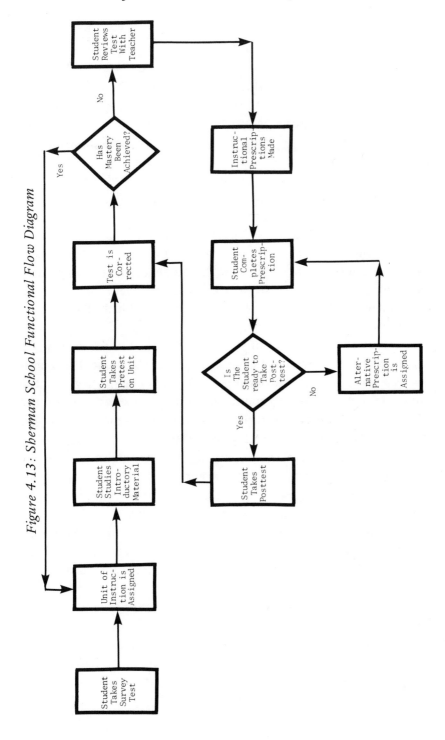

Figure 4.13: Sherman School Functional Flow Diagram

places the book with the "tear-off" sheet in the first or appropriate page of the prescription on a table near the door. This enables the helper to hand the assignment and the book to the student coming to the terminal room from the review room. In case the student passes the test, the new printout will indicate the study guide to be read before the pretest is taken. The terminal room also contains the study guides which are handed to students going on to a new unit along with a new printout.

Step 4. After the student has picked up either (a) an assignment for missed objectives or (b) a study guide for a new unit, the student goes to a study room where the student works on the assignment. If it is a missed objective (one at a time), the student will have *one* textbook that will be used to do a problem set. The study teacher will help the student on that assignment and, when finished, the student can use the teacher's editions to check his work with the help of either student checkers or teachers.

Once the assignment of study guide is completed, the student goes to the next station in the program. If the student has been assigned a new unit and has been working on a study guide, the next station is the testing room, where the pretest is taken and the instructional sequence returns to step one. If the student had failed a test and was working on an assignment dealing with a missed objective, then upon completion of the assignment of the first objective missed, the student goes to the review/quiz room. There the review/quiz teacher determines whether the student has learned the objective missed on the previous test.

Step 5. If a teacher, through the use of quiz cards or any other approach, determines that the student does understand the objective, then the student can go back to the terminal room and pick up the text assigned for the next objective missed on the previous test. If the objective passed on the quiz is the last objective or the only objective missed on the previous test, then the review/quiz teacher can send the student to the testing room. On the "tear-off" sheet is listed the next test to be taken, which the quiz teacher can circle to assign it to the student.

Step 6. If the quiz teacher thinks the student does not understand the objective, then the teacher can select from the prescriptions listed on the printout alternative experiences for that objective. This is indicated by simply circling the sequence number of the optional prescription on the printout. QT or update is also written on the hard copy so the aide will notice that a file update is needed when the "tear-off" sheet is returned. The student will then leave the quiz/review room and go:

(a)   to the terminal/book room for a textbook and then to the study room; or

(b)   to the seminar or lab room if that prescription had been assigned as an optional experience.

Step 7. The student doing an optional assignment after completion always returns to the review/quiz teacher for either reassignment or permission to go to testing.

Step 8. When finally returning to testing, the student must take his "tear-off" sheet so it can be stapled to the UOML. This is because if optional assignments have been made, the aide can update the prescription record of the student so that on the new "tear-off" sheet those assignments already given will have an asterisk (*) in front of them, enabling the review/quiz teacher to know what has already been assigned. After completing an assignment or study guide, the student returns it to the book cart in front of the terminal room so that it can be recycled back into the instructional process.

Several changes from the previous cycle are apparent. First is the use of the survey test to place the student within the curricular plan. Second is the addition of a step where alternative prescriptions can be assigned when the student is not ready to take a posttest. Third, if mastery is not achieved on a unit test, the student reviews the test with the quiz teacher.

Other Changes. No changes were made for the 1974/75 school year in any of the reports used in the CMI system. An abbreviated form of the Student History Report, called the Unit Achievement List, Figure 4.14, was created for use in parent-

Figure 4.14: Unit Achievement List

```
REPORT REQUEST?
L,MR JONES,03/25/76,805,S

UNIT ACHIEVEMENT LISTING REPORT
********************************

RICHARD RICH          ID:    805    CURRICULUM: SHERMAN MATH


DATE: 09/08/76    REQUESTED BY: MR JONES
SCHOOL NAME :TEST
GROUP: TEST GROUP 2
                                TEACHER NAME: MR. LORENZ

ACTIVITIES SINCE:  3/25/76

                                                     NUMBER OF
       UNIT       DATE BEGAN   DATE COMPLETED         DAYS  TESTS
       ----       ----------   --------------         ----  -----

*UNIT 1-1     INTRODUCTION TO SETS
                  4/ 1/76      4/ 5/76                  2      2

*UNIT 2-1     TERMS USED IN ADDITION AND SUBTRACTION
                  4/ 1/76      4/ 5/76                  2      1

 UNIT 3-1     MULTIPLICATION AND DIVISION THEORY
                  4/ 1/76      4/ 5/76                  2      3

 UNIT 18-1    EXTENDING SET THEORY & PLACE VALUE TO 1,000,000
                  4/ 5/76      4/ 5/76                  1      6

*UNIT 18-1    EXTENDING SET THEORY & PLACE VALUE TO 1,000,000
                  4/ 5/76      4/ 5/76                  1      1

*UNIT 5       INTRODUCTION TO FRACTIONS
                  4/ 5/76      4/11/76                  5      4

*UNIT 10-1    COMPARING FRACTIONS AND FINDING PARTS OF SETS
                  4/ 5/76      4/11/76                  5      2


# THE FOLLOWING ARE CURRENTLY ASSIGNED  #
-----------------------------------------

 UNIT 3-2     INTRODUCTION TO MULTIPLICATION AND DIVISION
                  4/11/76         -                    47      2

 UNIT 6-1     SET THEORY
                  1/ 1/76         -                   107      2


* THESE UNITS WERE COMPLETED BUT NOT MASTERED.

2   ACTIVITIES HAVE BEEN MASTERED SINCE :  3/25/76

UNIT ACHIEVEMENT LISTING REPORT COMPLETED.
```

teacher conferences. This report lists only the names of units completed and the date of completion. It also compares the student with the average student in the same grade as to number of units completed. The latter was added at the request of parents, who needed a frame of reference for their child's progress. The management component was changed in only one respect. The teachers decided to abandon all private record-keeping with respect to the mathematics course. Teacher grade books and other records were replaced by the reporting component of the CMI system, and the "tear-off" sheets had replaced the student's 3 x 5 card. The change was motivated primarily by the knowledge gained during the first year of operation that the computer's data base maintained accurate records.

The changes to the computer component for 1974/75 were numerous, but represented additional capabilities rather than design changes. The prescription module was modified to implement the automated prescription selection, fast mode prescribing, printing of the "tear-off" sheet, and later updating of a student's history file record with quiz teacher selection prescriptions. A somewhat oblique attack on the dynamic file growth problem was taken by allocating only enough file space for up to 20 units until the first student reached this unit. Then the files were redefined to hold 40 units. This procedure was designed to hold down file storage charges during the beginning of the year when the Student History File was relatively empty.

Surprisingly, one of the most difficult problems encountered in implementing the changes for the 1974/75 school year was printing of new study guides, tests, and related materials. The curriculum group who had restructured the curriculum had completed only 23 units when school started. A three-way race among the teachers developing the units, the printers, and the students began the first day of the school year. The staff of the school district's printing facility were working overtime and weekends in order to win the race. Unfortunately, the Title III proposal had not taken printing of new instructional materials into account. The printing problem served to emphasize the difficulties associated with locally developed instructional programs. In such programs, the design, development, and production of instructional materials is a time-consuming and expensive task. Changes in such programs cannot be taken lightly due to the level of effort and the costs involved.

Second Year Operations

Like the first year's operations, the second year began with a minor disaster. Rather than technical, the difficulties were instructional. The survey tests intended to distribute the students over the initial units in the curriculum did just the opposite. Of the 130 students taking the survey tests, 127 were placed in the first unit after the survey test. As a result, the beginning-of-the-year problems of the first year were repeated. The failure of the survey test to distribute the students was twofold. The test began with the topic of sets, that the fourth graders had never studied and the fifth graders apparently didn't master. Secondly, regardless of what unit was covered in the test, the criteria set for mastery was too high for the students involved. As a pretest, the survey tests were rather successful in that the percentage of correct reponses to the items varied across the curricular units in rather logical patterns. As a placement device, the survey tests were a failure.

The remainder of the changes made to the Sherman School CMI system paid off rather handsomely. The automated diagnosis and prescription procedures coupled with the use of a teacher aide as the computer terminal operator virtually eliminated the problems encountered the previous year. Having the teacher aide performing the mechanics of generating the "tear-off" sheet in parallel with the quiz teacher and student reviewing the test proved to be an excellent procedure. When backlogs did occur, the teacher aide was able to dispose of them quickly via the fast prescribing mode. A contributing factor was that the only role played by the teacher aide was that of computer terminal operator. Thus, when use of the terminal beyond the mathematics period occurred, it did not interfere with other duties, as was the case when a teacher perfomed the function.

Some interesting data was collected on how the teacher aide, the teachers, and students spent their time during the second year. The use of the computer terminal by the teacher aide as a function of the MICA commands is shown in Table 4.2. The time for performing the prescription function, the most common usage of the terminal, was 47 seconds. During the second year, the teacher aide was able to keep up with the student flow, and in an average mathematics period spent 6.75 minutes waiting for students. It was a common practice to sign in with the computer roughly 20 minutes before the class period to insure access to a 300 baud telephone line. Some time was also used after the mathematics class to finish up the day's work. On the average, a total of 78.04 minutes per day of computer terminal usage was needed. In the previous year, an average of 120 minutes was needed. The goal of performing all computer-related operations during the actual class period was rapidly being reached.

Table 4.2

Time to Perform CMI Functions at Computer Terminal

		Average Time
/P	Giving a student a prescription and entering test results.	47 seconds
/A	Updating a student's prescription on the request of a teacher.	93 seconds
/O	Assigning a student a new unit on the request of a teacher.	17 seconds
/R	Generating a student history report.	67 seconds

Table 4.3

Allocation of Teacher Time

Instructional Station	Average # of Interactions per Hour	Average Duration of Interaction	% of Hour Engaged in That Type of Interaction (Instructional)
Review/Quiz Teacher	15	148 seconds	74%
Study Room	43	39 seconds	84%
Seminar Teacher			84%
Individual Help	19	48 seconds	52%
Group Help	2.5	114 seconds	16%
Lab Help	13	44 seconds	16%

The staff had worked hard to delegate noninstructional responsibilities. Students got all of their own materials, parent volunteers helped answer reading questions in the test room, and aides corrected test papers. The task the teachers kept for themselves was to teach. The data of Table 4.3, based upon 20 class sessions, shows they were quite successful. On the average, 80 percent of teacher time was spent in one-on-one instruction or with small groups. Out of the remaining 20 percent, only 2.85 percent was devoted to material handling and 2.33 percent to disciplining. The remainder of the time was devoted to moving about the room and waiting for students.

The teacher time allocation varied slightly as a function of the role. The review/quiz teacher devoted 74 percent of the time to instruction, while the study room and seminar teacher devoted 84 percent to instruction. The nature of the interaction differed, with the review teacher having fewer but longer interactions. The other two functions involved more frequent but shorter contacts with the student. Such results are in keeping with the functions performed by these teachers. The remarkable result is the minimal time devoted to material handling, only 2.85 percent, showing that the teachers were really freed from clerical-level tasks.

To determine how students spent their time, six students were observed in the study room for a number of days and their time budgets measured. Two students each at a slow, average, and fast rate of progress were observed. The data in Table 4.4 show these three levels of students allocated their time quite differently. Surprisingly, an average of 17 percent of the study room time was spent waiting for help; recall that there was a single teacher in the room. Roughly 27 percent of the period was devoted to working on assignments. The most dramatic difference among the three levels of progress was that slow-progesss students spent 27.5 percent of the class period "goofing off"—looking around, fiddling with things, etc.—while fast-progress students devoted only 7.67 percent of the hour to this category of behavior. In addition, slow-progress students asked for and received correspondingly less help. The interesting aspect of the data is that even under individualization, students spend less than a third of their time in a study room actually working on assignments.

From the time budgets shown here, it is clear that the computer-related functions are becoming quite efficient. The teacher aide is able to keep up with the work load. Teachers are spending a high proportion of their time in instructionally related tasks. Only the students appear to have relatively low amounts of time devoted to instruction. This latter observation is probably accounted for by the student-teacher ratio in the study room. The study teacher interacted with 43 students during the class period. The class composition varied during the period. Although 17

Table 4.4

Student Time Allocation in the Study Room, N = 6

Task	Slow	Average	Fast	Total for All
Wait	14.18	20.83	16.34	17.54
Working on Assignments	21.23	26.81	32.83	26.94
"Goofing Off"	27.50	16.39	7.67	17.10
Help	3.82	7.17	4.82	5.49
Moves	2.20	4.33	2.46	3.15
Other	6.00	8.72	1.82	5.87

students were always in the room, 21 students entered the room, and 21 on the average left the room during the hour, having completed their tasks. Unfortunately, data was not collected for the seminar room, where only 6.14 students per hour were served by a single teacher. Perhaps a much better student time allocation might have been observed.

Elimination of the private record-keeping in conjunction with the use of the teacher aide as the terminal operator significantly increased the utilization level of the reports. The Group, Unit, and Contact Reports were generated weekly, and Student History Reports were generated upon request. Early in the school year, some students discovered the teacher aide would generate their Student History Reports if they said a teacher wanted it. The generation of Student History Reports increased until a teacher's signature was required. The new Unit Achievement List report was also used on a routine basis for parent-teacher conferences.

Other than the printing problems, the restructuring of the curriculum achieved a much improved match between the educational and computer components. The vexing mechanical problems were eliminated and new procedures such as the Unit Objectives Missed List resulted in a good match between testing and prescribing. With the advent of a curricular plan with a large number of units, the teachers recognized the potential for greater curricular flexibility. Early in the year a planning sheet was devised to be used in charting individual student paths through the curriculum. The planning sheet has the structure of the curriculum represented by circles. The homeroom teacher draws lines linking these units in the order deemed best for each student. Its primary use is for students not making progress or for front-running students interested in a certain topic. Through the use of the existing Objective Module in the MICA computer program, assigning curricular units in arbitrary sequence was not a problem. As soon as use of the curricular planning sheet becomes a common practice, POS procedures similar to those used by PLAN* and IPI could be implemented.

The nature of computer-related failures changed during the second year. In the past, when the computer failed, it would be inoperable for long periods of time. The pattern of failure changed to one of failures of short duration, usually five to ten minutes; and the probability of a failure during the class period dropped to .18. During the period from November 28 to March 4, which included an end of a semester, the computer was in operation 91 percent of the possible time during the class hours. This change in pattern reflects the hardware configuration of the UNIVAC 1110, which had dual CPU's and two levels of core memory. When a failure occurs, the computing center staff is able to reconfigure the hardware and resume operations rather quickly. The failed unit can be tested and repaired while the rest of the computer is operating. Such "graceful degradation" contributes to a much lower rate of long-duration computer failures. When the hardware reconfiguration is automated, most of the small-term periods of inoperability will be eliminated. The staff of the University of Wisconsin's Computer Center also had invested a significant effort to locate and correct the many hardware errors and operating system errors attendant to the new computer system. This effort contributed greatly to the improved level of performance of the time-shared mode of operation used by Sherman School.

Comparison with a Non-CMI School. One question of interest was the nature of the contribution of the computer component to an individualized program of instruction. In order to study this question, one of the other schools using the Sherman School Mathematics Program was selected as a comparison school, designated as School B. During the second year, it operated in the same fashion as did Sherman School, except it employed manual rather than computer-based data processing. Since the school had a somewhat lower enrollment, 100 students, it had only four teachers in the two grades. However, they were assisted by three teacher aides and three parent volunteers. A computer printout of all the prescriptions for each test, in unit order, was produced to facilitate the prescriptive process. A rather extensive evaluation questionnaire was administered at the end of the year to the teachers and students in both schools. The complete results are too voluminous to be reported here and are given in Chapin (1975). The differences in teacher attitudes towards the instructional program were sharp. The Sherman teachers felt that all students were doing satisfactory work or better in the program, while School B teachers thought only the high-ability students benefited. The Sherman teachers felt they were able to act in a more ideal teacher role, while the School B teachers devoted too much time to the mechanics of the program. In addition, the manual system was unable to keep students and teachers supplied with the information needed for the instructional paradigm to run smoothly. While the student bodies of the two schools were not matched in any deliberate way, their average scores on the STEP 5th grade math concepts, Spring form, were similar. In terms of number of units completed as of March, 1975, Sherman had a mean of 15 units while School B had a mean of 10. Except for the displacement of the means, the distribution of students over the curriculum was quite similar, but a somewhat larger number of Sherman students were engaged in higher-numbered curricular units. In both schools, roughly 10 percent of the students were capable of finishing the two-year program in one year. Although there were some differences in achievement, the major differences were in the teacher attitude towards the total instructional situation. The teachers using CMI felt freed of the mechanics of the system and able to devote a high proportion of their time to teaching. The teachers without computer support were less satisfied with the instructional system and encumbered by the mechanics of the system. It was also determined that the "medical clinic" instructional paradigm does not work well with only four teachers, even when additional aides and parent help are provided.

Summary of Second Year's Operations. By the end of the second year's operations, the design of the Sherman School CMI system was essentially completed. The changes to the instructional paradigm and the curriculum had resulted in a smoothly functioning system. The operational strains of early years had disappeared and occasional computer failures were treated as minor inconveniences. The fine-tuning of the total CMI system had been to the benefit of both teachers and the students. The teachers were free to do what they like best—teach—and the students were devoting less time to procedural matters and more to instructionally related activities. The comparison with the non-CMI school showed that the computer component was essential if teachers were to manage individualized instruction. In addition, student progress under CMI was greater than in the non-CMI school. Because of the level of development achieved, focus of the CMI project turned towards the problem of multiple schools supported by a single computer program.

The Third Year

During the course of the second year of operation, teachers from schools throughout the city of Madison visited Sherman School. They were impressed with the degree of individualization and the smoothly operating system. Near the end of the second year, all elementary schools in the district were asked if they would like to participate in the next year's effort. Seventeen schools volunteered, a number in excess of what the small staff and funds could handle. The list was pared down to six schools geographically distributed across the city. Five of these schools were already using the Sherman Mathematics curriculum and one school would use it for the first time. A substantial effort was devoted to creating sufficient instructional materials, study guides, tests, etc., so that all the schools had equivalent curriculum. In addition, some specialized furniture was needed to make the system function smoothly in the additional schools.

As was the case in past years, a rather short preservice training session was held for the teachers in the six schools before school began. Overall, the problems in bringing up five additional schools were not severe. The total system had been fine-tuned at Sherman School and most of the problems had occurred before; hence, their solutions were known. Due to the efforts expended on curriculum improvement during the Summer of 1975, the mathematics program now contained 87 curricular units. As a result, the print shop was faced with another year of intense effort to produce study guides, tests, etc., faster than the students could use them. The redesign of the beginning-of-the-year placement tests was yet another problem solved. One unanticipated problem occurred in a school in a high socioeconomic status neighborhood. The students were going through the curricular plan at a high rate. The mathematics curriculum had been tailored over the years to the Sherman student body. This new school had a different student body, hence the curricular match was not as good. It was necessary to supplement the mathematics program in this school to provide a higher level of difficulty and greater breadth to the program. In this same school, the staff elected to retain the self-contained classroom. The test scoring and computer terminal usage was the same as at Sherman School, but all other functions were performed by a single classroom teacher for his or her own group of 25 students. Each of the other four schools also adapted the instructional model to fit their local needs, but the changes were not as extensive as in this school. At Sherman School the only change made was to use student runners to provide input for the teacher aide at the computer terminal. Rather than have individual students perform this task, a student was assigned to each room, carrying the UOML and tear-off sheets to the terminal operator and bringing back books and tear-off sheets. In addition to reducing traffic among the rooms, to be a runner was a motivation to get a unit done early. However, all students eventually got their turn as runner.

At the beginning of the third year, the six schools employed six copies of the MICA computer program and shared the unit and prescription file. Each school had its own student data and student history files. While this arrangement was possible, it was quite expensive in terms of storage costs. At midyear a preliminary version of MICA-level 5 was put into operation to reduce the costs. However, the very generalized I/O capabilities of the ASCII FORTRAN proved to be very expensive to use, and they were replaced by local routines to bring the operational costs back in line. By the end of the third year, the computer costs were averaging $7.31 per hour, a considerable drop from the $16 per hour of the first year.

Due to the requirements of the Title III project, a considerable amount of effort went into evaluation. Teacher and student attitudes towards the CMI system as well as student achievement were measured. Comparisons were made among the six schools using CMI as well as between schools using "traditional" instructional models. These studies are reported in detail in the 1976 Title III report (Chapin, 1976). From a CMI point of view, the important feature of these studies was the utility of the computer component for obtaining evaluation data. The Unit, Group, and Student History Reports obtained at various points in time during the school year were very useful. One of the specific areas of interest was how well Title I students, the disadvantaged, fared within the program. Within each school these students were identified as belonging to an additional group within the Group File. Thus, to obtain reports dealing with only these pupils, it was simply a matter of specifying the group. Through the use of similar techniques, it also was possible to evaluate a variety of curricular and instructional model issues. For example, it was possible to determine how many times each textbook was used as a prescription and to identify little-used books. It was also possible to identify instructional units where students spent excessive time or were tested too frequently. Such units became candidates for revision during the Summer. The computer component, used with some imagination, proved to be a very powerful tool in performing evaluation.

The third year of operation was an unqualified success. The five additional schools made the transition to computer support quite smoothly. Due to the characteristics of these schools, none of them turned out to function identically to Sherman School, yet all used basically the same curriculum. In addition, the MICA computer program supported all six schools with ease. During the year, a major transition was made from MICA-4 to a preliminary version of MICA-5, again without disastrous consequences. The computer-related operational costs appeared to have stabilized, and any further improvements here will be a function of the rate structure of the computer facility. Although adding the five schools went smoothly, it was also clear it takes a full school year for classroom teachers to become comfortable with the CMI system. The behavior patterns observed in these five schools followed those seen earlier in Sherman School. For example, first-year teachers under CMI rarely use reports, since they have not had them in the past. It also takes the better part of a year for the teachers to realize the computer component is for their own personal benefit and is not something imposed upon them by the school. Once this realization is reached, teachers begin to use reports, rely upon the stored data, and take advantage of the instructional model. However, this state is not reached until late in the first school year, as it takes time to adjust to these new classroom conditions.

Some experimental uses of the MICA computer program were also initiated during the third year to demonstrate the versatility of the CMI concepts. The MICA system was used to support 12 experimental curricula and information systems. Several reading programs, one locally developed, were supported. One of the most unusual curricula was a high school physical education program. A trial social studies curriculum based upon the Wisconsin State Department of Public Instruction Social Studies Skills list also was supported, and the system was used in an alternative high school to implement a student-faculty evaluation system. A referral teaching system for special education students was also implemented using MICA. All of these 12 applications of the MICA system were activated as pilot or demonstration projects. However, they clearly indicated the versatility of the computer component, and some may become full-scale projects in the future.

Summary

The case study in this chapter was presented to show the reader the developmental pattern of a particular CMI system. The Sherman School CMI system had its origins in the efforts of a handful of classroom teachers and University graduate students. From this beginning, it has grown to a medium-scale CMI system in multiple schools. The course of this growth has never been smooth, yet through the cooperative efforts of many people, goals have been reached that were never envisioned in the early days of the project. That these goals have been reached is due to a highly competent and dedicated project staff, and very strong support in the school district's administration—elementary school principals, area coordinators, director of research, and the superintendent. Without this administrative support, the CMI project would have faltered in its earliest hours. A key ingredient has also been sufficient funding at critical times. The original Teacher Corps money came at an opportune time. The Title III funding and the strong support of Mr. Russell Way, Wisconsin Department of Public Instruction, was crucial to expanding the CMI system beyond Sherman School. In the case of the Sherman School CMI system, there appears to be a rather fortuitous pattern of the right events occurring at the right time. Because of this, the original goals of developing a small-scale CMI system have been completely met and the level of aspiration has risen considerably as current efforts are on a medium-scale CMI system.

It can be seen from the system improvement cycles performed that the development of educational systems and CMI systems in partuclar is an iterative process. Within this process there is a high degree of interaction among the six components of CMI. During the first year of operation, there was a severe mismatch between the curriculum plan and the computer component. In addition, the effort was plagued by computer-related problems. By the second year, the curricular mismatch had been corrected, and computer-related failure minimized. At the third, a smoothly running system had been achieved. The fine-tuning of the instructional model in the first three years at Sherman School resulted in marked changes in the conduct of the mathematics program. While the basic instructional model remained, the proportion of time devoted to its operation dropped, and teachers were able to spend 80 percent of their time in an individualized program in one-to-one instruction with students. At the same time, the teachers assumed a much more managerial orientation towards the program. The computer-generated reports were used as a part of normal practice to support managerial activities. One of the clear trends was the automation of the instructional level of management. The use of a teacher aide as a terminal operator, computer-selected prescriptions, and the imminent use of optical scanners have automated nearly all the clerical-level tasks associated with the unit-of-instruction cycle. The extension of the CMI system to other schools already using the mathematics curriculum revealed that there is a predictable pattern of teacher reaction to the introduction of the computer component. It was also clear that the present project was not properly funded or staffed to provide adequate preservice and inservice training to aid teachers in making the transition. Those persons introducing CMI into a school need to devote considerably more attention to teacher training and inservice efforts. Due to the excellent human factors work done on the MICA procedures, the teacher aides learned to use the computer terminal very quickly and they required only minimal training.

The several curriculum improvement cycles and the production problems attendant to printing study guides, tests, etc., made it clear that locally developed individualized curricula are too expensive. When the teachers at Sherman School initiated their efforts, few individualized programs were available. However, there are a variety of such programs currently available in many subject matter areas. As a result, when the CMI effort is expanded to other subject matter areas, commercially available materials will be used. Flanagan (1967a, 1969) recognized this in his original conceptualization of PLAN. The present experience shows the wisdom of his approach.

Another major insight gained from the first three years' experience was that an important function is the management of CMI. Chapin (1976) has stated: "The key to successful experiences in computer managed instruction lies not in the technical issues, but in the ability to manage computer managed instruction in the school. The questions of where and how materials are stored, what instructional materials are available, who performs what task, where are those tasks performed, how students flow from task to task and space to space—these are questions of human engineering that are as important as the questions of computer engineering. This was not recognized fully at first, nor was the necessity for proper instructional furniture realized. This and the increasing need to teach the staffs how to manage CMI are reflected in a budget which calls for as much money being put into human engineering, planning, materials, and people as go into machine time. CMI just creates potential by freeing teachers from clerical tasks, and gives them a new level of information. How that time and information are used in the instructional interaction with a student is where payoff will occur or not occur."

The day of reckoning for the Sherman School CMI project had not quite been reached when this chapter was written. One more year of Title III funding remained to support the use of additional subject matter areas, and to develop MICA-6 to be used on the school system's own computer. The school district is in the process of determining if a medium-scale computer will be obtained. Such a computer will be able to support both the administrative data processing and a medium-scale CMI system. The crucial issue is whether or not the CMI effort has become an integral enough part of the schools to be supported wholly by the school district. In Sherman School, at least, loss of the computer component would be disaster for the teachers who have invested so much to bring the system to its present level and to enjoy the freedoms it has brought. Whether this feeling can be translated into continuing operational funds after June, 1977 remains to be seen.

Chapter Five

A CMI Computer Program

In the present chapter the computer program employed in the Sherman School Project is described. The presentation is intended to provide both educators and computer specialists with some insight into the characteristics of CMI computer software. In order to meet this goal, the software used in the Sherman School Project has been described at a variety of levels. Some areas are described at a global level, others at a technical detail level. The intent is to provide the reader with the rationale of the software as well as an understanding of how it was accomplished.

The CMI computer program used in the Sherman School Project had its origin as a class project in a course taught by the author (Baker, 1973). The six students in the class were responsible for the total development from conceptualization to the operational program. They christened the program with the mnemonic MICA (Managed Instruction with Computer Assistance) and the name has been retained throughout its several iterations. MICA-1 was the original version produced by the students in the Spring of 1972. MICA-2 was the version used during the 1973-74 school year; it was primarily a more refined version of MICA-1. MICA-2 also underwent some iterative improvements during the 1973-74 school year. MICA-3 was used in 1974-75, and has been designated the baseline version of the program. Mr. Thomas Lorenz rewrote extensive sections of the computer program and developed a more complete set of program documentation. Thus,

MICA-1 and MICA-2 were abandoned; however, conceptually all three versions were identical. The changes incorporated in version 3 were primarily operational streamlining and quality improvements in critical program areas. Two additional versions, MICA-4 and MICA-5, have been developed, but their description will be deferred until later in the chapter. All versions of the MICA program were written to be used on the UNIVAC 1100 series computers operating under EXEC-8. MICA 1-4 were written in FORTRAN-V and were based upon six characters per computer word. MICA-5 was written in ASCII FORTRAN and is based upon four characters per computer word.

System Concept

The basic design goal of the MICA computer program was to provide the computer support necessary for a small-scale CMI system in which a teacher manages an individualized program of instruction in a single subject matter area. In order to meet this global goal, a number of subgoals were defined and a basic design philosophy adopted. The definition of the subgoals was accomplished by examining the needs of the Sherman School Mathematics Program in detail. The subgoals were then defined at a higher level of generality so that the computer program meeting these goals would not be specific to the local context. The first subgoal was that integration of the computer into the classroom should have minimal impact upon existing practices; the goal was as much political as technical. When teachers have designed and implemented a local instructional program, they are proud of their system and confident of its capabilities. Hence, to have outside persons insist upon modifications in order for the computer to be used is clearly unacceptable. In addition, there is a natural reluctance to readily accept technological innovation in a labor-intensive situation such as a classroom. Thus, all the computer should do is to make current procedures more efficient, at least initially. This does not rule out building additional capabilities into the computer program for future use when the teachers are more at ease with the computer-based system. Second, the computer-based procedures should be simple to understand and use. Such a design goal stems from the fact that teachers using the system are not sophisticated with respect to computer-type operations. The teacher-computer relationship should be such that the actions to be performed by the teacher are as simple and as self-evident as possible. The teacher must feel the computer system is in a subservient role and under the control of the teacher. These roles can easily be reversed by involved, complex procedures. Simplicity also minimized the training time necessary for a teacher to learn to use the system. The third subgoal was that the system be cost-effective. Instructional funds are difficult to obtain under most circumstances, and local funding for instructional uses of computers typically has a rather low priority. Hence, one must design a system towards minimum operational costs. The MICA design goal, based upon 165 pupils enrolled and 30-40 students processed by the assignment teacher each day, was $12 per day at 1972 computer rates—totaling $2,160 for a 180-day school year or 7.3¢ per pupil per day.

In addition to the basic design goal and the three subgoals, global design concepts also were established to guide the design effort. The two primary design concepts underlying the MICA software system were as follows: First, the MICA software system should be independent of the grade level, the subject matter, instructional philosophy of the curriculum, and even the degree of individualization desired. The system simply provides a framework which may be used by the school to build a "tailor-made" CMI system. By treating the curricular structure as data which is independent of the actual workings of the system, a high degree of adaptability could be achieved. Consequently, the MICA software system could be used in the classroom to support instructional programs ranging from conventional group-oriented to completely individualized curricula. Second, all actual educational decisions are made by the teacher—the system acts only as an information source. The idea of the system as an information source is an important aspect of the system concept both in terms of eventual acceptance of the system and the underlying educational philosophy. Since the system acts merely as an information source, teachers are always free to ignore the system-provided information and proceed with an action of their own choosing. This approach follows a suggestion as to the development of future CMI systems made by Glaser (1967): "In the future, it is conceivable that the teacher might be presented with suggested alternative student prescriptions which she can accept, reject, or modify."

The concepts underlying the MICA design were intended to provide for the development of a reasonably general purpose, small-scale CMI computer program. It would be able to handle a broad range of curricular plans, a reasonable range of instructional models, and have enough inherent flexibility to cope with changing requirements.

Functions Performed

The functions performed by MICA are, for the most part, independent of each other. For purposes of description only, they are presented in an order which assumes they are all being used. The primary functions of MICA are to: (a) diagnose student progress; (b) suggest instructional alternatives as a function of the diagnoses made; (c) record this information; and (d) make such information available upon request. In each area where a decision must be made, the system is capable of providing a list (menu) of alternative instructional units, instructional methods, or evaluative procedures from which the teacher makes a selection. When such choices are mechanical in nature, that is, when a choice is directly dependent on previously stored information, and that dependency can be specified, the system is capable of recording the dependency and bypassing any unnecessary steps of rote selection on the part of the teacher.

Initially, the data base for the system is developed by curriculum specialists or teachers. This data base is a representation of the curriculum in terms of instructional units, behavioral objectives, or study guides. Associated with a unit are data describing the prerequisites of the unit, instructional methods for attaining these objectives, instruments for evaluating whether the objectives have been met, and prescriptions for achieving an objective on subsequent attempts or for proceeding beyond the mastered unit. The categorization of a unit (i.e., what comprises a unit, a subunit, a superunit, a co-unit, etc.) is arbitrary and left to the choice of the curriculum experts and teachers. One of the system's functions is the building and maintaining of the data which reflect the units and their structural interdependence.

An associated system function is the building and maintenance of student instructional history data, which among other things contains information describing the student's past achievements in the curriculum. These data are valuable for tracing a pupil's path through the curriculum and for studying the curriculum itself.

A major function performed by the MICA software system is that of reporting. A number of different summary reports can be produced at the computer communications terminal upon teacher request. These reports provide the teacher with detailed instructional histories of pupils or groups of pupils, as well as status summaries of the instructional program from a number of points of view.

One system capability not originally included in the MICA system concept but added at MICA-2 was that of self-protection. Computer system failures can and do occur; hence, procedures must be designed to minimize the impact of such failures upon the integrity of the data base. During the first year of operation, a number of protection schemes were tried before one was adopted.

Capacities and Hardware Requirements

MICA-3 was designed as a small-scale CMI system to assist in the management of one curriculum in one content area for no more than 1,000 students. MICA's capacities in terms of curriculum, resources, and student body and the associated file size requirements are discussed below.

In addition to a student body not exceeding 1,000, the maximum capacities for curriculum or resource information are: 4,000 instructional units, 16,000 prescriptions, 4,000 tests, 63 learning method classifications, and 63 student group classifications. These capacities imply that a maximum of approximately 15 million characters of mass storage, and 380,000 characters of core storage are required* to hold MICA's maximum data base.

The Sherman School Project data base during the first year involved 165 students, 36 units, 2,100 prescriptions, 140 tests, 2 learning methods, and 7 groups of students. When in operational use, the data base required approximately one million characters of mass storage and 48,000 characters of core storage.

In addition to the hardware implications of the file sizes described above, MICA also assumes the computer and its operating system support an interactive capability. At least one terminal such as a keyboard terminal or alphanumeric display is required for teacher interaction with the MICA system. MICA's file creation function assumes the computer system has card-reading equipment. File creation could be done interactively, but such an approach would be inefficient. Also, for efficient operation, MICA's report-generation function requires a line printer and a magnetic tape unit for large-volume reports.

Examination of the basic concepts underlying MICA and the functions it performs reveals it is fundamentally an interactive management information system. Data is collected from the classroom via the computer terminal, stored in the data base, and made available in the form of lists of information (menus) or as summary reports. All of these are classical management information system functions.

---

*These figures were derived by summing the products of the capacities and the associated record sizes. The record size definition is given in a later section of this chapter dealing with file definition.

Data Base Design

Since the MICA software system is an interactive management information system, having a good data base design was fundamental to achieving the stated design goals. There were a number of areas in which considerable preliminary designing and "trade-off" studies were performed before the final data base design was achieved. The three most important considerations underlying these studies were: First, flexibility was needed in order for the system to accommodate instructional program descriptions and decision data from a variety of curricular plans. Second, efficient data storage and access were required to minimize overall system costs in terms of operational expenses and mass storage charges. Third, a data base design was needed that could provide computer programmers with a powerful, yet conceptually simple, data base management capability. Several different data base designs were investigated, and the one described below appeared to be the best within the existing context.

The MICA data base consists of five major files and a dictionary. The technique used to access the information in these files was the indexed sequential approach (Dodd, 1969). Each record in a file is assigned a record number. Random access to this record via the record number is achieved by converting the number to a mass storage address location. Within MICA, the indexing concept was extended to include access to individual data items as well. Dictionaries of data items, such as student names, curricular units, and prescriptions, were established and each item assigned a relative index number within a given dictionary. A major advantage of the dictionary approach is that only the index number is stored in a file record element, not the original data item, resulting in a significant reduction in record size in the major system files. The indexing scheme in conjunction with the dictionaries also solved the problem of efficient cross-file linkages. Any index number extracted as a data item in one file is the record number of a record in its own file.

File design adaptability was achieved through the use of file header records for each file, based upon a common header design. The file header essentially holds a specification for each data item contained within a record in terms of its name, relative location within the record, and number of characters allocated to the data item. Another feature of the file design was the use of repeated sections within each of the records. Certain of the files within the MICA system are dynamic; the amount of information within a record is dependent upon the number of instructional actions taken by the teacher. Dynamic record growth is best handled by variable length records or linked records. However, data base management systems providing either of these capabilities were not available on the computer employed and are costly to develop for a fixed word length computer. Consequently, fixed length records with repeated subsections within the record were used to provide a pseudo-variable length capability

File Headers

Each file in the data base has a header record, describing the file and the structure of its records. The header of a file contains a description of the record fields, specifying where they begin within a record, their length, and in some cases whether or not they are repeating fields. The information in a header serves several purposes:

(1) it is used by any of the MICA programs for accessing or searching specified fields within a record;

(2) it is used to provide a verbal description of the corresponding file, for purposes of record-keeping and file expansion; and

(3) it is used to make changes to the actual structure of a file.

Figure 5.1 illustrates the general format of a file header. The first three words are the same as the header of a definition table, i.e., they specify the number of records in the file, how many of those are active, and the length (number of computer words) per

Figure 5.1: General Format of a File Header

Computer Word													
1	NUMBER OF RECORDS IN THE FILE												
2	NUMBER OF ACTIVE RECORDS IN THE FILE												
3	NUMBER OF WORDS PER RECORD												
4	SIZE OF FILE IF CORE-RESIDENT												
	0	1	2	3	4	5	0	1	2	3	4	5	Characters
5	6-Character Description of Field 1						SW		SC		NC		
7	Field 2												
9	Field 3												
.	:												
.	.												
.													
28	Up to 12 fields may be defined within a record												

SW is the starting word within the record or item of the field*

SC is the starting character within the word of the field

NC is the number of characters of the field

*In the special case of repeating fields, SW_1 is the starting word of the first field, NCPRF is the number of characters between the starting word of the first field and its being repeated.

SW_1	NCPRF

record. The fourth word contains the size of the file if it is core-resident. Subsequent two-word pairs describe a field within a record. The first word contains an alphanumeric verbal description or abbreviation identifying the corresponding field within a record. The second word of the pair specifies the computer word where the field starts within the record, and how many characters it comprises. These two-word pairs are repeated for each field within a record. A special format is used for elements which can repeat within a record.

Dictionary Design

The MICA system employs four definition tables, referred to generally as dictionaries. The prescription definition table contains representations of all the unique prescriptions a teacher can assign to pupils. The unit definition table contains entries describing the instructional units constituting the curriculum being supported by MICA. The method definition table lists the alternative instructional methods available to a teacher. It should be noted that certain instructional methods may be appropriate to particular instructional units; however, this table defines the complete set of available instructional methods. The total set of evaluation procedures employed in the curriculum are defined in the test definition table.

The definition table entries may be a verbal description, an abbreviation, or a code that is understood by the system's users (teachers, curriculum specialists, etc). The tables also eliminate unnecessary repetition of lengthy descriptions throughout the files. The linear position of an entry in a definition table serves as that entry's index or identification number within the computer programs and the files. Reference to that entry throughout the other portions of the system's data and programs is made via this identification number. In addition to being used as an internal identification number, the index of a definition table entry also determines the corresponding relative position of the entry in a file. An example of this scheme is given in Figure 5.2.

Figure 5.2: Definition Table and File Relationship

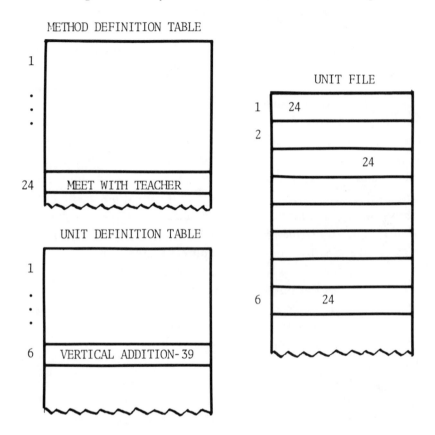

In Figure 5.2, the 24th entry of the method definition table is "MEET WITH TEACHER." The entry index itself is the means of identification to the computer program. Throughout the system, reference to this method is by identification number 24, rather than by the full verbal description. Similarly, the unit whose description is vertical addition-39 is assigned identification number 6, the position of the definition in the unit definition table. This same index, 6, is also used as the index into the unit file, where the sixth record contains an internal description of the prerequisites, methods, and tests associated with the unit, vertical addition-39. Each entry of a definition table takes up the maximum entry length, since blanks are placed in any remaining character spaces not used by the entry. When an entry is dropped, the last computer word of the definition is modified to reflect inactive status of the definition. Hence, by inspecting the last word of an entry in the definition table, one can determine whether the entry is still active.

Figure 5.3 illustrates the format of the definition tables in the dictionary. Each definition table also has a corresponding header. The header serves to describe the entries in the definition table in a general fashion for consistency and communication among different system programs. The information in the header allows for a general treatment of the definition tables for purposes of searching, updating, report generation, etc. It also permits an easy transition to another computer system or addition of definition tables for system growth. Data in a definition table header specifies the number of entries in the table, how many of those entries are "active" definitions (i.e., have not been dropped), and how many computer words comprise a table entry.

File Structure

In addition to the dictionary, the data base is composed of five files: the Unit File, Prescription File, Student Data File, Student History File, and Group File. In the following descriptions they are referred to as the UTF, PRF, SDF, SHF, and GRF files, respectively. A file is made up of records, which in turn are broken up into fields or items. For example, the unit file consists of several records, each of which describes a different curricular unit. Data item-access is achieved via a record buffer for each file maintained in core memory.

Unit File. The unit file contains the curriculum plan for the subject matter in the system. Each instructional unit maintained in the file has associated with it the prerequisites that must be completed before this unit can be started by a student. In addition, there are up to five alternative "instructional methods"

Figure 5.3: Dictionary Table Header and Definition

Definition, Table Header

Computer Word	1	NUMBER OF RECORDS IN FILE										
	2	NUMBER OF ACTIVE RECORDS IN FILE										
	3	NUMBER OF WORDS PER RECORD										
	4	SIZE OF FILE										
		0	1	2	3	4	5	0	1	2	3	4	5
	5	E N T R Y						0	1	0	1	2	3
		F L A G						0	4	2	4	0	1

Definition Table Record

		0	1	2	3	4	5	Character Position
Computer Word	1	DICTIONARY						
	2	TABLE						
	3	ENTRY						
	4						F	
	.	.	.	.		.		
	.	.	.	.		.		
	.	.	.	.		.		
	n-3							
	n-2							
	n-1							
	n						F	

where F is the activity flag.

available from which the teacher can select as vehicles for achieving the unit. Associated with each alternative instructional method are evaluation procedures, either pretest, posttest, or both, depending upon the school's needs.

The curricular plan is assumed to be predefined by curricular specialists in terms of learning objectives and the relationship among these objectives. That is, the curriculum content and structure is implemented in a "unit-of-instruction" approach, where a unit of instruction is defined as a set of instructional activities designed to achieve a set of specific learning objectives. The computer programs are such that any of the curricular structures described in Chapter Two can be employed. A record exists in the Unit File (UTF) for each instructional unit, and it is assigned an identification number, determined by its position within the Unit Definition Table of the Dictionary. The record corresponds roughly to a node in the curriculum graph, where each lower node in the graph connected by an edge is a prerequisite for that unit. A record in the Unit File can contain up to 12 prerequisites in the form of identification numbers of other units. Up to five instructional methods can be specified (also by identification number) along with up to six pretests and posttests associated with each instructional method. The first word of a Unit File record contains the number of prerequisites and number of instructional methods for the unit; each method subsection begins with an identification number of the method and the number of pretests and posttests to be used for that method. Because the number of pretests and number of posttests is specified within the record, there can be any combination to fill the six positions, e.g., six pretests and no posttests, one pretest and five posttests, etc. A Unit File record can consist of up to 20 computer words of 36 bits each. Figure 5.4 illustrates Unit File header and the layout of a record in the Unit File.

Prescription File. Each record in the prescription file corresponds to a particular assessment instrument, i.e., a test. The contents of the record consists of up to 20 scoring patterns that

Figure 5.4: Unit File Header and Record

Unit File Header

INITIALLY	Ø			
INITIALLY	Ø			
				20
O P E N O B	1	2	2	
N P R E R Q	1	2	2	
N M T H D S	1	4	2	
P R E R Q S	2,2	0	2	
M E D O B	6,18	0	2	
N P R E S	6,18	2	2	
N P O S T S	6,18	4	2	
T I D O B	7,18	0	2	

Names of Items (left of table)

Item Specifications (right of table)

Unit File Record

Character Position

Computer Word		0	1	2	3	4	5
	1			NUMBER OF PREREQUISITES		NUMBER OF METHODS	
	2	PREREQ. 1		PREREQ. 2		PREREQ. 3	
	3	PREREQ. 4		PREREQ. 5		PREREQ. 6	
	4	PREREQ. 7		PREREQ. 8		PREREQ. 9	
	5	PREREQ. 10		PREREQ. 11		PREREQ. 12	
	6	METHOD ID		NUMBER PRETESTS		NUMBER POSTTESTS	
	7	TEST ID 1		TEST ID 2		TEST ID 3	
	8	TEST ID 4		TEST ID 5		TEST ID 6	

Can Be Repeated
Up to 5 Times

can be applied to the results of a test taken by a student. The first word of the record contains the number of patterns used. (A pattern is one of many ways in which test scores can be analyzed.) A pattern is represented by a low and high criterion (a criterion consists of those specific test score values with which the evaluator is concerned) and between one and nine ranges of items for which test scores will be calculated. Following this information, a number of prescriptions (up to eight) are specified, two per computer word. No distinction is made internally as to whether these prescriptions are remedial or forward. The beginning of each pattern also contains parameters specifying the number of ranges in the pattern and the number of prescriptions which are applicable in case of a pattern match. The manner in which this information is employed is explained in the prescription module section. Figure 5.5 illustrates the layout of a record in the Prescription File.

Group File The Group File (GRF) contains one record per administrative group, such as a homeroom group defined by a teacher or other supervisor external to the system. As students are added to the system, their identification numbers are added to the

Figure 5.5: Prescription File Record

	0	1	2	3	4	5
1	NUMBER OF PATTERNS					
2	# RANGES	# PRESCR.	LOW CRITERION		HIGH CRITERION	
3	LO RANGE 1	LO RANGE 2	LO RANGE 3	LO RANGE 4	LO RANGE 5	LO RANGE 6
4	LO RANGE 7	LO RANGE 8	LO RANGE 9	HI RANGE 1	HI RANGE 2	HI RANGE 3
5	HI RANGE 4	HI RANGE 5	HI RANGE 6	HI RANGE 7	HI RANGE 8	HI RANGE 9
6	PRESCRIPTION 1			PRESCRIPTION 2		
7	PRESCRIPTION 3			PRESCRIPTION 4		
8	PRESCRIPTION 5			PRESCRIPTION 6		
9	PRESCRIPTION 7			PRESCRIPTION 8		

Computer words 2 through 9 can be repeated up to 20 times within a record.

Figure 5.6: Group File Record

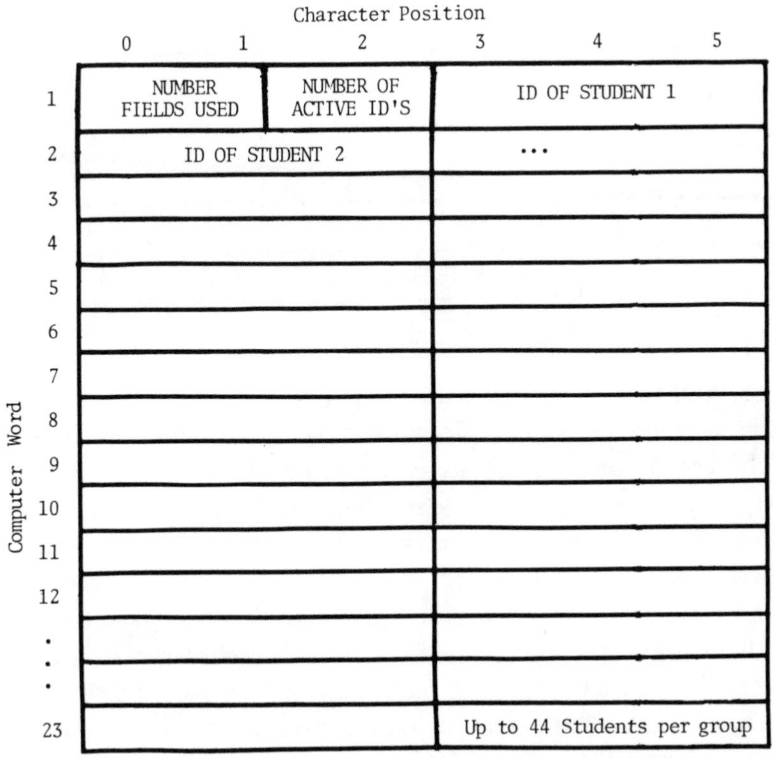

Character Position

	0	1	2	3	4	5
1	NUMBER FIELDS USED		NUMBER OF ACTIVE ID'S	ID OF STUDENT 1		
2	ID OF STUDENT 2			...		
3						
4						
5						
6						
7						
8						
9						
10						
11						
12						
.						
.						
.						
23				Up to 44 Students per group		

Computer Word

record in the Group File corresponding to their group. In this manner, the system has a record of which students are in a particular group, and can generate reports accordingly. A group consists of up to 44 students. The first two fields in the group record specify the number of fields (three per word) being used in the group record, and the number of active students, i.e., students who are currently using the system. The remainder of the record consists of three character fields containing student identification numbers. As indicated in Figure 5.6, a record has 23 computer words.

Student Data File. The Student Data File (SDF), shown in Figure 5.7, contains descriptive information about each student. It

Figure 5.7: Student Data File Record

	0	1	2	3	4	5
1						
2			N A M E			
3						
4	GROUP	GRADE	ZONE		BIRTH	
5	SEX	CURRENT UNIT		OPEN		STATUS

is used primarily for identification purposes. For each student, there is a record in the file consisting of five computer words. Each record contains the student's name (18 characters or less), his group, grade, and sex (one character each), a zoning code indicating where he lives (two characters), and his birthdate (three characters). The last character in the last word of the record, the active flag, is set to an asterisk if the student is no longer enrolled in the school. The position of a student's record within this file determines his identification number, which is used internally by the system as well as externally by teachers to refer to the student.

Student History File. There is a record in the Student History File (SHF) corresponding to each record in the Student Data File. The record describes the instructional history of a student: units selected, tests taken, prescriptions assigned, etc. A record within the SHF file, shown in Figure 5.8, consists of up to 1,792 words made up of repeated sections. Each section corresponds to an instructional unit assigned to the student (in the form of a unit identification number), the date it was selected, who selected it, the instructional method used, who selected the method, and a subsection for each test taken.

A subsection of the record contains the information relevant to the evaluation procedures and the consequences of the pattern of item responses. This subsection contains the evaluation (test)

Figure 5.8: Student History File Record

1	LENGTH OF ITEM	UNIT ID		DATE	
2	WHO SELECTED UNIT	METHOD	WHO SELECTED METHOD	NUMBER OF TESTS FOLLOWING	OPEN
3	TEST ID		DATE		OPEN
4 5	BINARY VECTOR OF ITEM RESPONSES (UP TO 72 ITEMS)				
6	FIRST PRESCRIPTION CHOSEN		SECOND		
.	THIRD		FOURTH		
.	ETC.		ETC.		
.	ETC.		ETC.		
12	ETC.		ETC.		

Can Be Repeated Up to 4 Times

identification number, the date administered, and the identification index for each prescription chosen by a teacher as a function of the item response pattern. The item responses for up to 72 items are recorded as a bit pattern with a 1 denoting incorrect, 0 correct, and left most bit item 1. The subsection may be repeated up to four times for each unit section in a student's history record.

Software Design Philosophy

The design of the MICA computer program was based upon a modular approach where each module was as self-contained as possible. It was felt that a modular structure would lead to an easier implementation, and that future program modifications would be simpler to incorporate. Under this design philosophy, the system concept was subjected to a lengthy task analysis, and a hierarchy of modules defined. Where a major module had several distinct functions to perform, the module was divided into several smaller submodules. These submodules were relatively self-contained and independent of other modules. Where possible, functions performed by several modules or submodules were isolated in a single utility subroutine for efficiency. The resulting set of utility routines are then available for use throughout the program, which simplifies the routines using them. Within this general modular framework, the software structure of the MICA system consists of a series of cascaded drivers. For the most part, each major module contains a driver to control the interactions among its submodules. The major modules themselves are coordinated via a master driver, or controller. The individual modules or submodules are activated through the use of control statements which appear in the input stream, be it batch or interactive. After a module is activated, it is responsible for interpreting and acting upon the input stream, returning control to the next higher module upon encountering the proper terminating control image. When MICA is running under a job supervisor (*viz.* An Operating System), the supervisor acts as merely a supermodule of the MICA controller, activating MICA when the proper control image is encountered. In recent years, the design philosophy used for the MICA program has become known as the "top-down" approach. However, it has been a basic design technique among skilled software designers since the earliest days of computer programming. The group designing MICA made particularly effective use of the philosophy.

Software Structure

The MICA software consists of six major software modules, whose interrelationships are depicted in Figure 5.9, plus a set of utility subroutines. A brief overview of these modules is provided below. Then each major software module is presented at a more detailed level to expose the implementation of the module. Very brief descriptions of the underlying utility subroutines are also presented to complete the software package.

The Controller is the focal point of the software, serving as

Figure 5.9: MICA Software Components

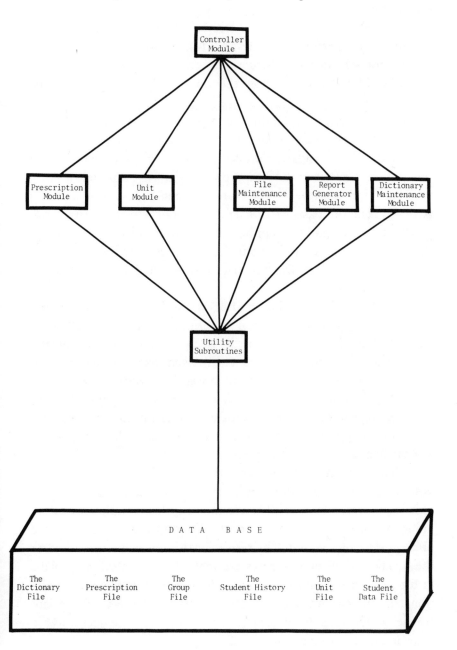

the means of communication between the user and the system capabilities and between different system modules. User requests are directed to the Controller, which calls upon the appropriate module(s) to perform the desired function(s). For example, a request for selection of instructional units is made by the user to the Controller; it calls upon the unit module to perform the proper function.

The Prescription Module is the most flexible of all the modules in terms of possible use. It has three capabilities: given the results of an evaluation procedure, it is capable of determining (on the basis of prestored user-supplied patterns) whether or not a unit has been mastered, or to what extent it has been partially achieved. On the basis of this data, together with other user-supplied data, the module supplies the appropriate prescriptions in the form of next units or remedial activities. The module also is capable of recording the prescriptions selected in the student's history record.

The flexibility of this module stems from the fact that the decision-making aspects of the functions are performed by the teacher. On the other hand, it is the ability to tie specific prescriptions to the diagnoses (as derived from evaluation procedures) which make the system potentially very powerful and time-saving. Because diagnosis and prescription are important and are used repeatedly in the unit-of-instruction cycle, the Prescription Module provides the teacher with considerable management assistance at the instructional level.

The Unit Module utilizes the data from the Unit File describing the instructional units in the curricular plan. When a unit is requested by a teacher for a pupil, this module locates the unit's record and determines if the pupil has met all the prerequisites of the unit. The results of this check are presented to the teacher. If all prerequisites are met, the Unit Module displays in list fashion the unit, alternative assessment techniques, instructional methods, and evaluation procedures. After an appropriate course of action is decided upon by the teacher, the decisions are recorded in the student's history file record.

The Report Generation Module provides information on students, the curriculum, and the system in a concise, organized fashion. The report generator is able to collect data on individual students or groups of students and on single instructional units or groups of units. The data are organized according to user-specified groupings or time divisions and printed in a pre-defined report format.

The File Maintenance Module is used both externally by the user and/or internally by the system (but still directed by the user). The Controller can call upon the File Maintenance Module for initializing, updating, and deleting information in the data base. For example, the File Maintenance Module is called upon by the Controller when the user is in the process of initializing or updating curricular information in the form of units, their components, and their relationships. By the same token, the Controller may call upon the File Maintenance Module to update information concerning a student's progress. It is important to note that throughout the process of receiving or sending data, key data elements are verified, and all production processes are checked to assure integrity of the data base.

The Dictionary Maintenance Module is used to change the names of students, prescriptions, units, etc., contained in the definition tables. It provides the capability to correct keypunching errors, spelling errors, and similar mistakes.

The Utility Subroutines are a collection of diverse but necessary functions. One set is concerned with initializing and terminating the MICA program. Another set performs a very detailed level set of functions such as manipulating character strings and number conversions. The most versatile set is that of performing file access functions. All the major modules and their submodules access the data base via utility routines. In addition, the data fields with a file record are obtained via the utility routines. All information from the external environment, whether it is from a card reader or an operator at a keyboard terminal, is obtained via one of the utility routines.

MICA Module Descriptions

Controller Module

The Controller Module is the focal point of communication between the user and the major modules in the MICA program. Access is achieved via a simple job control language (JCL) implemented by the Controller Module. The commands in the MICA job control language are as follows:

Command	*Description*
/C	This command causes termination of the current processor and control returns to the Controller.
/D	Transfer control to the Dictionary Maintenance Module (DMM).
/F	Transfer control to the File Maintenance Module (FMM).
/H	This command indicates the file headers are to be filled in with the information on the punched cards following the command.
/U	Transfer control to the Unit Module (UTM).
/P	Transfer control to the Prescription Module (PRM).
/R	Transfer control to the Report Generation Module (RPM).
/@	Terminate the MICA run.
//	This command indicates a comment follows on the same input line. The command has no effect upon the currently active processor.

The flowchart of the Controller Module is presented in Figure 5.11 using the standard flow chart symbols listed in Figure

Figure 5.10: Symbol Description System, Flow Chart

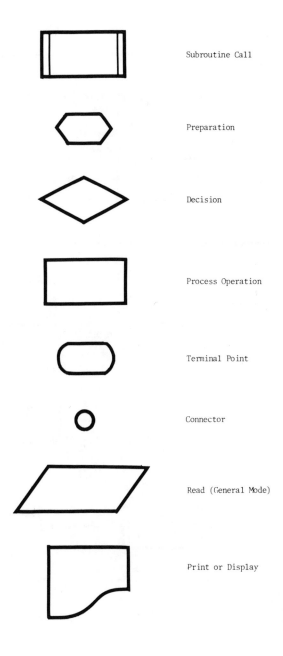

Subroutine Call

Preparation

Decision

Process Operation

Terminal Point

Connector

Read (General Mode)

Print or Display

Figure 5.11: MICA Control Module Flow Chart

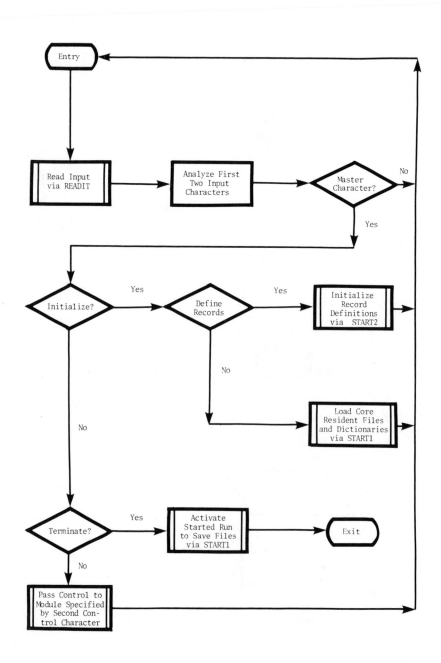

5.10. In normal use, the appropriate JCL command precedes or describes the operation to be performed by MICA. It is either punched into the first two columns of a card in the batch mode or entered as the first two characters of a line on a keyboard terminal. The Controller gets this input image—the image of the punched card or the line from the terminal—via the utility routine READIT, which is the only routine allowed to communicate with the external environment. If the first read position does not contain the master character, /, the Controller prints the error message, ILLEGAL COMMAND, and begins the process over again with the next input image. When the master character is present in the first read position, the Controller proceeds to extract the character in the second read position. Before checking the legality of this second character and doing the appropriate processing, the Controller determines if any initialization is required. If a special initialization flag is not set (=0), then one of two types of initialization must occur, depending upon the second character in the command. If the second character is an H, then the record definition initialization procedure is activated by a call upon routine START2, which reads the record definitions from cards according to the appropriate format to create the file header records for the dictionaries and five major files. Once the file header records are created by START2, the rest of the file creation is performed under control of the File Maintenance Module. If the second character is other than an H (a default condition transparent to the user), the second and more normal initialization procedures are performed. Routine START1 is called to transfer the file headers, and dictionaries, from disk to core memory, since these must be core resident before MICA can function. After completing the appropriate initialization, if any, control is passed, with few exceptions, to the appropriate module according to the second character previously extracted. If the second character is illegal—neither a @, P, U, R, F, D, nor C—an error message will be printed and the Controller will proceed to the next input image. The occurrence of an H as a second character after initialization is complete (initialization flag = 1) will cause the generation of an error message.

MICA's // command is transparent to the Controller. That is, the utility routine READIT never returns an input image with a // in the first two read positions. Upon encountering such, READIT fetches the next input image. The // feature allows the user to insert comments or notes on the hard copy of the printed output during the interactive session.

The modules, with one exception, return control to the Controller either normally or nonnormally. A nonnormal return means the processor module encountered a JCL command in its input stream before its processing was complete. Since this input image resides in a buffer available to the Controller, the Controller needs only to decode the command according to its second character and step through the switching decisions previously discussed. A normal return implies that the processor did not encounter any "unexpected" JCL commands; and, consequently, the Controller must search for the next command by fetching the next input image. The one exception to the normal, nonnormal returns is the return from the Prescription Module (PRM). Under certain processing conditions within PRM, it is desirable to transfer control automatically to the Unit Module (UTM) without inputting a /U command. A special flag is used in the call to PRM and UTM. Upon return from the PRM, the Controller checks the value of this flag to determine if a direct call on UTM is desirable, or if it is, in fact, a normal return.

The /@ command is used to terminate the use of the MICA program. The Controller is responsible for saving certain files and variables so that no information is lost between successive executions of MICA. The actual saving process is done via utility subroutine START1. Using features of the Operating System, it sets up a started run, a job to be executed in the batch mode, to save those files whose contents were modified during the use of the MICA program. When the started run is executed, these files are written to magnetic tape, thus completing the termination process.

Unit Module

The Unit Module may be thought of as the "starting point" for use of the MICA system. It is through this module that information regarding available instructional methods and evaluation procedures for a particular instructional unit are obtained. A brief description of the workings of the Unit Module, a sample interaction with the module (Figure 5.12), and a flowchart showing the logic of the module in Figure 5.13 are presented below.

The Unit Module may be entered directly from the Controller, or as a result of a forward unit choice made in the Prescription Module. Upon entering from the Controller, the terminal operator (teacher) is asked to enter the pre-assigned ID number of the student for whom a unit is to be chosen. In Figure 5.12, student 123 was selected. The system reads the desired student's record in the Student Data File and the Student History

Figure 5.12: Sample Unit Module Interaction

```
/U
  ? STUDENT #
123
  ? ENTER UNIT NAME FOR JOHN JONES
2 - DIGIT ADD
  ? PREREQUISITE UNITS
  ? 1. NUMBER FACTS
  ? 2. 1-DIGIT ADD
  ? #
  ? UNIT #
1
  ? AVAILABLE METHODS:
  ? 1. TEXTBOOKS
  ? 2. FILMSTRIPS
  ? METHOD #
1
  ? AVAILABLE PRE-TESTS:
  ? 1. TEST1
  ? 2. TEST2
  ? PRE-TEST #
2
  UNIT SELECTION COMPLETED
```

Figure 5.13: Unit Module Flow Chart

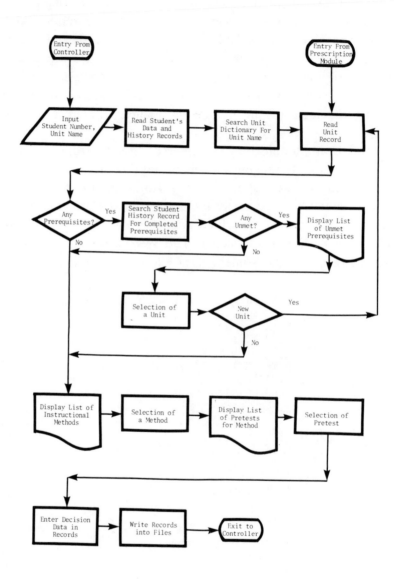

File, and Responds by typing the student's name and requesting the desired unit. If a mistake was made or the student's name is wrong, the operator may enter a /U to try again. Otherwise, the operator should simply type the name of the desired unit, in this case, "2-DIGIT ADD." At this point the selected unit record is read into core and checked for the existence of any prerequisites to the unit. If any prerequisites are present, they are checked against the list of completed units stored in the student history record. If any of the prerequisites have not been completed by the student, they are displayed at the terminal, and the teacher may assign one of these prior units in lieu of the original specified unit. This is done by entering the number typed to the left of the desired unit (see Figure 5.12). If the teacher wishes to allow the student to proceed without completing the prerequisites, he or she may press "return."

When a unit is decided upon, the unit record is examined and the list of instructional methods available for achieving this unit is presented to the teacher. To select a method, the teacher merely types the number printed to the left of the desired method. Next, a list of available pretests is obtained from the unit record and presented to the teacher. Again, to select a test the teacher enters the number printed to the left of the desired pretest, and the system responds by typing "UNIT SELECTION COMPLETE." When a list contains only a single item, the computer will automatically select it and store the number 1 in the appropriate data element.

The student history record is then updated by entering the selected unit number, instructional method, pretest, and current date in the record. The student data record is updated by inserting the selected unit number as the current unit. These records are then written back into their respective files, and control is returned to the Controller Module.

Prescription Module
The prescription module provides the greatest part of the

computer assistance needed by the teacher at the instructional level of management. It implements four functions: diagnosis, prescription, test selection, and data storage needed to manage the unit-of-instruction cycle. The flow chart of the prescription module is presented in Figure 5.14. A typical interactive sequence is given in Figure 5.15. When a /P command is entered by the terminal operator, the Controller Module passes control to the prescription module. Upon entering the module, the operator is asked to enter the student's identification number. In Figure 5.15, student 102 was entered. The student's history file record is retrieved and the assigned pretest or posttest extracted. A message is displayed containing the name of the test and of the student and asks for the test results. If the names in the prompt message are incorrect, the operator can enter /P again and provide the correct information. The sequence numbers of the items or objectives failed are entered, separated by commas. These results are recorded in the student history file record currently in the core buffer. The test ID is used to obtain the prescription record from the prescription file. The prescription record contains the information enabling the module to select and display the appropriate prescription menus. The module then checks for unit mastery. This is determined by comparing the test results with the test criterion specified in the prescription record. The test results (lists of right or wrong responses) are compared with the prestored user supplied criterion for up to 20 patterns. Each pattern contains one or more ranges specifying the lowest and highest numbered item to be considered. Each pattern range is compared to the list of item numbers entered by the operator. Each time a test item number falls within a given range definition, a counter is incremented by one. After all pattern ranges have been compared with the list of item numbers entered, the counter number is compared to the criterion lower, upper bound in the prescription record. This criterion is met if the counter value lies within these bounds. If the criterion is not met, then the prescriptions contained in the record are displayed in menu format for use by

Figure 5.14: Prescription Module Flow Chart

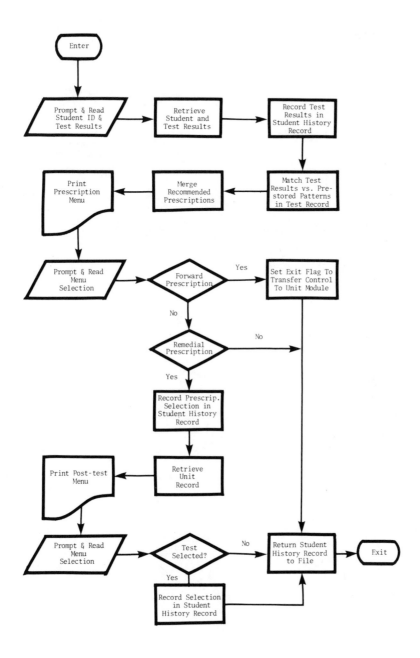

Figure 5.15: Prescription Menu and Selection Format

INTERACTIONS	EXPLANATIONS
MICA READY	
/P	The prescription module is called.
?STUDENT #	MICA prompts the student's ID#.
102	
?ENTER PRE1? TEST RESULTS FOR JACK CARR	MICA displays the name of the test
9.	the student should have taken, the student's name and prompts the entering of test results.
?REMEDIAL PRESCRIPTIONS:	MICA displays a menu of remedial
? 1. MEASUREMENT	prescriptions from which the
? 2. STAR UNIT *A TELLTIME1	teacher may choose, and then
? 3. STAR UNIT *B TELLTIME2	prompts her choice.
? 4. STAR UNIT *G LENGTHWEIG	
?ACTIVITY #	
1.	
?AVAILABLE POST-TESTS:	MICA displays a menu of post-tests
? 1. PT17A	associated with the originally
? 2. PT17B	assigned method, and prompts the
? 3. PT17C	selection of one of them.
?TEST #	
1	
PRESCRIPTION SELECTION COMPLETED.	MICA's message indicating that all
MICA READY	communications with the prescription module concerning this student are complete.
/P	In this next example the teacher determined that either the student number entered is incorrect or the student has taken the wrong test.
?STUDENT #	
40	
?ENTER PRER2 TEST RESULTS FOR KARI MILLER	
/C	
MICA READY	
/P	In this example the student meets the criteria for the assigned unit.
?STUDENT #	
156	
ENTER PT12C TEST RESULTS FOR LYNN BAER	
.	
?NEXT UNIT:	A menu of new units is displayed
? 1. SG13	and a choice prompted.
?UNIT #	
1	
PRESCRIPTION SELECTION COMPLETED.	
?AVAILABLE METHODS:	The Unit module is automatically
? 1. SG13	called for the selection of an
? 2. SGTAPE	appropriate method and pretest for the selected unit.
?METHOD #	
1	
ONLY ONE PRETEST IS AVAILABLE: PRE13	
UNIT SELECTION COMPLETED.	
MICA READY	

the operator. If no test results were entered, it is assumed the unit was mastered, and control is transferred to the unit module where the next unit is assigned. Once the prescription menu is displayed, the operator selects the prescriptions of interest by entering the sequence number appearing at the left. It is mandatory that the first prescription be selected, as it identifies the objective being remediated. Once the prescriptions are selected, their dictionary numbers are stored in the student history file record of the student. The prescription module then displays the list of available posttests, and the operator selects one by entering its number. Test selection completes the prescriptive process. After the student history record is written on the disk, control is returned to the Controller Module, which responds with MICA READY.

File Maintenance Module

The File Maintenance Module (FMM) provides a link between the user and the data base of the MICA system, regardless of whether portions of the data base are in rapid-access (core) storage or mass storage. Unlike the Unit and Prescription Modules, the File Maintenance Module is not meant to be used interactively, though it certainly can be. Rather, it is to be used in a batch environment to make time-consuming changes to the system's data base.

The File Maintenance Module is composed of three submodules: the Student Data Module (SDM), the Prescription File Module (PFM), and the Educational Unit Module (EUM). The three modules are controlled by a driver in the File Maintenance Module, and perform the functions of adding records, modfying records, and deleting records according to predefined operation (function) codes located in the first column of each input image (card). The three routines are logically the same, since they manipulate their respective files according to the same function codes; the only significant difference among them is in the actual sequence of operations carried out to fulfill the functions desired by the user. The table presented below defines the three submodules of the FMM and their relationship to the various files.

CODE (in Columns 1-3)	Submodule Called	Main File Manipulated	Other Files Referenced
SDM	Student Data Module	Student Data File	Group File (GRF) Student History File (SHF)
EUM	Educational Unit Module	Unit File	Unit, Method, and Test Definition Tables (UTD, MED, TED)
PFM	Prescription File Module	Prescription File	Prescription and Test Definition Tables (PRD, TED)

The File Maintenance Module (FMM) serves to route user requests to the appropriate submodule to create or update a file, as depicted in Figure 5.16. Upon being activated by the MICA controller, as the result of a /F as input, the FMM reads in a code specifying the type of file maintenance to be performed. If the three-letter code read in is one of these shown above, the File Maintenance Module turns control over to the appropriate submodule. That module then takes control of any further input, output, and file maintenance pertaining to its file(s), until an END card is encountered, at which point control is returned to the File Maintenance Module. The process continues in this manner, transferring control to a submodule as designated by the three-letter code, and getting back control from the submodule when an END card is reached. The File Maintenance Module returns to the Controller when a MICA control card (slash in column 1) is encountered.

Although each submodule has its separate control, independent of the File Maintenance Module, every submodule returns control when either an END card or a MICA control card (slash in Column 1) is encountered. It is up to the File Maintenance Module to determine what condition exists on return from a

Figure 5.16: File Maintenance Module Flow Chart

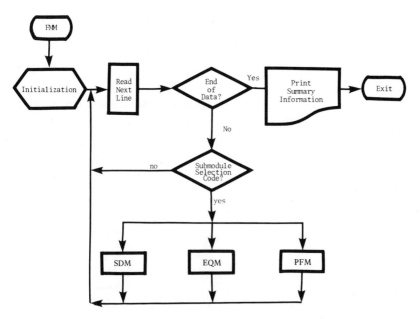

submodule and either select another submodule or return to the Controller, as is appropriate.

Another concept common to all submodules is one of definition by use. This means that, in general, when a component (be it unit, test, method, or whatever) is encountered in the input stream which has no entry in a definition table, an entry in the table is made for the new component. In this way, a unit, for example, may be referenced before it has been completely defined in the file. This is not the case when an attempt is being made to drop such a component, nor when a student name is concerned, as students may have the same names. Furthermore, an attempt to add a name already existing in a definition table (except for a student name) is marked as an error and ignored.

All data input to one of the three submodules have common codes in column 1, used for specifying whether data is being added to, deleted from, or changed within a file. These codes are:

+ or blank	information to be added;
-	to be dropped;
$	to be changed or located;
*	to replace or change to.

When an error is encountered, the information which was being built, dropped, or changed is not recorded in the file, and an appropriate error message is printed. In the case of the Prescription File Module and Educational Units Module, data following an error is ignored until the next major unit of data is found, which is the beginning of a unit or test, respectively. Figure 5.17 illustrates how a data deck may be set up for the File Maintenance Module.

Student Data Module. The Student Data Module (SDM) is the submodule that adds, drops, or changes data in the Student Data File. The form depicted in Figure 5.18 is used to collect the student data to be entered via key punched cards. The format of the cards is specified by the card column assignments given on the form. Each line of input information is read by the Student Data Module on a line-at-a-time basis, and the processing performed is depicted in Figure 5.19. SDM inspects each line of data to determine if it is additional data or the end of the data stream. Until an end of data is encountered, the following occurs: Each line of data passes through a function check which inspects the flag in column one of the input to determine whether data is to be added, dropped, or changed. The files are inspected to ascertain if there is room for additional student data. If capacity has been reached, the data is refused. If the data is "new," there is no identification number for the student associated with the data; hence, the next available identification number is assigned to the new student. If a new group is indicated, a check is made to see if the system can accommodate it. If so, it is added to the group roster. Header entries affected by this new data are updated. This includes (1) number of active students in the system, (2) number of records in the SDF, and (3) number of members in the student's group. A subroutine then writes this new data into the

Figure 5.17: File Maintenance Module Data Input

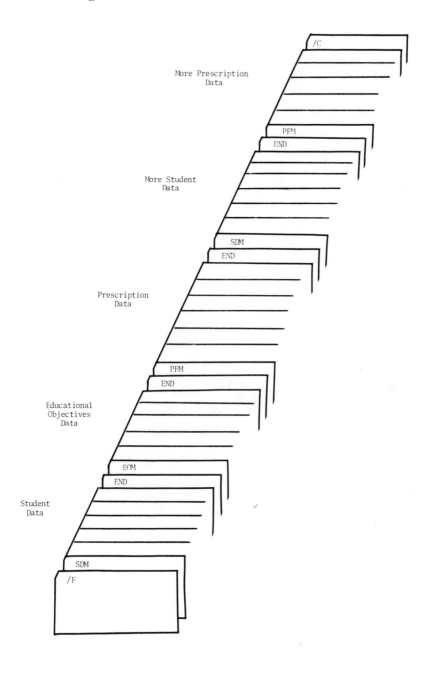

Figure 5.18: MICA Student Data Form

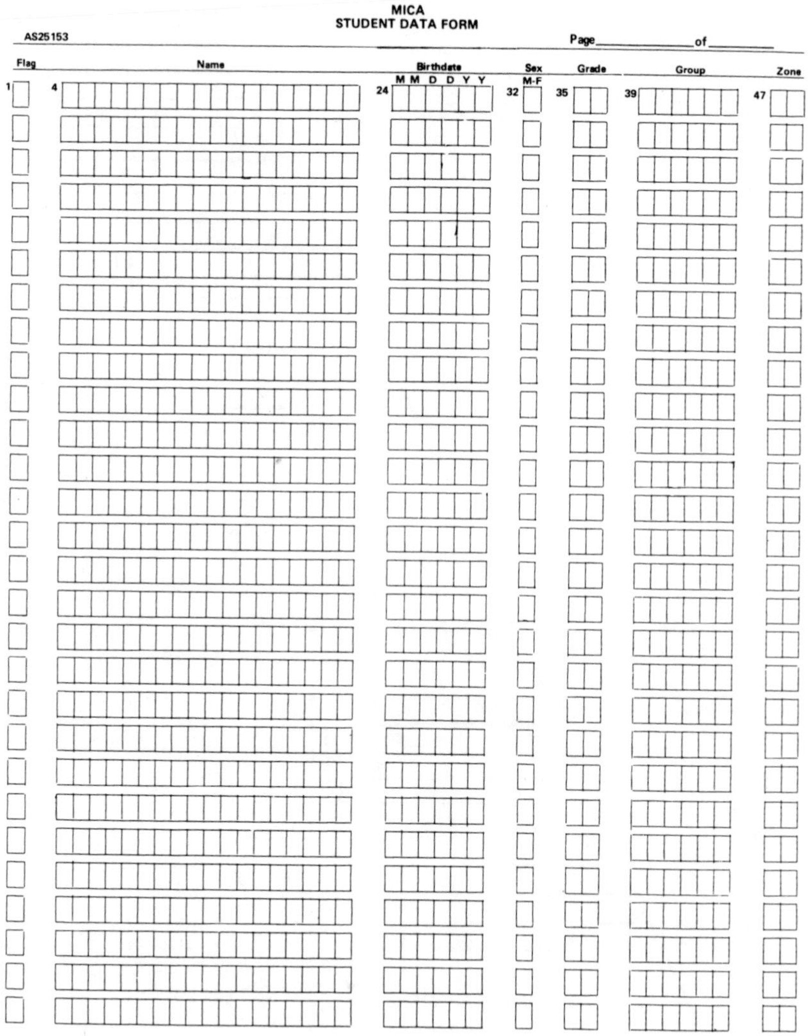
MICA
STUDENT DATA FORM

AS25153

Page ______ of ______

Flag | Name | Birthdate (M M D D Y Y) | Sex (M-F) | Grade | Group | Zone

1 | 4 | 24 | 32 | 35 | 39 | 47

Figure 5.19: Student Data Module Flow Chart

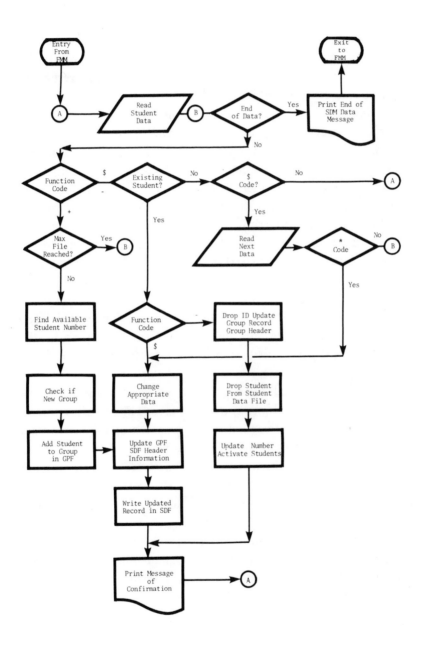

Student Data File in the appropriate student record and into the appropriate group record of the Group File. To assure that the information has been entered, the user obtains a printed message of confirmation of the input. The corresponding record in the Student History File is initialized to zeroes. (Now the student is active in the Student Data File.) The computer program returns to the input data stream, and reads the next line of data.

If one wanted to drop a student or change a student record in the Student Data File, the file is searched (searching on name, birth data, and sex) for the specified student. If the student's record is located, the data line will be checked according to its flag. Depending on whether it is a change or a drop, different procedures are followed. If the student is not found in the Student Data File, the program prints an appropriate message to the user notifying him of the error; the program then returns to the incoming data stream. If the flag signals drop data, the student's group record is updated and his ID is dropped; then the Student Data Module updates the number of active records in the Student Data File Header. To assure that the information has been deleted, the user obtains a printed message confirming the drop. The computer program returns to the input data stream, and reads the next line of data.

If the flag signals change data, the program reads the student's present record into the buffer area. The next line of data from the data stream is converted for buffer use, and verification is made of the asterisk in column one, denoting that this line of data is indeed the modified data. If the asterisk is not located, an error message is printed to the user, and the module returns to the input data stream. This procedure alleviates any problems of nonsequential lines of data. If everything is in order, the program will change the information in the student's record to correspond to the nonblank fields in the line of "change" data by writing the new data into the student's data record. If the student is being changed to a new group and there is room in the new group for him, he is dropped from his old group and added to his new group.

The student's group record and/or student data record are written into their files. To note the change of data, a message confirming the change, which includes both the old and new record, is printed. The program returns to the input data stream and reads the next line of data.

To protect against errors in flag characters, anything other than a plus, blank, minus, or dollar sign is assumed to be an error. Should an error in the flag character be detected, the user obtains an error message and the program returns to the input data stream to read the next line of data. When all data have been processed and the "END" card is read, the Student Data Module returns control to the File Maintenance Module.

Prescription File Module. The Prescription File Module (PFM) is responsible for the creation and updating of prescription records maintained in the Prescription File. The routine is accessed through the File Maintenance Module (FMM) when the FMM receives a PFM card as input. The processes of creation and updating are actually composed of the three functions of addition, deletion, and changing of records. These functions, although directed toward whole prescription records, accomplish a task in a step-by-step fashion. Each step of a task or process is initiated by reading a card containing a flag character in column 1, a card code in columns 2 and 3, and data on the remainder of the card. Prescription record information is composed of four data types: test, response patterns, pattern ranges, and pattern prescriptions. The card codes correspond to the information types are: "TE" (test), "PA" (pattern), "LO" (low-high range), and "PR" (prescription). The Prescription File Module is organized into a hierarchy of sections. The hierarchy results from the sequence of file maintenance operations that must be performed in a specified order. The order of the data cards by card code must be the following: first, the TE card to identify which test is involved; second, a PA card specifying which pattern within the test is being affected; and third, a LO or PR card containing range or prescription data, respectively, for the pattern in the test previously declared. Multiple LO and PR cards having data for a single pattern may follow a PA card during the creation of a prescription record. Multiple pattern definitions (one PA plus multiple LO and PR cards) having data for a single test may follow a TE card during the creation process. Due to the potential impact of errors arising from a deletion or change in a prescription record, changing or deleting a single datum requires that its test and pattern be explicitly declared on a TE and PA card, respectively. The layout of the form used to prepare the data cards processed by the Prescription File Module is shown in Figure 5.20. The full pattern-scoring capability of MICA was not used in the Sherman School Project; hence, a single low-high range was associated with each pattern.

The processing performed by the Prescription File Module is depicted in Figure 5.21. Upon entry from the File Maintenance Module or the completion of a creation or update task, the Prescription File Module initiates a task by reading a card. The flag character and card code are extracted from the card during the read operation. A test is made to see if the end of data (END in columns 1-3) card was just read to direct control back to the File Maintenance Module. In the absence of an "END" card, the card code is decoded to direct control to the appropriate section of the Prescription File Module. If a TE is encountered, the processing of all functions at the record level is performed. The test name is fetched from the data portion of the TE card. The test definition table is searched for the presence of the test name. The prescription record of the test is returned by the search if the test exists in the dictionary. Then one of two tasks is initiated, depending upon the flag character on the TE card. The test name can be dropped from the dictionary and the prescription file, or the data can be modified. When the test is not already defined, the test name is added to the test dictionary, a prescription record is initiated for the test, and the headers of the test dictionary and prescription file are updated. For both new and existing tests, the next card is read and the process advances to the PA section.

Figure 5.20: MICA Prescription Form

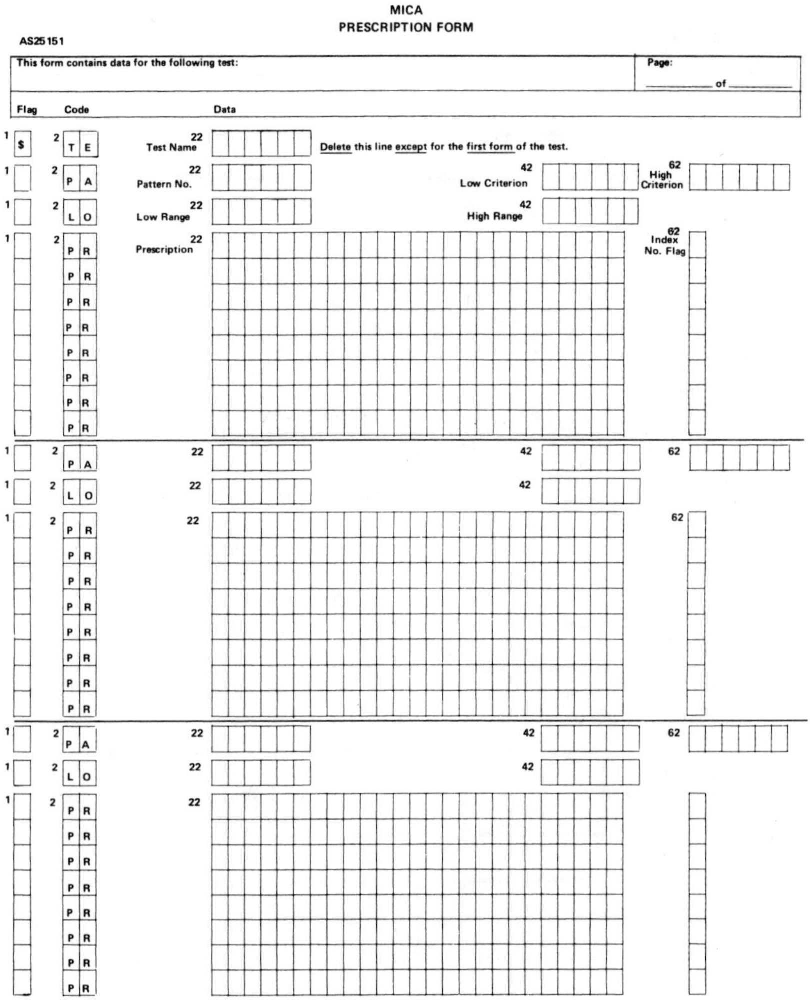
MICA
PRESCRIPTION FORM

AS25151

This form contains data for the following test:

Page: ______ of ______

Flag Code Data

1 $ 2 T E 22 Test Name — Delete this line except for the first form of the test.

1 2 P A 22 Pattern No. 42 Low Criterion 62 High Criterion

1 2 L O 22 Low Range 42 High Range

1 2 P R 22 Prescription 62 Index No. Flag

P R

P R

P R

P R

P R

P R

P R

1 2 P A 22 42 62

1 2 L O 22 42

1 2 P R 22 62

P R

P R

P R

P R

P R

P R

P R

1 2 P A 22 42 62

1 2 L O 22 42

1 2 P R 22

P R

P R

P R

P R

P R

P R

P R

Figure 5.21: Prescription File Module Flow Chart

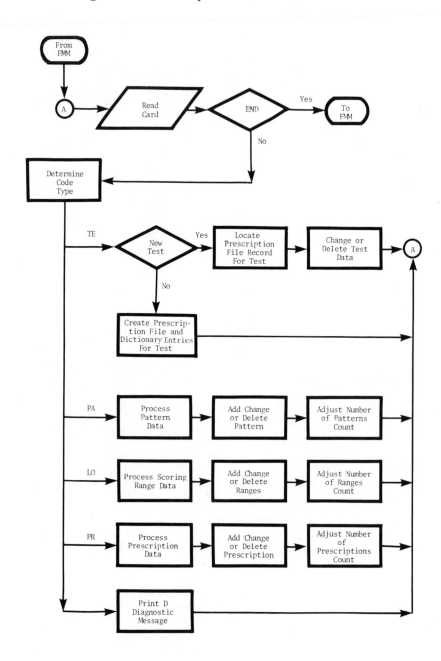

The PA Section (Pattern) processes all functions performed at the test pattern level (i.e., adding a new pattern, deleting a pattern, or changing a pattern). The absence of a PA card code on the first card used by this section generates an error message, and the error sequence is executed. The data portion of the PA card contains the pattern number and the low and high criteria of the pattern. Validity checks are performed on all data. If an error is detected, the process is terminated with an appropriate error message and the error sequence is executed. One of three tasks (add, delete, or change) is initiated, depending on the flag character. Finally, the number of patterns is incremented and the next card is read. Normally, the process advances to the LO and PR sections.

LO section (LOW-HIGH Range) processes all functions performed on the low-high range pairs of a pattern. Upon entry to the LO section, the flag character is evaluated to determine which type of operation is to be performed. If the flag character is a + or blank, a check is made to determine if there is room to add the range data to the pattern. Lack of room for the range data generates an error message, and control transfers to the error sequence. Error-free data is added to the pattern, and the count of ranges is incremented. If the flag character is a $ or -, the specified range is located in the pattern. The - flag character directs the deletion of the specified range data and the count of ranges is decremented. The $ flag character causes the next card to be read. The range data from the second card replaces the original data in the pattern. With the completion of either task, a message of confirmation is printed and control is returned.

The PR section (Prescription) processes all functions that are performed on the prescriptions of a pattern. Prescriptions are identified by either their internal dictionary index or their literal name. Upon entry to the PR section, the flag character is evaluated to determine what type of operation is to be performed. If the code is a +, the pattern is checked to see if there is room to add another prescription. The prescription type is checked to see if it is valid (F for forward, R for remedial). If the prescription is identified by its internal index number, a check is made to see if the number is reasonable. When all the checks are passed, the prescription is added to the pattern, the number of prescriptions in the pattern is incremented, and control returns to the point where a card is read to add additional ranges and prescriptions to the pattern. If the code is $ or -, the pattern is searched for a prescription matching the prescription specified in the data area of the card. For the case of the flag character being a -, the prescription is dropped from the pattern and the prescription count is decremented. For the case of the flag character being a $, the next card is read. The prescription on the next card replaces the prescription specified on the "$PR" card and the change is reported.

Educational Unit Module. The Educational Unit Module is responsible for the creation and updating of records in the Unit File. The module is accessed through the File Maintenance Module when the characters EUM are encountered in columns 1-3 of an input card. A record in the Unit File contains the definition of one unit in the curriculum plan. The definition consists of the prerequisite unit(s), instructional method(s), and tests corresponding to a particular instructional method. For each instructional method within a unit, at least one pretest or one posttest must be specified. The layout of the forms used to prepare the cards containing the several types of data is shown in Figure 5.22.

The Educational Unit Module has a specialized subsection to process each of the four data types and an initialization section. As was the case with the preceding modules, the Educational Unit Module accomplishes its tasks in a step-by-step manner with each step controlled by the information contained in the card. The processing sequence employed by the Educational Unit Module is shown in Figure 5.23. Upon entering the Educational Unit Module from the File Maintenance Module, an input card is read. A test for the end of data card ("END" punched in card columns 1-3) is performed and, if met, the last unit record created is written into

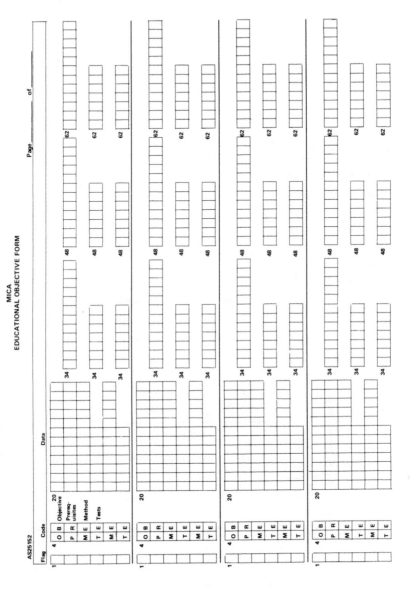

Figure 5.22: MICA Educational Objective Form

Figure 5.23: Educational Unit Module Flow Chart

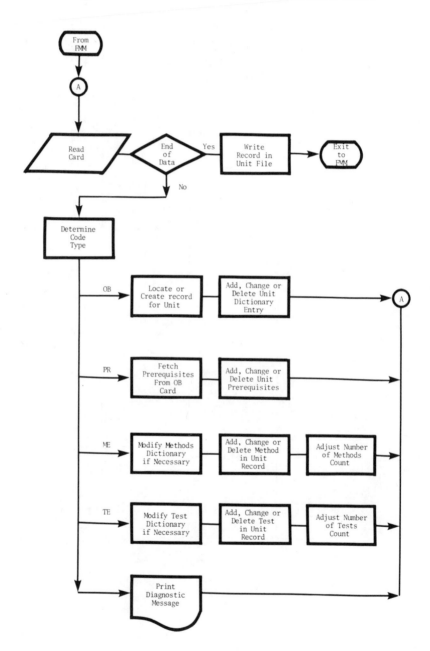

the Unit File and control is returned to the File Maintenance Module. If it is not the END card, the card code is checked for validity. Valid codes are "OB," "PR," "ME," and "TE." They direct control to the Objective, Prerequisite, Method, and Test specialized sections, respectively. An invalid card code causes an error diagnostic, and the error sequence is initiated.

The OB section processes all functions performed at the record level (i.e., dropping, initiating a change, or addition of a unit record). The unit name for the task just initiated is fetched from the data portion of the OB card. The unit definition table is searched for an occurrence of the unit name. The flag character is then evaluated to determine what action is required to complete the step. If the flag character is a +, the unit is added to the dictionary, and its definition table index number is retained for use as the index into the Unit File to the record defining the unit. Provided the unit is found in the dictionary and the flag character is a -, the unit is marked as dropped and the transaction is reported. Control is then returned to the initialization section. If the flag character is a $, the next card is read. If the flag character-card code is a "* OB," the objective name on the second card replaces the objective name in the dictionary, and control is returned to the initialization section to determine the next step.

The PR section (Prerequisites) processes all functions performed on the prerequisites of a unit. Upon entry to the PR section, the prerequisite unit(s) are fetched from the data portion of the PR card, and the flag character is evaluated. If the flag character is a +, the prerequisite unit(s) are added to the unit record, and control is returned to the initialization section for any further steps for this task. If the flag character is a -, the prerequisite(s) specified on the PR card are deleted from the unit record, and control returns to the initialization section. If the flag character is a $, the next card is read and the unit on the change card replaces the corresponding unit in the record specified on the "$ PR" card. Control is transferred to the initialization section for initiation of the next step or task.

The ME section (Method) processes all functions related to the instructional methods of a unit. Upon entry, the method name is fetched from the data portion of the ME card. The method is found in or added to the method dictionary. The flag character is evaluated to determine what action is to be performed to accomplish this step. If the flag is a +, the method is added to the unit record, the number of methods is incremented, and control is returned to the initialization section. If the flag is a -, the method is dropped from the unit record, the number of methods is decremented, and control is returned to the initialization section. If the flag is a $, the next card is read. If its flag is a *, the method in the record, specified by the first card, is replaced by the method specified on the second card. Control is then transferred to the initialization section.

The TE section (Test) processes all functions on the tests of a method of a unit. Upon entry to the TE section, the test names are fetched from the data portion of the TE card and added to the test dictionary if they are not already there. The flag character is then evaluated to determine what action is to be performed next to accomplish this step. If the flag is a +, the test(s) are added to the method, the number of tests for the specified method are incremented, and control is returned to the initialization section. If the flag is a -, the test(s) are dropped from the method, the number of tests is decremented, and control is transferred to the initialization section. If the flag is a $, the next card is read, and if the second card's flag is a *, the corresponding tests of the second TE card replace the specified tests of the first card in the record. Control is returned to the initialization section for the next step or task.

Dictionary Maintenance Module (DMM)

The Dictionary Maintenance Module implements, via a key board terminal, the interactive editing of method, prescription and student names stored in the dictionaries of MICA's data base. The Dictionary Maintenance Module is available through the file maintenance portion of the program by typing a "/D." The change of a definition table entry requires the input of two lines. The first line is composed of a flag character in column 1, a card code in column 2, and data starting in column 3. The second line has a flag in column 1 and data starting in column 2. The Dictionary Maintenance Module is composed of an initialization section and a separate section for each definition table within the dictionary. The flow chart of the Dictionary Maintenance Module is given in Figure 5.24.

The initialization section is responsible for initiating the two-step task of changing a definition table entry. The first line of input is prompted. The flag is checked to make sure it is a $ and the card code is decoded to determine to which dictionary the data portion of the line refers. Control is then transferred to the section which manipulates the appropriate dictionary. If the flag or card code is vacuous, a diagnostic is displayed, followed by the initiating prompt.

The M section (Method) receives control when the card code is an "M." The data portion of the line contains the literal name of the method to be changed starting in column 3. The Method Dictionary is searched for the input name. When it is found, the second line of input is prompted and read. The new method name is extracted from the input line, starting in column 2. The original method is replaced by the new method. Confirmation of the change is reported and control returns to the initiating prompt.

The P section (Prescription) receives control when the card code is a "P." The data portion of the line contains the index number of the prescription which is to be changed. The prescription is fetched from the Prescription Dictionary and since it could be a forward prescription (i.e., a unit name), the Unit Dictionary is searched for an occurrence of it. If a match is found, a warning is displayed. The prompt of the second line is displayed and the second input line is read. The new prescription is fetched from the data portion of the line starting in column 2. The original prescription is replaced by a new one and the change is confirmed. Control is transferred to the initiating prompt.

Figure 5.24: Dictionary Maintenance Module

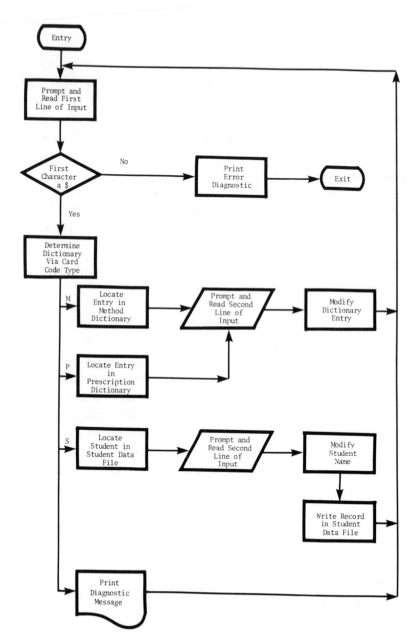

The S section (Student) receives control when card code is an "S." The data portion of the line contains the student's ID number starting in column 3. The student's record is fetched from the Student Data File. The new name is prompted by displaying the original name and the response is read. The new name replaces the original name in the student's record and the record is written back into the file. The change is confirmed and control is returned to the initiating prompt.

Report Module

The Report Module (RPM) is designed to generate standard reports based on data maintained in the system files. The data are aggregated according to user specified groupings and/or time divisions. Then the reports are printed. Reports may be requested interactively with immediate response displayed on the user's CRT or keyboard terminal. A batch run may also be used to generate reports. It is recommended for the more expensive and/or lengthy reports. An additional advantage of generating reports in batch mode is the capability of writing the reports in a print file which is saved on tape. The print file of reports may be printed several times, obtaining as many copies as are required at any time in the future at a fraction of the cost of the original run.

The following discussion of the report Controller and each of the report submodules corresponds to the flow charts shown in Figure 5.25.

Report Controller. The Report Controller is initiated when the "/R" job control statement is entered by the user. Its responsibilities include: reading the report requests, directing output to the appropriate print file, extraction and varification of information from the request that is common to more than one report, and transfer control to the specified submodule. Note: the design allows for the future addition of other reports with a minimum of modification to the existing structure. The Controller first scans the input line which caused the RPM to be called. If the control statement includes the command to SYM (make multiple

Figure 5.25: Report Module Flow Chart

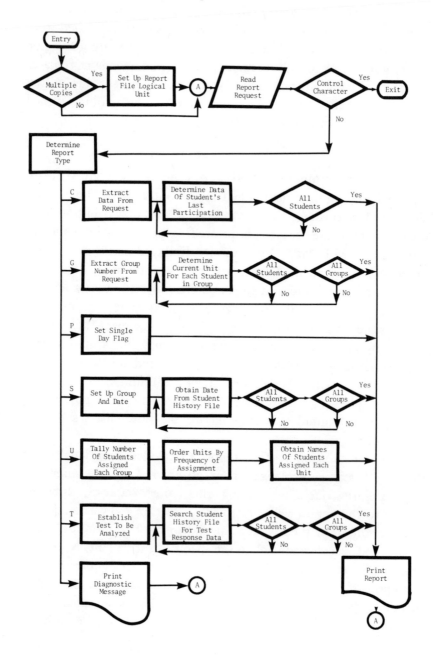

copies of) output, the print file is dynamically assigned to the run and all reports are written into the print file until a "/R" job control statement is encountered without the SYM command. Absence of the SYM command causes the reports to be printed at an interactive terminal. The Controller then reads the report request and extracts information from it. The request is in free format with the fields (parameters) of the request separated by commas. The first two fields are common to all reports. The first field is one alphabetic character in length, specifying which report is being requested. The second field is of variable length (zero to 24 characters) containing the name of the individual or department requesting the report. For the unit and test reports, the third field contains the name of a unit. If any errors are detected during the initial extraction of information from the request, a diagnostic is displayed; control returns to the reading of the next request. When the request is determined to be valid, control is transferred to the appropriate submodule.

Contact Report Submodule. This submodule receives control when the first character of the request is a "C." The Contact Report lists those students who have not participated in the program since a user-specified date. This was shown in Figure 4.6. The third field of the request contains the date which is the retrieval criterion. If the date is valid, i.e., in the past, the report is generated. The report is by group as defined by the students assigned to the groups of the group file. Each line of the report is a summary of the current status of a student meeting the request criteria. The information includes his name, ID number, last unit, method and test assigned, and the date it was assigned. For those students who have not been assigned a unit, a note to that effect replaces the above summary. With the completion of the report, control returns to the Report Controller.

Group Report Submodule. This submodule receives control when the first character of the request is a "G." The group report summarizes the last assignment given to each student of a group. This was shown in Figure 4.5. The third field of the request specifies the identification of the group to be reported. The group record is read from the Group File. The student ID's are fetched from the group record. In turn, the student ID's are used to locate and read the students' data file record and history file record. From these records, each student's name, current unit, instructional method, and test assignment are fetched and printed. Upon completion of the report, control returns to the Report Controller.

Unit Report Submodule. This submodule receives control when the first character of the request is a "U." The unit report lists the names of students currently assigned to the unit. It was shown in Figure 4.4. The third field of the request is either blank or contains the name of one of the units of the curriculum. If a unit is specified, it is the only one reported. If the third field is blank, all the units are to be reported. The student data records are searched in turn for all students working on each unit, and the units are sorted in decreasing order of the number of students working on the unit. The report output consists of the unit names; and, for each unit, the total number of students currently working on the unit followed by their names and ID's.

Student History Report Submodule. This submodule receives control when the first character of the request is a "P" or "S." The "S" specifies the report is for all student history information since a specific date or all information since the last unit was assigned for a single student or group of students. The layout of the Student History Report was shown in Figure 4.3. The third field of the request is the date, which may optionally be entered for type "S" reports and is required for type "P" reports. The fourth field is an integer followed by an "S" or a "G." The integer specifies an ID number and the "S" or "G" identifies it as a student or group ID, respectively. Once the parameters of the request are evaluated, the student data and student history records are read in turn for the specified student(s), and the report is printed. The information output consists of the student name(s) and ID number(s), the names of all units started and method selected, and all test names, results, and prescriptions. With the completion of the report, control is returned to the report Controller.

The "P" specifies a Participant Report is to be produced. This report has the same format as the Student History Report but contains data only from the date specified in the third field. It is used primarily by the terminal operator to determine if the student's record in the Student History File is accurate.

Test Report Submodule. The Test Report summarizes the performance of all the students who have taken a particular test or all the tests for a particular instructional unit. The layout of the report was shown in Figure 4.7. The third field of the request is the name of the unit associated with the test. The fourth field is the name of the test to be reported; optionally, all tests for a given unit can be reported. The final field in the request specifies the number of items in a test when a single test has been named in the fourth field. Once these initial specifications are determined, the Student History File is searched for students who have taken the test(s). The binary vector of item responses for the test is used to calculate the number of times the test has been taken and the item difficulty of each item. If more than one test is to be reported, the data is presented by test within unit.

Utility Routines

All major modules of MICA (and submodules) described thus far make use of the utility routines for performing common functions. These routines eliminate duplication and allow modules a higher degree of machine-independence. The following utility routines are employed:

ADIC— Add to DICtionary

  Calling sequence: CALL ADIC (DICTIN, DEFNTN, ID)

  Input conditions: DICTN is the number of the definition table ("dictionary" number) to which a definition is to be added. DEFNTN contains the definition to be entered (number of words dependent on the definition table referenced).

Output conditions: The definition contained in DEFNTN is entered into table number DICTN; ID is set to the identification number of the entry. If the table is full, the entry is not made and ID is returned with a value of Ø. DICTN and DEFNTN are unchanged.

CHAR—   CHARacter retrieval

Calling sequence: N = CHAR (STARTC, NUMC, LOC)

Input conditions: STARTC is the starting character position from which characters are extracted (positions numbered 0-5). NUMC is the number of characters to be extracted. LOC is the computer word from which the specified number of characters is to be extracted.

Output conditions: The characters are extracted and returned as the value of CHAR right justified, zero-filled.

Note 1:   The field of characters extracted cannot extend over computer word boundaries, e.g., one cannot retrieve the last two characters of a computer word and the first three characters of the following word with a single call to CHAR.

Note 2:   CHAR makes use of the 1108 FORTRAN V FLD function, not generally available on all systems.

CLEAR—   CLEAR a record on a file and its I/O buffer

Calling sequence: CALL CLEAR (FILEN, RECN)

Input conditions: FILEN is the number of the file of which a record is to be cleared; RECN is the number of the record to be cleared.

Output conditions:	Record number specified, RECN, of file specified, FILEN, is cleared (set to Ø), and I/O buffer of FILEN is cleared.
Alternate entry:	CLEAR4. Same calling sequence, input conditions and output conditions except the file's I/O buffer retains its original contents.

CTON— Convert to Numeric

Calling sequence:	CALL CTON (ANUMBR)
Input conditions:	ANUMBR contains a number in alphanumeric (fieldata) format.
Output conditions:	ANUMBR contains the same number converted to numeric format, right justified, zero-filled.
Note:	In the conversion, leading blanks are ignored, trailing blank(s) terminate the number. This routine depends on the input argument being in 1108 fieldata format.

FRD— File Read

Calling sequence:	CALL FRD (FILEN, RECN)
Input conditions:	FILEN is the number of the file being read from; RECN is the number of the record being read.
Output conditions:	Record number RECN of file number FILEN resides in the buffer (in core) corresponding to the file. (Each file has a correspondent core buffer, e.g., SDEN has SDFB, OBEN has OBFB, etc.) FILEN and RECN remain unchanged, as does the record on the file.

FWRT—   File WRITE

        Calling sequence: CALL FWRT (FILEN, RECN)

        Input conditions: FILEN is the number of the file on which a record will be written, RECN is the number of the record where the buffer will be written.

        Output conditions: The buffer corresponding to the file specified will be written out as record number RECN of the file, destroying any previous contents of that record. The buffer, FILEN, and RECN remain unchanged.

GET—   GET a specified field from the specified buffer

        Calling sequence: CALL GET (FILEN, CMPNNT, WCMP, WSMP, VALUE)

        Input conditions: The record from which the field is to be extracted resides in its correspondent buffer in core.

                FILEN identifies the file whose record (i.e., buffer) is being referenced.

                CMPNNT is the index into the file's header which entry describes the location of the field to be extracted.

                WCMP is the number which, in the case of a repeating item in a record, identifies which item is being referenced.

                WSCMP is the number which, in the case of a repeating field within an item, identifies that field.

                In the case of nonrepeating items or fields, WCMP and WSCMP are 0, respectively.

Output conditions: None of the input arguments are changed. Nothing in the record or header is changed. VALUE contains the value of the field desired, right justified, zero-filled.

Example: CALL GET (OBFN, NPRE, METHDN, Ø, VALUE).

NPRE = 6; the sixth word of the OBF file header describes the field.

METHDN = 3; the field is to be extracted from the third item in the buffer on return, VALUE will be the value of the third NPRE field in the buffer.

MOVE— MOVE some characters from one place to another

Calling sequence: CALL MOVE (FROM, FCHAR, TO, TCHAR, NCHARS)

Input conditions: FCHAR and TCHAR are character numbers (not limited to 0-5); FROM and TO are areas in core; NCHARS is the number of characters to be moved.

Output conditions: NCHARS characters are moved from FROM, beginning at character position FCHAR, to TO, beginning at character position TCHAR. FROM remains unchanged and input arguments (except TO) remain unchanged.

Example: CALL MOVE (LINE, 19, OBNAME(3), 3, 12)

Before call: LINE: THIS LINE CONTAINS ABCD EFGHIJKL IN COLU

OBNAME: OBJECTIVE IS RESTUVWXYZ 0 2345

After call: LINE: THIS LINE CONTAINS ABCD EFGHIJKL IN COLU

OBNAME: OBJECTIVE   IS   RABCDEFG
            HIJKL2345

NSCAN—   Number SCAN

Calling sequence: CALL NSCAN (POS, VALUE, ENDC)

Input conditions: POS is a position or column number of LINE at which scanning is to begin (or resume).

Output conditions: VALUE is the value of the first number encountered in LINE after column POS; ENDC is the character immediately following the number picked up; POS is the position or column number of LINE immediately after the number picked up.

PACKD—   PACK DATE

Calling sequence: CALL PACKD (MO, DA, YR, MDY)

Input conditions: MO is a month
                      DA is a day
                      YR is a year

Output conditions: MDY is the value of month, day, and year packed into three characters in numeric format.

READIT— READ IT (where IT is an input image from card or keyboard terminal)

Calling sequence: CALL READIT

Input conditions: None

Output conditions: LINE, a 14 word array in COMMON, contains the line image read in, MFLAG also in common, is equal to
                          7 if column 1 is blank
                          6 if column 1 is *
                          5 if column 1 is $
                          4 if column 1 is -
                          3 if column 1 is +

2 if column 1 is /
1 otherwise.

SADIC—   Search and Add to DICtionary if not present

Calling sequence: CALL SADIC (DICTN, DEFNTN, ID)

Input conditions: DICTN is the number of the definition table (dictionary) which is to be searched for DEFNTN, whose contents is a definition.

Output conditions: 1.   If the definition is found in the specified definition table, ID is the identification number of that definition table.

                       2.   If the definition is not found, it is added to the table, and the header is updated to reflect the updated number of definitions.

                       3.   If the definition is not found and the table is full, a value of 0 is returned as the ID.

SDIC—   Search DICtionary

Calling sequence: CALL SDIC (DICTN, DEFNTN, ID, INDEX)

Input conditions: Same as SADIC.

Output conditions: ID is the identification number of the definition if it is found in the table. INDEX is the actual index into the table where the definition begins (not necessarily the same as ID). If not found, ID = 0.

START1— MICA Initialization-Termination

Calling sequence: CALL START1

Input conditions: None

Output conditions: 1.   All Dictionaries and File headers are read from disk to core.

2.   All Dictionaries and File headers written from core to disk.

START2— File header definition

Calling sequence: CALL START2

Input conditions: None

Output conditions: Contents of all file headers are set to user specified values.

UPACKD— UnPACK Date

Calling sequence: CALL UPACKD (MO, DA, YR, MDY)

Input conditions: MDY is the value of a month, day and year packed into 3 characters in numeric format.

Output conditions: MO is the month
DA is the day
YR is the year

VERT— Virtual Memory

Calling sequence: CALL VERT

Input conditions: One copy of VERT required for each random access file desired.

Output conditions: Record numbers are converted to mass storage locations and records are read or written via direct access on the drums or disks.

Note: This routine was written in UNIVAC 1108 symbolic assembly language to provide a direct access capability.

Programming Languages

The ground rules for writing the MICA software were that the programming was to be done in the FORTRAN IV subset of UNIVAC FORTRAN V; and whenever non-subset language features were to be used, they should be identified by comment cards or isolated in a subroutine. However, there were two major deviations from the FORTRAN IV subset. First, due to the character manipulation requirements of the program, use was made of the FLD function to extract 6-bit characters from the 36-bit computer words. This function appears primarily within the utility subroutines. Second, the FORTRAN-V compiler available under the UNIVAC executive system (EXEC-8) had a serious design defect, since it treated all files whether on drum, disk, or tape as sequential tape files. An interactive data base management system based upon sequential file searching would have been so slow and expensive as to preclude developing the MICA system. The VERT program, written by Mr. Paul Stevens of the University of Wisconsin Computing Center, provided a virtual memory capability via direct access to drums or disks, thus circumventing the defect. VERT was of necessity written in symbolic assembly language and, therefore, is unique to the UNIVAC 1100 series computer. The structure of MICA is such that the programmer essentially doesn't know VERT is used, as all file accesses are via subroutines written in FORTRAN. Thus, VERT could easily be replaced by other direct access techniques on other computers. A detailed examination of the listing of the MICA-3 program will reveal other FORTRAN V features that have crept into the software. These ground rule violations constitute a management failure on the part of the author.

Additional Development of MICA Software

During the 1973-74 school year a number of operational deficiencies in the Sherman School instructional model were exposed (see Chapter Four for a detailed account). The major design changes were to automate the prescribing process and to use a teacher aide rather than a teacher as the terminal operator. To accomplish this, a number of minor changes were made to the prescription module. The prescriptions in the prescription file were assumed to be rank ordered in terms of their utility. The prescription module was modified to automatically select the highest ranked prescription. An option was provided through which the operator could select explicit prescriptions. The sequence numbers used in the selection process were replaced in the menu display by the prescription's dictionary index number. A fast prescribe mode was implemented where the prescription menu was not displayed and the "best" prescription was automatically assigned by the prescription module. Upon completion of the prescription process, the prescription module prints a "tear-off" sheet for the student. The /A command was added to the job control language to allow the quiz teacher to select additional prescriptions to be added to a pupil's student history file record under the current unit. Since the prescription module is used, the procedures are similar. The major new feature was the appearance of an asterisk before any prescription already assigned. A fast and slow mode were also implemented for these procedures. The /S command was added to provide the terminal operator some flexibility. Under this command, a REST option allowed the operator to leave the room for more than five minutes without the terminal loosing its telephone connection due to a "time-out." The TALLY option caused a printed summary of the day's transactions to be printed. The number of times each of the job control language commands were used, the number of accesses to each file, and the number of each type of report generated were printed. This same summary was printed when the /@ command was used to terminate a run. The file backup procedures were changed to rely upon the computing center's daily file dump tapes. Internally, the "check-point" procedure was implemented and coupled with the fast prescribe procedures to provide sufficient protection against computer storage failures. Although the basic structure of the program was unchanged, a sufficient number of small changes were made to allow the teacher aide to be the terminal operator. The resulting program was designated MICA-4.

The major software development efforts during the 1974-75 school year were devoted to solving the multiple current unit and multiple school problems in order to enable MICA to become a medium-scale CMI program. The original MICA conceptualization was that of a single curriculum managed via a single computer terminal. The success of the first year of the Sherman School project was such that a number of other schools wanted to use the computer both for the mathematics program and for other subject areas. The basic design of MICA, the UNIVAC FORTRAN V used to implement it, and the operating system, EXEC-8, was such that each computer terminal required a separate copy of the MICA program in the computer, although the files could be shared. Such an approach is both expensive and not a good use of computer resources. Fortunately, in the Fall of 1974 UNIVAC made an early version of the ASCII FORTRAN available. The ASCII FORTRAN has two features which made it ideal for programming CMI programs. First, it has the capability to directly access mass storage devices such as drums or disks—thus correcting the deficiency of FORTRAN V resulting from the magnetic tape orientation. Second, the ASCII FORTRAN generates reentrant object code, enabling a large number of computer terminals to employ a single copy of the MICA program. The ASCII FORTRAN immediately solved the direct access problem, eliminating need for the symbolic assembly level VERT routines. The ability to generate reentrant object code eliminated the multiple program problem and would minimize storage costs in a multi-school environment. Because of these features, a decision was made to redesign MICA to take advantage of these features and make the transition to a multi-curriculum, multi-school, medium-scale CMI system. To accomplish this, design changes were needed in four areas. First, in order to handle more than one subject matter area, the capability for a student to have more than one active instructional unit was needed. Achieving this capability would require changes to the design of all of the MICA modules except the Controller. Second, instructional models other than the Sherman School mathematics model were to be supported. A number of these employed dynamic instructional groups. Consequently, a capability to create and store data, and to report by instructional groups was needed. Again, the design of the major modules would be affected. Third, incorporation of the preceding changes as well as technical considerations dictated that the data base be redesigned. The primary technical considerations were to reduce the number of file buffers used in core memory, reduce the number of cross-file linkages needed to collect data, and make it possible for a number of schools to share a common data base. These requirements were met by merging the prescription file and the prescription definition table at the expense of large disk file records. Restructuring the prescription file in this manner would allow a single file to be shared by several schools employing a common curriculum. It also makes it possible to contain several different subject matter areas within a common prescription file. The student data file and the student history file were merged and then split into a current student history file and an archival student history file. The current student history file would greatly increase the efficiency with which actions dealing with a student's current instructional status could be processed. Since most of the reports relate to current instructional units, the efficiency of the report module would be improved. The redesign of these files also impacts the design of nearly all the MICA modules. Fourth, a planning capability was needed to enable teachers to develop sequences of units for individual students—a program of studies, in PLAN* terminology. A planning module would allow a sequence of eight units to be stored for each student. When a forward prescription was made, it would be according to this sequence. A message would be printed when the sixth unit in the sequence was assigned to alert the teacher of the need for a new list of units for the student. In addition to these four major areas, a large number of lesser changes were included in the MICA-5 design. These changes were aimed at making the computer program more flexible, able to handle groups of students as well as individual students, and able to cope with a greater variety of curricular plans and instructional models. An extensive set of file editing capabilities were also added to allow the terminal operator to make changes in the dynamic files as faulty information was encountered. To simplify the processing of tests, a module was included to perform test scoring using input from an optical scanner. A DATUM 5098 mark reader was to be used to input multiple-choice test results and unit objective missed lists. The use of the desk top optical scanner would automate one of the last of the manual procedures in the original Sherman School Mathematics Program.

The major restructuring of the MICA program had its impact primarily at the programming level. The procedures employed by the terminal operator were those of MICA-4, with the addition of new features and capabilities. However, these were all incorporated within the basic MICA operational framework. Numerous small changes in the size of tables, buffers, and arrays would also be needed to change the basic capacities in terms of the number of students, units, groups, and schools needed by a medium-scale CMI system. At the time this chapter was written, MICA-5 was in the final check-out stages, with the final documentation in preparation. The overall capabilities of MICA-5 are considerable, and it should prove to be a very useful CMI computer program.

Summary

The preceding discussion of the MICA software system was intended to illustrate the magnitude of the software conceptualization, design, documentation, and implementation effort required by CMI. Although MICA is operationally very simple, such simplicity is deceiving. A major software effort was required to achieve the simplicity. The basic impression the reader should acquire is that development of such software should not be taken lightly. In the present case, six months were devoted to conceptualization and design, but only six weeks to actual programming and check-out of MICA-1. In addition, it has been refined over a four-year period, leading to the "state of the art" version, MICA-5. The impact of the early emphasis upon conceptualization rather than implementation has paid off handsomely. Despite the MICA software system being sophisticated with respect to CMI software, it does not push the state of the art from a programming point of view. Well-known techniques, such as index sequential, file headers, etc., have been employed in a straightforward manner. None of the programmers involved have employed "tricky" or "cute" programming techniques to meet the design requirements. The lack of such practices has greatly facilitated the modifications and extension efforts. Another significant factor in the development of MICA has been the insistence upon a high level of documentation, both before and after software implementation. These efforts have also provided returns with respect to software reliability. Only a few situations have been encountered in the life span of the MICA program where a system failure was due to errors in the software. The history of the MICA computer program also illustrates the dynamic nature of CMI software and the need for some generality in the basic design. A CMI computer program must be able to adapt to changing requirements, improved procedures, and deeper insights in order to support instructional management. The MICA program has performed well in this regard. Over the years a large number of changes have been incorporated into the MICA software without disturbing the basic design or the day-to-day operational usage. The versions of MICA-1 to MICA-4 vary only in detail, not basic design. Only when it was decided to support multiple curricula and multiple schools did the underlying design prove to be limited. MICA was conceptualized as a small-scale CMI system for a single subject matter area. Consequently, some major changes were necessary to provide a medium-scale CMI capability. However, even MICA-5 employs the basic concepts developed by the students who created MICA-1, illustrating the soundness of the underlying concepts.

The pattern of development also shows the need for a consistent level of high-quality programming support to design and implement the software needed to keep the computer program current. In a very real sense, the computer program is never finished; it grows, adapts, and becomes more sophisticated in parallel with the other five CMI components. Only when there is a well-conceptualized underlying design can the software keep pace with its environment.

Chapter Six

The Educational Component of CMI

The introduction of a management information system into the instructional setting has an impact upon each of the four educational components of CMI. The primary focus of this impact is evident in the emergence of the concept of the teacher as a manager. As was indicated in previous chapters, the role of the teacher in instructional management is not well defined in existing CMI systems. However, development of an adequate conceptualization of the teacher as a manager is crucial to the long-term viability of CMI. Consequently, the bulk of the present chapter is devoted to examining the teacher as a manager. Less attention will be devoted to the relation of CMI to curricular issues and to diagnosis and prescription.

The Teacher as a Manager

Despite the early recognition of the managerial aspects of teaching, the concept of a teacher as a manager is not well formulated. In the classroom, the teacher is both an educational delivery vehicle and the manager of an instructional system. In the former role, lectures are given, pupils are shown how to perform various tasks, etc. In the latter role, the teacher sets goals, monitors each pupil's progress toward those goals, and allocates resources to the pupils. In addition, the teacher performs other functions, ranging from supervising of pencil sharpening to evaluation of curriculum in the various subject matter areas.

During the course of a school day, a teacher performs many different instructional and managerial functions, and the boundaries between them are indistinct. In the traditional instructional setting, this lack of distinction is of minimal importance. However, the existence of the computer and reporting components in a CMI system results in a much sharper distinction between a teacher's instructional and managerial roles. A common observation made by teachers and administrators after the introduction of CMI in a school is that it has resulted in a considerable emphasis upon the managerial aspects of the teacher's role. Despite this recognition, the concept of the teacher as a manager has proven very troublesome for the field of CMI, from both the point of view of the teachers and the CMI implementer. The former have been thrust into an expanded role with little preparation for the role. The latter have a limited idea of the managerial goals and functions to be supported by computer-based services. Because the concept is ill-defined, CMI systems have floundered rather badly once they have provided the immediate clerical level support services, such as test scoring, data collection, data storage, and rudimentary status reports. In addition, most CMI system implementers have been hard pressed to select a direction for future development. Thus, unless some clarification of the teacher's role as a manager can be provided, CMI will stagnate at or near its present level of development, as did CAI after its initial burst of development.

The obvious place to turn for assistance in developing a fuller concept of the teacher as a manager is the field of management theory. One would hope that the management theories developed in the commercial and industrial environment could provide the ideas, concepts, functions, and principles that could be adapted to the educational setting. The field of management theory, like modern educational theory, originated around the turn of the century. There is even a certain degree of parallelism between the development of educational theory and management theory that will be of interest. A full and detailed presentation of management theory is well beyond the scope of the present Chapter, and the reader is referred to George (1972), *The History of Management Thought*, for an excellent review of the field. However, a brief synopsis of the field of management theory is presented below to provide a context for the discussion of the teacher as a manager.

According to Minor (1971) the state of development of management theory has reached the point where there are a number of different schools of management thought, each with its own beliefs and adherents. The number of names of these schools depends upon the particular author reviewing the field. George (1972) lists the following schools of management theory: Scientific Management, Behavioral, Management Process, and Quantitative. Minor (1971, p. 145) lists the following schools: Classical, Human Relations, Structuralist, Behavioral Humanist, and Decision Making. Although the labels applied to the schools vary, the principle architects of the various schools are the same. The two schools of immediate interest are: Scientific Management and Classical. George (1972) considers these to be separate schools, calling the latter Management Process, while Minor (1971) merges them under the classical label. For present purposes they shall be treated as separate schools.

Scientific Management

The Scientific Management school originated in the pioneering work of Frederic W. Taylor, and was defined in his book, *Principles of Scientific Management* (Taylor, 1911). Taylor had been an engineer with various steel companies, beginning with the Midvale Steel Company where he rose from pattern maker in 1874 to chief engineer in 1884. He was an astute observer and quickly recognized numerous failings in factory operations. Principally, he noted that no standards existed for either performing various tasks or for the amount of output expected of workers, and that management decisions were based upon experience or rule-of-thumb rather than data. The era was also one of considerable labor strife, with force being the primary managerial tool. Within this context, Taylor conducted experiments ranging from techniques for cutting metal, procedures for handling material, to time and motion studies, over a period of many years. The important facet was that he was interested in better ways of performing factory operations, and he attacked the problems via a systematic, empirical approach. The final outcome of many years of such experimentation was expressed as a set of principles of management based upon the methods of scientific inquiry. Taylor's four principles of management were:

First: Develop a science for each element of a man's work, which replaces the old rule-of-thumb method.

Second: Scientifically select, and then train, teach, and develop the workman, whereas in the past he chose his own work and trained himself as best he could.

Third: Heartily cooperate with the men so as to insure all of the work being done in accordance with the principles of the science which has been developed.

Fourth: There is an almost equal division of the work and the responsibility between management and the workmen. The management takes over all work for which they are better fitted than the workmen, while in the past almost all of the work and the greater part of the responsibility were thrown upon the men. (Taylor, 1911, pp. 36-37).

In addition to enunciating these four principles of management, Taylor also developed the mechanisms for putting them into operation. He was quite careful to distinguish between his principles of scientific management and the mechanics of management. He originated many of the now standard procedures for task analysis, inventory control, and management reporting. The key mechanisms employed by Taylor to improve production were the following: He would perform a task analysis of a particular job, breaking it down into its component parts and determining how each contributed to the job. The result of the analysis would be a redesign of the job so that greater productivity would be achieved. He would also select workers who showed some aptitude for performing the particular job. Once this was done, he would establish standards for the output to be achieved by the worker using the new job methods. He was a strong believer in incentive payments; the workers who could achieve greater output than standard would receive higher pay. Superimposed upon this was a recognition that the worker needed supervision. Taylor developed what he called functional foremen. A worker might report to several different foremen, each a specialist in a particular aspect of the job being performed.

Compared to the productivity achieved by traditional management procedures, factories employing "Scientific Management" achieved dramatically higher output levels. Because of its demonstrable gains, Scientific Management soon became the dominant management philosophy of the early 1900's, and its impact upon management practice is still important. Probably the greatest deficiency of Scientific Management was its treating of the worker as an object. Although Taylor selected workers, trained them, and relieved them of unnecessary management responsibilities, he did so only to improve productivity. The worker was considered an extension of the machine, whose primary motivation was monetary. Thus, his call to management for improved working conditions, less physical fatigue, and allowing each man to develop to his fullest potential was rooted in a desire to increase productivity rather than humanitarian concerns. The crucial aspect of Taylor's work was the establishment of standards both in terms of how the work was to be done and for the amount of output. These standards also included a means for determining whether the worker met the standards.

The Classical School

The founder of the classical school of management is generally considered to be Henry Fayol, who was the managing director of the Commentry mine pits of the S.A. Commentry

Fourchamboult. His book on management, *Administration Industrielle et Generale,* was published in France in 1916. An English edition was published in Great Britain in 1929, but did not attract attention in the United States until it was republished in 1949 under the title, *General and Industrial Management.* Although Fayol's ideas were developed around the turn of the century, they did not have their major impact upon American management thought until much later. Massie (1965) states that "Fayol has been looked upon as the pioneer in administrative theory by most writers in the classical tradition." George (1972) credits Fayol with the "first comprehensive statement of a general theory of management." Due to the rather belated discovery of Fayol's work by American writers, his ideas were in a sense retrofitted into their management thought.

Whereas Taylor's Scientific Management had its origins in the shops and was primarily concerned with the lower levels of management, Fayol's experience was at the highest levels of management of a large corporation. Consequently, Fayol viewed management from a much larger perspective than did Taylor. In addition, he believed that management was universal and was basically the same whether an industry, a school, or a unit of government was being managed. Fayol expressed his view of management via five functions and 14 principles. The five functions were: (a) planning, which consisted of considering the future and establishing a plan of action to cope with the future; (b) organization, which involved the creation of a structure for the enterprise to enable it to achieve its objectives; (c) command, which was the execution of plans; (d) coordination, which consisted of unifying the activity and efforts of all those in the organization; and (e) controlling, or insuring that tasks were accomplished in accordance to the plans. Massie (1965) has indicated that the emphasis upon structure within the definition of an organization has become a major characteristic of all classical management theory.

One of the characteristics of early theorists, in both

management and education, was the propensity for defining principles. Some authors viewed their principles as immutable laws. Fayol, however, viewed his management principles more in the sense of flexible guidelines to be applied as the situation demanded. Briefly stated, his 14 principles were:

(1) Division of work
(2) Authority and responsibility
(3) Discipline
(4) Unity of command
(5) Unity of direction
(6) Subordination of individual interest to general interest
(7) Remuneration
(8) Centralization
(9) Scalar chain, i.e.: the line of authority
(10) Order
(11) Equity
(12) Stability of tenure of personnel
(13) Initiative
(14) Esprit de Corps

Most of these principles are self-evident. However, several are keys to Fayol's overall view of management. He was a strong believer in an explicit chain of command, with each individual reporting to only one person at a higher level of management. In this, he differed sharply with Taylor, who proposed that a worker have many, up to eight, supervisors. According to Massie (1965), the ideas of unity of command, scalar chain, and specialization were central to Fayol's thinking. Another facet of Fayol's approach was that he was quite flexible in the manner in which various elements and principles were to be employed. He emphasized that their use was a "matter of proportion."

A large number of other persons have contributed to the development of classical management theory, some working in parallel with Fayol and others building upon his work. The article by Massie (1965) is a good summary of this work as well as an excellent statement of the status of classical management theory.

A number of principles defined by the early writers have become basic principles in current classical theory (Massie, 1965). These are the scalar principle, unity of command, exception principle, span of control, organizational specialization, and the profit center. As was discussed above, the scalar principle is the basis for the hierarchical management structure. Under the scalar principle, there should be a clear, unbroken line from the company president to the lowest level worker. The modern emphasis upon the line and box organization charts used by industry and government to represent their management structures stems from the application of the scalar principle. Unity of command was originally conceptualized to mean that no one person should receive orders from more than one superior. However, in practice this is unobtainable, so that many qualifications to the principle have been added to make it workable. The exception principle is based upon the idea that the routine functioning of an organization should be delegated to subordinates. Only those important issues or exceptional items should be reported to superiors. Thus, only exceptional conditions are managed by higher level managers. This principle is widely employed as the basis for management reporting practices, and many computer-based management information systems implement management by exception reports. Span of control delimits the number of persons reporting to a given level manager. Span of control within a management hierarchy is important, as it defines the network of relationships existing among the managers. Massie (1965) reports that span of control remains one of the focal points of controversy between classical management and other emerging theories. Organizational specialization stemmed originally from Taylor, although others have extended the concept to higher levels of management. A task analysis of a company results in the departmentalization of a company into homogeneous units, with the dimensions upon which the departmentalization is based depending upon the nature of the company. The basic idea is that each department performs a specialized function, such as sales, production, accounting, etc., within the organization. Such departmentalization, coupled with the scalar principle, tends to simplify management. The profit center idea was not among Fayol's concepts, having been developed by Alfred P. Sloan, for use by General Motors Corporation. The basic idea was that very large corporations should be composed of essentially self-contained subunits. Each of these units in turn operates as a separate company attempting to maximize its profits. The concept facilitates the management of large companies by allowing top management to perform Fayol's five functions at the profit center level. Many city school systems have adopted the profit center idea under the guise of decentralized administration. One supplementary concept incorporated by some classical theorists is that of accountability. According to Massie (1965) it is "the obligation to carry out responsibility and exercise authority in terms of established performance standards." In the late 1960's and early 1970's governmental bureaucracies dealing with education discovered accountability, and instituted far ranging and often ludicrous schemes for achieving accountability within the educational domain.

Classical management theory appears to be the predominant school of management with respect to actual practice. In regard to theory building, it has a number of limitations. The principles of classical theory were developed upon philosophical grounds often based upon the experience of actual managers. Because of this, the classical approach does not meet the requirements of a theory in a scientific sense and its principles have been attacked on a number of grounds, chiefly their "arm chair" nature and unstated basic assumptions. That classical thought does not constitute a tight theory is not surprising, since its architects did not have theory building in mind. The second criticism of classical theory is its limited concern for the individual. Classical theory does not take into consideration what today would be called the sociological and psychological aspects of management. In one sense, classical management theory has been concerned with the mechanics of viable organization, but not with the people who manage or are managed.

Other than the quantitative school, none of the other schools of management listed by George (1972) or Minor (1971) are as clearly defined. These other schools arose primarily in reaction to the dehumanized nature of management based upon Scientific Management and the classical school. Like their predecessors, these later schools tend to be rather loosely structured and based upon the work of particular persons. These schools have drawn heavily upon the work of psychologists, primarily in the field of industrial relations, and upon sociologists. The emphasis is upon the psychological needs of workers and upon the social structure of the industrial environment. These schools have made important contributions to management thought, especially in regard to changing the view of the worker as an extension of the machine and in the area of management's interpersonal relationships with workers. The development of these schools must be put in the context of labor relations of the period 1920-1940, when labor unions gained their present status and power.

The quantitative school has its origins in an entirely different line of development, stemming from the operations research groups developed during World War II. These groups were interdisciplinary teams of engineers, military officers, physicists, psychologists, etc. They attacked a given problem, such as the development of RADAR, from many points of view simultaneously. The emphasis was upon developing quantitative models to represent the operations involved. These models could then be manipulated in various ways to determine the resultant outcomes. The quantitative school has also relied heavily upon the fields of probability and statistics for techniques upon which to base decision making. In contrast to the early schools of management, that were based upon the experience of managers, the quantitative school had its origins in the academic world with sophisticated mathematical and statistical techniques being applied to management problems. Crucial to this school is the capability to measure and express important variables in quantitative terms.

There is an interesting corollary between the fields of

education and management in terms of the role of theory. In both fields there are large numbers of practitioners (managers and teachers) who conduct the affairs of companies and schools on a day-to-day basis. These persons are highly pragmatic and use whatever management techniques they find will work in their situation. In both fields, there are theorists who are attempting to formulate the basic nature of the processes underlying what managers and teachers do. These theorists are interested in understanding the phenomena and advancing the field. Unfortunately, the teachers and managers have little interest in research, (too remote) or in theory (too little practical value). The practitioners also devote little, if any, time to reading professional literature. The net result is that the direct impact of theory upon practice is very difficult to ascertain on a short-term basis. However, significant changes in practice in both fields take place over the long term. Whether theory leads or follows these changes is not always clear.

Relation of Management Theory
and Education

Of the several schools of management theory, only Scientific Management has had any significant impact upon the field of education. Schools of management thought such as the Behavioral (George, 1972), Human Relations, Structuralist and Behavioral Humanist (Minor, 1971) have their roots in the behavioral sciences of which education is a part. Because of the unique relationship between a teacher and pupils, education has a strong tradition in the behavioral sciences. As a result, much of what these behavioral schools of management were trying to achieve in the business world was already a part of the educational environment. In many respects, educational thought led management thought in these areas, although there is considerable parallelism. The parallelism results from both fields sharing the research and theories developed in psychology and sociology. However, the impact of new developments in these two fields is much more immediate in the field of education than in management, due to the practitioners in the former having a behavioral science orientation. The quantitative school of management also lags development in the field of education. Since the turn of the century, education has had a strong quantitative tradition. Work of pioneers such as Rice (1897) and Thorndike (1903) established a strong interest in the role of measurement and quantitative methods. Again, many of the goals of the quantitative school have long been a part and parcel of education. In recent years, there has been considerable cross fertilization with the educational measurement techniques being used in management research and the techniques of operations research being used in education. Nonetheless, the quantitative tradition in education precedes the quantitative school of management by one or more generations.

The major impact of management thought upon education was made by Scientific Management. This impact has been two-fold, first in the area of educational administration, and second in the instructional area. The book *Education and the Cult of Efficiency* by Callahan (1962) presents a thorough documentation of the impact of Scientific Management upon both practice and theory in public school administration. He credits two persons, Frank Spaulding and Franklin Bobbitt, as being the most influential in applying Taylor's Scientific Management to education. Spaulding's contribution was in the area of administration of public schools. Bobbitt's was in the explicit conceptualization of the school as a factory. During the first decade of the present century the public schools were under severe attack from the press, politicians, and businessmen for being poorly managed (see Callahan, 1962, Chapter 3, for a detailed presentation of these attacks). The field of educational administration was in its formative years and was not sufficiently mature or organized to counter these attacks. Simultaneously, Taylor's Scientific Management had made a dramatic impact upon the productivity and efficiency of industry and was widely advocated as the management panacea. It was no wonder that the school administrators turned to Scientific Management as a vehicle for countering these attacks. The year 1913 appears to be a critical year in education: Spaulding's address to the annual meeting of the Department of Superintendence of the National Education Association, and Bobbitt's article appeared in the twelfth yearbook of the National Society for the Study of Education. Both dealt with the application of Scientific Management to education, although from different points of view. Spaulding (1913) began by defining the products or results of the educational system—the average daily attendance of pupils, average length of time required for a pupil to complete a unit of work, and the quality of the education a school provides. The latter was essentially defined in terms of academic achievement in the various subject matter areas. He then compared schools differing in "quality of education" in terms of cost per pupil and investment per pupil. He also presented extensive comparisons of various subject matter offerings in terms of their cost per pupil recitation and the number of pupil recitations per dollar. Thus, he was able to compare the various academic subjects on a cost basis. Callahan (1962, p. 73) states: "Spaulding's concept of scientific management obviously amounted to an analysis of the budget. By a study of local considerations he meant a study of the per pupil costs and pupil recitation costs. His scientific determination of educational value turned out to be a determination of dollar value. His decisions of what should be taught were made not on educational but upon financial grounds." In later chapters, Callahan traced the impact of Spaulding's conceptualizations of Scientific Management upon both the nature of the public school superintendency and upon the training of school superintendents. In essence, the impact was to change the role of the superintendent from that of an educator with a strong interest in the process of education, to that of a business manager, interested in unit costs. What Spaulding and the several generations of school administrators who followed him had done was to adopt the mechanics of Taylor's approach without comprehending the underlying philosophy based upon scientific inquiry. Thus, to increase the efficiency of the schools, i.e., lower costs, one simply increases the number of students per teacher, invests less in physical plant, etc., and achieves minimal "unit costs." The unfortunate heritage of this aspect of Scientific Management can be seen in most communities where the superintendent's annual report is primarily financial, and little attention is given to educational issues.

While Spaulding seized upon Taylor's principles of Scientific Management to reduce education to financial terms, Bobbitt used them to convert the school into an educational factory. The basic theme of Bobbitt's (1913) paper was one of speculation on how the principles of Scientific Management could be employed by managers and supervisors in education. Central to this speculation was the concept of the teacher as a worker, and of building principals and school superintendents as management. In keeping with the times, Bobbitt (1913) specified 11 general principles of management and supervision that had universal applicability. For the first seven principles he provided examples of how they would function within the educational context. The final four principles were stated without elaboration. The first two principles deal with standards and were to be applied to pupils.

Principle I.. Definite qualitative and quantitative standards must be determined for the product.

Principle II. Where the material that is acted upon by the labor process passes through a number of progressive stages on its way from the raw material to the ultimate product. Definite qualitative and quantitative standards must be determined for the product at each of these stages.

He then used the production of steel rails for railroads as an example of how a product is manufactured to exact specifications. Like modern writers, he then used elementary school arithmetic to show how one could establish educational standards. He suggested that "the ability to add at a speed of 65 combinations per minute, with an accuracy of 94 percent, is a definite specification, as can be set up for any aspect of the work of a steel plant" (Bobbitt,

1913, pp. 11-15). He also recognized that if standards were to be established, scales of measurement would be needed to determine if the standards had been met. Standards were also a double edged sword, as Bobbitt (pp. 27-28) felt that teachers and building principals could be evaluated on the basis of how well their students met the established standards. Like modern authors, Bobbitt hedged a bit when it came to subject matter areas such as social studies, where a specific product is more difficult to define. The question of who establishes the standards was answered by Bobbitt by analogy with industry. He believed that it was a factory customer who determined the specifications of products. Hence, specification of the educational products did not belong in the hands of educators, but were the responsibility of society and of business and industry in particular. However, he did allow that educators would be needed to translate the general specifications of what industry wanted in terms of bookkeepers, accountants, etc., into precise educational standards—thus reducing educators to the role of educational engineer. Like Spaulding, he also employed Scientific Management to affect the financial side of education. He stated: "We cannot standardize teaching costs until we standardize the teaching product. The school that secures the greatest amount of product for the money is the most economical school." The section on standards was summarized by Bobbitt as follows: "(1) As a foundation for all scientific direction and supervision of labor in the field of education, we need first to draw up in detail for each social or vocational class of students in our charge a list of all the abilities and aspects of personality for the training of which the school is responsible. (2) Next we need to determine the scales of measurement in terms of which these many different aspects of personality can be measured. (3) We must determine the amount of training that is socially desirable for each of these different abilities, and state these amounts in terms of the scales of measurement. (4) We must have progressive standards of attainment for each stage of advance in the normal development of each ability in question. When these four sets of things are at hand for each differentiated social or vocational class, then we shall have for the first time a scientific curriculum worthy of our present age of science." It should be noted that Bobbitt did not call for the same standards for all pupils. He also recognized that standards needed to be relative to where a pupil was within the curriculum. He was, however, quite explicit that standards and a means of comparing pupils against these standards were necessary. The second section of Bobbitt's article was devoted to methods, and involved only a single principle.

Principle III. Scientific management finds the methods or procedures which are the most efficient for actual service under actual conditions, and secures their use on the part of the workers.

This principle comes directly from Taylor's work on finding the best methods for performing a particular job. Once such a method was discovered via experimentation, then it was the job of management to insure that the method was used. Bobbitt proposed that a staff in a school district's central office, called the planning department, should establish such methods, rather than the teachers. Having the latter develop the methods was against Taylor's fourth principle, on the separation of management and worker responsibilities; besides, it was too complicated for teachers. Once the staff of the central office had established such methods, all teachers would be required to use them, as they were the most efficient method.

The next three principles stemmed directly from Taylor's second principle, dealing with the selection and training of workers.

Principle IV. Standard qualifications must be determined for the workers.

Principle V. The management must train its workers previous to service in the measure demanded by its standard qualifications, or it must set up entrance requirements of so specific and detailed a nature as to enforce upon training institutions the output of a supply of workers possessing the desirable qualifications in the degree necessary for entrance into service—competency-based education in today's jargon.

Principle VI. The worker must be kept up to standard qualifications for his kind of work during his entire service.

These three principles were aimed at the teacher as a worker, rather than at the pupils. Bobbitt explained that the characteristics of workers in each occupation were different: a jockey should be small, a policeman brawny, and a lawyer keen and alert. Thus, teachers should have qualifications. He recognized the qualifications of a primary grade level teacher were different from those of a high school teacher. He stated: "The nature of the work and the methods to be employed point out the qualities of personality that should be possessed by the worker." He used the term personality in a broader sense than is the current use of the word. He felt academic standards for teachers were well established but that personality criteria for teachers were also needed. Such standards were to be empirically based, much in the same way that Taylor had determined specifications for the qualifications of workers in a bicycle factory. The fifth principle was a call by Bobbitt for schools to define a standard product, which the teacher training institutions would then produce. He felt public schools devoted too much time bringing the graduates of teacher training institutions up to the level of performance needed by the schools.* Consequently, if the schools could establish standards and the teacher training institutions produced teachers to these standards, the schools would be assured a supply of well-trained workers. Principle VI recognized that even initially well-trained teachers would eventually become outdated and that initial training does not develop skills to their optimum level. Therefore, he proposed that teachers have the opportunity to exercise aspects of the "standard" teacher's personality and to organize and control incentives. The former was described in terms that today would be called "inservice training" for teachers. The theme

---

*It should be noted that the majority of elementary school teachers at this point in time had only one or two years of "normal school" training beyond high school.

underlying these three principles was that well-qualified, well-prepared, and continuously trained teachers would be more efficient and productive workers than those who were not. Borrowing from Taylor's bonus plan, he proposed that teachers who used the standard methods and secured maximum results should be rewarded by increased salaries, professional promotion, and social recognition.

The last major principle was concerned with the problem of getting teachers to carry out the instructions of school administrators.

Principle VII. The worker must be kept supplied with detailed instructions as to the work to be done, the standards to be reached, the methods to be employed, and the appliances to be used.

Bobbitt was a bit ambivalent with respect to the application of this principle. On the one hand, he called for teaching to employ only those best methods and appliances to achieve the stated educational standards. On the other, he felt that even within these methods, the teachers could work out the details for themselves. He did not want a method to be applied in a lockstep manner in all schools, since he recognized that individual differences existed among children and among schools. Yet, he did not allow a teacher to deviate too far from the methods produced by the planning office. His ambivalence was limited to methods; in the areas of the work to be done and educational standards, he was firm.

In his principles, Bobbitt had essentially applied Taylor's work to education. Through his article, Bobbitt showed how the school could be modeled after the machine shop or factory. He indicated that schools could achieve as dramatic an improvement in productivity as had the shops, if the school were operated on this factory model and administered via Scientific Management. While Spaulding's impact was upon school administrators, who quickly adopted a cost accounting approach to education, Bobbitt's contribution was to reduce education to a very mechanistic procedure with teachers as workers in the educational factory and administrators as management. As we shall see below, Bobbitt's article has had a profound effect upon curriculum theory that continues up to the present time.

Kliebard (1971) has examined the impact of Scientific Management upon curriculum theory. He showed that the immediate consequence of Scientific Management theory upon curriculum was in the area of standards. Since students should be prepared for very specific occupational roles, Bobbitt had called for standards to be established by business and industry. Thus, specific curricula should be designed to produce "products" i.e., students who would be capable of fulfilling these roles. The result was highly differentiated curricula based upon a student's vocational plans. Kliebard (1971) stated: "Educate the individual according to his capabilities has an innocent and plausible ring; but what this meant in practice was that dubious judgments about the innate capabilities of children become the basis for differentiating the curriculum along the lines of probable destination for the child. Dominated by the criterion of social utility, those judgments become self-fulfilling prophecies in the sense that they predetermined which slots in the social order would be filled by which class of individuals." Although this curricular philosophy waned after World War II, it still exists in the form of the "track" system employed by many schools. According to Kliebard (1971), the second aspect of the educational standards called for by Bobbitt had a much deeper impact upon curricular theory. If the schools were to produce standard products, then one must specify the characteristics of these products and the standard units of work by which these characteristics were achieved. Thus, if the schools were to produce a common laborer, there would be a specific set of skills and knowledge such a person would need to fulfill his role as a laborer and as a citizen. These would be achieved by having the student complete a set of standard units of work. By the 1920's Bobbitt was joined by others, such as W.W. Charters and David Snedden, who campaigned to reform the curriculum along the lines called for by the principles of Scientific Management. The concept of predetermination required that characteristics of occupational roles be defined very explicitly so that appropriate educational standards could be set. Charter's contribution was to show how to specify the requirements of an occupational role. The technique used was "activity analysis," where persons engaged in a role recorded what they actually did. These records were then analyzed and a curriculum designed to train persons to fulfill the role. The role studied by Charters was that of a woman, and he designed a curriculum for Stevens College that would provide "specific training for the specific job of being a woman" (Charters, 1926). Obviously, this was a project completed before the days of women's liberation and affirmative action. A side effect of this effort to define the occupational roles was the creation of a vast range of product diversification. To cope with the diversity, it was necessary to be even more explicit, to standardize the units of work needed to produce the products. It was in this area that Snedden (1925) contributed. Following the lead of Gilbreth and Gilbreth (1917), who developed a set of standard motions, Snedden defined standard curricular units. Like Gilbreth's standard motions, these could be combined in various ways to create a curriculum for a given vocation. The basic curriculum elements under Snedden's approach were very minute, such as a single spelling word. Clearly, Snedden's curricular approach is the intellectual forefather of what is now called the "Behavioral Objectives Movement."

Kliebard (1971) points out an interesting pattern in Bobbitt's writings. In his early writings (Bobbitt, 1913), he was a strong proponent of Scientific Management as the basis for curriculum theory. By 1926 (Bobbitt, 1926), he was beginning to express curriculum ideas that were at variance with the basic tenets; and by 1934 (Bobbitt, 1934), he had nearly completely rejected his earlier work. However, later curriculum theorists, especially those in the Behavioral Objectives Movement, neglected to note this reversal.

Although the school-as-a-factory metaphor declined during the 1930's, probably due to failure of the business-industrial model during the great depression, it has had a recent revival. Kliebard (1971) credits this second revival to the electronic revolution, to the central role of behaviorism in education, and to the survival of the 1920's doctrine of social efficiency. According to Kliebard, what has happened is that the concept of standardized units of work, now called behavioral objectives, has become permanent in the curriculum theories of the 1960's and 70's. He states: "Current curriculum practice seems to take the form of drawing up endless lists of minute design specifications in behavioral terms and then finding the right 'media mix' by which the product can be most efficiently manufactured." One of the characteristics of the behavioral objectives movement is that the success of instruction is based entirely on the factor of results, i.e., did the student achieve an arbitrarily defined level of mastery? Kliebard goes on to state: "Such a sharp dichotomy between ends and means is precisely what resulted from the introduction of the assembly lines in the first industrial revolution. Work became important only in so far as it was instrumental in achieving the desired product. The success of the assembly line depends upon the fact that it reduces the process of production to units so simple that the predicted outcome is assured." This criticism of behavioral objectives was recognized in a slightly different form by Krathwohl and Payne (1971), who admitted that behavioral objectives tend to become very concrete and deal only with the specifics of a subject matter area. Both Kliebard (1971) and Callahan (1962) concluded that under Scientific Management the child became the raw material of a school-factory turning out a standard product or products meeting the specifications of social convention.

One of the strange phenomena of the Behavioral Objectives Movement is that it does not admit its basis in Scientific Management. Writers such as Mager (1962), Popham (1969), Popham and Baker (1970), Tyler (1950), and Glaser (1967) do not cite Taylor, Bobbitt, or Snedden. These authors tend to treat behavioral objectives as a modern phenomenon arising out of a curriculum philosophy divorced from the work of Bobbitt and Snedden. That such is not the case can be shown quite easily. Since in actual practice, the behavioral objective becomes the standard unit of work, the criterion-referenced test the standard, the goal of education becomes one of having the student achieve mastery, i.e., meet the standard. Like the factory, proponents of behavioral objectives are interested only in outcomes. It is productivity that counts, not the process. Hence, any instructional process is acceptable, as long as it enables the student (worker) to master the behavioral objective (produce the product). As a result, many curricular plans based upon behavioral objectives also use instructional models based upon stimulus-response psychology. The latter tends to be mechanical in nature, with the student stepping through the instructional sequence with little thought as to what he is doing other than eventually meeting the criterion. Like Scientific Management, the student is simply an extension of a machine that methodically punches out a standard product.

Although Glaser (1967, 1969) does not relate his instructional model to the work of Taylor and Bobbitt, it is a modern explication of the school-as-a-factory model. To make this parallelism clear, each of the six points of Glaser's instructional model is related below to Scientific Management.

1. *"The goals of learning are specified in terms of observable student behavior and the conditions under which the behavior is to be exercised."*

A basic tenet of Scientific Management is that precise product specifications can be made. Glaser has essentially restated Bobbitt's first principle calling for definite qualitative and quantitative standards for a product.

2. *"Diagnosis is made of the initial capabilities with which the learner begins a particular course of instruction. The capabilities that are assumed are those relevant to the forthcoming instruction."*

Under Scientific Management, qualifications of workers for particular jobs were established. Workers who possessed these qualifications were then selected and assigned the jobs. Diagnosis is an integral part of determining which workers have the desired qualifications.

3. *"Educational alternatives adaptive to the initial profile of the student are presented to him. The student selects or is assigned one of these alternatives."*

Considerable emphasis is placed by Scientific Management upon using the best production methods. This part of Glaser's model, in essence, calls for the use of a production method corresponding to the capabilities of the student, thus fulfilling Bobbitt's third principle, calling for using the methods or procedures which are most efficient for actual service under actual conditions.

4. *"Student performance is maintained and continually assessed as the student proceeds to learn."*

This part of the model calls for procedures that are analogous to the quality assurance techniques applied to the production line. In the factory, data is collected and analyzed to insure products meeting specifications are produced and that the desired level of output is maintained.

5. *"Instruction proceeds as a function of the relationship between measures of student performance, available instructional alternatives, and criterion of competence."*

Glaser assumes there are a number of steps in the instructional sequence, each subject to management. This part of the model is analogous to Bobbitt's second principle, calling for definite qualitative and quantitative standards for the product at each stage of production. It is also a restatement of the basic idea that the best methods should be used as required by the conditions.

6. *"As instruction proceeds, data are generated for monitoring and improving the instructional system."*

The improvement of the production process via data collected during its operation was a key element in Taylor's approach. Under Scientific Management, very detailed records relating to all aspects of production were kept and used to maintain the factory. In addition, one continuously searched for better ways to produce a given product.

The basis of Glaser's instructional model (Glaser, 1967; Glaser and Rosner, 1975) is even more apparent when one examines its implementation in his "Individually Prescribed Instruction" project. Under IPI, much of the basic model, especially that dealing with pupil characteristics, is reduced to a minimum, and a clear production line approach is taken. The unit-of-instruction cycle described in Chapter Two becomes the predominant feature, and the students engage in a rather mechanical set of procedures centering on a standard unit of work. Under IPI, students spend a disproportionate amount of time on the mechanics of pretest, curriculum embedded tests, and posttests. The main focus of the student's efforts is aimed at achieving mastery on these criterion-referenced tests, i.e., producing a standard product.

Like Callahan (1962), Kliebard (1971) felt that the application of Scientific Management to education has had dire consequences. Kliebard (1971) concluded; "In education, as in industry, the standardization of the product also means the standardization of the work. Educational activity which may have an organic wholeness and vital meaning takes on significance only in terms of its contribution to the efficient production of the finished product. As in industry, the price of worship at the altar of efficiency is the alienation of the worker from his work—where the continuity and wholeness of the enterprise are destroyed for those who engage in it. Here, then, is one great threat that the production metaphor governing modern curriculum theory poses for American education. The bureaucratic model along with its behavioristic and technological refinements threatens to destroy the satisfaction that one may find in intellectual activity in the name of efficiency."

CMI and Scientific Management

All of the CMI systems described in Appendix A can be shown to make some use of the concepts and techniques of Scientific Management. However, the greatest use of the school-as-a-factory model is in CMI systems designed for use in training situations and in the elementary schools. CMI systems used in military training schools, such as the NAVY CMI system (Mayo, 1974) and AIS (Rockway and Yasutake, 1974), are explicitly based upon a production line philosophy and largely justify their cost on the basis of efficiency of production. Elementary school systems individualizing on the basis of rate of progress, such as IPI/IMS (Cooley and Glaser, 1968), PLAN* (Flanagan et al., 1975), and Sherman School (Chapin et al., 1975), are also production line schemes. In all of these CMI systems, a standard unit of work exists. This standard unit of work is typically a curricular unit composed of a number of behavioral objectives, and the curriculum consists of a number of these units. For each unit of work, a standard exists in the form of a criterion-referenced posttest that must be achieved by each student. Once assigned a unit of work, the student proceeds through the unit-of-instruction cycle until the standard product is produced, i.e., he or she achieves mastery on the posttest. The unit-of-instruction cycle is a closed loop feedback system allowing the student to iteratively produce the standard product. The pretest, curriculum embedded tests, and the diagnosis and prescription procedures serve only to bring the student's product up to the standard desired. When a standard product has been produced, the student acquires the next unit in the curricular plan, and repeats the production process. This basic unit-of-instruction cycle is repeated until all units have been produced at the set standards, or until the school year ends. Within this unit-of-instruction cycle the student is essentially the machine producing a standard product, and the teacher is the machine operator. At the instructional level of management, the teacher fulfills a role similar to the production line worker. The teacher provides the student with the raw materials, work sheets, books, etc., monitors the student via tests, and evaluates whether the standard product has been produced. When the student does not produce the standard product, the teacher uses diagnostic procedures to determine the problems, prescribes additional resources, and sets the student in motion again. This is analogous to making adjustments in a production machine or modifying the method used to produce the product. Like the fifth part of Glaser's instructional model, these procedures provide a degree of adaptation to the capabilities of the student, but the teacher is responsible for assuring that the student produces the standard product defined for each unit of work.

Due to the reliance upon individualization with respect to rate of progress, the CMI systems based upon the school-as-a-factory model place considerable emphasis upon throughput, i.e., number of units completed. This emphasis is analogous to productivity in the factory. Although the idea behind rate of progress schemes is to allow each student to proceed at his own rate, it is assumed progress will be made. Progress is defined as completing a unit. Hence, the course level of management in CMI systems is designed to manage throughput. The management emphasis is upon the number of units completed, the amount of time spent by a student on a unit, and the number of attempts needed to produce the standard product. The Program of Studies used by PLAN* enables the teacher to assign a sequence of units to a student and then to monitor the progress of the student relative to the assignment. The performance expectations used by WIS/SIM (Belt and Spuck, 1974) establish the level of productivity a student should achieve during a semester in terms of number of units completed. Consequently, most of the reports generated by CMI systems are related to the management of throughput. For example, IPI/IMS (Hsu, 1974) reports the day a unit was completed, the total number of units a student has completed to date, as well as the status of students relative to the curricular plan. Project PLAN* reports when units are started and completed, and lists all units completed by a student to date. The

Sherman School Project uses unit reports to locate each student in the curricular plan, and the contact report to identify students who were not producing. All of these reports have their origins in the detailed record-keeping used by Taylor (1911) to monitor the productivity of the factory. Bobbitt (1913) had also put a heavy emphasis upon record-keeping so that the efficiency of teachers and schools could be determined. Only through such reports could the number of units produced and their cost be determined. In both the factory and the school, the number of units completed is important as a measure of productivity. At the course level of management, the teacher's role is analogous to that of a production line foreman. The foreman is responsible for keeping all of his machines and their operators producing at an optimal rate, and producing goods meeting the specifications. However, the foreman's role is rather limited (Miner, 1971, p. 83) as he does little planning or supervising. The foreman primarily controls and coordinates in order to achieve productivity. Similarly at the course level of management, the teacher monitors the progress of each student, evaluates whether the class or a group is at an appropriate place in the curricular plan, and attempts to maintain an acceptable level of productivity of all the students. Since Taylor's fourth principle was explicit about relieving workers of management responsibilities, Bobbitt and others did not view management above the production line level as part of the teacher's role.

Scientific Management had as its goal the management of simple repetitive tasks, such as those used on the factory production lines. As a result, it places very little emphasis upon the management of the total corporate entity. Consequently, as was noted earlier, CMI systems based upon this management philosophy focus rather narrowly upon the unit-of-instruction cycle. These CMI systems place considerable emphasis upon instructional and course level management, and have no or little program level management capability. As in industry, the principles of Scientific Management can play an important role at certain levels of the enterprise, but they should not be the basis of the total management approach.

CMI and Classical Management Theory

One of the consequences of Scientific Management has been that teachers view themselves as workers, albeit professional workers, rather than managers. As was shown above, this point of view results in production line oriented CMI systems, with the major management emphasis upon productivity. In sharp contrast, classical management theory has little or no production line orientation, and its emphasis is upon the smooth functioning of an organization. While the classroom teacher hardly constitutes an organization, there are many management functions within the classroom that can be related to classical management theory. In order to expand upon this theme, the major aspects of classical theory are related to CMI in the paragraphs below.

Under classical management theory, planning plays an important role, and there can be several levels of planning involved in instructional management. The overall course of action to be taken by students is essentially defined by the curricular plan, whether it be in the form of a textbook or curriculum guides. Consequently, the level of planning performed by a teacher using CMI is usually that of planning sequences of units within the curricular plan. The best example is the Program of Studies (POS) used by PLAN*, where the teacher must lay out a sequence of units for each student in each of the four subject matter areas. PLAN* provides a variety of schemes for these unit sequences, varying from predefined to completely arbitrary teacher defined sequences of units. Once the POS has been decided upon, it can be stored in the computer and used for other management purposes. The instructional options display of the IPI/IMS (Hsu, 1974) also provides the teacher with a limited planning capability. The application of the MICA program to teacher education (Baker *et al.*, 1974) allows the student and the professor to plan a sequence of instructional modules analogous to the POS of

PLAN*. In its later years, the Sherman School Project (Chapin *et al.*, 1975) employed a planning mechanism similar to the POS of PLAN*. A weaker form of planning at the unit level is provided by the performance expectations of WIS/SIM (Belt and Spuck, 1974), where the predicted number of units to be completed constitutes a minimal plan for the student. Within an individualized curriculum, there is a considerable need for planning above the simple level of unit sequences or performance expectations. The teacher needs to be able to look ahead and ascertain the status of the class or students at a future point in time. For example, the teacher may want to focus upon a given theme at a particular point in the future. It would be extremely useful for planning purposes to have reports predicting pupil status relative to the curriculum as of a future date on a classroom or other group basis. In this vein, IMS-3 (McManus, 1971) reported pacing data to the teacher indicating whether or not the class will complete the curricular plan at the current rate of progress. However, IMS-3 did not provide predictions for future points in time. CMI systems could provide a much more sophisticated and useful capability to support planning at the instructional and course levels of management.

Despite the current emphasis upon management of single courses via CMI, future CMI systems will need to support the teachers' planning efforts at the program level of management. At this level there are complex planning problems involving the interrelationships among subject matter areas, allocation of resources, and budgeting of time. These problems exist under traditional instruction and are magnified under individualized or personalized instruction. The planning then becomes pupil based, and the potential variation and resulting complexity looms large. Although no current CMI systems provide significant support for the program level of management, there needs to be considerable fundamental work done in regard to the planning function at this level. Techniques need to be developed to plan the curricular sequences when interdependent courses are involved. Planning mechanisms for both short-term and long-term allocation of instructional and other resources need to be implemented. Finally, planning techniques providing a forecasting capability will be needed to give a teacher sufficient lead time to implement management decisions to cope with the anticipated events. Computer based support for program level management would be of considerable value. Unfortunately, none of the existing CMI systems support the planning function at the program level.

Organizing involves the creation of structure to enable the enterprise to achieve its objectives. The structure of most school settings is predetermined, so that there is little that can be done with regard to the primary organizational structure of a school district. However, teachers have considerable flexibility as to organization within the classroom. Elementary school teachers in particular use a variety of organizational arrangements to achieve particular purposes. At the college level, the instructor also has flexibility in an organizational sense. Courses can be arranged into lecture sections, laboratory sections, structured by student interest, etc. In many instructional settings, the organizational structure is dynamic, changing as a function of the topics under study as well as a function of student performance. In elementary school reading, for example, the use of reading groups whose number and membership is continuously changing is very common. One of the ways in which CMI systems can support the teacher or instructor is to provide data and reports to facilitate these dynamic organizational schemes. At least one CMI system, WIS/SIM (Belt and Spuck, 1974), provides the teacher with assistance in this area. It produces a report suggesting groupings of students for instructional purposes, typically those students who are to work on a given curricular unit. The basis for such groupings is whether a student has completed the prerequisites for a given unit. A computer program compares the student's history record against the curricular plan to determine the units for which he has completed the prerequisites. *De facto* groupings can be created under PLAN* by assigning students a common POS, but PLAN* does not suggest how to group students as a formal procedure as does WIS/SIM. The mechanisms currently employed for dynamic organization of the classroom are rudimentary, and much more sophisticated algorithms are available. These grouping or clustering algorithms (see Baker, 1972b) can make use of extensive vectors of information in the forming of instructional groups. It would be a simple matter to group students on the basis of an information vector containing demographic data, achievement data in several subject matter areas, and a pattern of curricular units completed. For example, the outcome of such a grouping algorithm could be the creation of groups for a science class that are homogeneous with respect to reading achievement, mathematics achievement, and science units completed. Under CMI, such grouping procedures can be performed upon request. This would allow dynamic reorganization of the class within and across subject matter areas.

Since most CMI systems involve a single teacher and a class of students, many of the constructs of organization as construed by classical management theory, such as a line and staff organization, profit centers, and unity of command are difficult to employ in the CMI environment, due to the lack of an extensive organizational structure. Even at the college level there are at most two or three levels of management. The Keller Plan, for example, employs an instructor, a graduate student assistant, undergraduate proctors, and graduate student laboratory assistants. Keller (1968) described the duties of this staff, but did not specify an organizational structure for the staff. One of the interesting and unanswered questions pertaining to CMI is the relationship of the organizational structure of the educational institution and the characteristics of the support provided by the CMI system. Anglin (1976) has investigated the relation of school organization to the decision making latitude of teachers. He found wide differences among four types of school organizations in both the level of decision making and in the nature of the decisions made by the classroom teachers. His results are germane to the issue of the characteristics of schools where CMI is likely to be successfully implemented. An additional peculiarity of CMI as it relates to organizing is that CMI systems primarily support the lowest level of the organizational structure. Most industrial management information systems have the inverse, since they are designed to support high level management.

Within classical management theory, commanding is the execution of plans. In the classroom, this management function is divided between the student and the teacher. Both are involved in execution of plans as the student actually executes the units of instruction in a plan. The teacher is responsible to some degree for insuring that the student properly executes the planned sequence of units. In addition, the teacher is responsible for higher level plans, such as the total curricular plan or a total educational program plan. The amount of support provided by CMI systems with respect to the execution of these plans is minimal. The reporting systems allow a teacher to maintain plans that have been put into effect, but few are designed to support the managerial control of the execution of a plan. No CMI system provides for the storage of teacher plans at a level higher than a sequence of units.

Coordinating consists of unifying the activity and efforts of all those in the organization. Under classical management theory this presupposes that a common goal is present but only vaguely recognized. Thus, coordinating under CMI tends to be associated with the instructional goals of individual students or groups of students. The teacher can coordinate the efforts of students working on a common curricular unit so as to facilitate their work. The teacher can coordinate the use of specialized equipment so as to insure its availability at the proper time and its maximum utilization. At the program level of management, coordination is an important function. The activities in the various subject matter areas need to be closely coordinated to achieve the overall goals of the total educational program. Again, CMI could play an important part in supporting the teacher's coordinating role.

The last of Fayol's management functions was controlling,

which insured tasks were accomplished according to the plans. Existing CMI systems place considerable emphasis upon the controlling function. Most of the reports are concerned with keeping track of the student relative to the curricular plan or segments of the curricular plan. However, they do not support the controlling function for higher level plans or program level plans. The unit-of-instruction cycle employed by most CMI systems also provides the basis for a detailed level of control. The unit pretest and unit posttest results are used by the teacher to control the student's accomplishment of the instructional plan of an individual curricular unit. Egan (1973) provides a very detailed level of control by managing students relative to an instructional flow diagram. Within these unit-of-instruction cycles, the student has not adhered to the plan until he has mastered the unit. Thus, the teacher asserts control to assure that the student follows the cycle and achieves mastery. In addition, the teacher maintains control to assure that the student follows the proper sequence of instructional units. At the college level and in the training situation, the controlling function is more evident than in the elementary school. At these levels, the instructor can have a number of persons, assistants, proctors, etc., working directly with the students. Consequently, the instructor must control these next level personnel to insure that the plans are properly executed. The professor report of the TIPS system provides the professor with data from each of the quiz sections that can be used to evaluate the performance of quiz section leaders. On the basis of the data, the professor can initiate controls to bring teaching assistants into accord with the plans.

Most of the 14 management principles due to Fayol (1949) apply to large organizations; hence, they have limited applicability to instructional settings. The key principles—unity of command, scalar chain, and specialization—have some application to CMI. In military training situations (see Mayo, 1974; Rockway and Yasutake, 1974) there is a clear unity of command and a scalar chain of command, due to the dependence of the military on hierarchical organization. College level CMI systems are similar in that teaching assistants report only to the instructor. The Sherman School system described in Chapter Four made use of a high degree of specialization but completely violated the unity of command and scalar chain principles. The teachers each performed a specialized function within the instructional model, yet a student could be managed by any of the teachers at various points in time. The Sherman School model is a good example of Taylor's functional foremanship rather than of Fayol's principles. The basic flavor of Fayol's management principles was a place for everyone and everyone in their place. Modern instructional settings often are deliberate attempts to violate this idea. Many instructional schemes are a reaction to neat rows of desks with students reciting upon cue. At the elementary school level in particular, most modern instructional schemes have an aura of purposeful disarray with considerable student movement, little obvious discipline, and considerable flexibility with respect to activities and time utilization. Thus, many of Fayol's principles of management tend to be of limited value to the conceptualization of CMI systems. However, most of Fayol's management functions are directly applicable to CMI systems. Such application requires some attention as teachers currently do not manage at a very high level within the organizational structures emphasized by classical management theory. The teacher's managerial role is akin to that of a middle level manager. They don't set the major goals but are responsible for meeting them.

The importance of the classical school of management to CMI is not so much in its direct application but rather in its conceptual level. The current heavy reliance of CMI upon Scientific Management results in the teacher being viewed as a low level manager. Persons involved in CMI need to look at the teacher's managerial role from the point of view of the classical school. In doing so they will of necessity need to raise their conceptualization of the role of the teacher as a manager. Rather than emphasizing the production line aspects, higher level functions such as planning, organizing, coordinating, etc., will come to the fore. When performing these managerial functions, the teacher will need both a different kind and a different level of support from the computer component. While there may be some controversy among management theorists as to the relative merits of the classical school, for CMI it can provide a useful tool to raise the level of conceptualization of the teacher as a manager.

Some Issues Related to the
Teacher as a Manager

The primary conceptual basis for the management of instruction under CMI is that of Scientific Management. This management philosophy has been embedded rather insidiously within CMI by means of the common denominator of behavioral objectives and the unit-of-instruction cycle. The early work of Bobbitt (1913), Snedden (1925), and Taylor (1911) has reappeared with a new label in the work of Mager (1962), Glaser and Reynolds (1964), and Popham and Baker (1970). The result of the application of Scientific Management to instructional management has been a heavy emphasis in CMI systems upon the management of throughput in the guise of individualized rate of progress. In its initial efforts to provide the teacher with support of the mechanics of individualized or personalized instruction, CMI implementers have essentially ignored educational goals in favor of the production of units. The managerial reports are aimed at keeping track of a pupil's productivity rather than what educational goals he has accomplished. To truly manage an educational program, managerial emphasis must be changed from that of productivity to that of educational goals. Although the behavioral objectives movement tends to read a different interpretation into his work, this has been Tyler's point of view in recent years (see Tyler, 1964; Fishbein, 1973). Computer managed instruction needs to provide the vehicles, data, reports, etc., that will enable teachers to establish educational goals rather than productivity as the basis for instructional management. The focus of most CMI systems upon a single subject matter area or treating multiple courses as independent courses has also hindered management at the educational goals level. Most of the higher level goals espoused by the various commissions on goals (see NEA, 1918; NEA, 1938; NEA, 1961) cut across many subject matter areas. Independent management of courses tends to preclude managing towards such goals. In addition, many college level and training school CMI systems have no interest in educational goals spanning many courses. However, even in these situations there is a need for management above the behavioral objectives, standard unit of work level. It appears that education has developed a split between what Perrow (1961) has called official goals and operative goals. The official goals are those such as stated by the NEA Commissions. The operative goals are those actually pursued by the organization. In the case of CMI systems the operative goals are the behavioral objectives or instructional units rather than higher level educational goals.

In the beginning of the present section it was noted the teacher is both a worker and a manager within the instructional setting. Because the teacher is fulfilling both of these roles, essentially simultaneously, it is difficult to clearly separate them. Many decisions made by a teacher and the resulting actions can be both instructional and managerial. The situation is further compounded by the teacher managing at the instructional, course, and program levels. Within the industrial realm of interest to management theorists, there are few direct analogies. The closest approximation is the management performed by professional persons such as doctors or nurses. According to Minor (1971, p. 86), a number of writers have felt that there are large differences in the managerial aspects of professional organizations and administrative organizations. The former would encompass law offices, medical clinics, and schools, while the latter would include government, factories, and the military. The majority of the effort in management theory has been directed at the management of administrative organizations. In a study of professional organizations, Hall (1967) found that these organizations had two primary characteristics: First, in professional organizations the authority and power tends to shift from the managers to the professionals. Second, as the level of professionalization increases, the level of bureaucratization decreases. In the case of classroom teachers, these two factors coupled with the split between teachers and administrators due to Scientific Management have resulted in teachers having a dominant role in the management of instruction. Most classroom teachers and college instructors are relatively free of bureaucratic intrusions into their classroom domain (Bidwell, 1965). Because they operate quite autonomously, it is difficult to extricate the managerial roles fulfilled by teachers, and to date there has been virtually no research on the teacher as a manager. The author was unable to find a single study dealing with the topic. A generally agreed upon observation is that CMI tends to bring about an emphasis upon the teacher as a manager. However, this observation has not been substantiated by empirical research to date. If this shift does occur, it would seem advantageous to define the nature of the role much more explicitly than is the present case. Such a definition of the teacher as a manager would allow teachers to prepare for the role rather than have it thrust upon them, as is so often done. The lack of role definition was very apparent in the Sherman School Project when the additional five schools were brought into operation. A very distinctive pattern of teacher behavior was noted, and a full school year was required before teachers were comfortable with the CMI system. Initially, teachers were very suspicious of the role of the computer and doubtful that it would help them personally. As the year progressed, teachers became comfortable with the mechanisms of the CMI system. Finally, near the end of the year, they began to perceive how the reports could be useful. If a clear managerial role definition existed, such a long period of adjustment would not have been needed. Because of the lack of role definition, it is imperative for CMI implementers to consider preservice and inservice teacher training as important. Considerable effort should be expended in not only showing how the CMI system functions, but also in assisting the teachers in perceiving their managerial role. It is necessary to provide continuing assistance in helping teachers make the transition to a more managerial role. An often overlooked aspect of inservice training is the inclusion of substitute teachers. A substitute can step into a classroom for a day without knowing how to cope with the mechanics of the computer related procedures. However, without proper training, a substitute cannot be used for any extended period of time. The lack of properly trained substitute teachers can prove to be a serious problem in schools with high absentee rates among its teachers. Team teaching situations such as in the Sherman School Project are less susceptible to this problem than are self-contained classroom. However, properly trained teachers, both regular and substitute, are necessary if the CMI system is to function properly. PLAN* (Flanagan *et al.*, 1975) has an extensive set of preservice training procedures as well as a consultative service to assist in the transition. All CMI systems need to pay much more attention to this aspect of the system.

Even if the managerial roles of teachers were more clearly defined, implementers of CMI systems face a major problem relating to the kind and level of support the CMI system provides for these roles. One of the early outcomes of the Sherman School Project was a realization that teachers are hard pressed for time to perform both instructional and managerial functions. In computer terms, they operate a real-time system. Within the real-time framework, they must perform the various management functions as well as instruct. Like the busy factory manager, they have difficulty attending to all facets of their responsibilities. Consequently, a CMI system must provide managerial support that in some sense is optimum. What constitutes this optimum is highly situationally dependent and is a function of the management goals. The optimum support for a throughput model is far different from that of an educational goals model, and is different for different instructional models. However, such optimum support should have the following characteristics: (1) The CMI system as seen by both the teacher and the pupils must be operationally as simple as possible. Since time is extremely valuable in the instructional setting, the simpler the system, the less time it demands. (2) The support provided for the managerial roles should reduce, not increase, the teacher's work load. The CMI system should enhance the teacher's ability to fulfill a given managerial role. (3) The CMI system should be perceived as being useful by those who use it. The reports generated and the data provided should be of specific use to the performance of particular managerial roles. Too many CMI systems have provided capabilities—data base query via a keyboard terminal being the favorite—that have absolutely no utility with regard to instructional management. Because teachers are pressed for time, CMI systems should be designed to relieve the teacher of routine management functions in addition to routine clerical functions. For example, in the Sherman School Project it was shown that instructional level diagnosis and prescription can be automated with ease. One of the original impetuses for needing computer support in the Sherman School Mathematics Program was to assist the teacher in the diagnosis and prescription procedures, as they were consuming a large proportion of the teacher's time. Yet, in a few years the process was completely automated and managed on an exception basis by the quiz/review teacher. There needs to be a conscious effort made to examine CMI systems for routine managerial functions that can be partially or completely automated, as these functions often are both at a low level of detail and time consuming. Once relieved of the functions, the teacher can manage at a higher conceptual level as well as have more time for instructionally related activities.

With a few exceptions, CMI systems have not included the school administrative hierarchy among those it supports. In most situations, this is due to CMI systems being developed to support a given teacher or instructor. In these cases, the conceptualization of the system was deliberately limited to the needs of the classroom teacher. College level CMI systems, in particular, have no intent of serving the needs of anyone beyond the course instructor. At the elementary school, a somewhat different situation exists. Although the CMI systems such as Sherman School, IPI/IMS, and WIS/SIM were developed to support the classroom teacher, a role for the building administrator lurks in the background. In the elementary school, the school principal tends to fulfill a leadership role with respect to instruction. The principal often is the catalyst, if not the moving force, in establishing educational innovations, acquiring resources, etc. While not actually managing instruction, the principal does have a vested interest in the overall success or failure of the instructional program in his school. In addition, the principal is also the teacher's supervisor in the administrative hierarchy. These two factors pose a difficult problem for CMI systems at the elementary school level—to what degree should the system provide the school's administrative hierarchy with instructionally related data? The obvious danger is that the summary data such as test scores, number of units completed, and discrepancy between performance expectations and accomplishments, would be used to evaluate teacher effectiveness. Bobbitt (1913, pp. 27-28) was quite explicit that instructional data should be used for this purpose. He stated "A teacher who fell short of the standard was unmistakably shown to be a weak teacher and the supervisor would have incontestable evidence of inefficiency against the weak teacher who cannot or refuses to improve. This knowledge would enable management to instantly overcome one of the most difficult problems in the schools—that of getting rid of inefficient teachers." Under Scientific Management the productivity of a teacher was measured by the number of standard units of work produced by the students. Such a point of view is an anathama to teachers, as it does not take into account the distribution of pupil characteristics across classrooms and schools. Nonetheless, evaluation of teachers on the basis of student performance remains an implicit factor. For example, Spuck and Owen (1974) have recently suggested using WIS/SIM for this purpose. As a result, teachers tend to resist schemes providing the administrative hierarchy with detailed instructionally related data. Such resistance stems in part from adoption of the Scientific Management concept by school administrators that they are management and teachers are workers. As such, management evaluates the productivity of the workers. Despite this long-standing division, one cannot completely shut off the access of administrative organizations to instructionally related data. The school superintendent and the building principals bear a responsibility to the public for the quality of education provided. In order to meet this responsibility, the administrative organization must be able to evaluate, hopefully in educational terms rather than financial terms, the various educational programs. To do so requires data rather than informal observation. This legitimate need for instructional related data can readily be met by CMI systems via the reporting system. The data provided by Group and Unit Reports obtained at various points in time can be used for evaluation purposes. Additional reports can be developed based upon aggregation of information in the student history files and related to curricular data in the Unit and Prescription files. Aggregation across classrooms and schools can be used to obtain data used for curriculum evaluation. The evaluation of the Sherman School Project for Title III purposes (Roecks, 1976) made extensive use of the reporting capabilities of the MICA computer program. Since instructionally related data is prone to abuse, nearly all elementary school CMI systems have avoided reports for the administrative hierarchy. Inclusion of such reports would further heighten teachers' apprehensions about the role of the computer component in CMI. Even without such reports in the initial system capabilities, it is highly likely that school principals and the superintendent's staff will exert pressure to obtain summary data for program evaluation purposes. It is the author's view that such reports are inevitable due to the relatively large costs associated with the use of CMI. The magnitude of the fiscal costs will force the administrative organization to justify the budget item. They will in turn require some form of reporting. The problem faced by the CMI designer is to provide the data in a manner meeting the needs of the administration, yet not compromising the CMI system in the eyes of the teacher.

The major thrust of the preceding has been upon the dependence of CMI systems upon the philosophy of Scientific Management. Callahan has shown that in the mid-1920's school administrators turned to Scientific Management as a panacea for dealing with the critics of the public schools. In the field of administration the result was to change the role of school administrators from that of educators to that of financial analysts. Under Scientific Management, educational issues were reduced to cost ratios, such as cost per pupil, cost per recitation, etc. Callahan (1962) documents quite elegantly the damage done to the American educational system due to school administrators embracing the mechanics of Scientific Management. He states: "It seems, in retrospect, that regardless of the motivation, the consequences for American education and American society were tragic. And when all of the strands in the story are woven together, it is clear that the essence of the tragedy was in adopting the values and practices indiscriminately and applying them with little or no consideration of educational values or purposes. It was not that some of the ideas from the business world might not have been used to advantage in educational administration, but that the wholesale adoption of the basic values, as well as the techniques of the business-industrial world, was a serious mistake in an institution whose primary purpose was the education of children. Perhaps the tragedy was not inherent in the borrowing from business and industry, but only in the application. It is possible that if educators had sought "the finest product at the lowest cost"—a dictum which is sometimes claimed to be a basic premise in American manufacturing—the results would not have been unfortunate. But the record shows that the emphasis was not at all on producing the finest product but on the lowest cost" (Callahan, 1962, p. 244). The adoption by CMI systems of Scientific Management via behavioral objectives and the unit-of-instruction cycle carries the implementation process one step further. As Kliebard (1971) shows, the behavioral objectives movement carried Bobbitt's work into the design of curricula, but actual educational programs based upon Bobbitt's approach failed due to their unmanageability. However, CMI systems have the data processing support necessary for the school as a factory model to succeed. There is a real danger that CMI will be the vehicle by which Scientific Management is extended to the classroom, thus completing the process so vividly described by Callahan (1962). The extension is quite insidious because behavioral objectives proponents do not admit of their ancestry, and CMI system designers do not recognize the production line analogy in the processes and procedures they implement. Unless educators quickly recognize the school-as-a-factory basis of the majority of CMI systems, especially at the elementary school level, the impact of Scientific Management upon the classroom could be as disastrous as it was upon school administration some 50 years earlier.

Curricular Issues

In 1897 Rice first proposed that curricula should be designed so they can be managed. Despite the antiquity of this concept, relatively little effort has been devoted to developing the management aspects of various curricula. The existence of CMI systems has brought the issue to the fore again, as one of the foundations of instructional management is the curriculum. Consequently, the present section devotes attention to the aspects of curriculum related to their manageability via CMI.

When done properly, the design of educational programs should be based upon educational goals and subject matter content, with specific curricula being the end products. The design process is an iterative one in which these three components interact. The starting point is the major goals of American education defined by various commissions over the past seven decades. These periodic redefinitions (see NEA, 1918; NEA, 1938;

NEA, 1961) serve to provide the broad goals of American education much in the sense of Perrow's (1961) official objectives. Due to the broad nature of these goals, they must be expanded, made more specific, and their interrelationships exposed to be useful in educational program development. The end result of this expansion is a set of educational goals intermediate to the broad societal goals and the instructional goals of specific curricula. These intermediate educational goals are not subject matter specific, and their achievement may require contributions from many different subject matter areas. For example, achieving an educational goal of being able to formulate a decision based upon the evaluation of data can be the result of experiences in many different subject matter areas. These second and lower level goals are very difficult both to define and to make operational. Human beings appear to have a strong propensity for leaping from a single high level goal to many low level, highly detailed goals. In this cognitive leap, the intermediate educational goals are completely bypassed. The Behavioral Objectives Movement is especially prone to this pattern, as it tends to discuss only the lowest level of educational goal. Such behavior is not unique to the developers of educational programs, since classic examples of this syndrome can be found in many fields.

Once a set of educational goals defined at a number of different levels of abstraction have been determined, the educational designer should look for experiences in a number of subject matter areas that would contribute to achieving the goal. This linkage process is performed across the total goal domain. When the total linkage network has been completed, those experiences belonging in a given subject matter area are identified. These experiences constitute the building blocks used by the curriculum designer. The curricular entities associated with these experiences are then restructured according to the logical structure of the content area in a way that facilitates their use in instruction. This final reordering takes into account learning sequences, pupil developmental characteristics, resource requirements, etc. This final reordering constitutes what are called curricula. The crucial feature of this design process is that there is a known linkage between the resultant curricula and the educational goals they are designed to meet. In the case of an educational program, the interdependencies and joint contribution of experiences in several curricula to the achievement of higher level educational goals would be explicitly defined. Due to subject matter specialization and asynchronous curriculum development, goal oriented design is rarely achieved.

The approach to curriculum design underlying most CMI systems is not that described above but one based upon task analysis. These techniques were originally developed by Taylor (1911) to break a task into its simplest elements so that they could be restructured into a more efficient sequence to achieve the desired results. Under such a task analysis, there is no question as to what the ultimate outcome will be, because a known entity was disassembled. When all the elements are performed, a predetermined product will be produced to a certain set of specifications and the goal achieved. The behavioral objectives movement has made the same basic assumption relating to an initial known entity when applying task analysis to curricular design. Unfortunately, the behavioral objectives specialist does not start with a known entity, but with one that has been partially disassembled before he begins his task analysis. Specifically, he starts with an existing subject matter—one that has been separated from the educational goals domain described earlier. Task analysis techniques are then applied to the subject matter area, independent of any educational goals considerations. A common practice is to analyze existing textbooks and extract the behavioral objectives implicit in the content of the book. The end product of this task analysis process is endless lists of minute design specifications in behavioral terms (Kliebard, 1971). However, the behavioral objectives approach does not provide any mechanism for reconstructing the original entity. Consequently, there is no means for recovering even slightly higher educational goals from the lists of behavioral objectives, as there never was a connection with them. Thus, the initial entity, the goal domain, cannot be recovered. Tyler (1964) makes this clear when he compares the concept of addition to the behavior of being able to add two-digit numbers. The behavioral objectives specialist is content that the student can reach criterion performance on a test of adding two-digit numbers. He has no means for ascertaining if the student has acquired the concept of addition. This must be inferred when the student has achieved mastery on tests of one-digit, two-digit, three-digit, etc., addition tasks. The task analysis approach results in curricular units and behavioral objectives as independent entities unrelated to educational goals. Perhaps the ultimate in this regard is the capability for teachers to obtain behavioral objectives from an objectives exchange.* On numerous occasions, the author has asked elementary school pupils what they had accomplished. The reply is invariably, "I finished Unit 6." When asked what they had learned, the response become vague, as they really don't know what the unit contributed to their education.

The end product of a curriculum design process based upon task analysis is a set of instructional units in a given subject matter area. These units, in turn, are composed of detailed subject matter oriented behavioral objectives. Under this approach, little attempt is made to link the behavioral objectives to intermediate or higher level educational goals. As a result, it is not surprising that existing CMI systems do not provide program level management. The educational consequence of using task analysis in curriculum design has been to focus the teacher's attention on the ground rather than the horizon. It would be an extremely simple matter to provide descriptors linking curricular units to those higher level educational goals to which they contribute. The CMI system could use these descriptors to generate reports indicating a student's status relative to broad educational goals. Given these kinds of reports, a teacher could manage at the educational goals level

*Instructional Objectives Exchange, W. James Popham, Director, Center for the Study of Evaluation, University of California, Los Angeles.

rather than at the units completed level. Parents are interested in whether their child can read; they are provided no information in this regard when told that the child has completed six units in word skills. It was observed above that CMI systems do not provide for program level management functions. The present section suggests the logic of the behavioral objectives-task analysis approach precludes program level management, since the behavioral objectives movement has divorced subject matter from educational goals. In addition, each subject matter area is treated as an independent domain. As a result, there is no vehicle for ascertaining the joint contribution of several subject matter areas to a common educational goal. Perhaps when teachers have a few years of managing multiple independent courses under a common CMI system, they will recognize the inadequacies of course level management. Then they will make demands for curricular designs facilitating program level management related to achieving educational goals at several levels of abstraction.

Most CMI systems employ curricular plans providing some flexibility in regard to the order in which a student may take the units, the exception being a linear plan. Thus, in addition to rate of progress, a degree of individualization is provided by the way in which a student sequences the units he undertakes. In the strand structure, he can be at different places in each strand. Within a block plan, no required order is imposed. Under a tree structure, a student may skip around with regard to units, but must complete prerequisites before proceeding to a higher level in the tree. A given student may be at a very high level in one part of the tree and at a low level in another. Unfortunately, most such curricular plans are disguised "lockstep" curricula, since eventually all students completing a curriculum complete the same units. The mere fact that a student is free to move about in the curricular structure and proceed through it at his own pace does not negate the fact it is a lockstep curriculum. Few, if any, CMI systems implement curricular plans involving goal differentiation, where the curricular structure for a given pupil is unique to that pupil.

Most CMI developers have seriously confused curricular flexibility with goal differentiation. Failure of the student to complete units within a curricular structure may mean he had a unique curriculum; but the goal differentiation was achieved by accident, not by deliberate allocation of units as a function of the students' needs and goals. Similarly, the capability to be assigned units from various parts of a curriculum does not constitute goal differentiation if eventually the total curriculum must be completed. The computer component of CMI can easily provide the capability for assigning each student a unique set of curricular units both within and across various subject matter areas. From a procedural point of view it is a simple matter for CMI systems to cope with a unique set of instructional units for each student. PLAN*, for example, can do this through a teacher designed POS. The basic issue in the use of curricular units for goal differentiation is not procedural, it is educational, since not all educators feel goal differentiation is a viable concept. For example, Glaser (1967) feels goal differentiation should not be used in the basic skills courses typically found in the elementary school. The design of Individually Prescribed Instruction reflects this point of view. It provides some selection flexibility at the unit level but none at the behavioral objectives level. A student completing the mathematics curriculum essentially will have "mastered" all objectives. Despite this, some goal differentiation could be employed at the elementary school level to take student interests and abilities into account. In mathematics, for example, not all students need to be exposed to sets; yet, for certain students, sets can provide valuable mathematical insight.

At the college level, where students have a range of backgrounds, goal differentiation can be used within even introductory courses. A common curricular plan is to have a set of required units covering the core requirements of the course and optional units chosen by the student. BIO-CMI (Allen, Meleca, and Meyers, 1972) uses this arrangement, as does the Keller Plan (Keller, 1968; Sherman, 1974). The menu selection curricular plan allows the teacher or the student to select a sequence of modules unique to a student's goals. A number of college level CMI systems (see Countermine and Singh, 1974; Merrill, 1974) employ the menu selection technique, but they do not indicate whether it is used for goal differentiation or for curricular flexibility within a fixed curriculum.

As a concept, goal differentiation has considerable appeal, but in practice it is difficult to manage. In basic skills courses, teachers are reluctant to allow students to avoid units for fear the topic will be needed at a later point in time. Self-selection of units by students also enables them to avoid important but difficult topics. To be effective, a unique curricular plan for each student needs to be based upon an adequate set of information. Information such as curricular plans completed, ability, interests, future needs, etc., is needed to intelligently plan a unique sequence of units for a student. Unfortunately, teachers typically do not possess this data in a form that can be used to design curricular sequences for individual students. They must rely primarily upon either their judgment or externally designed sequences. The sheer mechanics of highly differentiated curricular plans also deters their use, as the preparation time required of the teacher can be extensive. Compromises between goal differentiated unit sequences and lockstep plans are provided by the use of required plus optional units, and by the POS used by PLAN*. The former allows the teacher or student some flexibility but reduces the sequence planning load. The latter provides predefined unit sequences which can be modified or supplanted by the teacher. Both schemes provide a degree of goal differentiation that is probably commensurate with our present level of understanding. One needs to proceed with some caution in this area, since unique curricular sequences based upon differentiated educational goals for each student can be a thinly disguised implementation of the concept of predetermination.

Some Curricular Details

The definition of the minimum management entity is

important to CMI systems from both a computer component and a management point of view. If the curriculum is fractionated to an excessively fine level of detail, too much instructionally related data gets generated in the classroom. The teacher is then faced with an excess of information that must be reduced to workable proportions. Although most curricular plans supported by CMI fractionate the curriculum to the behavioral objectives level, very few CMI systems employ objectives as the minimum management entity. For the most part, they use the instructional unit as this entity. The instructional unit provides considerable information compression for management purposes, while not overburdening the computer component. The greater the level of detail in the curriculum design, the greater the amount of instructionally related data and data storage requirements. The use of units keeps the data base requirements within reasonable bounds. Excessive detail in the data base also results in more data processing in the report generation process. For reporting purposes one usually wants a degree of summarization to provide a better view of the situation. Thus, detailed data would need to be aggregated and analyzed for reporting purposes, but data storage at the unit level eliminates much of this data processing and simplifies the reporting process. Inspection of the reporting component of most CMI systems shows instructionally related data being reported primarily at the unit rather than the behavioral objectives level.

One of the outcomes of the Sherman School Project was the recognition that the use of CMI will force a greater degree of discipline upon curriculum designers. In manually managed instructional systems, inconsistencies in numbers of objectives per unit, unmatched item ordering in equivalent forms of tests, and the other mechanical problems described in Chapter Four can be tolerated. When the computer is used, such practices are not acceptable, as they can result in excessively large computer programs to cope with the unsystematic procedures. The computer component is at its best when there is considerable uniformity in the curriculum design, the layout of assessment instruments, etc. When this is true, the computer program is simpler, more efficient, and less prone to trouble. A considerable portion of the first year's effort in the Sherman School Project was in regularizing the curriculum packaging to obtain a good match between the computer capabilities and the curriculum. If the developer of the computer component is foolish enough to build in a software dependence upon a specific curriculum, CMI may force an undesired degree of curriculum stability. If such a dependence exists, changes in the curriculum result in changes to the computer program. Since computer programming is expensive, there will be considerable pressure to avoid making curricular changes that result in software changes, but the wrong component is controlling the decisions. An additional degree of curricular standardization can also be imposed when medium-scale or large-scale CMI systems are used. Due to the need to have consistent computer-based procedures, there will be a requirement for all schools to use a common curriculum in each subject matter area. If the curricular design is on the rigid side, this can cause considerable resistance from teachers or schools who feel the externally imposed curricular design is inappropriate for their pupils. This problem clearly faces commercially available CMI systems such as PLAN* and TRACER. PLAN* has met this issue by providing a range of curricular designs ranging from predefined by PLAN* to fully teacher designed. Viable medium-scale and large-scale CMI systems must provide sufficient flexibility to accommodate variations in curricular design. If they do not, they can impose a degree of curricular standardization that may be undesirable or even unacceptable.

Although many CMI systems provide some support for the curriculum improvement cycle, a higher level of support is needed. Since the computer component tends to impose curricular stability, the CMI system should provide a vehicle to counter the tendency. At the present time, only rudimentary curriculum improvement data, primarily test results, are provided. CMI designers should take a more extensive look at the curriculum improvement cycle and provide curriculum developers a wide range of data analysis, reports, and other support for this activity. For example, the effectiveness of diagnosis and prescription could be determined from data in the data base, and patterns of pupil paths through the curricular structure could be examined and related to achievement or other variables. Glaser (1967) made an important point when he included procedures for self-improvement in his instructional model. CMI designers need to do a better job in implementing this aspect of the model.

Due to the grassroots nature of many CMI systems, they often employ locally developed curricular plans and materials. Local development and production of curricular materials can be an extremely time consuming and expensive process. The author suspects, and Chapin (1976) insists, that unless there are highly mitigating circumstances, such developmental efforts are not cost-effective. At the elementary school level, in particular, there are a variety of well-developed textbook series and sets of individualized instructional materials in each of the subject matter areas. At this level, local curriculum development efforts often consist of simply selecting units from a range of such texts or rearranging units within a textbook series. Such changes often offer little educationally over the source materials from which they are derived. While locally developed curricula are possible in the elementary school, the corresponding instructional materials production can be a problem. In the second year of the Sherman School Project, the printing of locally developed instructional materials and tests became a significant cost and schedule problem. At the elementary school level, the approach taken by PLAN* in reading and mathematics provides a good model for local curricular development that appears to minimize costs. Under PLAN*, curricular plans were built around existing textbook series, providing flexibility in the utilization of curricular units, allowing supplementation via local units, and minimizing the number of printed sheets of paper associated with each unit. If a school does not minimize physical materials production, the cost of local curriculum development is also going to force curricular stability. Given the high quality of many existing elementary school curriculum materials, local school districts would be well advised to limit their efforts in this area. Their attention should be devoted to developing systems achieving educational goals via program level management rather than producing curricular materials.

Diagnosis and Prescription

Effective procedures for diagnosis and prescription are at the core of any instructional model, and CMI systems employ diagnostic and prescriptive techniques ranging from the teacher's clinical judgment to fully computer automated approaches. Like curricular design, diagnosis and prescription have been and will be impacted by CMI systems; hence, the present section examines this relationship.

The concept of educational diagnosis at a formalized level has its origins in the intelligence testing movement. The initial work of Binet (1916) in the area of individually administered intelligence tests was aimed at identifying students' ability to profit from classroom instruction. Similarly, the early work by Yerkes' group resulting in the Army Alpha group intelligence test was aimed at screening draftees who could not be trained as soldiers in World War I. During the 1920's and 1930's a large number of diagnostic tests were developed in various subject matter areas, particularly in the area of elementary school reading and arithmetic. Early editions of the *Mental Measurements Yearbook* (Buros, 1949) contained descriptions of many different types of diagnostic tests. These diagnostic tests provided descriptive data about each student relative to specific aspects of the subject matter area. The diagnostic test results were used by the teacher to understand the pupil's problems, and identified the areas in which the teacher should assist the student. In reading, for example, it was common to obtain a reading skills profile for a student from the diagnostic test. Then a remedial reading program based upon the profile was developed for the student. Interest in diagnostic tests appears to have waned during the late 1940's and 1950's, and they appear not to be widely used in an instructional context at the present time.

Diagnosis

From a conceptual point of view, there are two types of diagnoses—symptomatic and causative—and the differences in these two types are at a fundamental level. A symptomatic diagnosis is at a descriptive level; the diagnostician merely describes what can be observed. In a medical context, the doctor would note that the patient had a temperature of 102 degrees, was flushed, and was weak. In an educational setting, the teacher would report that a student had a test score of 12 on a reading test, had taken the posttest twice, and was three units below expected placement in the curricular plan at this time. In both cases, the diagnosis is a description of the person's status. A causative diagnosis is one in which the mechanism underlying the symptoms can be identified. For example, a physician would state that the disease was diagnosed as "strep throat" on the basis of bacterial culture. A reading teacher might state that a child's reading difficulties stemmed from a visual deficit. In most diagnostic situations, one strives for causative diagnoses, but often must settle for symptomatic diagnoses, due to the "state of the art" in the particular area. Medicine, for example, can provide causative diagnosis in many areas via a variety of techniques and is a reasonably mature field in this respect. However, even in a mature field such as medicine, the causative diagnoses made by practitioners are often speculative. By comparison, diagnosis within the field of education is at an embryonic level of development. Even in areas such as reading, where diagnostic procedures have been in use for many years (see Della-Piana, 1968), causative diagnoses are rare. Due to a rather primitive "state of the art," instructional diagnosis is symptomatic in nature. It is reasonably simple to observe that a pupil cannot add one-digit numbers, but it is quite another matter to isolate the cause. The latter requires diagnostic tools, information, and concepts that simply do not exist at the present time. Even if they did exist, if they were time consuming, complex, and expensive, they would probably not be used on a large scale, due to poor cost-benefits ratios.

The diagnostic procedures employed by CMI systems are symptomatic in character and are based upon the results of criterion-referenced tests rather than specialized diagnostic tests. The diagnostic information typically recovered from these tests is simply mastery or nonmastery of behavioral objectives. This data is often supplemented by information describing the student's status relative to the curricular plan, such as number of units completed, date of last testing, and his progress in relation to a performance expectation. All of the CMI systems listed in Appendix A depend upon test results for diagnostic data. However, a number of CMI systems—PLAN*, WIS/SIM, IPI/IMS—allow teachers to provide observational data in lieu of test results.

Because of the lack of formal procedures for analyzing instructional data from a diagnostic point of view, CMI systems do not produce a diagnosis labeled as such. Rather, they generate reports containing the data used by teachers as the basis for instructional diagnosis. The primary diagnostic procedure is clinical judgment based upon the teacher's or instructor's experience. However, even at a judgmental level diagnostic procedures can be difficult to perform. For example, failure to master a single objective as measured by a criterion-referenced test has a rather clear diagnostic interpretation. Failure to master several objectives on a given test does not have a simple interpretation. The teacher must weigh the relative importance of the several objectives, and relate them to pupil characteristics and to the total curricular plan. After doing this, the teacher formulates a symptomatic diagnosis that is acted upon. In all but two CMI systems, there are no formal mechanisms for assisting the teacher in this complex process. BIO-CMI (Allen, Meleca, and Meyers, 1972) provides a measure of assistance through categorizing test results by levels of Bloom's Taxonomy (Bloom, 1956). TIPS (Kelley, 1968) provides Boolean Algebra operators, enabling the instructor to express complex relationships among test results and other variables. While this scheme provides a considerably more powerful diagnostic tool than any other CMI system, it does require a sophisticated instructor. In addition, it is very easy to write such an expression but quite another matter to show that it is a meaningful expression when employed diagnostically. However, the basic outlines of educational diagnosis will emerge through the translation of teacher's clinical judgments into such diagnostic expressions, and then observing consequences of such diagnosis on a large-scale, systematic basis. Therefore, CMI designers would be well advised to follow Kelley's lead and incorporate similar diagnostic expressions.

Diagnostic techniques also need to be broadened in their scope. Due to the heavy reliance upon test scores, little diagnostic use is made of the pattern of pupil performance either within a given course or across courses. For example, it could be diagnostically informative to know that a given pupil invariably exhausts the available posttests and proceeds to the next unit on the basis of teacher certification. Another pupil might exhibit a highly variable number of objectives mastered on pretests, while rarely failing to master all objectives on a posttest. Such information is readily available in most CMI systems but is rarely presented in a form convenient for diagnostic purposes. Some information of this type is contained in reports generated by various systems. IPI/IMS (Hsu, 1974) reports the day of the school year that various actions were taken. PLAN* reports can be used to determine when units were assigned and completed. Typically, such data is not integrated with other diagnostic data so that it can be used in the manner indicated above. Patterns of performance across subject matter areas can also provide diagnostic information. For example, one might observe that when the progress made by a given pupil is slow, it is slow in more than one subject, suggesting a generalized problem rather than a course specific problem or perhaps an interdependence between courses for that pupil. In keeping with the need for greater emphasis upon educational goals rather than productivity, there should also be diagnostic procedures related to higher level educational goals. If, as was suggested earlier, there were links among curricular units and the goal domain, diagnostic procedures and reports pertaining to goals could be developed. Such procedures and reports would enable teachers to diagnose at a higher level than is presently the case. Again, the lack of program level diagnostic procedures is a function of the independent course orientation of present CMI systems.

Although Glaser's (1967) instructional model calls for the use of ancillary data such as pupil interests, intelligence, and family background in the diagnostic process, very little use of such data is made in CMI, including his own IPI/IMS system. The underlying problem is that very little is known about the educational significance of these factors at the behavioral objective level. The relationship of some of these factors to long term academic success is well known, but their role at the day-to-day level of instruction is obscure. TIPS (Kelley, 1968) provides for the use of both performance data and student characteristic data in diagnostic expressions. Perhaps the analysis of the effectiveness of these diagnostic expressions could be used to determine the usefulness of ancillary data at the detailed instructional level.

The diagnostic capabilities of present CMI systems is limited to symptomatic diagnoses. The diagnostic information given consists of names of objectives passed or failed, test scores, dates on which units or tests were assigned, and similar descriptive data. Other than TIPS (Kelley, 1968), none of the existing CMI systems appear to provide a mechanism for integrating this information into a diagnosis. Typically, they simply report the data, and the teacher interprets the data on a judgmental basis for the particular student or group of students. Recognizing that diagnosis is currently at a very rudimentary level, CMI systems need to be exploited as a vehicle for improving the diagnostic process.

Prescription

The complement of diagnosis is prescription. It is the allocation of educational resources or experiences as a function of the diagnosis. The medical analogy is prescribing a therapy, such as an antibiotic, known to "cure" a given disease. Similarly, in education, if a student fails to master an objective, there should be a resource, such as a filmstrip, that will enable him to understand the objective and achieve mastery upon the next testing. Educators have a long-standing belief in what is currently called aptitude-treatment interaction, i.e., the educational prescription should be unique to the characteristics of the pupil. Despite this long-standing belief, there is very little information available as to how one matches a prescription to a specific pattern of diagnostic information other than by clinical judgment. Even with Kelley's sophisticated Boolean algebra diagnostic expressions, the joining of a prescription to the diagnosis is done clinically. Ideally, one should have an algorithm for matching the "curative" power of specific educational resources to a diagnosis. However, there are no well recognized schemes for specifying the ability of various resources to respond to a given diagnosis. In many CMI systems, the only prescription is to simply restudy the textbook, while others assign filmstrips, audio-tapes, or media related materials. The basic rationale underlying the connection between these prescriptions and the diagnosis is that they cover the same material with a different set of examples or possibly a different orientation. As was described in Chapter Four, the prescriptions used by the Sherman School Mathematics Program were rank ordered from "best" to tutorial by the teachers who established the prescriptions for each instructional unit. PLAN*, while not prescribing for individual students, provides teachers with information relating to materials that can be used prescriptively. The majority of CMI systems leave the prescriptive process up to the instructor, who links available resources to the diagnostic information on a clinical basis. Typically, this linkage is between an objective failed and a textbook section.

Even when prescriptions are judgmentally connected to diagnosis, their creation is a significant task. A teacher or curriculum specialist must know the subject matter area, the specific objective, and the common reasons for a student to fail to achieve an objective. They also need a good understanding of the resources and activities constituting potential prescriptions. Finally, they must assign a prescription to a diagnosis such that it will be reasonably helpful for the majority of students who will receive the prescription. To do this is a difficult task even at the rudimentary level of assigning a prescription whenever an objective is failed. As one increases the level of sophistication of the diagnosis, the task of creating and allocating prescriptions becomes very complex and requires considerable insight on the part of the persons performing the task. It is also easy to underestimate the magnitude of the task of creating prescriptions. In the Sherman School Project, there were roughly 11,000 prescriptions assigned; of these, some 2,000 were unique. The creation of several thousand prescriptions in a single subject matter area covering only two grade levels was a major task. To do the same for four courses and eight grade levels would be a major undertaking requiring many persons and considerable resources, and would be of several years duration. In addition to being expensive to create, prescriptions are also difficult to keep current. Curricula in particular subject matter areas change over time, but the prescriptions are quite specific to the curricular objectives, the assessment instruments, and the resources. Consequently, curricular changes can easily make obsolete a portion of prescriptions. The prescriptions themselves can also become unusable due to the passage of time. The commonly used textbooks and workbooks wear out and are not replaced, the filmstrips become technically outdated, etc. As these resources and media are lost, they must be replaced by new ones that will serve as the basis for prescriptions. Thus, like the curriculum, diagnosis and prescription must be part of a continuous improvement cycle involving significant resources over a period of years. If a total improvement cycle is not employed, the dependence of the CMI system upon existing prescriptions will lead to curricular rigidity and obsolescence.

The existence of large numbers of prescriptions associated with a curricular plan can lead to management problems at the instructional level of management. For example, during the first year of the Sherman School Project, the teacher functioning as the computer console operator had to recognize and evaluate the usefulness of over 2,000 unique prescriptions. Only a small number were applicable at one time to a given student, but as students dispersed over the curricular plan, the range of prescriptions in use increased markedly. Fortunately, the teacher at the console was also instrumental in the creation of the prescriptions and had a good grasp of them. However, it is doubtful a teacher not as closely involved could relate 2,000 different prescriptions to the needs of 165 pupils in a coherent fashion. Unless a teacher spent a reasonable period of time each day reviewing the prescriptions likely to be used the next day, there is a low probability that the prescriptive process would be performed effectively. Any CMI system employing teacher selection among multiple prescriptions for each objective failed can overburden the teacher's ability to keep track of the prescriptions and use them properly. Consequently, the prescription process can lead to an increase of the teacher's work load. There are two alternatives to keep the load imposed by prescriptions at a reasonable level. First, only provide diagnostic data and have teachers prescribe on clinical grounds. This is the alternative chosen by the implementers of PLAN*. Second, automate the prescriptive process so that the teacher does not perform prescription as part of the instructional process. This alternative was chosen by Kelley (1968) and by the Sherman School Project. The first choice essentially maintains the status quo and has a minimal impact upon a teacher's existing prescriptive practices other than providing systematic diagnostic data. The second requires the teacher to have confidence in the prescriptions assigned by the computer component on the basis of the diagnosis. An additional justification for the automation of the prescriptive process lies in the characteristics of the prescriptions. Due to prescribing at the behavioral objectives level, the prescriptions tend to have a one-to-one relationship with the objectives. At the same time, the lack of a wide variety of available resources and limited information on aptitude-treatment interaction results in a restricted range of prescriptions for a given diagnosis. The net effect is that even when performed clinically, prescription becomes a rather routine procedure. Because of this, one can easily relegate existing diagnosis and prescription procedures to the computer component, and this has been done in 11 of the 28 CMI systems listed in Appendix A. Once automated, the exception principle could be used to manage the instructional level diagnosis and prescription process. As long as the computer based procedures function at an acceptable level, the teacher relies on them. When a prescription does not seem to be functioning for a given student, the teacher interjects herself into the prescriptive process. The use of the quiz/review teacher in the Sherman School Project is a good example of the use of the exception principle. When an objective was failed, most students received the "best" prescription automatically. When the student encountered problems, the quiz/ review teacher could override the prescription as well as assign alternative prescriptions. This scheme has worked extremely well and has eliminated what was once a major part of the instructional level management work load.

Although apprehensive at first about automated prescriptions, teachers quickly realize routine prescribing is a bore and best left to the computer. They are especially likely to reach this conclusion when the computer is merely implementing a judgmental connection between the diagnosis (objective failed) and a prescription that has been made by the teacher or a group of teachers. This leads to the interesting possibility of introducing what one might call the "best professional judgment" into the automation of diagnosis and prescription. One could involve the curricular developers, educational psychologists, and highly skilled teachers in specifying the prescriptions and their relation to diagnoses at the time the curriculum was designed. The curriculum package could contain not only the instructional units and the assessment instruments, but also the unique prescriptions appropriate to the specific diagnosis in a computer compatible medium. Thus, when a curriculum was adopted, the instructional level diagnosis and prescriptive procedures could be readily automated. Though expensive, to do so is well within present capabilities. The real question is whether teachers would have as much confidence in a CMI system embedding "best professional" judgment rather than their own. Given teachers who have used a CMI system employing automated prescriptions for a few years, the transitional problems would seem to be minimal. In case of both teacher developed and "best professional judgment" prescriptions, the computer component could be used to monitor the utilization and effectiveness of individual prescriptions. The improvement of prescriptions and any assignment algorithm could become part of the curriculum improvement cycle. At some point, when the theory of aptitude-treatment interaction becomes well developed, best professional judgment can be supplanted by analytical tools for connecting diagnoses and prescriptions.

Summary

One of the major impacts of CMI has been to bring about an awareness of the managerial role of the teacher. Such an awareness found the field of education ill prepared, since the concept of the teacher as a manager was not well developed. Consequently, the instructional models and the computer supported procedures have served to define the teacher's managerial role. The resulting emphasis of course level management upon productivity (units completed) and of instructional level management upon a standard product (behavioral objective achieved) was shown to be the educational implementation of Taylor's Scientific Management. The unfortunate aspect of the adoption of this management philosophy and its school-as-a-factory orientation is that teachers are allocated only low level managerial functions related to productivity. In an attempt to broaden the definition of the teacher as a true manager, the classical school of management was examined. This school emphasizes higher level management functions, such as planning, coordinating, organizing, and commanding, that are also an integral part of a teacher's managerial role. Because of their Scientific Management basis, present CMI systems provide little support for the teacher's involvement in these higher level management functions.

From a managerial point of view, a major deficiency of existing CMI systems is their inability to assist the teacher in managing towards achievement of educational goals rather than productivity. The task analysis basis of the behavioral objectives movement has lead to a "top-down" approach to curricular design with no mechanism for reintegration in a vertical sense. In addition, subject matter insularity also works against achieving educational goals cutting across subject matter areas. If the teacher is to truly become an educational manager, CMI systems will need to provide mechanisms for program level management aimed at achieving intermediate and higher level educational goals.

The twin procedures of diagnosis and prescription are currently at a rather rudimentary level. Diagnosis tends to consist of lists of objectives failed, and prescriptions are typically additional pages in a textbook dealing with the objective failed. Present diagnostic and prescriptive procedures are relatively simple as well as routine; hence, roughly a third of the CMI systems automate these procedures. Since a theoretical basis for diagnosis and prescription appears to be in the very distant future, CMI systems need to be employed as a vehicle to study and improve these procedures.

Chapter Seven

The Computer Component

In the present chapter, three facets of the computer component will be explored—systems considerations, software issues, and software life cycle. The systems considerations will deal primarily with the use of computers and computer-related equipment. The software issues focus upon how one approaches the implementation of management information systems. The final topic, software life cycle, was included because most developers of small-scale CMI systems do not plan for the long-term existence of their system, and this leads to a number of problems. The rationale underlying the discussion of all three topics was one of attempting to examine the way in which the particular topic and CMI interact. Most of the areas discussed are standard topics in computer applications, yet they take on special characteristics within the context of CMI.

Systems Considerations

The use of a computer to support a management information system involves a number of systems considerations that are primarily hardware oriented. The sections below deal with four of these—modes of computer usage, data collection, reliability, and computer configurations. The primary interest is in how these relate to CMI and contribute to an effective, efficient computer component.

Mode of Computer Usage

In Chapters Two and Three it was seen that CMI systems have employed both batch and time-sharing modes of operation. Under the former, the data collected in the classroom is physically transported to a central computer facility where it is processed and the printed reports produced are returned to the classroom in the same manner. A widely used variation of the batch mode is Remote Job Entry (RJE). The data processing procedures under RJE are identical to the batch mode, but the computer input-output equipment is located in the school building rather than at the computer facility. The RJE approach essentially makes the batch mode more convenient for the user of the computer. When the batch mode of computing is used, under either conventional batch or via RJE, it has a number of influences upon the operational characteristics of the CMI system. Without a RJE capability, the input data and the printed output must be physically transported to and from the central computer facility (see Baker, 1974b, and McManus, 1971, for extensive discussions of the problems associated with physical transport systems for instructional data). Under either approach to the batch mode, once the data has been entered into the computer, it is placed in a job queue and must await its sequential turn for processing. The speed with which the job is reached depends upon the length of the queue, the nature of the computing performed by the preceding jobs, and the computer resources needed to process the instructional data. Thus, the "turn around time," i.e., the time from submission of the job until the receipt of the results, can be highly variable. It can range from a few minutes when the computer has a small queue to many hours or more when the queue contains several large jobs. The advantage of the batch mode is that it is the least expensive mode of computer utilization, especially considering the usual discounts offered for non-prime time computer usages. PLAN*, for example, does all of its CMI data processing during the night shift. As can be seen from Appendix A, batch mode, and the RJE approach in particular, is by far the most common mode of computer usage in CMI systems.

The time-sharing mode allows one to place an interactive terminal, such as a CRT display or keyboard device, in the classroom. Under this mode, the teacher, teacher aide, or even a student can conduct a dialogue with the computer. The dialogue can be based upon the entry of instructionally related data, accessing information in the data base, or the generation of a standard report. Because the interactive terminal has direct access to the computer, the services of the computer are available to the user when he needs them, and there is essentially little or no delay between a request and a response.

With respect to data flow within a CMI system, the batch and time-sharing modes of computer usage are very similar. In both cases, instructionally related data such as test results, identification of units completed, etc., is collected in the instructional setting and entered into the computer, and the data received is processed and stored. The major difference lies in the level of responsiveness of the system. Due to the delays inherent in the batch mode, most CMI systems employing this mode use a predetermined operational cycle. They employ a daily or weekly cycle where all of the available instructionally related data is entered into the computer and the routine reports are generated on a scheduled basis. For example, PLAN* uses a daily cycle for data collection and reporting, with a superimposed weekly and monthly reporting cycle. The use of such a cycle enables one to establish routine procedures to insure that the cycle is performed properly.

Compared to the overall use of the central computer facility, the use of batch mode for small-scale CMI constitutes a low level of computer usage, both in terms of repetition rate of use and amount of computing performed. The operational cycle of CMI systems employing the time-sharing mode involves a higher level of activity but not much more total data processing than under the batch mode. Because of the man-machine interaction under the time-sharing mode, a dialogue takes place on a reasonably continuous basis. The computer must respond quickly to the user's requests. The amount of data processing and related operations per request is relatively small. However, the cost of achieving this quick response capability is quite high, due to the hardware and operating system software needed to provide the time-sharing mode.

The choice of whether to design a CMI system to employ the batch or time-sharing mode is somewhat dependent upon the scale of the CMI system. The interactive approach is quite attractive for small-scale CMI systems when one has access to a large-scale computer supporting time-sharing. In this situation, the CMI system is only one of many users of the time-sharing system, and the total system costs are distributed over many users. A large proportion of the CMI systems developed by persons associated with universities have employed the time-sharing mode. University computer charges are usually reasonable, the interactive terminals are easily obtained, and the total cost for CMI usage is quite low. More important than operational costs is the fact that a staff other than that of the CMI project bears the responsibility for the proper operation and maintenance of the time-shared computer system. To the CMI implementer, the time-sharing capability is a *given*. When a CMI system is of medium- or large-scale, the interactive approach requires considerably more computing resources. Instead of the CMI system being simply one of many users, it becomes a major user of the system. Consequently, there is a tendency to require the CMI project to provide a greater proportion of the resources needed to support and maintain the time-shared computer facility. Depending upon the CMI system, a point can be reached where it requires a dedicated computer. At this point the total cost of the CMI system rises sharply as costs, formerly amortized over many users and the institution, become the responsibility of the CMI project alone. At the present time, only the military CMI systems appear able to justify the costs associated with interactive computer systems dedicated to CMI.

With present technology, the Remote Job Entry approach to

the batch mode is able to support small-, medium-, and large-scale CMI. Although the RJE approach depends upon a variation of the time-shared mode to handle the input and output of data, it imposes a much lower load on the central computer than do interactive terminals. The data collected via RJE is placed in disk storage and the data processing task queued within the normal job stream. There is no requirement for immediate response to the person using the terminal. Thus, the RJE approach enables one to transmit instructionally related data to the computer easily, yet the data is processed by the computer at its convenience.

A final consideration in the choice between batch and time-sharing mode is that of who is going to operate the interactive terminal. One of the author's most cherished concepts was that of a classroom teacher seated at an interactive terminal orchestrating the individualized instructional program via the computer. In the case of the Sherman School Project, at least, this proved not to be a viable concept. The computer-related procedures quickly became routine, and the teacher at the console felt they did not require a professional level person. In addition, the use of a teacher as a computer terminal operator was not cost-effective. During the second year of operation, no problems were encountered when diagnosis and prescription was automated and a teacher aide was the computer operator. Full automation of the computer-based data collection procedures, via the use of the desk top scanner, completed the demise of the author's cherished concept. Completely automated use of the computer is a return to Flanagan's (1967a) concept that the computer should be an unobtrusive tool used by the teacher. Experience has shown the computer component is indispensable, yet its technical operation should be independent of the teacher's instructional roles. Richard E. Schutz, Director, Southwestern Regional Educational Laboratory, had expounded this view to the author since the mid 1960's. The Sherman School results lend considerable credence to his views.

Given the capabilities of present computer systems, the

choice between the use of a remote job entry terminal or an interactive terminal depends primarily upon the scale of the CMI system. Small-scale systems can readily use either and the choice depends upon the instructional model and costs. If the model does not depend upon immediate response to the instructionally related data, the RJE approach is appropriate and low-cost. Large-scale CMI systems are limited to the RJE approach by technical and economic considerations. The primary consideration is the scope of computer equipment and the costs associated with maintaining a large number of interactive terminals for CMI use. Existing computers can support a reasonably large number of remote job entry terminals, which in turn can service a large number of classrooms. Providing a sufficient number of interactive terminals for these same classrooms strains the capabilities of present time-sharing computers and the cost is far beyond what educational institutions can provide. Consequently, for the immediate future the RJE approach is the most viable for large-scale CMI systems. Medium-scale CMI systems can use either RJE or time-sharing with the choice dependent upon local conditions and funding patterns.

Data Collection

One key to the success of management information systems is "point of origin" data collection. In the case of CMI systems, the instructionally related data generated during the course of instruction and by the management of instruction must be captured and entered into the data base. Both the types of data collected and the means used to communicate it to the computer vary widely across present CMI systems. The most common data collected is test results. Some systems (Kelley, 1973; Mayo, 1974; WLC, 1973b) collect the responses of each student to each item. Others (Behr *et al.*, 1974) only note whether or not an objective was passed or failed. The TIPS system also provides for the entry of test scores obtained from other sources. The majority of CMI systems also collect data related to objectives or curricular units completed, although in some cases this information results from the processing of tests. A few systems (Behr *et al.*, 1974; Hsu, 1974) record teacher decisions such as prescriptions assigned and tests assigned.

The most rudimentary data collection scheme is based upon the use of information forms completed by students or teachers. In the case of test results, these are answer sheets. Other data, such as units completed, tests assigned, etc., can be collected via forms designed for the purpose. These forms are given to key punch operators, who enter the data into Hollerith cards via the key punch machine. The decks of cards produced serve as the input medium to the computer. Very few CMI systems rely entirely upon punched card input since, as an operational procedure, the use of manually punched cards on a daily basis is not desirable. It is a labor-intensive process, requires supervision, needs quality control, and can be very slow. Because of this, most CMI systems have turned to optical mark reading equipment as the primary data collection device. Punched card input is used mainly to build the initial data base, where a high degree of accuracy and control is needed in the file construction. As a data collection medium, punched cards are obsolete.

The field of education has a long tradition of using optically read test answer sheets (see Baker, 1971b, for a thorough discussion) and this tradition has carried over into CMI. There are a number of optical mark readers (OMR) available that can detect a pencil mark on a card or sheet. Two different approaches are used to process scannable sheets or cards. The first uses equipment such as the IBM 1230 or DIGITEK 100 to scan the sheets to produce punched cards. The punched cards are then used as the input medium to the computer. A number of the early CMI systems (Cooley and Glaser, 1968; Kelley, 1968; Silberman, 1968) used this equipment. The use of optical mark readers producing punched cards is rare, due to the above machines being obsolete and the adding of an unnecessary step to the processing sequence. The second and present approach is to use optical mark readers connected to the computer via telephone lines. Thus, as the data is scanned, it is entered directly into the computer, where it can be processed and stored. Equipment such as the IBM 2956 and the Hewlett-Packard 7260A employ Hollerith sized cards as the input medium. However, such cards impose some limits on the amount of information collected and the nature of the forms printed on the card. Sheet scanners such as the Decision 6500, OPSCAN 17, Datronics 5500, and the DATUM 5098 can handle the standard 8½ x 11" answer sheets. The OPSCAN 17 and Decision 6500 can score the full sheet, while the DATUM 5098 and Datronics 5500 scan somewhat less than half the page. The OPSCAN 17 also has the capability for hand-written numbers and forming editing. The DATUM 5098 is a desk top scanner of very small physical size. Within the various CMI systems this OMR equipment is used in a number of different ways. Systems such as PLAN*, AIS, and the Navy CMI system use the OMR devices instead of a conventional card reader as the input portion of the RJE terminal. PLAN* submits the cards in batches with identifier cards preceding and following the set of cards. MICA-5 can use the DATUM scanner in conjunction with the interactive keyboard terminal to enter test results. Although the Optical Mark Readers provide an extremely convenient way to collect data from the instructional setting, they do pose some constraints in the area of assessment. Under normal practice, the OMR answer sheets are used for multiple choice items. But not all assessment lends itself to the multiple choice format. Unfortunately, there is some tendency for the convenience of the equipment to force the use of multiple-choice questions even where they are not appropriate. With a bit of imagination the constraints imposed by OMR upon assessment can be avoided, while retaining the advantages of the approach. For example, the Development Mathematics Program supported by WIS/SIM uses a teacher observation schedule where the teacher simply checks observational categories on an optically scanned card (Belt and Skubal, 1974). Outside of the assessment area, the use of OMR sheets or cards presents few problems for data collection. The form appearing on the sheet or card can be designed to meet the needs of the particular CMI system with little difficulty. The scheme used by PLAN* is a good example of a parsimonious, yet efficient data collection scheme based upon the use of optical mark readers.

Interactive keyboard terminals can also be used as data collection devices. The terminal operator can enter data via the keyboard and the computer can prompt the data entry and respond to the data. The Sherman School Project described in Chapter Four used interactive terminals for all data input. Using an interactive terminal as a data collection device is a bit slow due to the man-machine dialogue and the low transmission rates typically employed. Consequently, the data collection procedures need to be parsimonious to reduce the time required to a minimum. A number of CMI and related systems have employed interactive terminals, chiefly cathode ray tube displays with keyboards, as test administration devices (Allen, Meleca, and Meyers, 1972; Anderson *et al.*, 1974a; Dick and Gallager, 1972; Griesen, 1973; Hsu, 1974). Under this computer-aided testing (CAT) approach, the computer displays the test items and the student uses the keyboard to enter his response. This approach, however, is not viable when one has many students, due to the large number of interactive terminals that would be required. The computer-aided testing approach appears to be best suited to college level or training institution CMI systems; it does not appear to be economically feasible for elementary school level systems. The best approach to the use of interactive terminals in CMI is one where they are used to conduct a dialogue with the computer while an optical mark reader is used to collect the item response data. Such a combination is reasonably quick, yet retains the responsiveness of the interactive terminal.

At least two CMI systems use hybrid approaches to data collection and entry. A very clever mix of remote job entry, interactive, and computer compatible data collection media is employed by Countermine and Singh (1974) at Penn State for their use of CMI at branch campuses. Optically scannable answer sheets are used to record a student's item responses. These sheets are read via an OPSCAN 17 optical mark reader and recorded on magnetic tape cassettes via a Texas Instruments 700 keyboard terminal. When scanning the sheets, the keyboard terminal serves no function other than to connect the scanner and the cassette recorder. When the sheet scanning is completed, the cassettes are replayed and their contents printed at the keyboard terminal. The operator is able to perform verification and error correction procedures upon the recorded data and rerecord the data on a second, error-free cassette tape. Upon completion of this process, the keyboard terminal is connected to the central computer via telephone lines and a computer program reads the contents of the cassette tape. The CMI data processing procedures are performed on the data and the reports produced on the line printer of the remote job entry terminal. This mixed approach provides excellent local control of the quality of the data, provides access to the computer when needed via the interactive terminal, and can produce reports via the line printer. It takes advantage of interactive computing and remote job entry while minimizing the costs associated with interactive computing. Hsu (1974) uses an interactive terminal in a rather unusual operational procedure. At the end of each school day a teacher aide uses the interactive terminal to enter the data found in a student's folder. The data entered by the teacher aide goes into temporary files in the computer that are edited and quality controlled by a programmer during the weekend. Only when all the daily transactions have been checked does the data enter the data base.

Where immediate response to the generated data is not required, the Remote Job Entry mode is adequate for most if not all instructional level management purposes. In addition, most of the course level management procedures revolve around procedures such as scheduling, pacing, and resource allocation that tend to be based upon reports such as the unit report, group report, and contact report. If a daily or weekly reporting cycle is adequate for course level management purposes, then the batch mode is also adequate. Ideally, one would like a teacher to request the relevant report when a decision needs to be made, rather than wait for the scheduled issuance of the report; and report generation upon request can best be done via an interactive terminal and the time-sharing mode. However, with some planning ahead on the teacher's part, even reports produced via batch procedures can be timely. It is interesting to note that in the Sherman School system, where reports upon demand are available, the three major reports were generated on a weekly basis.

System Reliability

Due to the reliance of teachers and students upon the computer component, the computer hardware and software must be reliable. The daily operation of the instructional program under CMI depends heavily upon the computer component performing its task accurately and in a timely fashion. Because computers are electronic devices, their computer programs are produced by humans, and many procedures are performed manually, complete reliability is difficult to obtain. Consequently, the designer of CMI systems must take this unreliability into account and provide means for minimizing its impact upon the classroom. The usual measure of reliability of electronic equipment such as computers is mean time between failure (MTBF). It can range from a few hours to many days, depending upon the size and complexity of the computer. Those CMI systems employing the interactive mode of computer usage are especially vulnerable to the effects of a low MTBF. They depend upon the man-machine dialogue, and when it stops, all computer-related operations stop. Remote Job Entry usage is also affected by MTBF, but computer failures are not as disruptive as they are under the interactive mode. If the computer fails, the terminal operator can wait until the system is operational again and resubmit the card decks, scan sheets, etc. Unless they are of very long duration, routine computer failures do not seriously interfere with batch-oriented CMI systems.

Computer hardware reliability varies widely as a function of the equipment and how it is used. Computer terminal equipment, such as CRT displays, keyboard terminals, optical mark readers, and printers, is normally very reliable. These devices are physically small and involve a small amount of electronics and electro-mechanical parts. In addition, they are designed for use with minimal maintenance. Although the computer devices used as interactive terminals or as Remote Job Entry terminals are very reliable, the telephone lines by which they are connected to the computer are a major problem. In talking to persons responsible for CMI and other computer-based systems throughout the country, the telephone lines are a common source of concern. In some geographical areas, little or no difficulty with the telephone lines is encountered. In other areas, the telephone service nearly precludes using remote terminals. There are several grades of telephone line quality as provided by the telephone companies. Often, switching to a higher grade of service can eliminate many problems. In the case of the Sherman School Project, the telephone company installed a "conditioned" line and completely eliminated many months of mysterious line difficulties. For most CMI systems, the only solution to telephone line problems is to cooperate closely with the telephone company to solve them. Monitoring equipment is available and it can be used effectively to isolate the problem and eliminate it. There are a number of alternatives to telephone interconnections, such as microwave, infrared, and laser beam systems, that can be used in limited geographical areas. However, the present cost of such equipment generally precludes their use for CMI systems.

There seems to be a direct relationship between the degree to which a computer is used and its reliability. Those computers having a low load factor, in terms of utilization of the total resources of the computer, are usually reliable. This factor was first brought to the author's attention by the low MTBF of the University of Wisconsin's computer facility. The director of the computer facility collected some informal data from other universities on systems reliability as a function of load. He found that the relationship held in a number of university settings and was not related to the manufacturer of the computer. Since most universities have a single large-scale computer devoted to academic and research computing, these machines tend to be heavily loaded. In addition, a large proportion of this load consists of student jobs and research projects that often can "clobber" the system, with the attendant system failure. Computer usage at universities also tends to be cyclic, with light loads early in a semester and heavy overloads near the end of semesters. The author suspects that most computer systems used by universities are poor choices for supporting CMI, since universities tend to use their computers rather heavily and have a very diverse work load. The moral of these observations seems to be that if one wants reliable service in a CMI application, implement it on a computer having excess capacity relative to the work load. Such a recommendation is anathema to budget controllers, as they invariably insist upon obtaining the minimum capacity needed for the existing work load. To do so simply means that the overall system becomes heavily loaded, and reliability decreases significantly, with real costs in terms of user time, etc., rising sharply. Another source of hardware system unreliability is the practice of changing computers periodically. Most computer facilities change computers roughly every five to seven years. When this occurs, the overall system reliability is sharply degraded. New computers seem to be inherently unreliable, despite the manufacturers' best efforts to break them in. Apparently the shipping process, a different work load, and new physical environment disturbs the equipment. From a reliability point of view, the worst possible combination is a new computer, a new CMI system, and a new set of teachers using the system. Hence, one should avoid this combination if at all possible.

Computer software also contributes to the unreliability of CMI systems. Each of the three levels of software involved—systems software, compilers and other languages, and the CMI program—can contribute to unreliability. All computers, from mini's to super computers, employ operating system software to allocate and protect the resources of the computer. These operating systems are large, complex computer programs and are difficult to perfect. As errors are detected, they are corrected, and periodically the manufacturer will consolidate all the changes into a new release of the operating system. For some reason, new releases seem to have more errors in them than the versions they replace. Most computer facilities devote considerable effort to checking new releases before they are put into daily use. The actual CMI computer programs are written using either standard programming languages, such as FORTRAN and COBOL, or employ one of the special CAI languages, such as IBM's COURSE-WRITER or PLATO's TUTOR. These languages depend upon compilers or similar software to translate the language into instructions performed by the computer. Like operating systems, the language software consists of large, complex computer programs. They also are subject to new releases and their attendant unreliability. What happens in both cases is that many iterations are required to correct all the errors in the software supporting the actual CMI computer programs. Just when stability is reached, the manufacturer or the computer center releases the next version of the software that "corrects" all the known deficiencies and adds new features and capabilities. As is obvious, the whole cycle begins again. The impact upon the operation of the CMI project is clear: systems software induced failures are high whenever new releases are put into use and low just before new releases are installed. Often the CMI project has no control of the cycle and must be prepared to live with it. If some control can be exercised, a CMI program should be run under the most stable systems software. Often computer centers will not accept and install new releases for many months after they are available to allow major problems to surface elsewhere. The key to system software reliability is stability. If your computer facility is prone to quickly installing each new release as soon as possible, they need to be educated as to its impact upon your CMI effort.

Despite one's best efforts to achieve both hardware and software reliability, systems will fail. The CMI designer needs to protect those in the classroom against such failures. Other than the loss of the operational capability, the loss of data is the most important effect of a system failure. The transaction in process during the failure can be completely or partially lost and the data base itself can be altered or in rare cases destroyed. There are a number of techniques that can be employed for coping with system failures. System failures can be handled at the operational level by manual data recording procedures which allow the instructional paradigm to continue functioning. In addition, the use of magnetic tape recording of every transaction between the terminal and the computer enables one to pinpoint when a failure occurred and then to update the files from that point via the manual records. Although the magnetic tape back-up provides both excellent recovery from a failure and data base protection, it is too expensive to use. A simple, but very effective, system protection feature is to "check point" data to mass storage as soon as possible. Computer programmers have a tendency to design programs in which once a data record is completed in core memory, it is retained in core until all other uses of the record are completed. Such a practice leaves the record open to loss via a system failure. Under the check pointing approach, as soon as the data record has received new data or otherwise has been modified, it is copied into mass storage. This minimizes the time period it is exposed to the possibility of a system failure. Check pointing does not prevent subsequent use of the record, as the original is still in core memory and can be used as before. Another approach is to copy the active files, such as the student history file, at the end of each day's use, onto magnetic tape. This technique also provides good protection against loss of the data base due to system failures occurring when the CMI system is not in use. In addition, most large computer facilities copy all mass storage files onto magnetic tape each day, so that major failures in the storage system results in the loss of no more than one day's changes in the files. This tape copying procedure coupled with the CMI daily tape provides a very good level of data base integrity, especially if the failure occurs when the CMI system is not in use. The staff of the Sherman School project eventually abandoned the daily recording of active files in favor of check pointing coupled with the computing center daily mass storage tape copy. Through the use of the one day student history report, the fast mode of prescribing, and the "tear-off" sheets, the computer terminal operator could quickly determine which student's records were used during a given day and whether or not the failure affected his record for the day. Once determined, the individual record could be updated via the interactive terminal in less than 20 seconds. The procedures just described are only a few of the many possible techniques to protect the data base from system failures and to restore it to its proper state. The CMI designer must include such procedures that are both effective and easy to use.

To achieve an acceptable level of reliability, the CMI computer component also needs to be protected against those who use it, i.e., be "fool-proof." Such protection can be implemented in both normal and abnormal operational situations. Normal operations need to be protected against inadvertent use of system features. Sufficient checks and in the interactive case, prompts, should be used to insure that the proper sequence of operations is being performed. Certain features, such as alteration of the static files, should be accessible only by authorized persons via a password or other such device. Thus, the user cannot inadvertently access an unintended file. Keeping the normal sequence of operations as simple as possible also enhances reliability. Users of the system will quickly develop a "feel" for how things function and readily detect improper uses of system features. When errors are made, the system design should make recovery from them as simple as possible. One should be able to repeat the sequence or replace a given operation without becoming involved in a long, complex recovery procedure. There is some tendency to design systems as if failures and errors will not occur. However, system reliability can be a function of how well the user and the system can cope with abnormal operations.

System reliability is also a function of the data entered into the data base. Once erroneous data enters the data base, it is difficult to detect, as it gets amalgamated with correct data and used as if it were correct. The best quality control procedures are those detecting bad data as early as possible, namely where it originates. Thus, teachers and students need to be trained in the correct procedures for filling in forms and answer cards or sheets. The completed forms should be visually inspected for correctness before leaving the instructional setting. The procedures used to enter the data into the computer should also perform quality control functions. PLAN* (WCL, 1973b) has an excellent set of quality control functions for its optical mark reader input. As each card is read, it is subjected to a series of checks, and certain errors are reported to the terminal operator. Obvious mistakes can be corrected by the operator and the cards resubmitted. Once the cards are read, the data is subjected to logical checks against the data base. Errors are not allowed to enter the data base but are reported to the teacher via the daily report. This two-level procedure provides a good level of quality control of the input data. Reliability of the data collection procedures can be enhanced considerably by proper design of the forms, scan sheets, etc., used to capture the data. Considerable attention should be paid to the layout of the forms. It is the simple things, like whether the item response positions go down or across the page, or whether the student number is in a position to be easily seen, that determine reliability. The forms, sheets, etc., should be carefully designed and then extensively pilot tested before they are used. How a student perceives and uses a data collection sheet and how the designer views it can be quite different. Again, simplicity is the key; complex, hard to understand forms will result in errors. Simple, easy to use forms will help minimize error and enhance system reliability.

A reliable CMI computer component depends upon four

factors. (1) A computer facility should have a good balance between the load imposed upon it and its computing capacity. If one has a choice, use a lightly loaded computer. (2) Stability of both hardware and software contributes greatly to system reliability. A computer system that has been used for a few years, with peculiarities that are well known, with a pool of knowledgeable users, and whose documentation matches its uses is normally a reliable system. (3) Reliability also depends upon having simple, systematic procedures for both normal and abnormal operations. Many times, the users of a CMI system can self-inflict major problems through improper use of the system. Making the system "fool proof" increases reliability. (4) A basic principle of quality control is to perform the error detection and correction procedures as close as possible to where the data was created. Those most familiar with the data are in the best position to insure that it is proper. Attention to these four factors in the design and operation of CMI systems should result in adequate levels of reliability.

Some Computer Configurations

In the developmental stages, most CMI systems have relied upon large-scale computers available through universities. As CMI systems become part of the instructional setting, there will be a need for computer configurations designed explicitly for CMI use. Three different computer hardware configurations are described below to illustrate potentially useful configurations (see Ashenhurst and Vonderhoe, 1975; Farber, 1975; and Wulf and Levin, 1975 for an extended discussion). The first configuration is based upon the computer network approach. A number of mini-computers are connected to the large-scale computer via telephone lines. In turn, each mini-computer has connected to it a number of remote job entry terminals. These can be directly connected or connected via telephone lines. Because the mini-computer at each of the nodes of a configuration has its own data processing capability, it can perform a number of functions. Primarily, it can act as a data concentrator for the large-scale computer. In this role, it performs editing checks on the data as it is read via card readers or optical mark readers. It can reformat the data to reduce the amount of data transmitted to the central computer. It can also establish queues of data needing the same data processing services; hence, making the processing more efficient. When reports are produced at the central computer, they are transmitted to the appropriate mini-computer. It in turn can route the report directly to the appropriate remote job entry terminal printer. Alternatively, the reports can be stored in a disk file for printing upon request of a terminal operator. The latter technique provides better operational flexibility. Figure 7.1 depicts a typical mini-computer network configuration.

There are two CMI systems making use of this type of computer configuration, IMS-3 (McManus, 1971) and PLAN*. IMS-3 employs a single mini-computer, a PDP-8, as a data concentrator. The mini-computer collects instructionally related data from optical mark readers (two OPSCAN-17's) that are in the same room as the computer, as well as from remotely located optical mark readers. The mini-computer collects the data, performs edit checks, and writes the data onto magnetic tapes. At a later point in time, a telephone connection is made with either a large-scale computer, an IBM 360/91, or a medium-scale computer, a Sigma 7. A job stream is initiated and the data on tape is transferred via the telephone lines to the mass storage devices of the larger computers as a card input file. Control cards in the job stream then initiate CMI computer programs to process the data in batch mode. When reports and other results are generated, they are transmitted to the mini-computer and stored in a report file. The reports are then printed via a line printer connected to the mini-computer.

In the PLAN* computer network there are IBM 3755 remote job entry terminals connected via telephone lines to the IBM 370/155. PLAN* also makes provision for the use of mini-computers as remote job entry terminals. The most common terminal consists of a Hewlett-Packard 2100 with optical mark

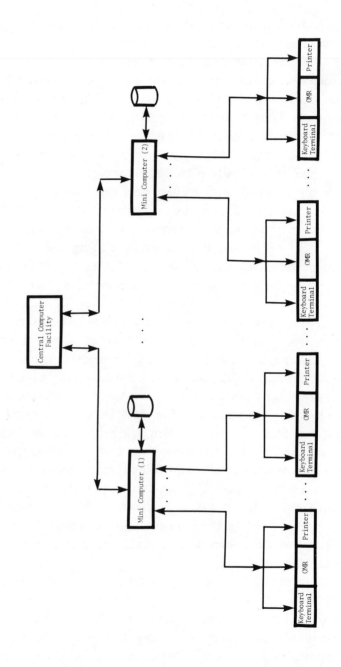

Figure 7.1: Typical Mini-Computer Network

reader and a printer. IBM System 3's are also used in this role. Available documentation (DeHart, 1974) does not indicate scope of the tasks performed by the mini-computers at the local sites. The author suspects that the mini-computers appear to the central computer as though they were IBM 3755 terminals. To do so would simplify the PLAN* software and make it possible for computers in the school districts to be interfaced with the system. Local schools could, of course, develop their own pre- and post-processing software to perform the quality control functions described earlier. It should be noted that the computer configurations used by PLAN* also support other educationally related computer services. These are SCORE, a computer-assisted test construction system, and administrative data processing, such as pupil scheduling, report cards, and similar functions. Sharing the computer network with other services amortizes the costs over a larger customer base, thus lowering the cost for individual services.

The second type of computer configuration, multiple mini-computers, is used by Project ABACUS of the U.S. Army (Howard, 1974). Multiple mini-computers, each performing a separate function, are configured to achieve the capabilities of a larger computer at a much lower cost. Figure 7.2 shows the hardware configuration and functional flow of the Computerized Training System (CTS) developed by GTE Sylvania for Project ABACUS.

There are six mini-computers (PDP-11/35) in the system, a system controller, a data base controller, and four display controllers. The system controller serves as the central computer, executing the primary CMI software, maintaining student records in its own disk files, and exercising supervisory control over the rest of the system. The data base controller is responsible for a set of disk storage devices containing the lesson material for the CAI mode of operation as well as the static files used in the CMI mode. Each of the four display controllers is responsible for 32 hard-wired student stations. These stations consist of a CRT display and a keyboard for data entry. The display controller

*Figure 7.2: Computerized Training System
Hardware Configuration*

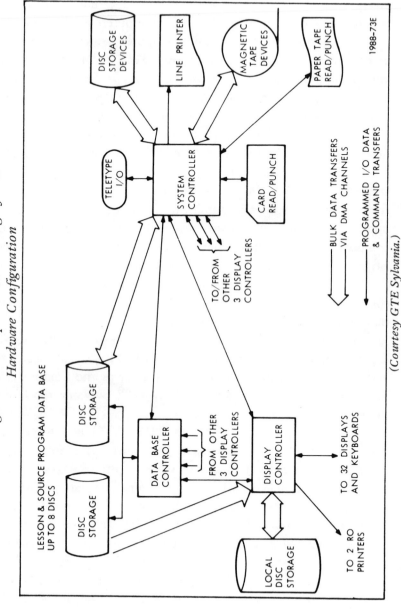
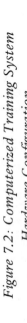

(*Courtesy GTE Sylvania.*)

handles the information flow to and from each of its terminals as well as serving as the connecting link with the rest of the system. The display controller has some local capability to respond to requests generated at a terminal. If it cannot handle the request, it passes it on to the system controller. The system controller can then call a computer program module to process the request. If necessary, it can also instruct the data base controller to locate information in its files needed to respond to the request. The data base controller transmits the necessary data to the system controller via direct computer to computer memory access channels. The four display controllers are each connected to both the data base controller and the system controller. Although such a configuration appears complex, it represents an approach that is becoming widely used. By partitioning the functions among several computers, the computer programming for a given computer is limited and specialized. The inter-computer coordination is handled by the system controller much in the way an operating system does in a large-scale computer. However, considerable simplification in this coordination is due to the dedication of the total system to CAI and CMI. The classes of information and its flow can be limited to those required by the application instead of meeting the needs of general purpose computing. In the CTS configuration, the system controller has its own complement of peripheral equipment: line printers, card read/punch, magnetic tape, and disk files. These can be used to input data and generate reports in the CMI mode. The multi-mini configuration is also employed by TICCIT (MITRE, 1974), but only two computers (NOVA 800) are used. One acts as a system controller, the other as the display controller. TICCIT is attempting to handle 128 color TV displays, each also having a keyboard device and audio output.

Because of the low cost of mini-computers, the ease with which they can be interconnected, and the wide range of available peripheral equipment, the multiple-mini configuration is attractive for CMI. It seems to be an especially viable approach to medium-scale systems where the computer configuration is dedicated to CMI. The major disadvantages to such configurations lies in the software area. Mini-computers generally use assembly level programming languages. If compiler level languages or special purpose author languages are available, they tend to limit the size and scope of the programs that can be written. Such configurations also require a high level of programming skill to develop the software needed to make the total configuration operate in concert. Once created, future development tends to be discouraged due to the rather close tailoring of the software to the hardware configuration and the particular application supported.

The final computer configuration of relevance to CMI is one implementing the distributed computing concept. The hardware configuration is similar to that of the mini-computer network depicted in Figure 7.1. But the small computers in the network are more powerful than a mini-computer. A representative computer would be one of the Harris-DATACRAFT 6000 series machines having a 24 bit word length rather than the 12-18 bit word of most mini-computers. The additional power of the computers in the network permits them to do more than act as data concentrators. As was the case with the mini-computer network, the small computers will have a number of terminals connected to them, both RJE and interactive. Inspection of the MICA software described in Chapter Five reveals that the proportion of the total CMI software package devoted to operational procedures is relatively small. The major portion is associated with the data base management procedures. The small computers are quite adept at controlling peripheral devices, but they do not have sufficient capacity to perform the data base management functions.

The large-scale computer at the apex of the network can easily handle the data base management functions, but it is not well suited to handling a large number of peripheral terminals. Under the distributed computing concept, CMI functions are allocated to the computer best suited to the function. The author had proposed a distributed computing concept for WIS/SIM involving a DATACRAFT 6024/5 and a UNIVAC 1110.

The DATACRAFT computer would be connected to up to 16 RJE terminals, each consisting of a GE Terminet 1200 keyboard terminal and a DATUM 5098 Optical Mark Reader. The DATA-CRAFT computer was in turn connected directly via a cable to the UNIVAC 1110 several city blocks away. The CMI software package was to be divided such that the UNIVAC 1110 contained a general purpose sophisticated data base management package and the CMI data base. The 6024/5 would contain the operational CMI software but no data base other than record buffers. In a sense, the DATACRAFT would be the master computer and the UNIVAC 1110 the slave computer. Operationally, the DATA-CRAFT would collect data via one of the RJE terminals, process the data and, if appropriate, transmit data back to the terminal. All access to the CMI data base in the UNIVAC 1110 would be via inter-computer messages. For example, if the DATACRAFT software wanted a record from the student history file, it would send a message to the UNIVAC 1110. The 1110 would call upon the Data Base Management package to locate the record in mass storage, place it in core memory, and then transmit the record via the inter-computer channel to the DATACRAFT. The latter would place the record in a buffer in core memory as well as copy it onto its own small disk memory. Once the record was in the DATACRAFT memory, it could be updated, data extracted from it, etc. If the record contents were modified, the record would be sent back to the 1110, where it would be written into the appropriate location in the data base via the data base management program.

The distributed computing approach is very attractive for CMI systems. Large-scale, sophisticated Data Base Management systems are very expensive to develop, and typically can only be executed on large-scale computers. Direct access to such systems from a small computer eliminates the need to locally develop this software. Also, these data base management systems can provide a wider range of capabilities than can locally developed software. Thus relieved of this major developmental burden, the CMI portion of the software can be more sophisticated. The distributed computing concept also can result in better overall system reliability. When the large-scale computer fails, the operational environment is in the small computer. The latter holds the working buffers, the operational software, and the communication lines to the terminal. The small computer can complete as much processing as possible, up to the need for data base access, inform the terminal operators as to the system status, and put the system in a holding state. This protects the use of the CMI system from total system failure. Of course, if the small computer fails, it is equivalent to a total failure, but the data base is protected. It would also be possible to have the CMI system reloaded in the large computer and have the terminal operators reestablish communication—thus, enabling the CMI system to remain operational even though the small computer had failed. The approach also provides a degree of protection against the problem associated with heavily loaded computers. The small computer can be dedicated to the CMI application with its RJE and interactive terminals and heavy communications traffic. The load generated by the small computer upon the large computer is minimal, consisting of requests for data base management services at the record level. The scheme removes a considerable work load from the large-scale computer and replaces it with a much lower level of load. The allocation of the work load is also much better in that each computer is performing tasks much more in tune with its capabilities. The removal of the time-sharing interactive procedures from the large-scale computer is particularly important.

Although the distributed computing concept appears to be relatively simple, it does involve some rather sophisticated software. The primary problem is getting the two computers to cooperate. Each computer must have the capability to interrupt the other and to pass messages across the inter-computer channel. Once received, the computer must respond to the message with the proper action. In the case of the small computer, the I/O routines requesting data from the large computer must automatically send messages to the large computer, which then returns the proper record. To the CMI programmer, it appears as if the request for a record from a file was satisfied by the small computer. Hence, the intercomputer traffic is transparent. In the larger scale computer, the operating system must recognize a request for service, bring in the data base management package, and pass the message and control to the package. When the record is found, it is made available to the operating system, which then establishes a communication link with the small computer and sends the record to it. These procedures would require modification of the operating system in both computers.

At the time of writing, WIS/SIM had not implemented the author's proposed use of the distributed computing concept. However, a large number of military computer based systems for weapons control, missile systems, command and control, etc., employ distributed computing systems of far greater complexity than that described above. The concept can provide CMI designers with the best of the capabilities of both small-scale and large-scale computers with a relatively small investment. The ability to dedicate the small-scale computer to CMI while exploiting the data base management capabilities of large computers is especially important for the development of medium-scale and large-scale CMI.

Software Issues

The computer component of the CMI system is embodied to a large extent in the computer programs executed by the computer. The programs determine what functions are performed, provide operational flexibility, control future growth, and to a considerable degree determine the operational costs of a CMI system. Whether one has a good or a bad CMI system rests heavily upon the quality of the conceptualization and the implementation of the CMI software. In the paragraphs below, a range of issues related to the design and implementation of CMI software is discussed. The intent is to expose those issues that tend to be obscure until after one has developed a system.

Since CMI systems are basically management information systems, there are a number of issues arising from the data base that is the core of such systems. There is a high degree of interaction among the data base design, the curricular plan, and the instructional model. This interaction determines the size of the data base and the costs attendant to storing and using the data base. The degree of fractionalization of the curricular plan can determine the level of detail which must be taken into account in the data base. The impact of curricular fractionalization also is seen in files, such as the prescription file and unit files, related to the curricular plan. However, the major impact is upon the student history file. The data base designer must decide upon the level of curricular detail to be stored for each pupil. If the curriculum has been fractionated to the objective level, and the reports are based upon objectives, then a student history record must provide space for recording each objective encountered by a pupil. If a great deal of instructionally related data is generated as a student employs an instructional unit, the student history record size also grows. In many CMI systems, there are pretest and posttest scores for each unit, within-unit test scores, and prescriptions that must be recorded for management purposes. The greater the instructional activity associated with each unit, the greater the data storage requirements. As a consequence, the data base designer needs to examine the worth of each data element to the total CMI system. Each element must be justified, as there are data storage costs and computer programming costs associated with each data element.

Dynamic growth of the data base as a function of time is also a problem for data base designers. At the beginning of the school year there is very little instructionally related data for each pupil. As the school year proceeds, the mass of data increases to a maximum at the end of the year. Because it is simplest, programmers tend to design the student history record to hold the maximum amount of data. Such fixed length records simplify programming but are expensive to store, since at the beginning of the school year there are disk file charges for essentially empty files. File records should be dynamic so that the record size is a function of the amount of data collected rather than being predefined. The problem of dynamic record growth can be solved by well-known techniques, but their implementation is usually beyond the resources of CMI implementers. Many of the data base management packages available for large-scale computers can handle the problem automatically in a way that is transparent to the programmer.

Another data base design issue is cross-file linkages. It is generally not feasible to put all of the data associated with a CMI system in a single, large file. For conceptual and practical reasons, multiple files are created, each containing a specific class of data. During operational use of the CMI system, data often is extracted from a number of different files as a function of data needed. For example, when performing the reporting process, data in a student history file record is used to access data in the unit file, prescription file, and student data file. Thus, an efficient means is needed to access data in one file as a function of data in another. There are a number of different techniques that can be used to achieve cross-file linkages. The dictionary approach used by the MICA software was based upon the indexed sequential technique. It proved to be a rudimentary, yet effective, means of achieving cross-file linkages. The cross-file linkage problem has the characteristic of being rather insidious. Programmers tend to design a file, develop the software to manipulate the file, and only belatedly recognize the interdependencies among files. At that point, a number of *ad hoc* solutions are implemented and the CMI software becomes hopelessly clumsy. Hence, the basic problems can be avoided easily at the data base design stage if one recognizes the need for cross-file linkages.

The scale of the CMI system also has an effect upon the data base design. When designing a small-scale system, the designer can have a relatively free hand. He can use relatively large file records, include data items of questionable value, and create many different files. He can do this because the curriculum is limited to a single subject area and the total number of students involved is small. Although the designer has been somewhat extravagant, the total size of the data base is small, the time to search the total file is low, and minor inefficiencies in cross-file linkages do not seriously degrade the performance of the system. The real impact of such practices appears when one attempts to expand a small-scale system into a medium-scale or large-scale system. The many small inefficiencies and extravagances become considerably magnified. The student history file record provides a good example. This record in the MICA-3 program contained 1,732 computer words of six characters each. If all 30,000 elementary school pupils in the school district were to be included in the file, it would require 1,732 x 6 x 30,000 characters of disk storage. These 311.76 million characters would require 11 of the commonly used 29 million character capacity disk packs, which is a large number of packs for a computer to support simultaneously for a single application. A related data storage problem is one of allocation of core storage to each interactive terminal connected to the computer. A number of time-sharing systems allocate blocks of core storage for programs and data to each terminal. The size of these blocks helps determine how many terminals can be maintained by the computer. Again, sloppy record design with its attendant large buffer requirements will make it difficult to employ these blocks efficiently.

The data base management program is a key element in the computer component, and most CMI designers develop their own package. When the CMI systems are small-scale, such programs can be constructed by specializing them quite narrowly to the problem at hand. The main problem associated with such programs is that they are difficult to adapt to changing conditions, due to limitations with respect to documentation and long-term software maintenance. None of the CMI systems described in Appendix A reports using a standard data base management system, such as IBM's IMS/VS, System 2000, Mark IV, or DMS 1100. Bratten (1968) used a general data base management and reporting system called LUCID to provide the data base management for IMS. While it was a general-purpose system at that time, it was only available on the computer at System Development Corporation. The availability of a sophisticated general purpose Data Base Management Package designed for CMI usage would be a considerable help (see Sibley, 1976, for an overview of the basic DBM designs). Such a program could eliminate many of the data base problems, such as dynamic growth, cross-file linkages, and resource utilization, that each CMI designer must resolve for each CMI system. Elimination of this major software package from the CMI implementation effort would be extremely helpful.

In addition to data base management software, the CMI field also needs programming languages designed specifically for its use. A number of CMI systems (Allen, Meleca, and Meyers, 1972; Anderson *et al.*, 1974a; Morgan and Richardson, 1972) have used CAI languages to program CMI systems. However, CAI languages, such as COURSEWRITER III and TUTOR, are ill suited for CMI use, as their conceptual base rests upon the lessons-and-frames approach of programmed instruction. Under this antiquated approach, the author expresses the actual instruction via the programming language. For example, if the student is to be asked a question, the question is embedded directly in the computer programming. Thus, if the question is to be changed, the segment of computer program must be recoded. The TICCIT system (MITRE, 1974) also used this approach. The use of programming techniques requiring expression of the curriculum as computer code is ill-conceived and incompatible with CMI. The programming techniques should provide absolute independence of the curriculum (courseware) and the software. Well-designed CMI systems place the courseware, i.e., the curricular plans, prescriptions, tests, etc., in the data base, not the software. When changes need to be made, they can be done via the file maintenance procedures rather than by reprogramming. The CMI computer program should be generalized to handle files, records, and elements and be unconcerned about the actual contents. A given

CMI computer program should be able to handle any of the various curricular plans described in Chapter Two without reprogramming. However, the computer programs are not independent of the instructional model; but, with some thought, a reasonable degree of independence can be achieved. The CAI languages also make little or no provision for the storage of student history data and other data in a data base. Allen, Meleca, and Meyers (1972) report having to add considerable special programming to COURSEWRITER III in order to use it for CMI. TUTOR is also weak in the data base management area. Gardner (1974) has developed a language for the Advanced Instructional System intended for CMI use. However, the language definition is primarily CAI oriented (based on TUTOR) and only a few record handling statements were included to meet CMI needs. It is the author's view that the use of CAI languages for CMI development is a very poor practice. One's time is better spent using one of the standard programming languages, such as FORTRAN or COBOL. At an earlier point in time, CAI languages could be justified, since they were one of the only vehicles for access to the computer via interactive terminals. At the present time, the time-sharing capabilities of most computers eliminate this reason. The fundamental deficiencies of CAI languages are two-fold: one, they do not provide for independence of courseware and software, and two, they do not provide a data base management capability.

There is a real need for a high level CMI programming language. Such a language should allow one to specify the data base design, define the data processing, conduct a man-machine dialogue if desired, generate reports, and communicate with a variety of peripheral devices. In addition, the compiler for the language should generate reentrant code, so that many terminals can share the same computer program. The approach taken by Merrill (1974) at Florida State University is a step in this direction. He employed a standard data base and a collection of useful subroutines. To build a CMI system for a given instructor, he programmed a driver routine that collects the appropriate subroutines and provides them with a controlling mechanism. The sequence of operations is then achieved when the driver program is executed. His approach has considerable flexibility, with a minimum of new software development for each new user. The technical details of this approach have not been published, but it could serve as the basis for a language development. Kelley's TIPS software could also provide a stepping stone to a CMI language. His data base definition scheme, with its arbitrarily assignable performance and attribute variables, is a good beginning. In addition, TIPS' ability to define decision rules in terms of these variables could be the basis for a flexible diagnosis and prescription component of a CMI language.

The closest approach to a CMI language is the Outcomes Analysis Procedure due to Behr (1976). The OAP language employs four types of variables—outcome, temporary, message, and pupil. The outcome variables are primarily test scores. The temporary variables are used to hold intermediate results during processing. The message variables are similar to those of TIPS and can be prescriptions or information. There are three types of pupil variables—pupil, network, and unit—that reference selected entries in a pupil's instructional history file record. The OAP language implements 16 statements that are similar in structure to the logical statements in FORTRAN. These 16 statements are organized into three major types—test statements, immediate action, and deferred action statements. Using the OAP language statements, Behr (1976) was able to express the diagnosis and prescription procedures implemented by TIPS and IMI/IMS (Sellman, 1975). The OAP language is only a procedural specification scheme and does not include either data base management or an authoring capability. Consequently, Behr's work, though a significant contribution, does not provide a complete CMI language definition. The development of a good high level language for CMI purposes is well within the state of the art. The basic problem is pulling together the resources and talent needed to design and implement a language.

One of the characteristics of a good CMI software package is flexibility. As teachers become more familiar with CMI, experience has shown that their level of expectation also rises. They recognize new services the computer can provide, inadequacies in existing functions, and an expanded role for the computer. As a result, the CMI software must have sufficient inherent flexibility to meet this higher level of expectation without major restructuring of the software. The software designer must approach CMI software with a "things are going to change" philosophy, and such changes should have a minimum impact upon the computer component. Achieving this goal requires that flexibility be designed into the software from the start. Unfortunately, there is a breed of computer programmers who philosophically cannot accept this point of view. They conceptualize software very narrowly to meet the stated requirements, akin to the budget controllers who force schools to buy computers with no growth potential. These programmers view software as having a short life span and investing resources in flexibility as a waste. At the other end of the continuum are those generalists who want to design the ultimate amount of generality into any application they program. Unfortunately, these persons rarely complete a project—and never for a reasonable cost. The author knows of several multi-million software efforts that were eventually abandoned because the generality desired became too complex to implement. Thus, one must find a middle ground, where the program has enough inherent flexibility to adapt to change over a period of time without the flexibility being too expensive. In reality, such flexibility is achieved at the conceptual and design stages of software development. The cost of implementation of reasonable flexibility program is only trivially more than that of a highly specific computer program, yet these costs will be returned many times over the life span of the program.

Three factors underly designing CMI software of sufficient flexibility: (1) The designer must look beyond immediate needs, concepts, and requirements when creating CMI software.

Typically, the persons dealing with the educational components are concerned with an immediate problem; even when pressed, they have difficulty anticipating next year's needs. The software designer has a somewhat freer hand. For example, he can anticipate additional reports and can design a report generator that can easily produce many different reports on the basis of parameters, rather than write a separate computer program for each report currently specified. Often the immediate needs of a given educational setting can be met by a rudimentary CMI system. By examining more sophisticated CMI systems, the software designer can see functions, capabilities, and features that will be needed in the future. These can be included in the original developmental effort. By looking ahead as far as possible, and borrowing liberally from other systems, the software designer can provide the flexibility needed to meet future needs. (2) Software modularity is also fundamental to flexibility and high quality software. A proper software fractionalization results in modules which are compact and conceptually independent. That is, a module does a single task, and coordination among tasks is accomplished at higher levels in the program. With the software structured around modules, one can add new modules and delete old ones without affecting the structure of the computer program. It was shown in Chapter Five how the MICA program employed a system of cascaded drivers, each controlling a level of modules. This approach is extremely flexible, allowing the program to be modified by minor changes to the drivers and the changing of software on a module basis. The worst possible situation is one in which a programmer entwines the control logic with the software performing various functions. Such highly entwined software quickly becomes unmanageable. Minor changes in one part of the program have second-order and third-order effects in remote parts of the program, for very obscure reasons. Non-modular, non-structured software often can be made operational only to collapse under its own complexity after a series of modifications. Like looking ahead, software modularity provides the necessary flexibility. (3) The final key to software flexibility is a good data base design. One is in a much better position to meet new requirements when the data base design has some generality. The practice of designing the data base to a specific set of variables and then programming the CMI software to these variables is very restrictive. More general schemes, such as that used by Kelley (1968), provide a much greater degree of flexibility. Attention to these three factors will result in CMI software that is better able to cope with changing needs. The designer of medium-scale and large-scale batch oriented CMI systems must create data collection and reporting procedures that can be used in a number of different school settings whose characteristics can be very different. When a few schools are involved, these procedures can be determined readily; but when the number of potential customers is large, achieving an optimum design for all is difficult. Consequently, the designer must try to create procedures that are acceptable, although not optimal.

The development of software for medium-scale and large-scale CMI systems employing interactive terminals under the time-sharing mode of computer usage involves a number of considerations beyond those under the batch mode, although the same computer programs often can be used without modification under both modes of operation. The primary software considera-tion is that medium-scale and large-scale interactive systems are not simply extensions of small-scale systems. For example, the MICA computer programs were developed for a small-scale interactive system. While MICA was quite flexible as a small-scale system, it could not be extended directly to a medium-scale system. It was limited by its data base design, by the operating system of the computer, and by the FORTRAN compiler. From the efforts to extend MICA from a small-scale to a medium-scale system, it became clear that an additional set of software issues was involved. The primary technical problem of medium-scale and large-scale interactive systems is one of multiple terminals accessing the computer programs and the data base. Access to the

CMI software from a number of different terminals is reasonably simple when RJE terminals are used, and difficult when interactive terminals are used. In the former case, the operating system services the terminals and places the data in mass storage files after input or before output. The data processing is performed by a single CMI program upon the sequential job queue. Under the time-sharing mode, multiple access of the CMI software from a number of interactive terminals is much more complex technically than for RJE terminals. Each interactive terminal is controlled directly from the CMI software so that a man-machine dialogue can be conducted. As was the case with RJE terminals, the computer's operating system provides the time-sharing capability, but it must also provide data processing upon demand rather than sequentially at a time of its own choosing. There are essentially two approaches to providing interactive multiple access to computer programs, multiple copies and reentrant code. A number of computer manufacturers provide for multiple access by the simple expedient of maintaining a separate copy of the computer program for each interactive terminal. In essence, they employ multi-programming techniques. The problem with this approach is that a complete copy of the CMI software is stored in mass storage for each interactive CMI terminal. Segments of each copy are transferred to core memory as they are needed to process the data from the terminals. Due to multiple copies, mass storage charges also are high. Although the production of multiple copies is a commonly used approach, it is becoming an obsolete technique. The "state of the art" approach to multiple access is via reentrant code. Under this approach a single copy of the CMI software is maintained by the computer. The actual instructions in the computer program are such that they cannot be modified during execution, and the software maintains separate working areas in memory for each terminal accessing the common software. Thus, rather than having complete multiple copies of the CMI software, a single copy with multiple working areas is used. The reentrant program technique has been used for many years to implement small routines such as mathematical functions, but in the mid 1970's much larger programs were developed using this technique. However, even the use of reentrant programs does not allow an unlimited number of interactive terminals to access a given program. The time-sharing system itself has limits as to the number of terminals it can service, due to the amount of core memory available for working areas and the operating system overhead. Some time-sharing systems also place limits upon the number of computer instructions contained in a reentrant computer program module (see MITRE, 1974, p. 50). Such constraints are often associated with the use of medium-scale and small-scale computers, and they can be very restrictive to the software designer and implementer.

The overall efficiency of medium-scale and large-scale interactive CMI systems also depends upon access to a common data base, especially when one or more curricula are shared. Normally, the operating system will perform the necessary procedures to prevent the technical difficulties associated with simultaneous file access. In some cases, it may be necessary to put additional file control in the data base management software to prevent unauthorized persons from performing file maintenance activities on the static files. When the static files relate to more than one subject matter area, there are additional file design considerations. One has the choice between assigning the curricular data such as the unit descriptions, prescriptions, and test specifications to unique files for each curriculum or integrating them in a single file. The use of several unique files for each curriculum has the advantage of conceptual simplicity, but requires considerable bookkeeping. within the computer software to coordinate the data processing and the files. Integration of files simplifies the computer programming, at the cost of a greater level of care required when maintaining the files. Both approaches are used and the final selection is one to be made by the designer. Dynamic files such as the student history file are best handled by having a separate file for each administrative unit such as a school. Separate files simplifies reporting procedures by limiting the area of search, makes file protection somewhat easier, and provides better control of file maintenance.

The software problems of interactive CMI systems, coupled with the state of time-sharing technology, limits the development of interactive medium-scale and large-scale systems. Though such systems are conceptually attractive, they require large-scale financing, considerable technical expertise in both hardware and software, and much managerial talent to develop. Consequently, small-scale will be the norm for interactive CMI systems for the near future.

Over and above the technical problems associated with going from small-scale to medium-scale CMI, the major software problem is that of not planning for the growth. The increase in scale is an extension of the need for flexibility described above. The software designer needs to decide quite early whether the CMI system will spend its life as a small-scale system or whether it has the potential to become a medium-scale or large-scale system. The growth problems will be few if the CMI system remains a small-scale system. However, if there is a possibility for growth, one should design and implement a larger-scale system. It is always possible to use a larger-scale at less than its full capabilities, but the reverse is not true. One way to approach the growth problem is to design the highest level system required, but to take an incremental approach to development. Behr (1976) has examined this issue in some detail and has developed a software design to cope with the increase in scale problem. Under this approach, the CMI system was conceptualized as a large-scale system. Then both the data base and the software were fractionalized into building block components. In the earliest stages of development, those blocks performing test scoring and reporting were to be implemented. As additional services are needed, appropriate components are added. The underlying concept is one in which a developmental ramp exists in which new capabilities are acquired by adding components in predefined blocks. The most difficult aspect of this approach is the incremental growth of the data base. Although Behr's approach is in the form of a concepts paper rather than an actual implementation, it can serve as the basis for design efforts.

CMI Software Life Cycle

When the typical CMI system is conceived, little thought is given to the full life span of the system. The initial efforts are concentrated upon system design and implementation. It is implicitly assumed that the system will exist for some unknown period of time. Little thought is given to what happens after the developmental team is disbanded, or to the use of the system by other persons. Despite this lack of attention, all software packages have a well-defined life cycle, and astute software developers take this into account when designing and maintaining software. The life cycle consists of a number of definite stages: design, development, improvement, stable system, and phase out, each requiring the attention of software specialists.

During the design phase, the software developer needs to consider the software life cycle. He must try to incorporate features that will facilitate each stage. This includes techniques such as embedding debugging capabilities in the software so that the operation of the system can be traced when errors are detected in the future. The use of modular software or "top-down," structured programming (McGowan and Kelley, 1975) concepts to create an easily modifiable software design is another life cycle consideration. During the developmental stage, the single most important life cycle consideration is documentation. The end product of the development phase is a baseline CMI system that must be accompanied by documentation for the programmer, the user, and the operational staff. Such documentation is crucial, as it is the only link between those who conceptualized and developed the system and those who follow. It is especially difficult in the university and college environment to get adequate documentation. Without adequate documentation, the remainder of the life cycle will be devoted to trying to understand what and why the computer program was written the way it was. The description of the MICA software given in Chapter Five is illustrative of the system level documentation needed.

Once the baseline system is operational, the improvement phase begins. The users of the system request additional or changed services from the system, and the programming staff finds areas of the computer program that can be improved. There is a signal from noise detection problem here. If one responds to each request for a change, the situation quickly degenerates into an endless series of small modifications to the CMI software. Due to their nature and frequency, the changes are not evaluated for their impact upon the basic concept or upon the quality of the programming. Many times a seemingly innocent change can cause second-order effects that are difficult to trace back to the change. The quality of the computer program is quickly degraded by such changes as the program is successively "patched," and eventually it doesn't match its own internal annotation nor the external documentation. One must resist the temptation to be overly responsive to both user and programmer requests for changes. It is a good practice to make changes on a scheduled basis. The pattern of change requests can reveal a fundamental need or problem. In addition, one can make one basic modification to the routines involved rather than a series of overlaid changes. The latter approach is more difficult to perform properly and requires a lengthier check out period of time. At some point in time, the CMI system becomes reasonably stable and the rate of requests for changes becomes small. During this phase, the system operates well and becomes an integral part of the instructional setting. The length of this stable phase is dependent upon many factors, not the least of which is economics. Eventually, the "state of the art" will bypass the system. The underlying conceptualization of the CMI software is no longer adequate and more sophisticated conceptualizations are in use. In addition, the software can no longer be improved by modification, as it is design limited. When this point is reached, one needs to return to the design stage and begin the life cycle of a new CMI system. The next generation design effort can be facilitated if a good documentation effort was maintained over the previous life cycle. Operational experience also should have been documented, ideas for future use recorded, and software changes documented. All of these can be valuable information sources for the next design stage. A new design for a CMI computer component can also take advantage of technological gains in both hardware and software. Computer technology changes very rapidly. Many new devices, such as cassette tape recorders, desk top optical scanners, and low cost terminals have appeared on the market in the past few years. A number of new devices appear each year which can be used in CMI applications. The general "state of the art" in computing also achieves considerable progress as a function of time. Improved concepts of time-sharing, better computers, and new software techniques such as structured programming are developed, rendering past efforts obsolete. Again, CMI needs to take advantage of these developments.

An often overlooked aspect of the life cycle of a computer program is configuration control. Configuration control is essentially the planning and controlling of changes to the computer program. Within small-scale CMI projects, the usual behavior is to make many small changes to the software; and, after a period of time, the basic computer program becomes overlaid with a maze of program patches. Because each change is small, little attention is paid to documenting the changes or even recording that the change was made. In this environment, programmer turnover can be a disaster. Each new programmer must not only learn the basic software package, but must wade through the patches, attempting to reconstruct the reason for the patches. One spends an excessive amount of time in the learning process rather than in productive work. The long-term effect of such uncontrolled software modification is an unmanageable piece of software, technically referred to as a KLUDGE. Such software is difficult to use and nearly impossible to maintain over a number of years. Computer manufacturers, software companies, and the military employ well-defined configuration control procedures to insure the orderly change of computer programs. Under these procedures, changes to the computer program are suggested, and a short form completed defining the change, why it is needed, the cost of making the change, and the impact of the change upon other segments of the program. The proposed change, then, can be evaluated in light of the overall computer program and a determination made as to its value. The military establishes formal change control boards to rule on proposed changes. Although a formal board is not needed in the CMI situation, it is a good idea to hold staff meetings to consider proposed changes. The person or persons proposing the change should document the change so that the whole staff can participate in its evaluation. Programmers are wont to communicate verbally, but the management should force documentation of proposed changes. Often a number of changes should be accumulated and treated as a group, especially if they deal with a common portion of the program. In this way, a single change to the program can be made instead of several individual changes. Once changes have been implemented, they should be thoroughly tested before being used in the operational setting. The most difficult aspect of software configuration control is that of employing it over the full life cycle of the computer program. Configuration control is a foreign concept to most university trained programmers. Unless pressured to participate in configuration control, they will quickly slip back into casual, verbally specified, changes. If the CMI software is to have a life span of more than a year, configuration control procedures should be instituted as soon as the design is completed.

Another factor to be considered in the life cycle of CMI software is changes in the computer hardware. Often the life cycle of a CMI system is not in phase with that of the computer it employs, and at some point the computer will be changed. In the university setting, the central computer facility tends to change computers roughly every five to seven years. Changing the computer is necessitated by the need for additional capacity, obsolescence of older equipment, and the desire to take advantage of new technology. The switch to a new computer can be detrimental to a CMI system; however, a number of precautions can be taken in the design and implementation stages to minimize the impact of changing computers. CMI software should be written in one of the standard programming languages such as COBOL or FORTRAN. For competitive reasons, the various computer manufacturers try to maximize the commonality of each language. There are standard definitions of these languages to further assist in creating program interchangeability across different manufacturers' computers. Although there is a high degree of commonality in the different implementations of FORTRAN or COBOL, each manufacturer inserts unique features. A programming ground rule should be to avoid the use of these unique features. Programmers will grumble a bit, but not using these features is rarely a serious problem. One also needs to avoid taking advantage of idiosyncrasies of the compiler. Often, programmers discover ways in which the compiler can be made to achieve non-standard results. Programmers like to take advantage of such tricks, but it is a bad practice. When the program is recompiled using a different compiler, the trick no longer works, and the fact is often difficult to detect. The use of symbolic assembly language also should be avoided, as it is unique to a specific computer. In some cases, it is necessary to use symbolic assembly level programming to control a given peripheral device. Such programming should be isolated in separate subroutines and documented in great detail. When changing computers, it will be necessary to reprogram these routines, and the documentation is quite helpful. Transition from one manufacturer to another can be accomplished, but this usually requires some additional effort. Transfer from a small to a large computer normally goes quite well, but the reverse is usually troublesome. If one programs in a standard language, avoids reliance upon programming tricks, and has adequate documentation, transition from one computer to another can be done with a minimum of problems. However, all such transitions require considerable advance planning to achieve a smooth transfer.

Summary
The computer component of CMI systems is dependent upon the "state of the art" in the computer field, as few computers are developed specifically for instructional uses. Thus, CMI employs the available computers, languages, and peripheral devices. At the present time, the use of remote job entry terminals is a standard practice in small-, medium-, and large-scale CMI systems. The interactive use of computers via the time-sharing mode is not as highly developed, since there are severe hardware and software limitations upon the ability of present-day computers to support large-scale interactive systems. As a result, few medium-scale and no large-scale CMI systems use interactive terminals in the classroom. The trend towards mini-computer networks, distributed computing, and other techniques will eventually provide the needed time-sharing technology.

CMI implementers have independently developed many different CMI software packages, but there is a considerable degree of underlying commonality in what these various software packages accomplish. Hence, there is a real need for programming languages to facilitate the development of CMI systems. At a minimum, there needs to be greater use of existing sophisticated data base management software packages. The data bases employed by CMI are such that these packages could be employed to great advantage. Hopefully, languages will be forthcoming encompassing both the data base management and the operational aspects of CMI in a simple, easy-to-use language. The seeds of this line of development are in the approaches taken by Kelley (1968), Merrill (1974), and Behr (1976).

Because the conduct of the classroom instructional management depends upon timely service by the computer, the computer hardware and software must be reliable. Interactive CMI systems are especially vulnerable to the lack of reliability. Experience has shown computer facilities having a light overall work load tend to provide the best level of reliability. In addition to being reliable, the computer component must be cost-effective, since CMI computer components are an "add-on" cost to the instructional setting. As a result, the operational costs associated with use of the computer need to be as low as possible. The widespread use of batch mode processing via remote job entry terminals is in part due to the lower costs of batch mode processing. It is also important that the computer programs and associated procedures be flexible and do not serve to force rigidity upon the educational component. The latter is the master and the computer the slave. Hence, the computer software should not impose unnecessary constraints upon the classroom. Finally, the designers of CMI software need to plan for the full life cycle of the computer program. If a CMI system is going to be used for more than demonstration purposes, it needs to be maintained via systematic procedures to insure its integrity.

Chapter Eight

Summary

The first phase in the development of CMI occurred in the years between 1966 and 1970, when the pioneering CMI systems were implemented. These early systems established the idea of using the computer to support the classroom teacher in the management of individualized instructional programs. Despite being developed independently for different academic environments, these pioneering systems exhibited a high degree of commonality in the functions they performed, and they established the basic outlines of what is now known as CMI. The viability of these early systems is attested to by the fact that two of them, PLAN* and TIPS, have been used continuously since 1967. The second phase of development, the implementation phase, began around 1970 and continues to the present. In this phase, the CMI concept has been used to develop a variety of additional implementations embodying the basic features of the early systems. The status of this second phase is indicated roughly by the many systems described in Appendix A. As additional CMI systems have been developed, the details of the functions performed have been adapted to meet local conditions and modified to meet the needs of individual instructors. This process has resulted in the superimposing of considerable variability upon the initial CMI approach, and it is difficult to formulate a concise definition of CMI. Thus, a major goal of the book has been to illustrate the "Gestalt" of CMI rather than to define CMI. In one sense, this Gestalt is described by the "state of the art" embodied in exemplar CMI systems used at the various academic levels. At the elementary school level, PLAN* (Flanagan *et al.*, 1975) and the Sherman School Project (Chapin *et al.*, 1975) are good examples. PLAN* is an excellent large-scale CMI system that delicately balances the management needs of a heterogeneous group of teachers with the need for systematization required by the computer component. It also illustrates the impact of economic realities upon the design and use of a large-scale CMI system. The Sherman School Project represents a small-scale CMI system that developed into a sophisticated medium-scale system. The developmental history of the Sherman School Project given in Chapter Four also illustrates the dynamic nature of CMI system development. The best example of CMI at the college level is Kelley's TIPS. A number of other college level CMI systems exist, but they tend to be particularized to specific courses and lack the flexibility and adaptability of TIPS to meet the needs of a range of college level instruction. The state of the art in the training environment is represented by two efforts. The Computer Managed Individualized Instruction System (Danforth, 1974) is an excellent system for a vocational school. The NAVY CMI system (Mayo, 1974) functions within a military training environment where large numbers of students are enrolled in a variety of courses. These five exemplar systems provide a good cross-section of CMI with respect to scale, academic level, and management information system design.

The Six Components of CMI

The field of CMI has completed its first phase of development and is in the midst of a second phase. What the third and subsequent phases will be depends to a considerable extent upon the way in which the six components of CMI are dealt with by the developers and users of CMI systems. To bring the major issues into sharper focus, the sections below reexamine these components. The frame of reference is where the field of CMI is now in respect to each component and the lines along which the author feels they should develop in the future. The latter are strongly biased by the author's view of CMI as a field and the reader may very well perceive a different future.

Curricular Plans

Due to the addition of the computer component to existing instructional schemes, CMI has caused little change in the curricular plans employed. At all academic levels, the curricular plans are heavily dependent upon the use of curricular units and behavioral objectives arranged in structures ranging from a simple linear sequence to complex trees. Within these structures, the primary dimension of individualization has been rate of progress through the plan. Despite this initial lack of impact of CMI upon curricular plans, there is a need to make such plans an integral part of the CMI system design. In particular, the curriculum designer needs to take manageability into account when creating a curriculum. New bases for structuring curriculum will need to be developed that will ease the management workload for the teacher, while raising the level of sophistication of the management. The present emphasis upon behavioral objectives in the curricular plans creates a considerable work load that is both low level and repetitive in nature. In order to raise the level of management of instruction, curricular plans need to be developed that emphasize educational goals. The salient deficiency of existing curricular plans, based upon behavioral objectives, is the inability to achieve upward integration. The top-down task analysis techniques used by the behavioral objectives movement lacks the ability to recapture the original intermediate and higher level educational goals. As a result, the managerial emphasis is upon the lowest level of detail rather than upon the higher level educational goals. Under CMI, curricular plans should be designed in such a way that the instructional managers can determine when a student has achieved a higher level educational goal. To do so requires much closer attention to the relation between the subject matter content domain and the goal domain. If program level management is to be achieved, multiple content domains will need to be related to the goal domain. Program level management will also require well defined interdependency networks for the several curricular plans involved. WIS/SIM has made initial steps in this direction in the areas of mathematics and science courses. These efforts need to be emulated by other CMI systems.

Inherent in the concept of individualization of instruction on a dimension other than rate of progress is the concept of highly differentiated curricular plans. Ideally, the teacher should be able to tailor the sequence of curricular entities employed and their characteristics to the abilities, interests, and past performance of an individual student. However, to do so requires a level of effort in the development of curriculum far beyond what is currently employed even in highly funded projects. Consequently, the majority of elementary school CMI systems make little provision for such curricular adaptability. They provide some flexibility within a curricular plan, but eventually all students complete the same lockstep curriculum. A number of college level CMI systems meet this problem by using a set of required units covering the essentials and student selected units to satisfy unique needs. Extension of the idea of curricular flexibility to a goal-differentiated curricular plan must be viewed with some caution. Goal differentiation, while having a plausible ring, carries with it the concept of predetermination. Thus, at the elementary school level at least, there appears to be both practical and philosophical bounds on the degree of flexibility one can design into curricular plans. College level and training school curricular plans may well include goal differentiation, since the students have made certain commitments by being enrolled in particular courses.

There are a number of factors associated with the use of CMI tending to lead to curricular stability. Factors such as data collection procedures, computer software, diagnosis and prescription, and reporting are all best performed for stable curricula. Due to the level of effort involved in making changes in these areas as a result of curricular changes, one resists the curricular changes. Consequently, these factors tend to inhibit changes in the curricular plan. However, the curricular plan should be free to be changed, as conditions warant, with little impact upon other procedures. A well designed CMI system should be independent of specific curricular plans and able to adapt to wide variations in curricular plans.

From a CMI perspective, the two crucial issues in the area of curricular plans are manageability and higher level educational goals. Curriculum designers will need to develop curriculum that can be managed at all three levels of management, yet do not impose an excessive managerial work load upon the teacher. What is meant by a manageable curriculum is not clear at present and the concept needs considerable attention. The management information system aspects of CMI make it possible to manage towards the attainment of educational goals, but present curricular designs based upon behavioral objectives virtually preclude this. The basic problem is that curriculum designers rarely document the intermediate and upper level educational goals embedded in a curriculum. The definition of educational goals is a non-trivial task, and one that must be done if sophisticated instructional management is to be achieved.

Instructional Models

The school-as-a-factory model borrowed from Scientific Management is at the core of the instructional models employed by most CMI systems. The unit-of-instruction cycle is basically a production cycle. The product is a completed curricular unit, and the standard of work is set by a criterion-referenced test. This instructional model is designed to allow the unit-of-instruction cycle to function as efficiently as possible, thus maximizing production. In the training environment, such a model can be appropriate, as the goal often is producing skilled technicians in a minimum time. At the elementary school level, this model is inappropriate, since it places its emphasis upon unit productivity rather than overall learning. Although most classroom teachers using CMI would find the school-as-a-factory model repugnant, most in fact employ such a model. Because the computer component was added to existing instructional schemes, the existing instructional models were absorbed intact into CMI. As a result, existing CMI systems appear to have fallen into the trap Taylor (1911) described as confusing the *mechanics* of management with the *principles* of management. The undue concern with supporting the clerical tasks of the unit-of-instruction cycle results in a focus upon mechanics. Broader instructional models need to be developed that encompass the total educational process and are based upon educational goals rather than on the unit-of-instruction cycle. In particular, much more emphasis needs to be given to instructional models achieving the upward integration lacking under models based upon the behavioral objectives approach. The instructional models used by CMI systems need to divest themselves of the standard unit of work and performance standards of Scientific Management. These should be replaced by more comprehensive and flexible instructional models, in which low level aspects of the model, such as the unit-of-instruction cycle, are allocated an appropriate niche rather than being the major focus of the model.

Diagnosis and Prescription

The state of the art in diagnosis and prescription is at a rudimentary level. Diagnosis consists essentially of a test score or a list of passed or failed objectives. The use of ancillary data, such as pupil characteristics for diagnostic purposes, is very rare. The majority of CMI systems have followed Glaser (1967) in using only performance data from the instructional setting for diagnostic purposes. However, no sophisticated diagnostic analyses are applied, the data is simply taken at its face value. Consequently, all the diagnostic procedures in use are symptomatic rather than causative in nature, simply describing the student's status. The prescriptions available for use with such diagnoses consist primarily of pages in textbooks, or presentations of material by various media. Few, if any, of these prescriptions have demonstrated "curative" powers with respect to the diagnosis that led to their assignment to the student. The connection between diagnosis and prescription is essentially a judgmental one where the hope is that students using the prescription will now learn the material. The rudimentary state of diagnosis and prescription cannot be laid at the door of CMI, as it is a function of the general status of the field of education.

A number of simple techniques can be used to raise the level of sophistication of diagnosis and prescription within CMI. For example, the running standardized grade placement used by the Stanford CAI project (Jerman, 1969) is easily implemented and quite useful. This index indicates whether a student is achieving below, at, or above his long-term average achievement level. Thus, the prescriber (computer or human) can assign materials appropriate to the student's present level. In addition, the index is useful managerially to monitor the student's pattern of achievement.

Better use can be made of existing diagnostic data by exploiting patterns existing in test scores or lists of objectives failed. It is easy to recommend this, but establishing meaningful interpretations of patterns of test scores or objectives missed is a difficult task. However, the data presently collected by CMI systems could be used to empirically identify the patterns occurring, and possibly attach some diagnostic significance to the patterns. Unfortunately, such patterns would be meaningful only for the curricular plan and instructional setting from which they were obtained. Hopefully, if some insight could be gained in this manner, some underlying structures and principles could be evolved.

Diagnosis and prescription are presently restricted to the unit-of-instruction cycle, yet there is a need for both at the course and program level. There is a need for diagnoses dealing with pupil progress, patterns of achievement across courses, and data relative to educational goals. These diagnoses are not easily extractable from information at the unit-of-instruction level. However, diagnosis and prescription above the unit-of-instruction level will be necessary if teachers are to do an adequate job of management at the course and program levels.

CMI implementers also will need to decide whether to automate diagnosis and prescription. There are essentially two options: (1) performing diagnosis via test scores, objectives missed, etc., and leaving prescription to be done by teachers on a judgmental basis; or (2) automating both diagnosis and prescription. The former greatly reduces the level of effort associated with creating a data base and has less impact upon a teacher's classroom practices. The latter will reduce the teacher's involvement in what is presently a routine mechanical process, thus freeing the teacher to teach and to manage at higher levels of management.

While diagnosis and prescription are currently at a rudimentary level, CMI holds great promise for significant advances in these areas. For the first time in education, a wealth of data is available detailing the diagnoses made, the prescriptions assigned, and the educational outcomes achieved. The data exists in the data base and is readily available for exploration and analysis. While the results may initially be curriculum specific, the potential exists for identifying underlying relationships and processes. A major obstacle is the lack of specific analysis procedures to elicit relevant information from the data. However, significant work can be done with present analysis techniques. Increasing the level of sophistication of diagnosis and prescription is a long-term effort, but CMI provides the vehicle for accomplishing this goal.

Management

The management philosophy embedded in the majority of CMI systems is that of Scientific Management. A consequence of the work of Spaulding (1913) and Bobbitt (1913) is that the teacher has been relegated to the role of a worker in the school factory. The academic production line is concerned with the students turning out a standard product—a mastered behavioral objective—and with levels of productivity, or rate of progress. The teacher's management responsibilities are at a low level, essentially consisting of keeping the production line producing at an acceptable level. This school-as-a-factory model is at the root of the conceptualization of all but a few college level CMI systems and is clearly the basis of systems designed for the elementary school and the training school. Under this approach, the instructional level of management is concerned with assuring that all students produce the same standard product. At the course level of management, the teachers' concern is productivity, and the curricular unit becomes the basic entity. The productivity of the school-as-a-factory is measured in terms of throughput, i.e., units completed. The reports received by the teacher, such as the group and unit reports, are designed to measure throughput. It should be recognized that individualization based on rate of progress is a thinly disguised throughput scheme, since progress is implicitly assumed. Even a cursory examination of most CMI systems reveals their basis in the school-as-a-factory model and their implementation of the procedures of Scientific Management. However, none of the CMI literature acknowledges the central role of this management philosophy.

A major source of conceptual difficulty for CMI is that the educational system and the teachers themselves view teachers as professional level *workers*, not *managers*. This has two consequences. First, the concept of the teacher as a manager is ill defined. Second, CMI systems primarily support management activities at the production line level. Educators in general and teachers in particular need to be disabused of the idea of the teacher as a worker. They need to raise the managerial status of the teacher. The teacher needs to become more of a middle- and upper-level manager concerned with the attainment of broader educational goals rather than with unit productivity. To achieve this, CMI systems used in elementary schools need to be extended in scope so that educational programs rather than single subject matter areas are managed. The unit-of-instruction cycle that is the present focus of CMI system can be fully automated and managed on an exception basis. With automation of this level, teachers can turn their attention to management functions, such as planning, coordinating, etc., at an educational program level. Rather than being concerned with the pupil's attainment of a specific behavioral objective, the concern would be with how achievement in several different subject matter areas contributes to attaining an intermediate or higher level educational goal. The management role of the teacher would emphasize the pattern of pupil progress, the interdependencies of his skills and attainments, and achieving a balance appropriate to the individual pupil. Thus, the teacher would devote attention to making it possible for the student to make coordinated progress in an educational program rather than measuring the student's productivity in separate isolated subject matter areas. Under this expanded managerial concept, the teacher would devote more time to studying reports, planning, and thinking about individual students, while time devoted to managing the mechanics of the unit-of-instruction cycle dropped to a minimum. A serious conceptual error, compounded by present CMI systems, is that an educational program can be managed via behavioral objectives and units completed. The inability of behavioral objectives style curricula to recapture the higher level educational objectives via upward integration precludes such management.

Developing an adequate concept of the teacher as a manager also entails recognition of the realities of the classroom. In a given school day and school year, there is a finite amount of time available to perform all the functions associated with a teacher's instructional and managerial roles. In computer terminology, the teacher functions in a "real-time" environment in which decisions are made, actions taken, and interactions with other persons occur on a dynamic basis. CMI systems with their data collection procedures, management reports, etc., essentially intrude upon this real-time environment. If, in addition, one expands the teacher's managerial role to include higher level management functions not presently explicitly performed, the time demands are further increased. Thus, there is a real problem for CMI designers to ascertain the kinds and levels of managerial support a teacher can effectively use in the school environment. A proper balance between the support provided by the CMI system and the load it imposes must be achieved. One of the interesting outcomes of the Sherman School Project was that the use of CMI reallocated the teacher's time budget in such a way as to provide much more time for instructionally related functions. Most of this time was gained via the automation of many clerical level tasks and through continual refinement of the instructional model.

A major contribution of CMI has been to focus attention upon the concept of the teacher as a manager. While the concept is not new, until the advent of CMI, the distinction between a teacher's managerial and instructional roles was indistinct. The addition of a management information system to the classroom provides the means for not only clarifying the concept but also expanding it in important dimensions. Present CMI systems do a good job of supporting the management concepts based upon the Scientific Management philosophy. However, this philosophy is a very limited·one and appropriate only to a production line or factory environment. Educators need to look seriously at other more sophisticated management philosophies to develop an expanded conceptualization of the teacher as a manager. The outcome of such an effort should be the conceptualization of the teacher as a high level manager concerned with educational goals and educational programs for individual students rather than productivity.

Computer

Despite the rarity of computers dedicated to CMI use, the level of technological sophistication of CMI systems is very high. One place or another, CMI systems are making use of the most recent advances in computer hardware technology, especially in the peripheral equipment area. CMI systems are using the latest in optical mark readers, cathode ray displays, hard copy printers, and keyboard terminals. This equipment sophistication is in part due to many CMI implementers having access to large-scale computers via colleges and universities. As a result, they are only indirectly responsible for financing the central computer facility and can devote their limited capital resources to sophisticated peripheral devices.

For the near future, the emphasis in the hardware aspects of the computer component will be upon remote job entry terminals consisting mainly of optical mark readers and hard copy printers. It should be noted that this is the basic configuration used by PLAN* since its inception. At the public school level, the trend will be away from college and university research computer facilities towards using the school district's own computer. For example, the State of Minnesota is trying an interesting approach (Anon., 1975) in which public schools are provided access to computers devoted to instructional uses on a state-wide basis. Whether this is an economically and politically viable concept remains to be seen. Another trend which will certainly have its impact upon CMI hardware is the use of multiple mini-computer configurations. Project ABACUS (Howard, 1974) already uses a six computer configuration. As the price of mini-computers continues to decrease, these configurations hold considerable promise for dedicated CMI systems at a reasonable cost. In many mini-computer systems, the peripheral devices already cost more than the computers.

One of the long-term trends in computing is the gradual improvement of the ability of computer systems to support the time sharing mode. Both large-scale computers and mini-computers are contributing to this trend. Medium-scale and large-scale CMI systems will depend very heavily upon the time-sharing mode to support the large numbers of remote job entry terminals and interactive terminals required. Eventually, CMI systems will support a keyboard terminal and a data collection device in each classroom. These devices will be used by students to input data, receive prescriptions, etc., on a continuous basis, and teachers will use them for obtaining reports. Even though such terminals will be interactive, it is doubtful whether there will be a computer operator assigned to the terminal. The terminals will operate on a semi-automated basis with a few function buttons initiating most activities. These devices will be intermediate to present remote job entry terminals and fully interactive terminals, performing the functions of both as the situation demands.

Although the computer hardware aspect of the computer component of CMI is quite sophisticated, the computer software lags behind. The majority of CMI software is coded in languages such as FORTRAN and COBOL specifically for a given project. However, neither of these languages is ideal for CMI. A number of CMI implementers have attempted to use CAI languages for CMI, but due to the lack of data base management capabilities, these are extremely poor vehicles for CMI software. As a result, there is a need for a high level language designed explicitly for the programming of CMI systems. Such a language would encompass data collection, data base management, data analysis, and data reporting within a conceptually simple structure. Although no such language exists, its basic dimensions can be seen in the work of Kelley (1968), Merrill (1974), and Behr (1976). A CMI language would greatly facilitate the development of small-scale CMI systems by individual instructors or small groups of persons. In addition to a high level CMI language, there is also a need for CMI software packages for general distribution. Only Kelley's TIPS and PLAN* appear to be developed to a level where they can be widely distributed. One or more such standard CMI packages would do much to increase the use of CMI. The development of a CMI language or standard packages is not beyond present capabilities. Their absence is due primarily to the limited resources available for development.

Reporting

One consequence of the Scientific Management philosophy

underlying CMI is that the reporting schemes are designed to manage throughput. Reports such as the Unit and Group reports are used to monitor a student's progress through the curricular plan. While these reports and others, such as the Contact report, are useful at the instructional and course level of management, they are primarily after-the-fact reports. Reports should be structured such that the teacher can anticipate future problem areas and initiate corrective action before the problem develops. The Program of Studies of PLAN* could be used in this fashion, but it appears to be primarily a scheduling device. Reports could also be developed which alert the teacher and students as to interdependencies among several courses. For example, WIS/SIM employs science units having mathematics units as prerequisites. Thus, difficulties encountered in the mathematics units have implications for the science units.

At both the course and program levels of management, reporting schemes are needed that relate student achievement to intermediate and higher level educational goals. With a well-defined relationship between the goal and content domains, such reports could be generated rather easily. Such goal oriented reports would enable the teacher to evaluate whether the student is making progress in problem-solving or understanding cause-and-effect, rather than tallying the number of curricular units completed.

The design of reporting schemes must balance the availability of information against its management utility. Too much information or the wrong information in a report can interfere with its function. Reports should be clear, concise, and useful. CMI systems also need to be more systematic in getting feedback from teachers as to the utility of reports. There is a bit of a "chicken and egg" problem here, as teachers rarely know what reports are useful until they have employed the reports. As a result, it often is necessary to modify the content and format of reports to meet teachers' needs. Also, as management concepts become more sophisticated, the content, purpose, and frequency of reports will change. Consequently, the reporting scheme and its underlying computer programs need to have considerable inherent flexibility. New reports should be added and old reports modified with some ease. Rigidly defined, difficult-to-modify reporting schemes can lead teachers to feel that the CMI system is not providing the management support needed.

The present emphasis upon reporting schemes designed to manage throughput is a function of the status of the concept of the teacher as a manager. As this concept becomes better developed, and alternatives to Scientific Management are employed, the reporting component will also change in character. Rather than emphasize throughput, the reports will need to stress planning, coordination, and other higher level management functions. From a technical point of view, such reports are easily generated. What is needed is a conceptualization of instructional management in which they would be useful.

The Evaluation Issue

A major difficulty faced by those interested in CMI is developing sufficient support at the local level for a long-term commitment to CMI. The present demand for educational accountability puts considerable pressure upon CMI developers to demonstrate the effectiveness of CMI. Unfortunately, Spaulding's heritage is the dominating factor in such demonstrations, and concepts such as cost per pupil and achievement gains per dollar dominate the evaluations. These demands for the evaluation of CMI in terms of cost-effectiveness are very difficult to meet. There are two primary reasons for this difficulty: First, CMI systems are typically the result of adding computer and reporting components to existing instructional programs, representing an additional cost. However, the improvement in pupil performance should have already occurred when the instructional program was put into operation. The contribution of CMI should be to make the program function properly and support its management. As a result, one usually cannot show increases in student achievement or a reduction in cost as a result of using CMI. Bureaucrats like to evaluate educational innovations in terms of student achievement, since they consider it to be the educational equivalent of profit. However, evaluating CMI on the basis of student gains is a lost cause unless one simultaneously introduces effective changes in the total instructional program. Second, CMI basically is for the teacher, not the student. The goal of CMI is to help the teacher manage individualized programs of instruction that were previously unmanageable. It allows the teacher to be more effective in coping with the complexities of such programs. In addition, CMI is a change agent upon the teacher. As a result of CMI, the teacher becomes more of a manager, devoting less time to the mechanics of the classroom and more time to management functions. Thus, *CMI should be evaluated with respect to its impact upon the role of the teacher, not upon student achievement or per pupil costs.*

The long-term goal of CMI is to improve the quality of education, but historically, those who evaluate education have been interested in minimizing costs, not maximizing quality (Callahan, 1962). As a consequence, CMI developers are often forced to play the costs game to justify their budgets. The per pupil costs data of PLAN* can be used to some advantage. For 1000 students the total direct cost of PLAN*, exclusive of additional teacher aides, would be $42,000, or roughly four relatively inexperienced teachers. The cost trade-off then becomes whether PLAN* or four teachers would have the greater impact. If we assume that there are 30 pupils per classroom, then adding four teachers drops the pupils per classroom from 30 to 27. This is hardly an educationally significant decrease in the student-teacher ratio; neither students nor teachers would notice much, if any, difference in the operation of the classrooms. Although the effects are hard to measure, it is the author's opinion that the impact of an elementary school CMI system upon variables such as student self-direction, teacher role, student involvement in planning, etc., is far greater than that of four additional teachers per thousand students. Due to their subtle nature, it is difficult to clearly demonstrate that these quality-of-education factors are worth the additional costs due to CMI. Basically, the whole evaluation issue becomes political rather than educational. A well-planned and continuous public relations campaign selling the advantages of individualized instruction supported by the computer will far outweigh any plan of data collection to show the cost benefits of CMI. *System developers should treat the evaluation of CMI as a political problem rather than a technical one.* Three groups should be the target of such a political approach. Teachers should be actively involved at all stages of the introduction and use of CMI. They should be given the best possible support via inservice training, immediate response to requests, and incorporation of their ideas. The goal is to have the teachers feel that the CMI system is their system and that the classroom cannot function adequately without it. The public should be well informed as to the overall instructional program and the role of the computer component. The public often has some ideas of CAI but rarely of CMI. Thus, it is necessary to use every opportunity to show what CMI is about. Parents in particular need to be shown, in terms they can understand, that CMI results in a better educational program. Finally, the administrative hierarchy needs to be made an integral part of the total process. They should be represented at all stages of CMI development and have a continuous involvement. Again, they need to develop a proprietary feeling with regard to the use of CMI. A well-planned *political* approach to the evaluation problem can be much more effective than tables-of-significance tests.

The major emphasis, at the present time, should not be upon evaluation but upon pushing the frontiers of instructional management. Present CMI systems are very rudimentary, the concepts of management too new, and the best relationships among the six components too nebulous to have CMI development terminated because of a bureaucratically imposed requirement to demonstrate cost-effectiveness. It is akin to asking the Wright Brothers in 1910 to provide an airplane that could fly coast to coast nonstop.

Since CMI developers are going to have to face the costs

issue, they need to be aware of where these costs arise, how to cope with them, and which of them can be ascribed to CMI. Chapin (1976) has made an important distinction between the costs of individualization and the costs related to the use of the computer. Most elementary schools have found that programs of individualization require teacher aides to assist with many of the mechanical aspects, such as materials distribution, test scoring, resource allocation, etc. It has also been found that specialized classroom equipment, such as file cabinets, audio-video equipment, and carrels, are required for a smoothly functioning program. Individualized programs of instruction also use a wider variety of textbooks and consume expendable materials at a higher rate than does traditional instruction. However, the costs of teacher aides, specialized equipment, and instructional materials should be ascribed to individualization *per se* not to the use of the computer.

There are three areas of direct additional cost due specifically to CMI; computer hardware, computer operations, and computer software. The computer hardware costs are typically associated with the purchase of terminal devices, such as optical mark readers, keyboard terminals, printers, and cathode ray tube displays. The total outlay depends upon the scale of the CMI system, but an OMR device and a keyboard terminal can be purchased for roughly $5,000 at 1977 prices. Since few CMI systems purchase computers, these peripheral devices constitute the main hardware cost. The primary operational cost is the purchase of computer time, usually on an hourly basis. The wide variation in the educational settings of CMI makes it difficult to accurately determine these costs. University computers are highly subsidized and their rates are much lower than commercial rates. Public schools tend to offer computing as an administrative service, and the small amount of computer resources devoted to CMI often disappears into the EDP budget. Computer software costs arise from the development and maintenance of the CMI computer program. Developmental costs in particular can be quite high, especially if the developmental group is inexperienced. Computer programs also tend to have a life of their own and require fairly constant attention, thus incurring continuing maintenance costs. Data base maintenance can also result in continuing costs: A number of files need to be reconstructed at the beginning of each school year, errors in the data base need to be corrected, and files have to be restored after system failures. Software and file maintenance can easily require the services of one full-time programmer.

The forcing function aspects of CMI upon the curriculum can result in additional costs associated with the curriculum improvement cycle. Instructional materials will need to be revised, better curricular plans devised, assessment instruments revised, and if locally prepared materials are used, considerable printing performed. None of these curricular improvement costs should be attributed to CMI, as they should be incurred as part of normal school operations. However, CMI often acts as the catalyst to get schools to do curriculum improvement where it has not been done for a period of time.

The totality of all these costs is difficult to assess due to the way in which most CMI systems are created and operated. The best gauge is the cost of PLAN*, which was $42 per student in 1975. This figure represents the computer-related operational costs, a majority of the expendables, and to some degree the cost of the curriculum improvement cycle for four subject matter areas. This cost also reflects the amortization of developmental costs and maintenance costs over a very large pupil base, which most CMI systems cannot do. Since PLAN* is offered commercially and must eventually make a profit, its per pupil costs represent a realistic cost for elementary school CMI systems supporting individualized programs of instruction.

The Achilles' heel of CMI is that it is an add-on cost to existing instructional programs. As long as these costs are low in absolute magnitude, a CMI project will not attract much budgetary scrutiny. However, as CMI becomes successful, the number of classrooms supported increases—as does the magnitude of the aggregated costs. Where one had a highly successful, inexpensive small-scale CMI system, we now have an expensive medium-scale CMI system. In this era of declining school enrollments and similarly declining budgets, creating even a moderate, easily identifiable new budget item is inviting a host of problems. As mentioned above, these problems should be approached from a political rather than a technical point of view. At the present state of development, one is in a better political position by limiting most CMI efforts to small-scale systems. The costs of such systems can be hidden budgetarily rather easily by keeping the computer operational costs low and diffusing all other costs in such a way they cannot be ascribed to the CMI project. For example, computer programming and file maintenance activities can be done by programmers who also support the administrative use of the computer. Thus, the fact that they also devote time to the CMI project can be obscured. At the college level, one is probably better off employing many different small-scale systems rather than a common medium-scale system. Again, diffusing the identifiable CMI costs across several different departments, each with its own budget and vested interests provides greater protection from the budget cutters than a single expensive system. Over the longer term, the use of multiple small-scale CMI systems, coupled with a well-planned public relations program, appears to be the best approach. The small-scale system can expand and contract as a function of the budget, but never entirely disappear. Yet, the public relations program makes the use of CMI an integral part of the way in which the schools operate. Thus, over the long term, say 10 to 20 years, CMI will become an established feature of the schools, and what were once add-on costs are now normal budget items.

A note of warning about outside funds, such as the various federal title monies available to the schools: While nice to have, these funds have the potential for being very detrimental to the well being of a CMI project. The infusion of outside funds tends to increase the scope of a project and result in a higher level of effort than would normally be involved. Once the project enlarges on these funds, the monies needed to continue at that level must come from local sources. However, few, if any, such projects successfully make the transition from outside to local funding at comparable levels. One needs to plan the use of outside funds very carefully. They should be used to accomplish tasks requiring such help but in a way that will increase capabilities but not the scope of the project. For example, one could use outside funds to design and implement the computer programs for a small-scale CMI system. However, it would be foolhardy to use outside funds to increase the scale of a CMI system from small to medium without guaranteed long-term local support for the expanded CMI system. Outside funds have the propensity for leaving a project high and dry just when the project is getting interesting. Consequently, one should view them with a jaundiced eye and utilize them in a very calculated fashion.

Some Underlying Issues

In the long term, the Scientific Management basis of most CMI systems is going to prove to be troublesome, especially in the elementary school. The basic danger is that CMI will be the vehicle through which the dominance of education by Scientific Management will be completed. Callahan (1962) has shown that School Administration has incorporated much of Scientific Management since Spaulding's early work. Bobbitt (1913) and Snedden (1925) tried to extend Scientific Management to the classroom but were defeated by the mechanics of implementing their curricular plans. However, their concepts live on in the behavioral objectives movement. Unfortunately, CMI provides the means of overcoming the mechanical problems that, in the past, have kept Scientific Management out of the classroom. The data collection procedures and the reporting schemes of CMI, coupled with behavioral objectives, provide the ideal vehicle for converting the classroom into a production line turning out a standard student with all of the appropriate behaviors attached like options on an automobile. A production line approach to education can be acceptable in the military, where there is a need for N radar technicians each month. In public education such a production line approach is unacceptable. An early warning of such unacceptability exists, since parents have insisted that some schools using CMI also offer traditional group-oriented instruction. Rather than use CMI to complete the imposition of Scientific Management upon education, it should be used to provide a much more open, flexible, and goal oriented educational system. There are capabilities inherent in CMI for providing curricular adaptability to individual students with an integrated educational program, and allowing teachers to become truly higher level managers. CMI developers need to realistically evaluate Scientific Management as the philosophical basis for instructional management. Upon doing so, they should reject it for all but specialized situations.

The data collection capabilities of CMI systems are the source of other philosophical issues. The data collected in the classroom can be used both instructionally and administratively. In the former use, the data is relatively benign, consisting of test results, units completed, and other data useful to the teacher and the student. The recent federal laws dealing with student access to records will inevitably be applied to CMI. Some lawyer will try to make a *cause* out of computerized records on individual students, but the problem is fundamentally nonexistent. Most CMI systems are designed such that each pupil either receives this data in the form of "tear-off" sheets or has access to summary reports. PLAN* schools typically post the daily report for all students to use. Problems with parents with respect to the data collected can be dealt with effectively by providing summary reports containing relevant information in a form easily understood by parents. When provided with such reports, parents will feel that the data benefits them; and, after a period of time they will accept CMI as a routine part of the school environment. Again, good public relations and complete candor about the nature and uses of the data will preclude most of the controversy associated with such data collection.

The greatest potential for inappropriate use of the CMI data base is in the area of teacher evaluation, not student related uses. One facet of Bobbitt's work was that teachers should be evaluated on the basis of student productivity. In the past, the data emanating from the classroom was so sparse and irregular, consisting mostly of once-a-year standardized tests and end-of-semester grades, that school administrators could not evaluate instructional programs or teachers. CMI alters this situation drastically, as a variety of data relating to productivity of teachers is readily available. It is a simple matter to generate reports by teacher showing number of units completed per student, number of students not meeting performance expectations, number of posttests taken per unit per student, etc. Such data can easily be used to measure the productivity of teachers from a production line point of view. Spuck and Owen (1974) have suggested the WIS/SIM system be used for this purpose within the IGE program. With such data, school administrators could hold teachers responsible for meeting production quotas, quality standards, etc., and the Scientific Management of education would be complete. Fortunately, few of the CMI systems presently generate such reports for administrators. However, as CMI becomes more widely used and a recognizable budget item, the demand for such reports will arise. CMI will then become a vehicle for teacher evaluation and its instructional utility badly compromised. Teachers will not be enthusiastic about using a CMI system in the classroom that also allows administrators to monitor their productivity. Consequently, those who design and operate CMI systems will need to face this problem with considerable finesse, since the very persons who will request these reports also control the budget. The implied loss of funds can be powerful motivation to get the programming staff to create and generate teacher productivity reports. Since the issue *will* arise, teachers, administrators, and CMI designers jointly will need to develop an appropriate solution. The elegant approach is one where the legitimate needs of administrators for instructional program evaluation data can be met without also evaluating an individual teacher's productivity. Achieving this solution will depend upon the educational context within which a CMI system operates and the negotiating skills of those involved.

The final underlying issue centers upon the computer as the master. This has several facets. Most of us at one time have encountered the clerk in the bank, or minor bureaucrat in a government office, who responds to an inquiry with: "I don't know, the computer did it." With the increasing dependence of business and government upon the computer for routine data processing, the degree to which responsibility is allocated to the computer increases. This occurs because the clerks, bureaucrats, etc., who deal with the public are, in a sense, far removed from the computer. The data they prepare enters a computerized data system that is often remote and not understood. Conversely, the outputs of the computer were achieved by mysterious means, and when problems arise there is no easy way to pin-point the cause. Under manual systems, one could find a person who performed the transaction and isolate what caused the problem. In the case of computerized systems, the data disappears into a disk pack and the data processing cannot be observed. Because of this, responsibility gets shifted to the computer, regardless of the actual locale of the responsibility. CMI can also engender a similar attitude within teachers, especially if the computer is perceived as a mechanism not under the teacher's control. For example, a student could ask the teacher why he was given a particular prescription. If the teacher has a limited concept of the CMI system, the reply could be "I don't know, the computer did it." Within the instructional setting, this state of affairs is unacceptable, as it implies that the computer is the master. Although it may not be possible for teachers to know every prescription, they should understand the principles upon which the diagnosis and prescription procedures are based. Every teacher must have a working knowledge of the total CMI system, so that the teachers can be confident of their control of the computer-based procedures. Such a working knowledge will enable teachers to bear the responsibility for the conduct of the classroom instruction, rather than ascribing it to the computer. Typically, it takes nearly a year for teachers to become comfortable with the computer-based procedures of CMI; hence, teacher training is very important. Each new group of teachers should acquire a good understanding of the CMI system via preservice training. During the course of the school year, frequent inservice training sessions should be held to help the teachers use the CMI capabilities as a management vehicle. As mentioned above, such inservice training also has political ramifications.

Since computer-based systems operate best in a stable environment, there can be a reluctance to make necessary changes. Such changes can involve procedural changes in the classroom and often require additional expensive computer programming. Consequently, one is prone not to make changes in an operating system. However, this is another facet of the computer-as-the-master problem, since computer-related considerations are imposing a stable state upon the instructional aspects. Reasonable stability is necessary for the smooth functioning of the instructional setting, but the computer component should not impose rigidity. The CMI system should be sufficiently flexible to easily accommodate changes. Without such flexibility, CMI can easily become the vehicle for instructional ossification.

Because no one explicitly states that the computer component is paramount, the computer-as-the-master is an insidious factor of CMI. The concept is implemented as the result of numerous small decisions, none of which seems important when it was made. The cumulative effect is one of a dominant computer component at the expense of the educational component. All computer related decisions should be evaluated in regard to their impact upon the relationship between the educational and computer components. When the issue is not clear-cut, one should bias the decision in terms of keeping the computer in the slave's role.

Need for CMI Related Research

In the late 1970's, CMI as a field is well into its second phase of development. The need for demonstrating what is CMI and implementing systems to illustrate the basic approach has drawn to a close. This is not to imply that the CMI concepts developed in the late 1960's are totally adequate, but that they have been shown to work quite well in practice. What is needed is a firm research base for the next generation of CMI systems. Due to the six components of CMI, the scope of this research is very wide. Each component is a fertile area of research of its own, as is the total CMI system. However, the primary area needing additional research is that of instructional management. Despite considerable attention devoted to this topic in the present book, the teacher as a manager is still a nebulous concept. The research attack on this issue should be two-fold: First, a number of alternatives to Scientific Management need to be conceptualized for use in the instructional setting. These management philosophies need to be oriented towards the attainment of higher level educational goals and towards the higher level management functions, such as planning, coordinating, etc., of the classical school of management. Second, comparative studies of these competing management philosophies are needed to determine their differential effects upon instructional management in a variety of academic settings. To conduct these studies requires the definition of variables and their measures so that differential effects can be observed. The identification of these variables is not an easy task, as they are primarily embedded in the teacher's role as a manager and are subtle variables. Essentially, these variables need to reflect the way a teacher manages in the instructional setting, and they should be sensitive to differing managerial philosophies. Easily obtained variables such as time or pupil achievement are only of limited value, as they probably are not sensitive to different management philosophies.

As the literature on industrial management shows (see McGuire, 1974), research in the area of management is difficult to conduct. When performed in the operational setting, it cannot seriously impact a company's business, as the risks associated with manipulating management factors in the operational setting can be quite high. Hence, both the number and scope of manipulative experiments is limited. Laboratory type experiments can be conducted, but they are most appropriate to the study of only one aspect of management. Due to the difficulties in conducting experiments, much of management research is descriptive in nature. In contrast to the field of management, education has a long tradition of in-the-field research, especially in the area of manipulative experiments. The operational environment in the schools is not as limiting as that of industry. Hence, the educational experimenter has had considerably greater latitude in making changes than has the industrial management researcher. Schools are quite amenable to making rather major structural and procedural changes in the interest of educational research. Often they make major changes just to try something different, i.e., innovate. Within this strong research tradition, one can easily conduct the kinds of research needed to study various management philosophies and teacher roles. The problem is one of logistics rather than access. To conduct research of this type, complete classrooms or schools need to be functioning under different approaches. Teachers need to be trained, data collection and reporting schemes developed, experiments designed, and measurements taken. Also, such experiments need to be conducted over a long enough time span for the differential effects of the management philosophy to occur and to be observed. One cannot conduct the usual two-week experiment and expect to observe effects of different management philosophies upon the teacher's role. Such effects may not be dramatic and will need to be teased from the experiment with some care. Despite the difficulties attendant to research on instructional management, it needs to be done. If it is not performed, Scientific Management will continue to dominate the conceptualization of instructional management.

A precursor to such research can be the careful exploitation of existing CMI systems. The data base maintained by a CMI system contains a wealth of data that can be examined from a number of points of view. In one sense, educational researchers need to go on a fishing expedition in these data bases. Such an expedition could answer questions like: What does instructional data look like? What are the predominant paths through the curricula? Are there observable differential results associated with prescriptions? Do teachers differ in their prescriptive practices, etc.? Exploring the data in this manner will provide a much better picture of what is actually occurring in instructional programs employing CMI. Once such a baseline is established, the creation of differing management philosophies could be attacked. The attack need not be head on, but could involve modifying certain aspects of an existing system and observing its impact. For example, one could install an "early warning system" within a CMI system to alert the teacher of a student's potential problems. The impact of the capability upon the way in which a teacher plans for such students and monitors them could be studied. The cumulative effect of many such studies could reveal the outlines of better management philosophies, different teacher roles, and perhaps far different roles for the computer. The development of such philosophies requires coordinated research within and across each of the six components of CMI. In addition, there are significant contextual effects arising out of the composite formed by the six components. Without a considerable degree of coordination, the research could become fragmentary and its cumulative effect would be minimal. The level of coordination is quite similar to that discussed by Baker (1967) with regard to large-scale research projects.

Another potentially rewarding area of research is the impact of CMI upon the student. The limited amount of available research (Dick and Gallager, 1972; Judd and O'Neil, 1974; Kelley, 1968, 1973; Wood and Lewis, 1974) indicates that CMI affects student attitudes, how students spend their time, and a number of nonachievement variables. Of particular interest are the results indicating students become more self-reliant and able to marshall the resources needed to accomplish a task (Wood and Lewis, 1974). Such research needs to be greatly expanded as it appears to be the best area in which to demonstrate the student benefits of CMI. It seems obvious to the author that even small gains in the ability of a student to assume responsibility for his educational program far outweigh larger gains on standardized achievement tests or in numbers of behavioral objectives mastered. A large body of well-designed research in these areas would provide a firm basis for justifying CMI as well as for developing more sophisticated management philosophies to implement the findings. Conducting such research can be greatly facilitated by the data collected in the classroom and stored in the CMI data base. What is needed are some imaginative ways of looking at existing data to provide the information to study the teacher's role as a manager and the impact of CMI upon nonachievement student variables. Such techniques will be a significant contribution to the field of CMI.

Conclusions

Since the feasibility phase of CMI has already been completed and the implementation phase is well along, the two basic questions are, "what is the impact of CMI?" and "what is next?"

The Impact of CMI

The immediate impact of CMI, based upon roughly ten years of experience, is clear. CMI has been found to act as a change agent in regard to a number of aspects of the instructional setting. The most common observation is that it results in a change in teacher role. This change is two-fold. First, the teacher is freed of many clerical-level tasks and is able to devote more time to instructionally related tasks. The greater the degree of computer involvement, the greater the gain in usable time. For example, the automation of diagnosis and prescription at the unit-of-instruction level releases considerable amounts of time for other uses. Second, there is a distinct shift towards a more managerial role for the teacher. The availability of reports allows the teacher to observe the status of the students relative to both the curricular plan and an instructional model—a capability that could be achieved only in a crude form prior to CMI. The teacher is now in a position to manage on the basis of data rather than intuition and judgment. Under CMI there is also a shift in pupils' roles towards more self-direction, assumption of responsibility, and independence (see Wood and Lewis, 1974). As a result, teachers find they spend less time directing students at a mechanical level and more time managing an instructional process. One direct result of such changes in the teacher's role is a more smoothly functioning program of individualized instruction. In keeping with the underlying Scientific Management philosophy, there are also demonstratable gains in throughput, i.e., units completed, although this is not a particularly good measure of the value of a teacher's management role.

Upon observing a number of elementary schools using CMI, Sidney Belt observed: "CMI allows good teachers to do better what they had already been doing and helps poor teachers to do better than they had been doing." CMI provides the good teacher with the tools to conduct individualization of instruction effectively. CMI provides the weaker teachers with well-defined procedures, plans, etc., to follow that will improve their classroom practices. The net effect in both cases is an improved instructional situation for the students. Finally, CMI is a forcing function upon curricular plans and instructional models. CMI forces a regularizing of procedures, imposes a need for a degree of systematization, and brings about a recognition of the need to be consistent within these two areas. Many practices condoned in a non-CMI situation cannot be used under CMI. Thus, CMI tends to force the "sloppiness" out of many classroom practices and procedures. Often this can be a major contribution of the introduction to CMI.

What Is Next?

While any predictions are speculative at best, the following paragraphs present the author's view of the likely next developments.

At the elementary school level CMI will continue to grow at a rather modest rate over the next five to ten years. Both the capabilities of the computer hardware and the sophistication of the EDP staffs in the public schools are increasing. Hence, the ability to either create or install an available CMI system at the local school level is becoming more general. The net result will be an increase in the total number of CMI systems and in the total number of classrooms managed via CMI. However, the worst possible fate for CMI would be a high pressure publicity campaign selling CMI as the solution to the schools' problems. CMI is clearly in its infancy and needs to mature in the schools at its own speed. Premature high visability with its attendant false promises could have a severe detrimental impact upon CMI in the public schools. It will also be detrimental if CMI is imposed upon classroom teachers by external forces. The best tactic is to enable a core group of teachers committed to CMI to initiate a small-scale local effort. After a few years of gestation, a successful CMI system will quickly diffuse throughout the remainder of the school system if adequate funding can be arranged.

The potential for CMI systems at the college level is probably much greater than at the elementary school level. College level courses tend to be quite autonomous, hence, accommodated by small-scale CMI systems. College instructors also tend to have some degree of sophistication in regard to computer usage and can readily employ yet another computer application. In addition, colleges and universities are under some pressure to improve their instructional practices, in particular to provide a more personalized rather than individualized form of instruction. Colleges and universities also support medium-scale to large-scale computer systems supporting time-sharing and other services. As a result, the developer or user of CMI is responsible only for the CMI software, not the total computer software support. Thus, using the available pool of programming talent, small-scale college level CMI systems are readily created and operated.

Although a number of different college level CMI systems are available, there seems to be little sharing of the associated computer programs. Perhaps this is a reflection of the situation-specific characteristics of most small-scale CMI systems. The exception to this pattern is TIPS (Kelley, 1968), which is used in a number of colleges and universities and in a diverse set of disciplines. The source code (FORTRAN) of TIPS should be made generally available so that local features can be added to what is basically an excellent computer program. Given the large potential audience, it is surprising that a number of CMI packages are not competing with TIPS in this market. The author suspects that a small-scale CMI system written in a file oriented BASIC language for a mini-computer would be quite popular in small colleges, if available at low cost.

Under the present Scientific Management approach to CMI, the training school environment has the highest potential for medium-scale and large-scale CMI. The school-as-a-factory model with behavioral objectives and management of throughput is appropriate in this setting. The military, in particular, employs this model, as any increase in throughput can be directly reflected in reducing training costs. All three branches of the military currently have CAI/CMI systems under development: The U.S. Air Force has AIS (Rockway and Yasutake, 1974). The U.S. Army has project ABACUS (Howard, 1974). The U.S. Navy has the NAVY CMI system (Mayo, 1974). However, the military is still enamored with CAI, and only the Navy system is a true CMI system. The other two systems are primarily CAI systems with a limited CMI capability. This emphasis is a bit strange, since there is such an excellent match between military training schools, Scientific Management, and CMI. The military appears to be looking for a means to automate instruction and minimize the total manpower devoted to instruction. In this context, CMI could provide a much better starting point than CAI, as the former would provide the vehicle for getting curricular plans, instructional models, and management procedures properly structured before going to CAI as a vehicle of instruction.

It also appears that a number of technical and vocational schools structure their curricula in a manner similar to that used by the military, whereby rate of progress is an important consideration. Vocational technical schools are also faced with increasing enrollments, and CMI could be used effectively to manage the highly individualized educational programs of these students. Although only one CMI system designed for use in such schools (Danforth, 1974) has been reported, a very large potential market for medium-scale CMI exists in these schools.

The future growth of CMI in the elementary school in particular needs to be directed away from the school-as-a-factory model. Most likely this will not occur in the near future, and CMI based upon the philosophy of Scientific Management will be the norm. This will be the case for two reasons: First, most developers of CMI systems do not realize that the school-as-a-factory model is the implicit basis for their system. Such implementers have focused upon the clerical tasks to be performed, and rarely take a look at the philosophical basis of *what* is being performed. Second, at present, viable alternatives to Scientific Management have not been developed in the context of instructional management. Implementing an alternative philosophy of management would require a massive reorientation of the thinking of teachers and administrators. Such a conceptually simple idea as managing instruction at the educational goals level rather than the behavioral objectives level is a monumental task. The goals are not readily available, curricular plans are not developed from an underlying goal structure, and managing for goals rather than objectives is not part of existing instructional models. Managing at a program level rather than at the independent course level involves similar conceptual dislocations. Presently, curricula are developed independently; and to define their interdependencies and common contributions to a set of educational goals is counter to present practice and perhaps present capabilities. Consequently, to ask teachers to manage at the program level seems an unlikely task at best. Unfortunately, Spaulding, Bobbitt, and Mager have done their work well—and undoing it is a nontrivial task. Thus, for the near future, it would appear that the majority of CMI systems will continue to unwittingly base their management procedures upon Scientific Management.

A Final Comment

The life cycle of most educational innovations involving technology follows a well-known pattern. The basic idea is formulated, a few prototype systems are developed, and based on demonstrations in a very limited context, the innovation is extolled as the solution to the school's problems. There is then a "jumping on the band wagon" phenomenon and the innovation proliferates. Persons using the innovation outside of the context of the demonstration environment quickly discover the pitfalls, costs, and disadvantages never mentioned by the touters. The use of the innovation quickly recedes, the band wagon jumpers get off, and a small band of dedicated persons remain to attempt to fulfill the unmet promises. The innovation then joins the list of ideas that never become an integral part of the educational scene. CAI is a classic example of this life cycle. Despite a high level of interest and funding, and two decades of effort, it is not part-and-parcel of the educational system. Hopefully, CMI will escape this fate and become an integral part of the educational system. In contrast to CAI, which was externally imposed upon the field of education, CMI has had its origins in the classroom. Because of this and its slow, low keyed developmental pattern, CMI seems to have a reasonable probability of success. Not that every classroom will be managed under CMI, but that a finite, yet not small, number of classrooms will be so managed. The author suspects that on a daily basis more students are involved in PLAN* in a single year than have been taught by all CAI systems used in the public schools since the advent of CAI. CMI will become part of the educational system in what will be a rather natural progression. At some point in time, a teacher will be able to select the type and level of services CMI will provide as easily as he or she now orders a slide projector (of course, in *some* schools it isn't very easy to order a projector, even in 1977).

The justification of the additional costs incurred by CMI will be the biggest deterrent to its widespread usage. This justification will be made more difficult by CMI having its greatest impact in an area where it is difficult to demonstrate impact, namely, the *quality* of education. The current thinking is that CMI will result in a change in the teacher's role towards one emphasizing instructional management. This shift should be accompanied by a greater emphasis upon those classical management functions, such as planning, coordinating, etc., currently performed at a minimal level. CMI will keep teachers better informed about their pupils, and will allow teachers to evaluate the consequences of instructional decisions, anticipate future instructional problems, and to effectively allocate a range of resources. None of these actions will necessarily contribute to specific gains in student achievement. However, they will contribute to a better educational environment, more smoothly conducted classes, and to optimization of instruction for individual students. The benefits may well be in students who have more confidence in their ability to identify a problem and to acquire resources to solve it; who know when to seek assistance and when not to; and who feel that school is an exciting place in which to learn. Quality of education is defined in terms such as these, not in the number of units completed, objectives mastered but not understood, or teacher productivity. Properly conceptualized and implemented, the major contribution of CMI should be to improve the quality of education.

References

Allen, M.W., Meleca, C.B., and Meyers, G.A. A model for the computer management of modular, individualized instruction. Columbus: Ohio State University, 1972, 15.

Anderson, T.H., Anderson, R.C., Delgaard, B.R., Weitecha, E.J., Biddle, W.B., Paden, D.W., Smock, H.R., Allessi, S.M., Surber, J.R., and Klemt, L.L. A computer-based study management system. *Educational Psychologist*, 1974a, *11*(1), 36-45.

Anderson, T.H., Anderson, R.C., Allessi, S.M., Delgaard, B.R., Paden, D.W., Biddle, W.B., Surber, J.R., and Smock, H.R. Multifaceted computer based course management system. University of Illinois, 1974b. (Unpublished paper.)

Anglin, L.W. The School Organization and Curriculum-Instruction Decision Making. Unpublished Ph.D. Thesis, University of Wisconsin, 1976.

Anonymous. Computer individualizes chemistry course. *Chemical and Engineering News*, June 17, 1974, *52*, 19-20.

Anonymous. *Preliminary Considerations for a Minnesota Instructional Management Support System*. Minnesota Educational Computing Consortium, August 20, 1975. (Unpublished paper.)

Ashenhurst, R.L., and Vonderhoe, R.H. A hierarchical network. *Datamation*, 1975, *21*(2), 40-44.

Baker, F.B. Use of computers in educational research. *Review of Educational Research*, 1963, *33*(5), 566-578.

Baker, F.B. Experimental design considerations associated with large-scale research projects. Chapter 5 in J.C. Stanley (Ed.), *Improving Experimental Design and Statistical Analysis.* Chicago: Rand McNally, 1967.

Baker, F.B. Computer based instructional management systems: A first look. *Review of Educational Research*, 1971a, *41*(1), 51-70.

Baker, F.B. Automation of test scoring, reporting, and analysis. In R.L. Thorndike (Ed.), *Educational Measurement.* (2nd Edition). Washington, D.C.: American Council on Education, 1971b.

Baker, F.B. A conversational item banking and test construction system. *Proceedings of the Fall Joint Computer Conference*, 1972a, *41*, Part 2, 661-667.

Baker, F.B. Numerical taxonomy for educational researchers. *Review of Educational Research,* 1972b, *42*(3), 345-358.

Baker, F.B. Teaching the design of CMI system software. *Educational Technology,* 1973, *13*(10), 33-35.

Baker, F.B. *The Sherman School CMI Project: The First Year of Operation.* Madison: Laboratory of Experimental Design, University of Wisconsin, 1974a.

Baker, F.B. Systems considerations. Chapter 7 in G. Lippey (Ed.), *Computer-Assisted Test Construction.* Englewood Cliffs: Educational Technology Publications, 1974b, 244.

Baker, F.B., Anglin, L., and Lorenz, T. A prototypic computer managed instructional system for competency-based teacher education. Department of Curriculum and Instruction, University of Wisconsin-Madison, 1974.

Behr, G. *Software Structures for Instructional Management Systems.* Unpublished Ph.D. Thesis, University of Wisconsin, 1976.

Behr, G., Berg, J., Jacobs, S., LeFaivre, R., Relles, N., and Underwood, J. *Managed Instruction with Computer Assistance: System Overview.* Madison: Laboratory of Experimental Design, University of Wisconsin, 1972.

Behr, G., Berg, J., Jacobs, S., LeFaivre, R., Relles, N., Underwood, J., Lorenz, T.B., and Chapin, J. *Managed Instruction with Computer Assistance (MICA): System Overview.* Madison: University of Wisconsin, 1974.

Belt, S.L., Marshall, J.L., and Romberg, T.A. Initial activities related to the computer-assisted management of DMP. Working Paper No. 109. Wisconsin Research and Development Center for Cognitive Learning. University of Wisconsin, November, 1972, 27.

Belt, S.L., and Skubal, J. Computer managed instruction: An application. *Association for Educational Data Systems Journal,* Fall, 1974, *8*(1).

Belt, S.L., and Spuck, D.W. Computer applications in individually guided education: A computer-based system for instructional management (WIS/SIM): Needs and specifications. Working Paper No. 125. Wisconsin Research and Development Center for Cognitive Learning, University of Wisconsin, January, 1974, 129.

Bidwell, C.E. The school as a formal organization. Chapter 23 in J.G. March (Ed.), *Handbook of Organizations.* Chicago: Rand McNally, 1965.

Binet, A. *The Development of Intelligence in Children.* Translated by Elisabeth S. Kite. Baltimore: The Williams and Wilkins Company, 1916.

Bitzer, D.L., Hicks, B.L., Johnson, R.L., *et al.* The PLATO system: Current research and developments. *IEEE Transactions on Human Factors in Education,* Vol. HFE-8 (June), 1967, 64-70.

Bloom, B. (Ed.). *Taxonomy of Educational Objectives: The Classification of Educational Goals. Part I: Cognitive Domain.* New York: McKay, 1956.

Bobbitt, F. Some general principles of management applied to the problems of city-school systems. *12th Yearbook of the National Society for the Study of Education,* 1913, 7-17.

Bobbitt, F. The orientation of the curriculum maker. Chapter 3 in

26th Yearbook NSSE, Part II. Bloomington: Public School Publishing Co., 1926. G.M. Whipple (Ed.).

Bobbitt, F. A summary theory of the curriculum. Society for Curriculum Study, November 1 Bulletin, 1934, *5*(1), 2-4.

Bolvin, J.O. Computer-managed instruction: The academic scene. In H.E. Mitzel (Ed.), *An Examination of the Short-Range Potential of Computer-Managed Instruction.* Conference Proceedings, November 6-8, 1974, National Institute of Education.

Bratten, J.E. Educational applications of information management systems. SP-3077/000/01. System Development Corporation, June 6, 1968.

Brudner, H.J. Computer-managed instruction. *Science,* 1968, *162,* 970-976.

Buros, O.K. (Ed.). *The Third Mental Measurements Yearbook.* New Brunswick, N.J.: Rutgers University Press, 1949.

Callahan, R.E. *Education and the Cult of Efficiency.* Chicago: The University of Chicago Press, 1962, 273.

Capson, M. *TRACER. Teacher's guide.* Menlo Park: Educators Alliance, 1974.

Chapin, J. (Ed.). *Madison Public Schools Computer Managed Instruction Project.* Madison: Madison Public Schools, 1975.

Chapin J. (Ed.). *Madison Public Schools Computer Managed Instruction Project. Third Year Continuation Proposal.* Madison: Madison Public Schools, 1976.

Chapin, J.D., Lorenz, T., Anglin, J.A., and Grass, B. An interactive management information system for the support of individualized instruction. Paper presented at the Annual Meeting of the American Educational Research Association, March 31, 1975, Washington, D.C.

Charters, W.W. Curriculum for women. *University of Illinois Bulletin,* March 8, 1926, *23*(27), 327.

Connolly, J.A. A computer-based instructional management system: The Conwell approach. Interim Report AIR 20091-11/70. Silver Spring, Maryland: American Institutes for Research; Washington Office, Institute for Communication Research, November, 1970.

Cooley, W.W., and Glaser, R. An information and management system for individually prescribed instruction. Working Paper No. 44. University of Pittsburgh—Learning R & D Center, December, 1968.

Cooper, M.K., and Tobey, G.R. A computer management support system for individually guided education. Unpublished paper, Portland: Portland Public Schools, 1976.

Coulson, J.E. (Ed.). *Programmed Learning and Computer-Based Instruction.* New York: Wiley, 1961, 291.

Coulson, J.E. An instructional management system for the public schools. TM-3298/002/00. System Development Corporation, June 12, 1967.

Countermine, T., and Singh, J. Instructional support system. In H.E. Mitzel (Ed.), *An Examination of the Short-Range Potential of Computer-Managed Instruction.* Conference Proceedings, November 6-8, 1974, National Institute of Education.

Cronbach, L.J., and Snow, R.E. *Individual Differences in Learning Ability as a Function of Instructional Variables.* Final Report U.S.O.E., 1969.

Danforth, J. Computer-managed individualized instruction. In H.E. Mitzel (Ed.), *An Examination of the Short-Range Potential of Computer-Managed Instruction.* Conference Proceedings, November 6-8, 1974, National Institute of Education.

DATUM, Inc. *Instructional Manual for Model 5098 Optical Mark Reader.* Publication 3047, Anaheim, California, 1973.

DeHart, G. PLAN: Program for learning with accordance with needs. In H.E. Mitzel (Ed.), *An Examination of the Short-Range Potential of Computer-Managed Instruction.* Conference Proceedings, November 6-8, 1974, National Institute of Education.

Della-Piana, G.M. *Reading Diagnosis and Prescription: An Introduction.* New York: Holt, Rinehart, and Winston, 1968.

duction. New York: Holt, Rinehart, and Winston, 1968.

DeNio, J.N. A computer-based test question system. In H.E. Mitzel (Ed.), *An Examination of the Short-Range Potential of Computer Managed Instruction*. Conference Proceedings, November 6-8, 1974, National Institute of Education.

DeVault, M.V. Computer managed system of mathematics instruction. University of Wisconsin, 1968. (Unpublished manuscript.)

DeVault, M.V., Buchanan, A.E., and Nelson, E.I. Description of the school context for the computer managed system of mathematics instruction project. Unpublished paper. Wisconsin Research and Development Center for Cognitive Learning, University of Wisconsin, November, 1969, 37.

DeVault, M.V., Kriewall, T.E., Buchanan, A.E., and Quilling, M.R. Computer management for individualized instruction in mathematics and reading. Teacher's Manual. Wisconsin Research and Development Center for Cognitive Learning, University of Wisconsin, September, 1969, 32.

Dick, W., and Gallager, P. Systems concepts and computer-managed instruction: An implementation and validation study. *Educational Technology*, 1972, *12*(2), February, 33-39.

Dodd, G.G. Elements of data management systems. *Computing Surveys*, 1969, *1*(2), 117-133.

Dunn, J.A. The development of procedures for the individualization of educational programs. Paper presented at Annual Convention of American Psychological Association, Miami Beach, Florida, September 5, 1970.

Egan, T.A. *A System for Developing Computer Managed Instruction Systems*. West Chester: West Chester State College, 1973, 127.

Farber, D.J. A ring network. *Datamation*, 1975, *21*(2), 44-46.

Fayol, H. *Administration Industrielle et Generale*. Paris: Dunod, 1925. First English translation, 1929; second translation by Constance Stores, London: Sir Isaac Pitman and Sons, Ltd., 1949.

Finch, J.M. An overview of computer-managed instruction. *Educational Technology*, July, 1972, *12*(7), 46-47.

Fishbein, J.M. The father of behavioral objectives criticizes them: An interview with Ralph Tyler. *Phi Delta Kappan*, September, 1973, *55*(1), 55-57.

Flanagan, J.C. Functional education for the seventies. *Phi Delta Kappan*, 1967a, *49*(1), 27-32.

Flanagan, J.C. Project PLAN: A program of individualized planning and individualized instruction. Paper presented at the Project Aristotle Symposium. Washington, D.C., December, 1967b.

Flanagan, J.C. Individualizing education. Invited address presented to Division 15, American Psychological Association, San Francisco, September, 1968, 31.

Flanagan, J.C. Program for learning in accordance with needs. *Psychology in the Schools*, 1969, *6*(2), 133-136.

Flanagan, J.C. The role of the computer in PLAN. *Journal of Educational Data Processing*, 1970, 7(1), 7-17.

Flanagan, J.C. The PLAN system for individualizing education. *Report of the National Council on Measurement in Education*, NCME, 1971, *2*(2), 1-8.

Flanagan, J.C., Shanner, W.M., Brudner, H.J., and Marker, R.W. An individualized instructional system: PLAN*. In H. Talmadge, (Ed.), *Systems of Individualized Education*. Berkeley: McCutchan, 1975, 210.

Freyman, J.M. The big class: TIPS keeps teachers in touch. *The Occasional*, 1973, No. 5, Exxon Educational Foundation.

Gagné, R.M. *The Conditions of Learning* (First Edition). New York: Holt, Rinehart, and Winston, 1965, 308.

Gardner, E.M. An overview of the CAMIL language (Air Force Human Resources Laboratory). Lowry A.F.B., 1974. (Unpublished paper.)

George, C.S., Jr. *The History of Management Thought.* Englewood Cliffs: Prentice-Hall, 1972, 223.

Gilbreth, F.B., and Gilbreth, L.M. *Applied Motion Study.* New York: Sturgis and Walton, 1917, 220.

Glaser, R. Adapting the elementary school curriculum to individual performance. In *Proceedings of the 1967 Invitational Conference on Testing Problems*. Princeton, N.J.: Educational Testing Service, 1967, 3-36.

Glaser, R. Evaluation of instruction and changing educational models. In M.C. Wittrock and D. Wiley (Eds.), *Evaluation of Instruction: Issues and Problems*. New York: Holt, Rinehart, and Winston, 1970.

Glaser, R., and Reynolds, J.H. Instructional objectives and programmed instruction: A case study. Chapter 5 in C.M. Lindvall (Ed.), *Defining Educational Objectives*. Pittsburgh: University of Pittsburgh Press, 1964.

Glaser, R., and Rosner, J. Adaptive environments for learning: Curriculum aspects. In H. Talmadge (Ed.), *Systems of Individualized Education*. Berkeley: McCutchan, 1975.

Gorth, W.P., O'Reilly, R.P., and Pinsky, P.D. *Comprehensive Achievement Monitoring*. Englewood Cliffs, N.J.: Educational Technology Publications, 1975.

Griesen, J.V. Independent study program at Ohio State based on computer managed instruction. *Communication News*, November, 1973.

Hall, R.H. Some organizational consideration in the professional-organizational relationship. *Administrative Science Quarterly*, 1967, *12*(3), 461-463.

Hambleton, R.K. Testing and decision-making procedures for selected individualized instructional programs. *Review of Educational Research*, Fall, 1974, *44*(4), 371-400.

Henry, N.B. *Individualizing Instruction*. 61st Yearbook of the National Society for the Study of Education. Chicago: University of Chicago Press, 1962, 337.

Hickey, M.E., and Hoffman, D.H. Diagnosis and prescription in education. *Educational Technology*, 1973, *13*(10), 35-37.

Howard, G.B. Project ABACUS. In H.E. Mitzel (Ed.), *An Examination of the Short-Range Potential of Computer-Managed Instruction*. Conference Proceedings, November 6-8, 1974, National Institute of Education.

Hsu, H. A computer-based instructional management system for elementary schools. In H.E. Mitzel (Ed.), *An Examination of the Short-Range Potential of Computer-Managed Instruction.* Conference Proceedings, November 6-8, 1974, National Institute of Education.

Jerman, M. The Stanford project computer-assisted instruction in elementary arithmetic and logic and algebra. *Teacher's Handbook.* Stanford University, Institute for Mathematical Studies in the Social Sciences, 1969.

Jerman, M. The Stanford project computer-assisted instruction in elementary arithmetic and logic and algebra. *Supplement to the Teacher's Handbook.* Stanford: Stanford University, Institute for Mathematical Studies in the Social Sciences, 1970.

Johnson, K.A., and Mayo, G.D. Navy CMI system. In H.E. Mitzel (Ed.), *An Examination of the Short-Range Potential of Computer-Managed Instruction.* Conference Proceedings, November 6-8, 1974, National Institute of Education.

Judd, W.A., O'Neil, H.E., Jr., Rogers, D.D., and Richardson, F.C. Development and formative evaluation of a five module CMI system for educational psychology. Technical Report 19, Austin: Computer Assisted Instruction Laboratory, University of Texas, 1973.

Judd, W.A., and O'Neil, H.F., Jr. Development and evaluation of a computer-managed instruction system for teacher education. Paper presented at Annual Meeting of the American Educational Research Association, Chicago, April, 1974.

Keller, F.S. Goodbye, teacher. *Journal of Applied Behavior Analysis*, 1968, *1*(1), 79-89.

Kelley, A.C. An experiment with TIPS: A computer-aided instructional system for undergraduate education. *The American Economic Review*, 1968, *58*(2), 446-457.

Kelley, A.C. Individualizing instruction through the use of technology in higher education. *Journal of Economic Education*, 1973, *4*, 77.

Klausmeier, H.J. I.G.E.: An alternative form of schooling. In H. Talmadge (Ed.), *Systems of Individualized Education.* Berkeley: McCutchan, 1975, 210.

Kliebard, H.M. Bureaucratic components of modern curriculum theory. In V.F. Haubrich (Ed.), *Freedom, Bureaucracy and Schooling*, 1971 Yearbook of Association for Supervision and Curriculum Development. Washington, 1971, 293.

Knipe, W.H. The computer at Grand Forks: Seeking the individual. *Educational Technology*, August, 1973, *13*, 44-46.

Kooi, B.Y., and Geddes, C.G. The teacher's role in computer assisted instructional management. *Educational Technology*, 1970, *10*(2), 42-45.

Kopstein, F.F. Why CAI must fail! *Educational Technology*, 1970, *10*(3), 51-53.

Krathwohl, D.R., and Payne, D.A. Defining and assessing educational objectives. In R.L. Thorndike (Ed.), *Educational Measurement* (2nd Edition). Washington, D.C.: American Council on Education, 1971, 768.

Kriewall, T.E. Data usage in an instructional management system. Unpublished paper. Wisconsin Research and Development Center for Cognitive Learning, July, 1969, 40.

Lippey, G. Computer-managed instruction: Some strategy considerations. San Jose: IBM. Unpublished paper, 1974a, 9.

Lippey, G. (Ed.). *Computer-Assisted Test Construction.* Englewood Cliffs, N.J.: Educational Technology Publications, 1974b.

Lipson, J.I. CMI application in the Chemistry Department of the University of Illinois at Chicago Circle. In H.E. Mitzel (Ed.), *An Examination of the Short-Range Potential of Computer-Managed Instruction.* Conference Proceedings, November 6-8, 1974, National Institute of Education.

Mager, R.F. *Preparing Instructional Objectives.* Palo Alto: Fearon, 1962, 60.

March, J.G. (Ed.). *Handbook of Organizations.* Chicago: Rand McNally, 1965, 1247.

Massie, J.L. Management theory. Chapter in J.G. March (Ed.), *Handbook of Organizations.* Chicago: Rand McNally, 1965.

Mayo, G.D. Computer based instructional systems. *Journal of Educational Technology Systems*, Winter, 1974, 2(3), 191-200.

McGowan, C.L., and Kelley, J.R. *Top-Down Structured Programming Techniques*. New York: Petrocelli/Charter, 1975.

McGuire, J.W. *Contemporary Management*. Englewood Cliffs, Prentice-Hall, 1974, 662.

McLean, L.D. It's almost time for CAI. *Interchange*, 1973, 4(4), 35-47.

McManus, J.F. Functional overview of score/IMS version 3. TM-5-71-01. Los Angeles: SWRL Educational Research and Development, 1971, 15.

McManus, J.F. Design of an instructional management system. Los Alamitos: SWRL Educational Research and Development, 1972, 178.

Merrill, P.F. Computer-managed instruction at Florida State University. In H.E. Mitzel (Ed.), *An Examination of the Short-Range Potential of Computer-Managed Instruction*. Conference Proceedings, November 6-8, 1974, National Institute of Education.

Minor, J.B. *Management Theory*. New York: Macmillan, 1971, 168.

MITRE. *An Overview of the TICCIT Program*. McLean: MITRE Corporation, M74-1, January, 1974, 65.

Mitzel, H.E. Computer technology: Its future role in basic education. *Journal of Teacher Education*, Summer, 1974a, 25, 124-129.

Mitzel, H.E. (Ed.). *An Examination of the Short-Range Potential of Computer-Managed Instruction*. Conference Proceedings, November 6-8, 1974b, National Institute of Education.

Morgan, K. Computer-managed geometry. In H.E. Mitzel (Ed.), *An Examination of the Short-Range Potential of Computer-Managed Instruction*. Conference Proceedings, November 6-8, 1974, National Institute of Education.

Morgan, K., and Richardson, W.N. The computer as a classroom tool: Project REFLECT. *Educational Technology*, 1972, 2(10), 71-73.

National Education Association. *Cardinal Principles of Secondary Education.* Commission on Reorganization of Secondary Education. Washington, D.C.: U.S. Bureau of Education Bulletin, No. 5, 1918.

National Education Association. *The Purposes of Education in American Democracy.* Washington, D.C.: Educational Policies Commission, National Education Association, 1938, 157.

National Education Association. *The Central Purpose of American Education.* Educational Policies Commission, National Education Association, 1961, 21.

Oakland Schools. *Student Achievement Monitoring,* narrative documentation, part 1. Pontiac, Michigan, 1972, 9.

Oakland Schools. *Student Monitoring System.* Pontiac: Oakland Schools, 1975, 16.

O'Reilly, R.P., and Hambleton, R.K. A CMI model for an individualized learning program in ninth grade science. Paper presented at the Annual Meeting of the American Educational Research Association, New York: February, 1971.

Perrow, C. The analysis of goals in complex organizations. *American Sociological Review,* 1961, *26*(6), 854-865.

Popham, W.J. Objectives and instruction. American Educational Research Association Monograph on Curriculum Evaluation. Chicago: Rand McNally, 1969, 32-33.

Popham, W.J., and Baker, E.L. *Systematic Instruction.* Englewood Cliffs: Prentice-Hall, 1970, 166.

Rice, J.M. *Scientific Management in Education.* New York: Century, 1897 (Arno Press reprint, 1969).

Rockway, M.R., and Yasutake, J.Y. The evolution of the Air Force advanced instructional system. *Journal of Educational Technology Systems,* Winter, 1974, *2*(3), 217-239.

Roecks, A.L. A brief look at the effect of Sherman math on mathematics achievement. Madison: Madison Public Schools, 1976. (Unpublished paper.)

Romberg, T.A., and Harvey, J.G. Developing mathematical processes: Background and projections. Working Paper No.

14, Wisconsin Research and Development Center for Cognitive Learning, April, 1969, 24.

Saettler, L.P. *A History of Instructional Technology.* New York: McGraw-Hill, 1968, 399.

Scanlon, R.G. Computer managed instruction: Present trends and future directions. Paper presented at Special Superintendents Seminar, IBM Education Center, San Jose, California, July, 1974.

Scriven, M. Problems and prospects for individualization. Chapter 8 in H. Talmadge (Ed.), *Systems of Individualized Education.* Berkeley: McCutchan, 1975, 210.

Seidel, R.J., and Rosenblatt, R.D. HumRRO CMI. In H.E. Mitzel (Ed.), *An Examination of the Short-Range Potential of Computer-Managed Instruction.* Conference Proceedings, November 6-8, 1974, National Institute of Education.

Sellman, J. Information processing to support enroute instructional management. Paper presented at Annual Meeting of the American Educational Research Association, Washington, D.C., April, 1975.

Shakhashiri, B.Z. Chem TIPS. *Journal of Chemical Education*, 1975, *52*, 588-592.

Sherman, J.G. *Personalized System of Instruction: 41 Germinal Papers.* Menlo Park, Calif.: W.A. Benjamin, 1974, 225.

Sibley, E.H. (Ed.). Special Issue: Data-Base Management Systems. *Computing Surveys*, 1976, *8*(1), whole issue.

Silberman, H.F. Design objectives of the instructional management system. SP-3038/001/000. Santa Monica: System Development Corporation, February 28, 1968.

Snedden, D. Planning curriculum research, I. *School and Society*, August 29, 1925, *22*(557), 259-265.

Spaulding, F.E. The application of the principles of scientific management. *Journal of Proceedings and Addresses of the National Educational Association.* 51st Annual Meeting, 1913, 259-279.

Spuck, D.W., and Owen, S.P. Computer managed instruction: A

model. *Association for Educational Data Systems Journal,* Fall, 1974, *8*(1), 17-23.

Steffenson, R.C., and Read, E.A. A computer program for management of student performance information: *Audiovisual Instruction,* 1970, *15*(5), 56-59.

Suppes, P.C., and Morningstar, M. *Computer-Assisted Instruction at Stanford, 1966-1968: Data, Models, and Evaluation of the Arithmetic Programs.* New York: Academic Press, 1972, 533.

Talmadge, H.E. (Ed.). *Systems of Individualized Education.* Berkeley: McCutchan, 1975, 210.

Taylor, F.W. *The Principles of Scientific Management.* New York: Harper, 1911, 144.

Thorndike, E.L. *Educational Psychology.* New York: Lemcke and Buechner, 1903, 677.

Tyler, R.W. *Basic Principles of Curriculum and Instruction.* Chicago: University of Chicago Press, Syllabus Division, 1950, 83.

Tyler, R.W. Some persistent questions on the defining of objectives. Chapter 6 in C.M. Lindvall (Ed.), *Defining Educational Objectives.* Pittsburgh: University of Pittsburgh Press, 1964, 77-83.

Vinsonhaler, J.F., and Moon, R.D. Information systems: Applications in education. Chapter 9 in C.A. Cuadra (Ed.), *Annual Review of Information Science and Technology.* Chicago: Encyclopedia Britannica, 1973, *8,* 277-317.

Weisgerber, R.A. (Ed.). *Developmental Efforts in Individualized Learning.* Itasca, Illinois: F.E. Peacock, 1971a, 361.

Weisgerber, R.A. (Ed.). *Perspectives in Individualized Learning.* Itasca, Illinois: Peacock, 1971b, 406.

Westinghouse Learning Corporation. *The PLAN* Curriculum Overview.* New York: Westinghouse Learning Corporation, 1973a, 465.

Westinghouse Learning Corporation. *The PLAN* Computer Manual.* 1974-75 Edition. New York: Westinghouse Learning Corporation, 1973b, 192.

Westinghouse Learning Corporation. *PLAN* Newsletter.* April, 1973c, No. 7.

Westinghouse Learning Corporation. *The PLAN* Curriculum Overview Mathematics Level, 1-6.* New York: Westinghouse Learning Corporation, 1975a, 107.

Westinghouse Learning Corporation. *The PLAN* Curriculum— Overview Language Arts.* New York: Westinghouse Learning Corporation, 1975b, 166.

Whipple, G.M. (Ed.). Adapting the schools to individual differences. *Twenty-fourth Yearbook of the NSSE, Part II.* Bloomington: Public School Publishing Company, 1925.

Wiel, R.V. *Project Basic Math.* Cedar Rapids: Cedar Rapids Community Schools, June, 1973.

Wood, J.D., and Lewis, J.W. A comparison of student utilization of time in IGE, PLAN, and traditional models of instruction. Paper presented at National AIGE Conference, Atlanta, Georgia, November, 1974.

Wright, C.E. Evaluation data and their uses in an individualized education program. Paper presented at Annual Convention of American Psychological Association. Miami Beach, Florida, September 5, 1970.

Wulf, W., and Levin, R. A local network. *Datamation*, 1975, *21*(2), 47-50.

Appendix A

CMI Systems

Coding Scheme

Academic Level
E   elementary school
S   secondary
C   college or university
T   training

Scale of System
S   small
M   medium
L   large

Curricular Plan
L   linear
B   block
S   strand
T   tree
M   menu

Dimension of Individualization
R   rate of progress
O   other

Assessment Procedures
L   placement
P   pretest
T   posttest
E   embedded tests
C   teacher certify
A   achievement
O   other

Diagnosis
T   test scores
O   objectives

Prescription
J   judgmental
A   automated
G   group assignment

Reports
G   group
S   student
T   teacher
U   unit
O   other

Management Level
I   instructional
C   course
P   program

Computer Mode
B   batch
R   remote job entry
I   interactive

Programming Language
F   FORTRAN
C   COBOL
3   COURSEWRITER-3
B   BASIC
T   TUTOR
A   Symbolic Assembly
O   other

Operational
Y   yes
N   no
?   unknown

CMI Systems

Author or Organization	Name	Academic Level	Scale of CMI	Curricular Plan	Dimension of Individualization	Assessment	Diagnosis	Prescription	Reports	Management Level	Computer Mode	Programming Language	Operational
[1] Allen, Meleca, Meyers	BIO-CMI	C	S	M	R	P,T	T,O	M	T,S	I,C	I	3	Y
[2] Anderson et al.	SMS	C	S	M	R	T	T,A		T,S	I	I	T	Y
[3] Behr et al.	MICA	E	S	L	R	L,P,T	O	A	S,G,U,O	I,C	I	F	Y
[4] Belt and Spuck	WIS/SIM	E	S	B,T	R	T	O	G	U,O	I,C	R	F	Y
[5] System Development Corp.	IMS	E	S	S	R	T	T	A	S,G	I,C	B	A	N
[6] Connolly	CONWELL	E	S	B	O	P,T	T,O	A	S	I,C	R		N
[7] Cooley and Glaser	IPI/MIS	E	S	L	R	L,P,C,T	O	A	S,G,U	I,C	R		N
[8] Cooper and Tobey	IGE/CMI	E	S	L,S	R	T	O	G	U,O	I,C	B	F	Y
[9] Countermine and Singh	ISS	C	S	M	R	T,C	T	A	S,G	I,C	R	F	Y
[10] Danforth	CMII	T	S	L	R	L,T	T,O	A	S	I,C	R,I		Y
[11] Dick and Gallager	CMI	C	S	L	R	P,T,A,O	T,O				I	3	Y
[12] Egan	ILS/*CMI	C	S	B	R	P,T,A	O	M		I	I	B	Y
[13] Flanagan	PLAN	E	L	L,B,S	R	L,P,T,A	O	M	S,G,U	I,C	R	C	N
[14] Hsu	IPI/IMS	E	S	B,L	R	L,P,C,T	O	A	S,G,O	I,C	R		Y
[15] Griesen	ISP	C	S	M	R	T,O	O		S,U	C	I	3	Y
[16] Judd and O'Neil	CMI	C	S	M	R	P,T	O		S,U	I,C	I	F	N
[17] Kelley	TIPS	C	S	L	O	T	T,O	A	T,S	I,C	B		Y
[18] Knipe	LOTT	S	S			P,T	T				B		?

410

CMI Systems
(Continued)

Author or Organization	Name	Academic Level	Scale of CMI	Curricular Plan	Dimension of Individualization	Assessment	Diagnosis	Prescription	Reports	Management Level	Computer Mode	Programming Language	Operational
[19] Mayo	NAVY CMI	T	L	L	R	T	T	A	T	I	R	F	Y
[20] Merrill	CMI	C	S	L,M	R	T	T,O			I,C	B,I	F	Y
[21] McManus	IMS-3	E	L	L	R	T	T		T,G	C	B,R	3	Y
[22] Morgan and Richardson	REFLECT	S	M	T	R	T,A	O	M	G,U	I,C	I	O	Y
[23] Rockway and Yasutaki	AIS	T	S	L	R	P,T	T	A		I,C	R		Y
[24] Selman	IMS/IMS	E	S	S	R	P,T	T	M	S,G,U,O	I,C	R		Y
[25] Steffenson and Read	SPINS	E	S		R	T					B		N
[26] U.S. Army	CTS	T	M	L	R						I		?
[27] Wiel	BASIC MATH	E,S	S	L	R,O	A						C	?
[28] Westinghouse Learning Corp.	PLAN*	E	L	L,B,S	R	L,T,C	O		S,G,U,O	I,C	R		Y

Related Systems

Author or Organization	Name	Academic Level	Scale of CMI	Curricular Plan	Dimension of Individualization	Assessment	Diagnosis	Prescription	Reports	Management Level	Computer Mode	Programming Language	Operational
[1] DeNio	KUMC-CMI	C	S	L	R	T	T		T	C	B		Y
[2] Gorth	CAM	E	L			P,T	T		G	C	B		Y
[3] Hayman and Lord	CMLL	C	S	M	O	T	T			C	I		Y
[4] Katin, Liu, Jemison		C	S	L	R	T	T				I		Y
[5] Oakland, Michigan	SAM	E	M	M		T			T,U				Y
[6] Seidel and Rosenblatt	HumRRO CMI	T	S	L	R	T	O			C			?
[7] Winter	FIS	T	L	L	R	P,C,T	T			C	I		Y

411

Index